Working With Animals

Animal Jobs Direct.com

Working with Animals

The Working With Animals publication is a comprehensive resource designed to help and inspire anyone who wants to work with animals. The subject matter is divided into three concise and informative sections: Careers with animals, Volunteering with animals and Jobs with animals.

When deciding on a career with animals, there are many different options to consider; many are well known animal career choices and others you may not have heard of or considered. Career opportunities with animals vary from dog trainer to zoologist, vet to wildlife photographer, marine biologist to pet sitter and many more. This section also has valuable training advice and links to useful organisations and training institutes. We hope to inspire and help you to find a suitable and rewarding career with animals according to your skills, experience and personal interests.

Volunteering is a great way to obtain hands on experience and a better understanding of the many different careers with animals. At the same time as giving you the tremendous satisfaction of helping animals in need, your volunteer work can also be an excellent career move. Many organisations will consider employing volunteers who can prove that they are competent and reliable even if they don't have the specific qualifications required in a job advert. The experience will enable you to gain valuable insight in the specific type of animal care that you aspire to work in.

The Volunteering with animals section contains details of over 600 animal volunteering opportunities, worldwide in over 96 countries. There are over 100 pages crammed with exciting animal volunteering options and web links directly to organisations that would benefit from your involvement as a volunteer. The opportunities are exciting and diverse. They include; working with endangered species, monitoring wild dolphins, feeding wolves, nursing sick animals, working in a cat houseboat sanctuary, assisting with wildlife recovery and release, attending to injured animals, walking dogs, grooming donkeys, transporting animals for re-homing abroad, caring for orphaned fox cubs, returning stray animals to their colonies after neutering, monitoring turtles and giving distressed animals some tender loving care. This section will show you how to gain valuable work experience, increase your chances of employment and at the same time to help animals in need.

You've chosen a career that inspires you, gained some volunteer experience, enroled on some training to improve your career and job prospects and now you are looking for a jobs with animals.

The Jobs with animals section contains job listings from various organisations in the animal care sector. The web links throughout this section point directly to the jobs on websites that are updated every time a new vacancy arises. This means that you have instant access to the latest jobs with animals. Browse this section for jobs with dogs, jobs with cats, wildlife jobs, horse jobs, veterinary jobs, zoo jobs, animal charity jobs and more. The team at Animal Jobs Direct are happy to provide you with any further assistance on training, careers, volunteering and employment. Contact us by phone on 0208 6269646 or by email: admin@animal-job.co.uk

ISBN NUMBER: 978-1-4452-3890-6

Table of Contents

Careers with animals

Introduction

Working with animals is an increasingly popular career choice. Many people instinctively have a desire to care for animals and begin working with them from an early age. For others, working with animals is a rewarding career change that enables them to fulfill a lifelong dream.

You may have no animal welfare experience and not be sure where to start or which career with animals to follow or what job opportunities may be available. However, having good work experience, life skills and being able to demonstrate a genuine interest in animal welfare, will ensure that you have a good chance of being employed in the animal care sector.

There is a huge amount to be learnt on the ground. It is possible to progress your career quickly if you are reliable, compassionate, committed, patient and able to develop a good understanding of real animal welfare issues.

A career with animals involves either working directly with animals: e.g. vets, vet nursing, dog wardens, RSPCA Inspectors, animal care assistants, rangers, dog and cat behaviourists, and handlers, or working in an office based position, e.g. management, administrative, fundraising or personnel positions.

To enjoy a successful career working with animals, it is important that you understand the physical and emotional needs of animals; you will need to be able to <u>recognise when animals are unwell</u> or unhappy and be able to pay particular attention to detail and to health and safety requirements. confined in a shelter or hospital need care twenty-four hours a day, seven days a week; therefore the working hours are unpredictable and varied and you will probably be required to work at weekends. Working with animals is usually grubby and can involve tough physical outdoor work; for this sort of career, you must enjoy being outdoors in all types of weather. You will need to be physically fit, healthy, hard working, have plenty of stamina, enjoy exercise and not be squeamish as some parts of the work can be messy and unpleasant. Some careers with animals may require you to live on site and to have a driving license.

The risk of being injured exists in all of careers working with animals and it is important to ensure you have sufficient training and that you feel confident being around animals before embarking on a career working with them. If you haven't spent time working with or caring for animals, it is worthwhile considering first working as a volunteer.

Volunteering is a great way to obtain hands on experience and a better understanding of the many different career options open to those wishing to work with animals. At the same time as giving you the tremendous satisfaction of helping animals in need, your volunteer work can also be an excellent career move. The experience will enable you to gain a valuable insight in the specific type of animal care that you aspire to work in.

For many employers, volunteer experience, interest, aptitude and commitment can be more important than initial entry qualifications. It is advisable to be well equipped with as many related skills as possible when seeking employment. Through volunteering, you will acquire new skills that will help you when applying for jobs or course placements. It is advisable for anyone wanting to work with animals, from would-be veterinary surgeons to animal care assistants, to do some sort of voluntary work before embarking on their chosen career.

If you are seeking a career change, volunteering can be an excellent way of landing your perfect job, as it is common for volunteers to be offered permanent positions. By enrolling as a volunteer you will gain a thorough and invaluable understanding of the work involved.

Training and qualifications can be equally important when seeking your career working with animals. There is fierce competition for animal care related jobs at all levels. If you don't have previous experience, an animal care qualification will greatly improve your job prospects. We have included training information as a part of each career option.

It is also worth considering enrolling on an online animal care course as this will enable you to study in your own time, at your own pace and at home. Here's a link to a selection of accredited online animal diploma and certificate courses. There's a great many to choose from including: Animal Behaviour, Animal Care, Welfare and Husbandry, Canine Science, Canine Studies, Professional Pet and Veterinary Assistant, Rescue Dog Trainer, Herpetology, Search and Rescue Dog Handler, Primatology, Birds of Prey – Rescue and Rehabilitation, Ornithology, Stable Management, Big Cat Studies, Professional Kennel Operator, Professional Pet Sitter, Professional Dog Walker, Feline Studies, Reptile Care, Welfare & First Aid, Equine Studies, Feline Behaviour and Psychology, Canine Psychology and Training, Cynology, Small Mammal Care, British Wild Mammals, Environmental Management, Ecology, Conservation, Canine First Aid, Canine Care, Canine Behaviour, How Dogs Learn, Puppy Training, Canine Nutrition, Bird Behaviour, Feline Behaviour, Feline Care, Feline Nutrition and Wolf Studies. For further information on training options visit Animal Jobs Direct (http://www.animal-job.co.uk).

There are many different options in this section; many are well known animal career choices and others you may not have heard of or considered.

We hope to inspire and help you to find an appropriate and rewarding career with animals according to your skills, experience and personal interests.

Animal Charity Careers

There are many different types of animal charities and consequently, a large variety of animal charity careers and jobs. Having a qualification will improve your job prospects. Consider studying an area of animal care that is of most interest to you. Here is further information about several online accredited diploma courses to help point you in the right direction.

Animal charities vary in type, size and function: Charities such as the RSPCA, Blue Cross, People's Dispensary for Sick Animals (PDSA), Battersea Dogs and Cats Home, Dogs Trust, National Animal Welfare Trust and Cats Protection operate a number of national programmes and initiatives. Most of them run clinics, hospitals and rescue homes around the country.

There are several large international animal welfare organisations - such as the World Society for the Protection of Animals (WSPA) and the International Fund for Animal Welfare (IFAW), These charities deal with worldwide animal welfare issues. Some focus on specific concerns such as farming; Compassion in World Farming and wildlife; World Wildlife Fund. The work of all these organisations largely involves campaigning to end animal suffering around the world. Most international charities run campaigns, projects that involve rescue and rehabilitation of animals and educational programmes. Consequently they need to recruit a number of people with varying skills that cover the work of the organisation, including management, administration, fieldwork, fundraising, education, human resources and animal care.

There are also many smaller regional animal charities - working locally to provide animal welfare services, promote animal adoptions and to deal with animal welfare problems. Many of these organisations are run by volunteers but they may also employ a small number of paid staff.

The primary role of some animal charities is campaigning for animal rights, e.g.: Animal Aid, BUAV, National Anti-vivisection Society and League Against Cruel Sports. Their work is mainly office based and most of these charities have few or no any animal holding facilities. Staff in these organisations may not necessarily have or need animal welfare experience, but will have skills ranging from management to IT.

Some of the current animal welfare issues include: intensive animal farming, inhumane slaughtering, hunting, the exotic pet trade, dog fighting, international animal cruelty/welfare problems and the overpopulation of domestic animals. In this guide, we have picked up on one of these issues - that of the problem of unwanted companion animals. We have chosen this issue as this problem has resulted in the huge growth in the number of animal welfare charities, and therefore jobs necessary to contend with this crisis.

The crisis of unwanted companion animals is heightened by:

1. The lack of legislation: the indiscriminate breeding and selling of animals by pet owners, puppy farms and cat, dog and small animal breeders (including those who may not be aware of the problem and therefore don't get their pet neutered and allow it to produce offspring), have all worsened the problem of there being too many animals and not enough homes. There are thousands of unwanted dogs, cats, rabbits, guinea pigs and numerous other species of small animals and exotics. Sadly, many end up in cages in rescue charities and most have little or no chance of being adopted. In addition, thousands of healthy animals are destroyed every year as there are simply not enough homes for them. The problem continues to worsen as breeders compete for trade by producing more unusual breeds of domestic or even exotic pets.

2. The lack of education/awareness: every year, thousands of animals are given up or abandoned by owners who were not fully aware of the long term commitment involved in caring for a companion animal. Many animals suffer a lonely, boring and uncomfortable existence due to their owners' lack of awareness of their needs - i.e. the correct amount of exercise, environment, nutrition and even the right climate necessary for some of the more exotic pets.

Many animal charities are responding to this and to other animal welfare problems by becoming more pro-active in their approach. Here are a few examples of animal charity initiatives and the different roles that some UK animal charities play:

- Take in unwanted and stray animals and re-home them to suitable homes, e.g.: Dogs Trust, Battersea Cats and Dogs Home, RSPCA, Wood Green Animal Shelter.

- Provide free or subsidised treatment for sick and injured unwanted, owned and stray animals, e.g.: Blue Cross, PDSA and Celia Hammond Trust.

- Offer reduced cost neutering schemes/vaccination clinics/veterinary care/micro-chipping, e.g.: RSPCA, Celia Hammond Trust, Blue Cross and Mayhew Animal Home.

- Provide an animal ambulance service and/or mobile clinics. e.g.: Blue Cross, PDSA.

- Respond to and investigate cruelty complaints, e.g.: RSPCA.

- Hold educational road shows and promote responsible pet ownership and neutering, e.g.: Dogs Trust.

- Assist owners who have social problems that affect their pets welfare i.e. domestic violence, substance abuse, e.g.: Dogs Trust

- Promote community initiatives such as Animal Welfare Officers and community nurses who identify and respond to animal related problems, e.g.: PDSA, Mayhew Animal Home.

- Provide 24 hour emergency service or help line and telephone advice, e.g.: RSPCA clinics and hospitals.

- Provide welfare boarding for owners who have social or financial problems, e.g.: Dogs Trust, Mayhew Animal Home.

- Provide training and behaviour advice for pet owners, e.g.: Dogs Trust

- Campaign for animal rights e.g.: BUAV and Animal Aid.

Most jobs in animal charities are highly rewarding and interesting, however, this type of work can also be challenging and stressful.

Animal charities and shelters are inundated on a daily basis with unwanted animals and requests for help with animal related problems - try visiting one or two and find out for yourself! As there is so much pressure on so few organisations, working for an animal charity can be stressful and highly demanding. Animal welfare charities don't receive government funding and are reliant on donations from the public. This means that many are forced to achieve their objectives with limited resources and therefore fewer staff. In many cases, staff perform duties way beyond their job descriptions without great financial reward. However, despite this, working for an animal charity can be an exciting and extremely rewarding career option.

If you're interested in working for an animal charity, becoming a member of one of these organisations could improve your chances of landing a job as you will receive regular updates and newsletters about their work. This will give you a better understanding of the work they do and you will be better informed for an interview.

If you're looking for a hands-on animal welfare career but have no previous experience working with animals, it may be worth considering taking an office job with in one of these charities. Expressing your interest in working hands-on with animals should give you a good chance of an interview if a suitable vacancy arises.

Another option is to seek voluntary work within an organisation that you would like to work for. It is quite common for organisations to offer paid employment to reliable volunteers with the skills they are looking for.

The staffing structure of animal charities depends largely on the size, nature and location of the organisation. There are careers that involve working hands-on with animals and there are also many roles that involve working less directly with animals. Many organisations don't have animal care facilities and therefore their vacancies are more office related. These charities make a huge impact and assist many animals through raising awareness of animal suffering, raising funds to assist hands-on organisations, and campaigning for better legislation for the protection of animals.

We have split the animal charity careers section into those careers that are hands-on with animals, and those that are more office related:

A: Hands-on careers: Animal Care Assistant (ACA), Animal Care Manager, RSPCA/SSPCA Inspector, Re-homing/Adoption Officer, Home Visitor, Animal Ambulance Driver and Veterinary Team.

B: Office careers: Chief Executive, Fundraising/media team, Campaigns Officer, Receptionist and Volunteer Co-ordinator.

A: Hands-on careers:

1. Animal Care Assistant (ACA)

Animal Care Assistants (ACA) are employed by most animal welfare charities that provide shelter, clinics or hospital facilities for stray or rescued animals. The main function of an ACA, is to provide for the needs of animals while they are in an organisation's care. This role is an excellent starting point for those who are unsure as to which animal career they ultimately wish to pursue.

Typically, an ACA has more direct contact with the animals than anyone else in the organisation. The role involves carry out the very important aspects of animal care on a daily basis - including cleaning, feeding, handling and exercise. Although this position is sometimes viewed as "the bottom of the ladder" (and this is reflected in the salary!), this is an extremely important and rewarding position.

The animals in the care of an organisation, are highly dependent upon the ACA. Having a competent and caring person in this role can make a very real difference to their physical, mental and emotional well-being. The quality of life for animals in care can be greatly improved by: carrying out thorough cleaning routines, ensuring the correct diet, providing mental and physical stimulation to alleviate the stress caused by confinement, observing animals closely for signs of ill health and stress and - most importantly - by being kind and compassionate. Depending on the size of the organisation, there may be some administration aspects to this role, such as record keeping, taking telephone calls and ordering supplies.

An Animal Care Assistant should be caring and patient, confident around animals, able to calm anxious animals and coax nervous ones, willing to use initiative, enjoy team work, not be squeamish, prepared to work hard and be physically fit, reliable and healthy. Working days usually start around 7:30 am, you may be required to work on a rota and be on duty five or six days a week - including weekends and bank holidays. ACA's work outside in all weathers - and the work can be noisy, smelly, stressful and tiring. In larger organisations, it may be possible to be promoted to a supervisor or kennel/cattery manager. With experience, it can also be possible to move into related careers such as: Animal Care Manager, Behaviourist, Veterinary Nursing or RSPCA Inspector. Animal Care Assistants may also be involved in the adoption process. This could include interviewing prospective animal adopters, assessing their suitability as owners and giving general animal care advice; it is therefore crucial to have good communication skills.

Real interest and enthusiasm can be more useful than a formal qualification, but training and qualifications are becoming increasingly important. Some organisations now require GCSEs/S grades - however, it is possible to start off as a volunteer or on a work experience placement. Some charities, such as the Dogs Trust and the RSPCA, train their own staff, and some provide NVQ training courses. The Animal Care, Welfare and Husbandry Dipoma is a recognised qualification equivalent to NVQ 3 and is available to study online. The Rescue dog Carer/Trainer Diploma and the Professional Kennel Operator Diploma are other examples of excellent qualifications for this career.

2. Animal Care/Welfare Manager

As no two animal charities are run in the same manner, it is difficult to clearly define the role of an Animal Care/Welfare Manager. Animal rescue centres/shelters vary in just about every way including: location, size, layout, facilities, types of animals catered for, policies and ethos.

The role of Animal Care/Welfare Manager role can be extremely demanding at times, as it involves having overall responsibility for how well the organisation functions on the ground to assist neglected and abused animals. Animal rescue centres are usually forced to function on tight budgets. This means many animal charities are short staffed, with employees often being required to work extremely hard, doing the work of several staff.

Whilst this role primarily involves having overall management responsibility for the welfare, health and well being of the animals, it may also entail some hands on duties. Depending on the size of the organisation, you could be responsible for some or all of the following: recruitment, daily cleaning and feeding routines, supervising staff, staff training, liaising with clients, and other organisations, overseeing veterinary clinics, dealing with contractors, re-homing, managing animal welfare initiatives and projects, behavioural assessments, administration, health and safety and maintaining high standards of care and hygiene throughout the organisation.

You need to be physically, emotionally and mentally fit. It helps to be calm and patient, it is important that you are kind and compassionate, have good organisational skills and solid management or supervisory experience. If you have no previous animal care experience working for an animal charity then a qualification such as the Diploma in Animal Care, Welfare and Husbandry, Canine Science and Behaviour Diploma, the Rescue dog Carer/Trainer Diploma, the Professional Pet Care and Veterinary Assistant Diploma and some volunteering experience will greatly improve your employment prospects. For the right person, this role can be a highly stimulating and extremely rewarding career.

3. RSPCA Inspector

The Royal Society for the Prevention of Cruelty to Animal's (RSPCA) vision is to work for a world in which all humans respect and live in harmony with all other members of the animal kingdom. The RSPCA operates as a charity with a mission to: "prevent cruelty, promote kindness to and alleviate suffering of animals". Inspectors are the public face of the RSPCA; they are required to undertake practical investigation work on behalf of the RSPCA. In Scotland, SSPCA Inspectors perform a similar role. Whilst the career of an RSPCA Inspector is a popular choice, the RSPCA currently only employs 300 Inspectors and the SSPCA employs 55 Inspectors.

There have recently been changes to the Animal Welfare Act, these have been helpful for RSPCA Inspectors as there is now a 'Duty of care' for animals - this is a legal phrase which means that someone has an obligation to do something. Prior to the Animal Welfare Act, people only had a duty to ensure that an animal didn't suffer unnecessarily. The new Act keeps this duty but also imposes a broader duty of care on anyone responsible for an animal to take reasonable steps to ensure that the animal's needs are met. This means that a person has to look after the animal's welfare as well as ensure that it does not suffer. The Act says that an animal's welfare needs include: a suitable environment (how it is housed), a suitable diet (what it eats and drinks), the ability to exhibit normal behaviour patterns, any need it has to be housed with, or apart from, other animals and protection from pain, suffering, injury and disease.

In essence, Inspectors are required to provide 24-hour cover for animals in need. They are required to investigate an initial claim of neglect or reported cruelty and if the problem is due to neglect, they work to provide practical animal care advice. In cases of cruelty they collect evidence, undertake interviews and possibly remove the animal from the situation. Later, they may be required to present evidence in court. RSPCA/SSPCA Inspectors also undertake animal rescue work - both in urban and country areas. In addition, Inspectors have the responsibility of visiting and checking other sites or establishments where animals are kept, such as farms, pet shops and markets. Inspectors are also required to follow up calls about lost/stray or suffering animals. Inspectors are home based, but work outdoors in all types of weather and may spend a fair bit of time on the road travelling to and from jobs. RSPCA Inspectors may be required to give presentations and talks to schools and other organisations to raise awareness of animal welfare issues This can be a highly rewarding career choice, as it involves a hands-on approach to preventing and alleviating animal suffering. However, it is an extremely demanding job, both physically and emotionally, and there are many challenges.

To enjoy a successful career as an RSPCA or SSPCA Inspector, you must have excellent people skills and be able to communicate well with a wide range of people. You must be compassionate and care deeply about animal welfare - previous experience of working with animals is desirable. You need to be physically fit, able to swim 50 meters fully clothed, and be able to remain calm in emergency situations. You are required to have a valid driving license. Applicants need at least 5 GCSEs/S grades (A-C/1-3) in English and a science subject, preferably biology. SSPCA, applicants need five GCSEs/S grades (A-C/1-3) including English.

The online Diploma in Animal Care, Welfare and Husbandry, the Animal Behaviour Diploma, the Rescue Dog Trainer Diploma, the Professional Pet Care and Veterinary Assistant Diploma and the Canine Science and Behaviour Diploma are examples of valuable qualifications.

This is a popular career choice and successful applicants are required to complete a challenging 12 month training course, where they major in animal welfare legislation and receive training in: investigation skills and interview techniques, court work, media and public speaking, mountain and boat rescue techniques and basic veterinary skills and animal-handling techniques. The SSPCA training takes place at the headquarters in Edinburgh and last for five months. The programme includes: in-house training, courses with other organisations, ongoing assessment and a final examination.

Useful contacts:

Royal Society for the Prevention of Cruelty to Animals (RSPCA): has a vision to work for a world in which all humans respect and live in harmony with all other members of the animal kingdom. The RSPCA operates as a charity with a mission to: prevent cruelty, promote kindness to and alleviate suffering of animals. Wilberforce Way, Southwater, Horsham, West Sussex, RH13 9RS.

Scottish Society for the Prevention of Cruelty to Animals (SSPCA): was established in 1839 to prevent cruelty to animals and promote kindness and humanity in their treatment. Braehead Mains, 603 Queensferry Road, Edinburgh, EH4 6EA.

4. Re-homing/Adoption Officer

Many animal charities take in or rescue animals and re-home them to caring new owners. These organisations operate sanctuaries, shelters or homes where the animals are rehabilitated and cared for until a new owner can be found. Most of these charities employ re-homing/adoption officers who are responsible for ensuring that the animals are re-homed to the right owners. It involves an in-depth process to ensure that the correct matches are made. A large part of this role involves making potential new owners aware of the responsibilities and commitments associated with having a pet. This is a crucial part of the job, as in many cases people are not aware of what this new commitment will involve - and this lack of awareness often leads to animals being given up again for adoption.

Re-homing/Adoption Officers spend much of their time meeting, interviewing and advising potential new owners. You need to be an articulate communicator with good interpersonal skills, have the ability to multi-task and make quick decisions, as well as have a thorough understanding about responsible pet ownership and what animals really need. The role involves: interviewing visitors who wish to adopt an animal, to determine which animal will best suit them and their lifestyle and offering advice to new owners about settling in their new pet and assisting if they experience problems. It may also involve facilitating behavioural classes to assist those who have recently adopted.

Ideally, you should have some experience of working directly with animals - preferably in an animal rescue environment. An animal care or animal behavioural qualification and previous customer care experience will improve your employment prospects for this rewarding career. The Rescue dog Carer/Trainer Diploma is also a valuable qualification for this type of work.

5. Home Visitor

Broadly speaking, the role involves conducting visits to the homes of potential owners. This is done to ensure that they are fully aware of the commitment of owning an animal and able to provide it with a suitable home environment. Many organisations employ Re-homing/Adoption officers to interview and match adopters with animals; once this has matching process is complete, a Home Visitor visits the new adopters in their home to ensure that the home environment is appropriate for the animal they wish to adopt. For example, most organisations that re-home dogs, would want to ensure that potential adopters have a garden that is suitably fenced. Those that re-home cats, may wish to ensure that the new owner has a suitable cat flap installed so that the cat can have outdoor access. In addition, there may be individual requirements for particular animals; some will have had a traumatic past and may have developed some behavioural problems or be unable to cope with certain situations - it is then the Home Visitors responsibility to ensure that the proposed new environment is suitable, to prevent the animal being given up again.

Home Visitors are required to be excellent communicators, able to represent the organisation and provide appropriate advice in line with the organisation's policies. Ideally, you should have prior experience of rescued animals and must have a clear and thorough understanding of the requirements of companion animals. You should hold a valid driving licence and possibly have your own vehicle as there is a fair bit of travelling involved. Home Visitors need to be extremely organised, able to prioritise and willing to deal with a high volume of work. Many organisations will wait until the Home Visitors' report before re-homing an animal - this means that there is an on-going pressure in this role to ensure that visits are carried out timely and efficiently to prevent unnecessary delays for the animal awaiting adoption.

Home Visitors also provide post adoption assistance to ensure that animals settle in without any serious problems. Ideally, you should have some experience of working directly with animals - preferably in an animal rescue environment. An animal behavioural qualification and previous customer care experience will improve your employment prospects for this career.

6. Animal Ambulance Driver

This role involves being responsible for the safe transport of sick, injured, recovering or stray animals. It is highly likely that you will have to deal with emergency situations such as road traffic accidents, and it is essential that you are able to respond quickly and calmly, and that you handle difficult situations well in stressful situations. You will be required to have a valid driving licence and previous driving experience (preferably of larger/emergency vehicles), as well as good local road and area knowledge. In addition, you may be required to have some animal care or first aid experience- and ideally should have previous experience in the handling of aggressive or dangerous companion and wild animals. You may be required to have a recent animal first aid qualification, be physically fit and able to attend to rescue situations, have good communication skills, pay attention to detail, work well on your own initiative, be resourceful and have good problem solving skills.

Some of the work will involve the routine transport of animals to and from rescue centres all around the country and this may involve very long journeys. You may also be required to provide regular transport locally for animals to and from veterinary practices and animal hospitals, and to collect stray dogs from police stations or overnight holding centres. Most organisations will provide on-going training, as it is essential that you remain up to date on the latest animal transport legislation. This role requires you to be compassionate and to have a thorough understanding of the needs of animals. You are required to continually consider the animals you are transporting - to ensure that their journey is as stress free as possible. For example: driving with extreme care, stopping regularly for water and exercise breaks, ensuring animals are comfortable and have clean bedding and that their environment is kept at an ideal temperature. Having vehicle maintenance skills will enhance your employment prospects.

The Department for Environment, Food and Rural Affairs (Defra) provides advice on transporting pets safely, legally and in comfort - this link will provide you with an insight into the basic requirements.

There are several useful qualifications that will assist you in this career. They include the Rescue-dog Carer/Trainer Diploma, Professional Pet Care and Veterinary Assistant Diploma, Animal Care, Welfare and Husbandry Diploma, Animal Behaviour Diploma, Animal Health Diploma and the Professional Kennel Operator.

7. Veterinary team

Rescue centres and animal hospitals are the most common places that employ veterinary staff in the animal charity sector. The Peoples' Dispensary for Sick Animals (PDSA) is one of the larger charities in the UK, employing approximately four hundred vets nationwide. The Royal Society for the Prevention of Cruelty to Animals (RSPCA) is also a large vet employer as vets are required to run the Societies' many animal hospitals and low cost clinics.

Some of the larger international animal charities such as the World Society for the Protection of Animals (WSPA), World Wildlife Fund (WWF) and the International Fund for Animal Welfare (IFAW), also employ veterinary staff. Working for these types of organisations will involve much international travel. Most international organisations require veterinary staff with a broad experience of working with a variety of animals. Many of the animals assisted by these organisations will be traumatised, having been rescued from appalling conditions such as bear baiting, puppy farms, poorly managed zoos, factory farms, bull fighting, working horses, whaling, etc.

The veterinary team employed by an animal rescue organisation/shelter usually consists of: Veterinary Surgeons, Veterinary Nurses and Animal Nursing Assistants. The size and number of each of these professionals depends on the size of the organisation and their objectives or type of work they carry out. The veterinary team is responsible for the health of all the animals cared for by the rescue centre. In a rescue or shelter environment, the veterinary roles broadly entail the following: maintaining health records, preventing and treating diseases, vaccinations, euthanasia, facilitating health clinics, neutering, education and dealing with any emergencies that arise. The veterinary team must be confident in the handling of companion animals. Most animals in rescue centres have experienced high levels of stress and as a result, they may be more likely to show signs of aggression and will require careful and competent handling.

Most animal rescue centres/shelters are inundated with unwanted animals and whilst in most cases, shelters are licensed to hold a specific maximum number of animals, in practice this may be impossible to adhere to. Often animals are dumped on the doorstep or given up with very little notice and as a result it is very easy for a rescue shelter to run over their stated license number. Having a large number of confined animals in one place is not ideal for a variety of reasons. Not least, the stress that this causes individual animals, as animal shelters - however well run they may be - are very unnatural environments for any species of animal. One of the biggest risks to the animals in these confined environments, is the outbreak and spread of diseases such as cat flu, kennel cough, parvo-virus, etc. Once these sorts of infections take a hold, they are very difficult to eradicate and may result in much suffering and even death. Veterinary teams working for animal rescue centres should ideally have had previous experience working in similar environments and must be confident in the prevention, detection and control of the spread of diseases.

Most animal rescue centres operate neutering programmes to control animal numbers and prevent unwanted animals. A large portion of the veterinary team's time may be taken up with the routine neutering work. Many organisations run mobile neutering units and therefore some of the neutering work may be done off site. Some animal charities offer community based veterinary advice projects, vaccination clinics and low cost veterinary procedures. For the veterinary team, this will mean playing a crucial role in the local community. This provides an excellent opportunity to educate people about responsible pet ownership and to play a hands-on role with animals in need. Many animal charities operate animal hospitals. These are very busy environments and they provide veterinary staff with an excellent opportunity to assist a large number of animals. Veterinary staff working in these situations are able to enhance their knowledge about a variety of conditions and problems that may not frequently be seen in private practice. Working for an animal charity may mean that you have to settle for a lower salary, however, there is plenty of job satisfaction to compensate.

As well as assisting with unwanted animals, rescue centers and international animal charities spend their time and resources helping neglected and abused animals. For the veterinary team this may mean providing emergency care or assisting suffering or distressed animals - this can be highly rewarding yet demanding and the veterinary surgeon may frequently be required to advise on, and carry out decisions regarding euthanasia.

B: Office careers:

8. Chief Executive (CEO)

Is in charge of determining policies and strategy for the organisation and is responsible for the overall operation and plans for future development. This role involves having overall management responsibility for the various departments and for managing budgets and finances. Ideally, you will have had previous animal care and charity management experience. It is essential that you understand the problems your organisation is working to solve, and that you have a thorough appreciation of how the organisation functions practically on the ground. The CEO usually reports directly to a Board of Trustees who are volunteers.

Useful contact:

Acevo is the Association of Chief Executives of Voluntary Organisations: connect, develop and represent the third sector's leaders, have over 2000 members and have been providing support and advice to their members for 20 years. 1 New Oxford Street, London, WC1A 1NU. Tel: 0845 345 8481

9. Fundraising/Media team

There is little or no government funding available for animal charities and they are therefore entirely reliant on donations from the public. Fundraisers are employed by most charitable organisations to ensure that sufficient funds are raised to carry out the animal welfare work. The fundraising team is normally headed up by a Fundraising Manager, who has overall responsibility for managing the team and for ensuring that budget targets are met.

Depending on the size of the organisation (and the income targets), the fundraising team may include some or all of the following positions: Events Officer, Fundraising Manager, Public Relations, Marketing Officer, Trusts/Grants Officer, Legacies Officer, Gift/Charity Shop Manager and Donor/Database Officer.

Raising funds is achieved through developing and managing a broad range of fundraising activities which may include: gaining corporate sponsorship, submitting grant proposals, soliciting private donations and legacies, running charity shops, promoting memberships and managing fundraising events. In order to be able to raise funds effectively, it is vital that public awareness is continually raised about the work of the organisation - therefore, most fundraising departments have a strong public relations and marketing elements to their work. As a part of this public relations aspect, the fundraising department may also be responsible for creating advertising campaigns, giving presentations, writing press releases and using all types of other media activities in order to increase public awareness about their organisation.

Having a proven track record in raising funds or of working in the charity sector will greatly improve your employment prospects. Experience is usually more attractive to prospective employers than formal qualification. Volunteering in this type of role could help you gain some of the necessary skills and experience. Having previous marketing, business or sales work experience is also helpful. Both the Institute of Fundraising and the Directory of Social Change run relevant training courses and these are particularly useful to those who are new to this type of work.

Useful contacts:

The Directory of Social Change (DSC): regards itself as the leading source of information and training to voluntary and community sectors worldwide. 24 Stephenson Way, London, NW1 2DP. Tel: 020 7391 4800

Working For A Charity: exists to promote the voluntary sector as a positive career option for those seeking paid employment in the sector. NCVO, Regent's Wharf, 8 All Saints Street, London, N1 9RL. Tel: 020 7520 2512

Institute of Fundraising (IOF): is professional body that represents fundraisers in the UK. Their mission is to support fundraisers, through leadership, representation, standard-setting and education, to deliver excellent fundraising. IOF, Park Place, 12 Lawn Lane, London, SW8 1UD. Tel: 020 7840 1000.

Chartered Institute of Marketing (CIM): are the leading international body for marketing and business development. Each year they help over 50,000 people at every stage of their career with training, qualifications and resources as well as enabling leading businesses to get the most from their marketing people. The Chartered Institute of Marketing, Moor Hall, Cookham, Maidenhead, Berkshire, SL6 9QH. Tel: 01628 427500.

Chartered Institute of Public Relations (CIPR): work to develop skills, raise awareness, rewarding excellence, supporting our members and giving public relations a voice at the highest levels. CIPR Public Relations Centre, 32 St. James's Square, London, SW1Y 4JR. Tel: 020 7766 3333.

10. Campaigns Officer

Campaign Officers are employed by campaigning animal charities who work to raise awareness about animal welfare issues or problems - with the ultimate aim of solving them. This is an excellent career choice for those who are passionate about animal welfare and wish to make a real difference for suffering animals.

Parts of the job may include: raising awareness among decision makers, celebrities and politicians, effectively utilising the media to broadcast awareness about the issue to a broader audience and preparing effective campaign materials and petitions.

You are required to have excellent social and communication skills, self confidence, public speaking skills, problem solving ability and a thorough general knowledge of current animal welfare issues. Whilst there are no specific qualifications for this career, previous campaigns experience is highly desirable and previous animal welfare experience will enhance employment prospects.

Useful Contacts:

The Born Free Foundation is a dynamic international wildlife charity, devoted to compassionate conservation and animal welfare. Born Free takes action worldwide to protect threatened species and stop individual animal suffering. Born Free believes wildlife belongs in the wild and works to phase out zoos. They rescue animals from lives of misery in tiny cages and give them lifetime care. Born Free Foundation, 3 Grove House, Foundry Lane, Horsham, West Sussex, RH13 5PL.

British Union for Abolition of Vivisections' (BUAV) vision is to create a world where nobody wants or believes we need to experiment on animals. 16a Crane Grove, London, N7 8NN. Tel: 020 77004888.

Fund for Replacement of Animals in Experiments (FRAME) works in researching alternatives to animal use in research, testing and education. Their long-term goal is the total elimination of laboratory animal use, through the development, validation and acceptance of replacement alternative methods. Tel: 0115 9584740

NAVS National Anti-Vivisection Society. Millions of animals suffer and die in cruel, unscientific, and futile experiments. The NAVS advocates the prohibition of all animal experiments and, pending the achievement of this aim, they may support partial measures of reform which would provide steps towards the abolition of vivisection. Millbank Tower, Millbank, London, SW1P 4QP. Tel: 020 7630 3340

Animal Aid is the UK's largest animal rights group and one of the longest established in the world, having been founded in 1977. They campaign peacefully against all forms of animal abuse and promote a cruelty-free lifestyle. They investigate and expose animal cruelty, and their undercover investigations and other evidence are often used by the media, bringing these issues to public attention. The Old Chapel, Bradford Street, Tonbridge, Kent, TN9 1AW. Tel: 01732 364546

Compassion in World Farming was founded over 40 years ago in 1967 by a British farmer who became horrified by the development of modern, intensive factory farming. They campaign peacefully to end all cruel factory farming practices. They believe that the biggest cause of cruelty on the planet deserves a focused, specialised approach. River Court, Mill Lane, Godalming, Surrey, GU7 1EZ. Tel: 01483 521 950

The International Fund for Animal Welfare (IFAW) works to improve the welfare of wild and domestic animals throughout the world by reducing commercial exploitation of animals, protecting wildlife habitats, and assisting animals in distress. They seek to motivate the public to prevent cruelty to animals and to promote animal welfare and conservation policies that advance the well-being of both animals and people. 87-90 Albert Embankment, London, SE1 7UD. Tel: 0207 587 6700

The World Society for the Protection of Animals (WSPA) believes that animals have biologically determined instincts, interests and natures, and can experience pain and suffering. It is their conviction that each individual animal has intrinsic value, and that it is the responsibility of humans to ensure that their welfare is respected and protected. 1st Floor, 89 Albert Embankment, London, SE1 7TP. Tel: 020 7587 5000

11. Receptionist

Receptionists play an important role as part of the team at any animal charity or hospital. They are responsible for the first impression received by a client (by phone or visit), and they provide the interface between visitors, staff, adopters, veterinary practices, other organisations and volunteers. Reception areas are invariably busy - with phones constantly ringing and a steady flow of people coming and going through the shelter.

Most animal rescue centres are under continual pressure with the number of unwanted, lost or abandoned animals they need to assist. The animal welfare charity environment can be highly stressful. To succeed in this role it is important that you have a calm disposition, are able to work well in a busy environment and that you are organised and able to effectively prioritise your work load. Depending on the size of the organisation, the role may include: answering and directing phone calls, providing animal welfare advice to callers, booking in animals that are being given up for adoption, maintaining up to date records about other animal welfare services, booking appointments for animal clinics, maintaining the adoption's/visitors diary, meeting and greeting visitors, processing payments and assisting with shop sales.

It is essential that you have a pleasant manner, excellent customer care skills and that you are able to communicate well with a cross section of people. Some animal welfare or hands-on experience of working with animals, as well as a customer care qualification is extremely helpful and will enhance your employment prospects.

Having a qualification will improve your chances of being selected for a job. There are several courses that offer excellent training and qualifications and if you wish to study at home there is an online receptionist course.

The British Veterinary Nursing Association (BVNA) Animal Nursing Assistant qualification includes a unit entitled 'Finance, Veterinary Reception and Administration'. Candidates can enrol on this course and undertake this specific unit - you do not have to continue to achieve the entire qualification. By undertaking and passing the multiple-choice examination successful candidates will be awarded a Unit of Achievement. If in the future, you want to progress this, you can undertake one or all three of the remaining units in order to gain the entire qualification. It is not essential for candidates to be enrolled at college to undertake this specific unit, however there are approximately 30 colleges in the United Kingdom who run the Animal Nursing Assistant qualification – see the useful contacts link below for further information.

Useful contact:

British Veterinary Nursing Association: offer an Animal Nursing Assistant qualification with unit appropriate for receptionists. BVNA, 2 Greenway Business Centre, Harlow Business Park, Harlow, Essex, CM19 5QE. Tel: 01279 408644.

12. Volunteer Co-ordinator

Most animal charities are dependent on voluntary help and therefore many employ a Volunteer Co-ordinator. This role includes having responsibility for recruiting, training and managing volunteers. It involves matching volunteers to suitable duties, supervising where necessary and assisting volunteers by providing resources and feedback. You may also be in charge of staff induction programmes and health and safety training.

The role requires you to have excellent communication skills, be highly organised, able to work on your own initiative, and to have a thorough understanding of the organisations' needs and priorities. Whilst there are no set qualifications for this type of work, previous supervisory/management experience and time spent working as a volunteer will enhance your employment prospects. There are several qualifications that are useful for this career, including: NVQ levels 3, 4 and 5 Management of Volunteers and Level 3 Certificate Managing Volunteers.

Useful Contacts:

Association of Volunteer Managers (AVM): has been set up with the aim to address the needs of those who manage volunteers in England regardless of field, discipline or sector.

Volunteer Development Agency: promotes and develops volunteering to build stronger communities.

Careers With Cats

Cats staying in a boarding environment are entirely reliant on the organisations staff for cleaning, feeding, stimulation and their general well-being. Being confined can be a frightening experience for some cats and for others it can be boring; good cattery staff will attend to individual problems and needs. Having a compassionate individual in this role makes a very real difference to the cats in boarding. Having a calm and cheerful disposition is essential for this type of work as cats will pick up on and respond to your mood and temperament.

There are several useful qualifications for those wanting to work with cats. These include, the Diploma in Animal Care, Welfare and Husbandry, and the Feline Studies Diploma, Cat Carer Diploma, Feline Behaviour and Psychology Diploma, the Advanced Feline Behaviour Diploma, the Professional Pet Care and Veterinary Assistant Diploma and the Feline Nutrition, Feline Care and Feline Behaviour Certificates.

Apprenticeships may be available for those under the age of 24. In England these are currently Apprenticeships (level 2) and Advanced Apprenticeships (level 3).

In this section, we have information about the following careers working with cats: Cattery Assistant, Cattery Manager, Cat Sitter, Cat Groomer and running your own Cat Boarding Business.

13. Cattery Assistant

Most careers with cats involve working in veterinary practices, animal rescue centres and boarding establishments. Animal Care Assistant jobs are often the starting point for this type of work. Before committing to voluntary or paid employment, it is a good idea to check that the cattery you intend to work for meets high standards. The Feline Advisory Bureau (FAB) has a list of recommended catteries that have been inspected and measured up to the FAB Standard for Construction and Management of Boarding Catteries. Both the construction and management of the cattery are taken into account and listing is a sure sign that the standards of cat accommodation and care conform to high standards.

Whilst the work is physically demanding, it also involves much hands-on contact with the animals and this can be extremely rewarding. The daily work in a cattery will invariably mean an early start, as the cats need to be fed and have their cabins cleaned. This first part of the day can be demanding, as the cats will be hungry and demanding attention! It is important that you are able to prioritise and work quickly and efficiently; speed is essential as you will probably be required to deal with a lot of cats.

One of the first jobs is to feed the cats and refresh water bowls. Some cats may be on medication diets or prefer different brands of cat food and there will probably be several different meals to make up. It is important to monitor each cat's daily food intake; cats can rapidly gain excess weight either through lack of exercise - or may overeat through boredom and this can lead to health problems. A cat that goes outdoors will nibble on grass and herbs as part of his diet. It is believed that eating vegetation helps cats to regurgitate hair-balls. This can be overcome by providing the cats with an indoor window box. Grass, catnip, thyme, sage, parsley or wheat and oats can all be sown indoors in a potting mixture. Your next job will probably involve emptying and scrubbing used litter trays and disinfecting each cabin; there is much bending and lifting involved and you need to be physically fit and have a strong back. Disease prevention is of paramount importance as viruses such as cat flu are easily transmitted and can cause much suffering and death. Having a clean environment and bedding is an important part of keeping cats happy. Whilst you are cleaning the cabins, you will need check on each cat. You will be looking out for signs of stress, such as ears pinned back, the cat hiding in a corner or not using the litter tray.

All cats are natural hunters - if their movement is restricted or they cannot go outdoors, they will become frustrated as they will be unable to exhibit their normal behaviour. Therefore, whilst a cat is confined in a cattery, it is very important to provide toys and games to keep ensure they are kept stimulated and exercised – both physically and mentally. Kittens and cats love newspaper tents, cardboard boxes and paper bags, sheet or blanket hammocks, scratching posts or logs and toys that encourage stalking and pouncing.

You will need to be aware of individual needs and to ensure that each cat in your care is given some individual attention. This is one of the more rewarding and pleasurable aspects of the job, so be sure to make time to interact with the cats each day. The remainder of your working day may involve playing with the cats, grooming them, preparing another meal at the end of the day and poop scooping litter trays. You may also be required to complete paperwork or keep records. The job could involve some interaction with the public when interviewing prospective owners at a rescue centre or when dealing with cat owners at a boarding cattery, so it is important that you are able to interact well with people and have good customer care skills.

Salaries for this type of work start from around £10,000 for a Trainee and may go up to around £17,000 depending on area based, qualifications, experience, responsibilities and hours worked. Some boarding catteries may offer accommodation and vehicle as part of your salary and it may be a requirement that you are able to drive. Once you have sufficient experience you may decide to go on to set up your own cattery or become a Cattery Manager.

Useful contacts:

Volunteering England:
Regents Wharf, 8 All Saints Street, London, N1 9RL. Tel: 0845 305 6979

Feline Advisory Bureau (FAB):
Taeselbury High Street, Tisbury, Wiltshire, SP3 6LD. Tel: 0870 742 2278

14. Cattery Manager

Cattery Managers are employed by private boarding, quarantine and charitable organisations to oversee the day-to-day running of the business. The role of a cattery manager can vary greatly and depends on the size and type of business or organisation.

At private boarding establishments:
The cattery manager is responsible for customer relations, advertising, recruitment, staff training, daily routines and maintaining high standards of care and hygiene throughout the cattery. The cattery manager may also be required to do some of the physical work such as cleaning, answering phones, or assisting with medications as necessary.

The cattery manager ideally needs to be physically, emotionally and mentally fit, have a calm disposition, be patient, kind and compassionate, have sound animal welfare experience, good organisational skills and recent management or supervisory experience. For the right person, the job of cattery manager can be highly stimulating and extremely rewarding. Salaries vary according to region and experience and range from £16,000 - £30,000. Often, once someone has worked as a cattery manager, they go on to running their own cattery business

Animal charity rescue and re-homing centres:
Vary in just about every way - including location, size, layout, facilities, types of animals catered for, policies and ethos. Most animal rescue centres are extremely busy caring for homeless animals; many of which have some sort of emotional or physical health problem. It is impossible for rescue centres to predict or plan the day as animals may arrive in varying states of need throughout the day and night. Reception areas are invariably busy with phones ringing constantly and a steady flow of people coming and going through the centre, either giving up animals or wanting to adopt an animal and this can create a feeling of chaos. This type of work involves working to assist neglected and abused animals and this can be emotionally and physically exhausting. Rescue centres are usually run on tight budgets and there is no government funding for animal charities. This means many places are short staffed and staff are required to work extremely hard.

A rescue centre cattery manager would be responsible for all or some of the following; animal care, daily cleaning and feeding routines, staff training, recruitment, managing staff, liaising with clients, veterinary staff and other organisations, dealing with contractors, adoptions, administration, maintaining high standards of care and hygiene. Salaries vary according to region and experience and range from £16,000 - £30,000.

15. Cat Sitter

This is an excellent career choice if you care passionately about cats and would like to run your own business working from home. Cat sitting is a kind and affordable alternative to a boarding cattery. The idea of cat sitting is simply that the owners' cats will stay in their own home environment where they receive individual care from a pet sitter who will visit daily. There is therefore the minimum disruption to the animal's routine. There is a unique online course called the Professional Pet Sitter Diploma - a valuable qualification for this type of career. This course can be tailor made to include more cat modules if you intend to work as a Cat Sitter and not general pet sitting.

Pet services are in high demand in the UK as more pet owners recognise that boarding can be a traumatic experience for their pet. Going on holiday is not the only reason that owners use a pet sitter; there are many other reasons such as going into hospital, moving house, building works, having a baby etc. Some of these reasons are more urgent and you may find that you don't receive much warning and have last minute requests for your services. It is a good idea to advertise your mobile phone number to ensure that you don't miss out on last minute bookings.

Some pet sitters set up their own businesses and others take on work from Cat Sitting companies – the latter is a good way of starting up as you should instantly have clients and will not have to incur any costs, such as advertising. If you do set up your own pet sitting business, it is a good idea to register with the National Association of Registered Pet Sitters (NARP). They are the largest Pet Care organisation in the UK; involved primarily with the proper care of Pets and Property and setting the standards for the Pet and House sitting industries. They have over 10,000 registered pet boarding/sitting businesses throughout the country and many people use their services to search for registered pet boarding businesses in their local area – a good way for you to get new clients. If you run your own pet sitting business, you will need to take out third party liability and care custody and control insurance.

The summer holiday months are the busiest in a cat sitter's diary and once you have established your business, you will find that the holiday months will book up long in advance. It is good practice to request that clients complete a profile form that will enable you to gather and record vital information about the cats you will be caring for. Find out about any specific medical problems, ensure that the owner leaves their vet's contact details with you and insist that the cats are insured. Request the details of someone you could contact who is authorised by the cat's owner to make decisions about the cat, should you not be able to get hold of the owner in an emergency.

It is advisable to inform your local vet of your business in case you need your local practice in an emergency or if a client's vet is too far away. Registering with your local vet is a good way of advertising your services for free.

Ideally you need to be mobile with your own vehicle and current driving license. If you enjoy interacting with cats, this could be a good way to work from home and earn extra income doing something you enjoy. Earning rates vary from between £12 - £20 per cat per night, depending on the area you cover - London rates can be higher. Offering additional services such offering to ensure that a client's home looks lived in, such as opening and drawing curtains, switching on lights, picking up post or deliveries, watering plants, etc. Some companies also offer cat grooming and have veterinary staff that will ensure that if a client requires a medical service, the cat's medication or insulin injections will be administered correctly, etc.

Having a qualification in animal behaviour or a Professional Pet Sitting Diploma will greatly improve your career prospects.

Useful contacts:

National Association of Registered Pet Sitters
National Home Boarding Register

16. Cat Groomer

Grooming is an important part of a cat's health and well-being – particularly for long-haired cats. Brushing encourages a healthy skin and good growth of a new coat, a regularly groomed cat will be happier, feel more comfortable and have a healthier looking and shinier coat. Therefore every cat, regardless of coat type, size, breed or age should receive regular grooming. In most cases, an owner can carry this out, however, some cats (mainly long-haired) may need professional grooming.

Working as a cat groomer can be very rewarding as grooming can prevent and alleviate suffering. Regular grooming can prevent problems such as excessive shedding and painful mats. It can help identify other problems, for example; sores, fleas, lumps, cuts, rashes and bad teeth, that might go unnoticed without the hands on attention. Grooming can prevent mats that pull tender skin and cause pain and lead to hot spots or wounds. Many thousands of dogs and cats are given up for adoption every year due to their owners having allergic reactions. Your work as a Groomer can in some cases help to reduce allergic reactions that owners may experience.

You should be manually dexterous with good hand to eye co-ordination and a good eye for detail. You must have patience and confidence to cope with the individual temperament of each cat. You need to be gentle and prepared to work calmly and not be rushed. You will need to have a love of working with animals and an understanding of animal behaviour. You will need to enjoy working with the public, have good customer care skills and be willing to deal with, in some cases, highly demanding cat owners.

The demand for professional groomers is increasing as more people have pets and there is a growing awareness about responsible pet ownership. Career opportunities are varied in this type of animal care and a good groomer should never be unemployed. Whilst there are varied career prospects, grooming isn't an easy or glamorous career. Be prepared to get dirty and be aware that you may have some unpleasant tasks such as dealing with ticks, fleas, lice and in some cases, severe matting. Most cats will find a grooming salon to be a potentially threatening environment and they may be fearful. There is always a risk of being bitten or scratched and if this happens, remember it is always your fault and not the cat's – never hit or shout at a cat if you are bitten or scratched, this is an occupational risk.

Career opportunities as a groomer include: working in an animal rescue centre, pet shops, home groomer, boarding kennels, veterinary practices, animal hospitals or working in or owning a grooming salon. If your dream is to run your own grooming business or salon, it is advisable to complete a start your own business course as well as grooming training. If you are considering setting up your own business, remember that the costs of setting up a grooming salon can be quite high as you will need to buy a variety of grooming equipment including clippers, etc. You may also need to consider hiring additional help to run a full appointment diary and to keep your salon open when you are not available. Working as a home groomer can also be fairly lucrative and there are less outlay costs – this is also a less stressful environment for most cats.

Cat grooming should not be undertaken as a career unless you have had some training. Ideally you should have had some hands on experience working with cats. Volunteer to assist a nearby animal charity or a local grooming salon, as this will give you an excellent opportunity to observe the many aspects of a grooming business. In addition, some salons may offer training on the job and this is another good way of getting into this industry. The Accredited Grooming Diploma is an excellent qualification to consider.

Some people start this career by studying for an NVQ/SVQ in Animal Care at Level 2 or 3. An NVQ/SVQ in Animal Care is also available at level 1, but grooming is not available within the qualification at this level. Private courses usually start with three months in the grooming school, followed by work experience for some months, returning to the school to prepare for exams. After at least 18 months' practical experience, Groomers can enroll for the City & Guilds Grooming Certificate - a two-part exam with a written paper and practical element.

Useful contacts:
The Pet Care Trust: has a list of centres that offer grooming qualifications Bedford Business Centre, 170 Mile Road, Bedford, MK42 9TW. Tel: 01234 273 933

17. Cat Boarding Business

Owning and running a boarding cattery can be both rewarding and fulfilling. The work is very demanding and comes with much responsibility; this career can easily become a way of life, as it is most likely that you will need to live on site. Buying a cattery will require a large up-front financial outlay, so it is worth first considering what you could reasonably expect as a return from your investment. Start by creating a business plan, this will give you a true picture of the type of income and profit you could expect to make. It is worth learning more about setting up your <u>own small business</u>.

Thorough research into demand and supply in your area is very important, first ensure that there is sufficient business available in your area and adequate demand for boarding services. If you intend to buy a going concern, it is worth employing the services of a financial advisor to examine the books first. This is not the sort of business that can be run part time, it is potentially a lifestyle change and a big financial commitment; first ensure that the business stands a good chance of success before you start to commit money and time. There is now government funding available in some parts of the country – this is worth researching, as you may be eligible for Defra grant funding towards your new cattery business.

Whether you build a cattery from scratch or take on an already established business, it is important to ensure that it conforms to the CIEH Model License Conditions. Local authorities are now enforcing these standards more stringently and won't license a cattery if you don't comply. Under the Animal Boarding Establishments Act of 1963, all boarding establishments are required to be licensed by the local authority. The license, which is granted in the name of the owner, is issued annually and all catteries must have a current license displayed in a public area of the business. Your local authority may attach conditions to the license and use the Chartered Institute of Environmental Health (CIEH) Model Licence Conditions & Guidance for Cat Boarding Establishments (1995) as a guide. Alternatively, they may adapt these guidelines to suit their own requirements.

During the year your local authority will usually make one or more visits to inspect your premises. An officer from your local Environmental Health Department or a veterinary surgeon appointed by the local authority normally carries this out. The license fee, which is decided on by each individual local authority, can vary enormously. If you are planning to purchase an existing cattery, you should check the terms of the license, as the license is issued to the owner personally rather than the business. It is important to find out if there are any reasons why the licence might not be renewed and to obtain permission in writing from the local authority to transfer the licence to your name. If you plan to build a new cattery you will need to apply to your local authority for outline and detailed planning permission, which can sometimes be a lengthy process. The local authority will provide the necessary paperwork and advice on how to continue. Building Regulations may apply to certain types of catteries. It is worth visiting several catteries to get a feel for the different designs and materials. You may decide to do the cattery design work yourself, the <u>Feline Advisory Bureau's</u> working drawings are useful for certain styles of cattery and these can be used to support your planning application. The FAB manual is a unique publication written with over 30 year's experience of working with boarding catteries. If you decide to employ a specialist cattery builder to construct your cattery, they will usually offer a complete package and make a planning application. Consider what material to use; UPVC is popular and practical as it is warm and easy to clean and maintain. There are some specialist companies that will assist with design and construction. It is worth visiting several catteries to get ideas on different designs.

As with all work with animals, running a cattery is extremely demanding and will involve getting your hands dirty. Whilst you may decide to hire animal care staff to assist with some of the work, you will still be ultimately responsible for the cats in your care. In order for your business to be successful and to attract returning customers, it is crucial that you have good people skills and that your customer care is excellent. Clients boarding their cats want to feel reassured that the cattery is well managed and that staff are caring, compassionate and genuinely interested in their pet's welfare. Offering extras such as cat grooming will help to enhance your business – there are specific animal grooming training courses available including the Accredited Grooming Diploma course. This qualification is worth having, as extra services will impress clients and ensure additional revenue for your business. Other qualifications to consider include the Feline Studies Diploma, the Professional Pet Care and Veterinary Assistant Diploma, the Cat Carer Diploma, the Feline Behaviour and Psychology Diploma and the Animal Care, Welfare and Husbandry Diploma.

Whilst there will be plenty of rewards in looking after the cats, there is much hard work involved in ensuring that their stay is stimulating and as stress free as possible. For this type of business, it is crucial that you are healthy and fit; the day will involve a lot of walking around the cattery to check on cats as well as lifting and bending if you are doing any of the cleaning. Other daily duties could include; liaising with clients, administering medication, grooming, bookkeeping and staff recruitment. If you intend to hire any cattery staff, it is imperative that they are well trained and that they have clear instructions about the standards required.

Even though the cats may be vaccinated, there is still a risk of disease spreading – particularly cat flu – and it is important that high standards of cleanliness are continually maintained. Having a disease outbreak will cause unnecessary suffering to the cats in your care and will do your business image a lot of damage. Once you have had an infectious outbreak, it is very difficult to completely get rid of the disease. Therefore, it is important that specialist animal accommodation disinfectant products are always used; these can be expensive but it is false economy to do without. Meal times are the highlight of the day for confined animals and so you will need to ensure that you serve good quality, nutritious, tasty food – again, this will cost more than the supermarket brands, so add this into your budget when you create the business plan. Some cats suffering from stress may go off their normal food and you might find yourself having to buy roast chicken, tuna or beef steaks to ensure that they eat something! Having a qualification in animal behaviour will also greatly assist you with this type of work.

Useful contacts:
Catteries for sale: Ladybird Kennels, Roman Road, Ingatestone, Essex, CM4 9AD Tel: 01277 356641
The Kennels Agency: Moorfield House, Mattishall Rd, Norfolk NR20 5BZ Tel: 01362 698855
Cattery Design: P O Box 146, Chipping Norton, Oxfordshire OX7 6WA. Tel: 01608 646454
Feline Advice Bureau (FAB): Taeselbury High Street, Wiltshire, SP3 6LD. Tel: 0870 742 2278

18. Cat Breeder
There is the option of cat breeding, but it is not a career we would recommend. One of the biggest worldwide animal welfare problems is the ever-increasing number of unwanted companion animals. Thousands of healthy cats are destroyed every year because there are simply not enough homes for them. Many of the unwanted cats that escape destruction are sitting in cages in rescue charities leading a boring and pointless existence with little or no hope of being re-homed. Most rescue homes are overflowing with unwanted cats. Knowing these sad facts, it seems wrong for us to advise further increasing the cat population by suggesting a career as a cat breeder.

Careers with Dogs

Dogs once existed as wild creatures; roaming in packs and surviving on their instincts. Humans domesticated them over 14,000 years ago – since then they have become our companions and we have become closely bonded with them. Dogs are highly social animals and many cultures consider them to be important members of the family and regard them to be man's best friend. In recent years, there has been an increase in the number of dogs owned as pets; now 22% of the population in Britain have at least one dog in their household.

Dogs are intelligent and they require both mental and physical stimulation, for which they are entirely dependent on humans. Being highly sociable, intelligent and adaptable has enabled dogs to learn to fulfill many roles that are extremely useful to society. For example, many are trained as working dogs of which there are several types including: assistance dogs, law enforcement dogs, rescue dogs, therapy dogs, herding dogs, guard dogs, detection dogs and war dogs.

There are many different careers and jobs available for those wishing to work with dogs. For most careers working with dogs, it is recommended that you have an NVQs/SVQs in Animal Care at levels 1 and/or 2 as a minimum education requirement. These are available through the College of Animal Welfare, some animal charities and through various other colleges around the country. You may be able to develop your career either by gaining experience and working towards NVQ/SVQ Level 3 in Animal Care, or by studying part-time for qualifications such as the EDEXCEL BTEC National Certificate/Diploma in Animal Management (Care) and the EDEXCEL BTEC National Award in Animal Management (Kennel and Cattery Management). Apprenticeships may be available for those under the age of 24. In England these are currently Apprenticeships (level 2) and Advanced Apprenticeships (level 3).

Training to consider is the Canine Science and Behaviour Diploma Course which is aimed at those with an interest in dogs, either in an employment capacity, or simply for pleasure. The Rescue dog Carer/Trainer Diploma is a valuable qualification for anyone wanting to work with dogs in an animal charity kennels.

Animal Jobs Direct offers a Diploma in Animal Care, Welfare and Husbandry that includes an entire module about dogs. In addition, the Advanced Canine Behaviour Diploma, the Professional Pet Sitter Diploma, the Professional Kennel Operator Diploma and the Search and Rescue Dog Handler Diploma, the Canine Science Diploma, Canine Studies Diploma, Canine Behaviour and Psychology Diploma, Canine Aggression Diploma, Canine Communication Diploma, the Professional Pet Care and Veterinary Assistant Diploma and the Cynology Diploma course are all valuable to those wishing to pursue a career working with dogs.

In this section, we have information about the following careers working with dogs: Kennel Assistant, Kennel Manager, Dog Home Boarder, Dog Trainer, Dog Handler (including Fire service, Search and Rescue, Customs & Excise, Army, Police & Private security), Assistance Dog Trainer, Dog Behaviourist, Dog Warden, Dog Groomer, Dog Walker, Dog Day Care Business.

19. Kennel Assistant

Kennel jobs are the starting point for most careers working with dogs. This type of work involves long hours and hard physical work. Candidates are required to have plenty of stamina and to be in good health. As well as being physically fit you also need to have common sense, an ability to follow instructions and good customer care skills.

Dedicated, compassionate and hard working kennel staff are highly valued in this environment. Dogs in boarding or welfare kennels are entirely reliant on the kennel staff for cleaning, exercise, feeding and stimulation. Having caring people with a genuine interest in dogs and their welfare doing this sort of work makes a very real difference to the quality of life for the dogs in the kennels.

Confinement in kennels is an unnatural environment for dogs, and has been known to cause physical and/or emotional ill health. Good kennel staff will pick up on and attend to individual problems and needs and provide environmental enrichment for the dogs to make their stay a more bearable experience. Having a calm and cheerful disposition is essential for this type of work as dogs will pick up on and respond to your mood.

Your daily work in a boarding, quarantine or welfare kennel will no doubt mean an early start as the dogs will need to be taken out for exercise and a toilet break. This first part of the day can be demanding as the dogs will in most cases, have been left all night in their kennels and will be desperate for attention.

It is important that you are able to prioritise and work quickly and efficiently, as you will probably have many dogs to deal with; speed is essential as all the dogs will be waiting their turn to go out.

After walking each dog, you will be required to clean the kennels. To prevent the spread of disease and to ensure that the kennel environment is clean for the dogs, it is important that this is done to a high standard. There is a lot of bending and lifting involved, as you will be required to poop scoop and scrub each kennel thoroughly and efficiently and replace bedding where necessary.

When you have completed these tasks, your work will involve preparing meals for the dogs. Again, this needs to be done efficiently and with speed, as the dogs will be hungry and waiting for their food. The dogs will have different dietary requirements and you may need to prepare a variety of different meals – normally they will each have two meals per day.

The remainder of your working day will probably involve more walks, games with the dogs, preparing another meal, cleaning and poop scooping, bathing and grooming some dogs and carrying out behavioural assessments if you are working in an animal rescue centre environment.

You will need to be aware of individual needs and able to ensure that each dog in your care is given some individual attention during the day. Hands on time, walking and playing with the dogs will be one of the more rewarding and pleasurable parts of this job, so make sure you get a chance to interact with as many dogs as possible every day! Formal qualifications are not essential for most jobs working in kennels but they will ensure you have a better chance of being offered a job, higher salary or more responsibility in your work. The Professional Kennel Operator Diploma, the Rescue Dog Trainer Diploma and the Diploma in Animal Care, Welfare and Husbandry are all excellent qualifications for this type of work.

Salaries for this type of work start from around £12,000 and may go up to around £18,000 depending on experience and responsibilities. Some boarding kennels may offer accommodation and/or a vehicle as part of the payment and it may be a requirement that you are able to drive. Once you have sufficient experience you may wish to go on to set up your own kennels or become a kennel manager

20. Kennel Manager

The role of a kennel manager can vary greatly and depends on the size and type of organisation. Broadly speaking, kennels can be divided into boarding/breeding kennels and charity/re-homing kennels – see descriptions below.

Private boarding establishments:
The kennel manager may be responsible for recruitment, staff training, daily routines, general management and maintaining high standards of care and hygiene throughout the kennels. You may also be required to do some of the physical work in the kennels. Formal qualifications are not always necessary, but good organisational or management skills and some experience working with animals or a relevant qualification is essential. Often, once someone has worked as a kennel manager, they go on to running their own kennel business. It is crucial to have some business experience or training as well as hands on experience working with dogs before setting up your own kennel business. It is more economical and less time consuming to buy an already existing kennels business than to set one up. You could expect to pay anything from around £200,000 for a kennel business and there are specific publications that advertise kennel business for sale – see useful contacts list below.

Animal charity rescue and re-homing centres:
Working for an animal charity is very different to the work of a private boarding or breeding business. As no two animal rescue centres are run in the same way, it is difficult to clearly define the role of a kennel manager in an animal rescue charity. They vary in just about every way including, location, size, layout, facilities, and types of animals catered for, policies and ethos. However, one thing they all do is to take in, care for and re-home unwanted animals.

Most animal rescue centres are very busy with the pressure of many unwanted, lost or abandoned animals; many of which have some sort of emotional or physical health problem. Reception areas are invariably busy with phones ringing constantly and a steady flow of people coming and going through the centre either giving up animals or wanting to adopt an animal and this can create a feeling of chaos.

The work of a charity kennel manager can be emotionally exhausting as it involves assisting neglected and abused animals. Animal rescue centres are usually run on tight budgets, as there is no government funding for animal charities. This means many animal charities are short staffed and staff are required to work extremely hard, often having to do the work of several staff.

Depending on the size of the organisation, a rescue centre kennel manager could be responsible for all or some of the following; daily cleaning and feeding routines, staff training, recruitment, managing staff, working with clients and other organisations, dealing with contractors, re-homing, behavioural assessments, administration and maintaining high standards of care and hygiene throughout the kennels.

The kennel manager may also be required to do some of the more physical work. There are no formal qualifications for this job but you need to be physically, emotionally and mentally fit, calm, patient, kind and compassionate, have sound animal welfare experience, good organisational skills and good management or supervisory experience. For the right person, the job of kennel manager can be highly stimulating and extremely rewarding.

The Canine Diploma courses as mentioned at the start of this Canine section are all excellent qualifications for this type of work.

Useful contacts:
Kennels for sale: Ladybird Kennels, Roman Road, Ingatestone, Essex, CM4 9AD Tel: 01277 356641
The Kennels agency: Moorfield House, Mattishall Road, Norfolk, NR20 5BZ Tel: 01362 698855
Kennel Design: P O Box 146, Chipping Norton, Oxfordshire OX7 6WA, UK Tel: 01608 646454

21. Dog Home Boarder

Home boarding services are in high demand as more pet owners become aware that putting their animal in kennels can be a traumatic experience. Many people now recognise that dog home boarding is a kind and affordable alternative to kennels. Confining any animal is never ideal; kennels can be a frightening and stressful experience for some dogs and for others a very boring one. The idea of dog home boarding is simply that dogs stay in a home environment where they receive individual care and are treated like one of the family.

To run a dog home boarding business, you will need to be home based. If you enjoy interacting with dogs, this could be a good way to work from home and earn extra income doing something you enjoy. Dogs can be messy – don't contemplate this career if you are house proud! To become a dog home boarder, you will need to either own your home or have permission from your landlord to allow dogs in your house. It is important that you have a secure garden and if you have any pets of your own, it is crucial that they get along with other animals.

Your day as a home boarder will be spent walking, playing and interacting with the dogs in your care. To ensure that they are well exercised and stimulated, it is likely that you will need to take the dogs out for at least two hours or for a minimum of three walks per day; you need to be physically fit and enjoy walking and exercise. It is ideal if you have open spaces near your home that are suitable for off lead dog walking. It is preferable to have a few options, such as woodland, park, beaches or fields so that you can vary the walking areas and prevent boredom for the dogs and yourself! If your home is not near a suitable walking area, you will need to buy a vehicle suitable for transporting several dogs at a time, for their walks.

Some home boarders set up their own businesses and others take on work from pet boarding companies. The latter is a good way of starting up, as you should instantly have clients and will not incur costs, such as advertising. There are several franchise type companies that are worth considering if you are contemplating running your own business – see useful contacts below.

If you decide to set up your own dog home boarding business, you may want to register with your local Association of Registered Pet Sitters, who set the standards for the Pet and House sitting industries. Many of your potential clients will use the services of an Association to search for registered pet boarding businesses in their local area and it is a good way for you to get new clients.

Going on holiday is not the only reason that animals are boarded; there are many other reasons such as going into hospital, moving house, building works, having a baby , etc. Some of these reasons are more urgent; you may find that you don't receive much warning and have last minute requests for your services. It is a good idea to advertise your mobile phone number to ensure that you don't miss out on last minute bookings.

The summer holiday months are the busiest in a dog home boarder's diary and once you have established your business, you will find that the holiday months will book up long in advance. It is good practice to request that clients complete a profile form, as this will enable you to gather and record vital information about the dogs in your care. It is advisable to arrange to meet up before the booking to find out more about the dog, daily routines and to discuss any specific requirements with the dog's owner. Going for a walk is a good way to conduct your initial meeting and will enable you to establish whether the dog is well socialised, is allowed off lead walks, what the dog's recall is like, etc. To help the dog settle well in your care, ask that his bedding, lead, bowls, toys and usual food is brought along with him – this will instantly help the dog to feel more at home.

Once you are established as a home boarder it is highly likely that you will have more than one dog staying at a time. This is a great way for dogs to meet other dogs and to have dog playtime. However, some owners prefer their dog not to be boarded with other dogs, and you will need to consider whether this suits you, or if you would need to adjust your prices accordingly, as this will affect your profits.

Find out about any specific medical problems, ensure that the owner leaves their vet's contact details with you and insist that the dog is insured. Request the details of someone you could contact who is authorised by the dog's owner to make decisions about the dog should you not be able to get hold of the owner in an emergency. It is advisable to inform your local vet of your business in case you need a vet in an emergency or if a client's vet is too far away. It is also worth gaining a basic animal/veterinary first aid qualification so that you are able to assist an animal in your care in case of emergency.

It is recommended that you request that the dogs in your care, are fully vaccinated, insured, micro-chipped and that they wear a dog collar with identity tag. If you run your own dog boarding business, you will need to take out third party liability and care custody and control insurance. Registering with your local vet is a good way of advertising your services for free and may result in some business for you.

The Professional Pet Sitter Diploma and the Diploma in Animal Care, Welfare and Husbandry and the Professional Dog Home Boarder Diploma are all excellent qualifications for this type of work.

Earning rates vary from between £12 - £20 per dog per night, depending on where you are based. Offering additional services such as grooming, pet taxi for dog collection, treats, etc are ways of increasing your earnings and enhancing your business.

Useful contacts:

National Association of Registered Pet Sitters

National Home Boarding Register

Examples of Dog Boarding Businesses:

Guardian Angel Services: Guardian House, Unit 28, South Hill Close, Norwich NR7 0NQ.
Tel: 0800 013 0026

Animals At Home: Tel: 01489 895015

Pals 4 Pets: 2 Croft Close, London NW7 4QL. Tel: 020 8201 1606

22. Dog Trainer

A career as a dog trainer requires you to have an affinity with dogs as well as plenty of patience and compassion. You will need to be self-motivated and able to communicate effectively with people and animals. You will need to have an understanding of and ability to work with dogs, as well as the confidence to handle dogs of all types, sizes and temperaments. It is crucial that the dog training procedure is an enjoyable and stimulating experience for the dog and that it is not a punishment!

Whilst there are no standard qualifications in this profession, it is advisable for anyone wishing to be a dog trainer to complete an animal behaviour course. It is crucial that candidates first have some experience of working with dogs before considering an Instructors course. If you haven't spent time working with or caring for dogs, it is worthwhile working as a volunteer before embarking on this type of career. Many animal charities run volunteer programmes, several offer work experience placements and some even offer NVQ training courses. All of these opportunities provide excellent ways to gain experience and build up your confidence for working around dogs. In addition, the following are useful qualifications to have for this type of work: Canine Science Diploma, Canine Studies Diploma, Canine Behaviour & Psychology Diploma, Advanced Canine Behaviour Management Diploma and the Advanced Animal Behaviour Diploma.

Although there are many training methods and courses available to anyone eager to get started - ranging from videos, books and college courses, it is advisable that you choose the course very carefully and avoid any course that uses punishment as a method of training. If this is suggested then they are not good courses! The dog training procedure should be an enjoyable and stimulating experience for the dog not a punishment.

The British Institute of Professional Dog Trainers runs an Instructor's course that is of use to those who have some dog training experience. The UK Registry of Canine Behaviourists keeps a register of trainers who have attained a high level of expertise and are respected in the profession. Both of these organisations provide advice to those wishing to become a dog trainer.

Most dog trainers are self-employed and charge according to their experience – this may be as much as £30 per hour in some parts of London. Many dogs taken in to rescue centres have behavioural problems and are in need of training before being re-homed. Some animal rescue centres employ dog trainers and behaviourists to work with the dogs brought into their centres. Whilst this can be extremely rewarding work, it can also be emotionally exhausting, as it involves assisting neglected and abused animals.

Useful Contacts:

The British Institute of Professional Dog Trainers: offers training for instructors. Tel: 01663 762772

Kennel Club Accreditation Scheme for Instructors in Dog Training and Canine Behaviour: this scheme is designed to give a personal, professional nationally recognised qualification for Dog Training Instructors. The scheme is flexible in its modular format to also cover training specialists, canine behaviourists, advisers and those involved in puppy/dog socialisation; rehabilitation; dog walkers/sitters; rescue/re-homing , etc. Tel: 0870 606 6750.

Association of Pet Dog Trainers: P.O. Box 17, Kempsford GL7 4WZ. Tel: 01285 810 811.

23. Dog Handler

Dogs are highly skilled creatures; they can detect human scents from several hundred yards away and are able to search restricted areas such as undergrowth far more efficiently than a human can. One-third of a dog's brain is set aside for scent detection alone.

Dog Handlers work with specially trained dogs. There is much competition for this type of work and there are not many positions. However, you will stand a better chance of employment if you are physically fit and have excellent vision. Although not essential, some experience with dogs might help – try volunteering at a local rescue centre or kennels.

Here are some examples of the different Dog Handler roles:

* Fire service – working with dogs to search burning and collapsed buildings for signs of life and other emergencies.

* Search and Rescue – this may involve mountain, cave, and water rescue, whilst searching for missing or injured people. There is a unique diploma course for this career: the Search and Rescue Dog Handler Diploma.

* Customs & Excise dog handler - usually employed at ports or airports, the work involves checking passengers, luggage and cargo for the detection of drugs and other banned substances.

* Army Handler/Trainer - could be involved in airfield defence and army support, and may be deployed in a land mine, war or casualty location. You must be at least 16 to join. To be a Royal Air Force police dog handler there is a minimum joining age of 17.5 years.

* Police dog handlers are involved in crime prevention, drug detection, explosives and firearms detection. As crime becomes more sophisticated, the use of dog handlers to assist in crime prevention is increasing. There is a minimum joining age of 18.5 years and you must have worked for at least two years as a Beat Constable. Applicants must be a British or Irish Republic subject, or a Commonwealth citizen not subject to work restrictions and they must satisfy a background report and security check.

* Private security companies - employ dog handlers for the protection of property. These companies usually recruit older people, although the need for agility and physical fitness remains.

Training encourages a dog to use its instinctive drives in a controlled situation and on command. One of the most important natural instincts is the dog's willingness to please the pack leader - the handler.

Trainee dog handlers learn: to understand the principles of dog training, the correct use of training and protective equipment, the correct use of training commands, both verbal and visual application of methods of search, an appreciation of the needs of a dogs' health and welfare and relevant legislation about dogs including the Dangerous Dogs Act.

The dogs learn: to always respond correctly to their handlers commands, attain a competent standard of general obedience, track a person over various surfaces, indicate dropped/lost property, search for and indicate missing persons or suspects, locate lost stolen or illegal property or substances such as drugs and carry out all criminal work exercises in a safe and controlled manner.

The hours can be long and varied and may include weekends, evenings and nights. Police dog handlers work shifts on a 24-hour rota that covers seven days a week. In the army and RAF, you may be called out at any time to deal with an emergency, and will work particularly long hours if involved in an operation. Much walking and running is involved, so handlers need to be physically fit. Most of the work is outdoors in all kinds of weather and terrain.

Dog handlers must have an affinity with dogs and enjoy interacting with them, have experience with dogs either as a handler or having owned a pet, be happy in their own company and that of their dog, be patient and self-confident and able to work in a team, be able to work with minimum supervision, be physically strong, have sufficient space to accommodate a kennel in their garden or a dog in their home and have a full driving licence.

There are good opportunities for dog handlers, provided that they have some experience within a suitable organisation and are sympathetic to dogs. A trainee dog handler usually attends a one-week familiarisation course. At the end of the week, the candidates and the dog training centre staff decide whether they are suitable. Dogs should be constantly rewarded and praised for hard work and given good food, care, exercise and protection. On completing the initial course, the dog and handler are assessed and if they have achieved the required standards they are licensed to become operational as a team. Re-licensing will occur annually throughout the working life of the dog to ensure the required standards are maintained.

In the Services, starting salaries are around £16,000 a year. An experienced handler in all areas may expect to earn £25,000. In senior positions, and those requiring specialist knowledge, earnings can be more than £30,000. Starting salaries in the police force are considerably higher.

There are several useful courses for this line of work and they include: Search and Rescue Diploma, the Rescue Dog Trainer Diploma, Animal Care Welfare and Husbandry Diploma, Animal Behaviour Diploma, Advanced Canine Behaviour Diploma, Cynology Diploma, Canine Behaviour & Psychology and the Advanced Animal Behaviour Diploma.

Useful contacts:

Police Service Recruitment

The British Army: Tel: 08457 300111

National Search and Rescue Dog Association (NSARDA)

Security Industry Authority (SIA): PO Box 9, Newcastle Upon Tyne, NE82 6YX. Tel: 0870 243 0100

National Association of Security Dog Users (NASDU): Unit 11, Boundary Business Centre, Boundary Way, Woking, Surrey, GU21 5DH. Tel: 01483 888 588

RAF Careers: Tel: 0845 605 5555

24. Assistance Dog Trainer

The role of an Assistance Dog Trainer is to enable people with sensory or physical disabilities to live independently with the help of their trained dog. Most trainers are employed by the registered charities that form the umbrella organisation, Assistance Dogs (UK). There are four types of assistance dogs:

Guide Dogs for the Blind: provide guide dogs, mobility and other rehabilitation services to meet the needs of blind and partially sighted people. Their trained dogs provide blind and partially sighted people with freedom and independence. They enable owners to cross busy roads, avoid dangers such as obstacles at their feet and to get around their homes with ease.

Hearing Dogs for Deaf People: alert their deaf owners to the sounds that many people take for granted. This provides deaf people with greater independence, confidence and security. Most of the dogs are selected from rescue centres or donated as unwanted pets. Deafness can be a very isolating and lonely disability; a hearing dog can offer a practical alternative to technical equipment – particularly for those deaf people who find such equipment restricting. There is also the added benefit of giving the recipient increased independence, greater confidence, companionship and a feeling of security. Hearing Dogs alert severely and profoundly deaf people to sounds such as alarm clocks, the cry of a baby, ringing telephones, doorbells, cooker timers, smoke alarms, etc.

Dogs for the Disabled: trains assistance dogs to help physically disabled children and adults to live a more independent life. Each dog helps with practical tasks, from opening and closing doors to picking up dropped items and even emptying the washing machine! Canine Partners assists people with disabilities to enjoy a greater independence and a better quality of life and, where possible, to help them into education and employment through the provision of specially trained dogs, whose well-being is a key consideration.

Seizure Alert Dogs such as Support Dogs: are dedicated to improving the quality of life for people with epilepsy and people with disabilities by training dogs to act as efficient and safe assistants. Their dogs are trained to assist and support their owners with their specific disability. Each dog is taught tasks tailored to his owner's needs, enabling the disabled person to lead a fuller and more independent life. Their Seizure Alert Dogs recognise signs that their owner is about to have a seizure.

Besides these assistance dogs, there is another category called:

Therapy Dogs: these dogs have gentle, friendly temperaments and they are trained to provide comfort to hospitalised and institutionalised patients. Pets as Therapy (PAT) is an example of an organisation that utilises therapy dogs. They provide therapeutic visits to hospitals, hospices, nursing and care homes, special needs schools and a variety of other venues. Their volunteers organise these visits with their own friendly, temperament tested and vaccinated dogs and cats. Since it's beginning, over 18,000 dogs have been registered into the PAT scheme. Every year some of these retire and new dogs - having first been examined and passed on health, temperament, suitability and stability grounds, join Pets As Therapy.

Today there are currently around 3,500 active PAT visiting dogs and 90 cats at work in the UK. Every week, these calm friendly dogs and cats give more than 10,000 people, both young and old, the pleasure and chance to cuddle and talk to them. The bedsides that are visited each year number a staggering half million.

The work of the Assistance Dog Trainer depends largely on the type of assistance dog being trained. Typically, the work involves supervising the training of puppies and young dogs, training dogs for advanced tasks, training dogs and clients together and providing support and aftercare. Assistance trainers often work with up to six dogs at a time for as long as six months.

A normal working week is about 35 hours, which can include evenings, weekends and bank holidays. Part-time work is sometimes possible. An Assistance Dog Trainer will spend much of their time handling and walking dogs outdoors in all weathers. A high level of fitness is required, as the role is a very active one. There is often quite a bit of driving involved when visiting clients, so it is imperative to have a full driving license. A trainer should have a natural affinity with all types of dogs, have a great deal of patience and perseverance, have initiative - be able to work well on their own and in a team, have a sense of responsibility, have strong interpersonal and communication skills and be confident with all kinds and age ranges of people. Young people can learn how to train dogs from the age of 18. It is advantageous to have had work/social experience with adults and/or children from various backgrounds. Specialist skills such as sign language and lip reading may be required.

No specific qualifications are necessary for entry to be a trainer, although you should be at least 18 years old and have a good standard of education as some organisations look for GCSEs/S grades or equivalent, including English. Having NVQs in Animal Care is advantageous as is the Animal Behaviour Diploma and the Canine Science Diploma. The Advanced Canine Behaviour Diploma, the Rescue Dog Trainer Diploma and the Advanced Animal Behaviour Diploma are also excellent qualifications. The various organisations as mentioned above, have their own separate entry requirements. For example, Hearing Dogs for Deaf People require you to have sign language skills – it is worth contacting each organisation for further information. Establishments that train Assistance Dog Trainers in the UK are usually charitable organisations of which The Guide Dogs for the Blind Association is the largest, training approximately 700 dogs a year. Hearing Dogs for Deaf People trains approximately 150 dogs a year.

A trainer will usually work at the centre of one of the charities, settling dogs into kennels and getting them into a routine. It is an advantage to have either worked or volunteered previously with dogs. Employers may offer sponsorship for apprenticeship training or for further study at college. There may be opportunities for promotion to senior and management posts. Some trainers become self-employed in areas such as dog obedience classes or private dog training. Others move into a related field such as Veterinary Nursing or RSPCA Inspector.

Useful contacts:
Canine Partners for Independence (CPI): is a charity providing very highly trained assistance dogs to severely physically disabled people keen to live independently in the community. Mill Lane Heyshott, Midhurst West Sussex GU29 0ED. Tel: 08456 580 480

Dogs for the Disabled: train specially selected dogs to perform tasks which people with disabilities find difficult or impossible to perform themselves, and provide these people with companionship, independence and security. The Frances Hay Centre Blacklocks Hill Banbury Oxon OX17 2BS. Tel: 01295 252 600

Guide Dogs for the Blind Association: breeds and trains guide dogs for visually impaired people to help them lead more independent lives. Burghfield Common, Reading RG7 3YG. Tel: 01926 337 244

Hearing Dogs for Deaf People: trains dogs to act as 'hearing' ears for deaf people thus offering a practical means to greater independence. Wycombe Road Saunderton Princes Risborough Buckinghamshire HP27 9NS. Tel: 01844 348 100

Support Dogs: dedicated to improving the quality of life for people with epilepsy and people with disabilities by training dogs to act as efficient and safe assistants. 21 Jessops, Riverside, Brightside Lane, Sheffield, S9 2RX. Tel: 0870 609 3476.

Pets As Therapy: sick patients often feel isolated, yet medical staff report that even the most withdrawn patience seem to open up and let the barriers down when their regular PAT visiting dog is around. The constant companionship of an undemanding animal, that gives unconditional love, is often one of the most missed aspects of patients lives. PAT was formed to help make this loss more bearable and speed recovery.

25. Dog Behaviourist

Dog behaviourists diagnose and treat behavioural problems in dogs, such as aggression and phobias. Behaviourists must be patient, compassionate and demonstrate a genuine love for and affinity with dogs. They must also enjoy working with people and be able to communicate effectively. This can be a very challenging yet rewarding job, as you will be helping to improve the lives of dogs and their owners.

The job entails meeting owners and their dogs to discuss problems, observing and handling dogs to assess problems and developing treatment programmes. Duties may include: setting up individual training sessions, consulting over the phone, visiting clients in their own homes and facilitating dog behavioural classes.

It is strongly advisable to have a recognised qualification; such as the Animal Behaviour Diploma, Advanced Canine Behaviour Diploma, the Rescue Dog Trainer Diploma, Canine Studies Diploma, Canine Behavour & Psychology Diploma, Cynology Diploma, Canine Science Diploma and the Advanced Animal Behaviour Diploma.

Most behaviourists are self employed, running their own businesses and charging according to their experience – this may be as much as £30 per hour in some parts of London. Some larger animal rescue centres employ their own behaviourists; this type of work can be extremely rewarding, as you will be helping to rehabilitate traumatised and suffering animals, however, it can also be emotionally exhausting.

Useful contacts:

The British Institute of Professional Dog Trainers: offers training for instructors. Tel: 01663 762772

Kennel Club Accreditation Scheme for Instructors in Dog Training and Canine Behaviour: this scheme is designed to give a personal, professional nationally recognised qualification for Dog Training Instructors. The scheme is flexible in its modular format to also cover training specialists, canine behaviourists, advisors and those involved in puppy/dog socialisation; rehabilitation; dog walkers/sitters; rescue/re-homing etc. Tel: 0870 606 6750.

Association of Pet Dog Trainers: PO Box 17, Kempsford GL7 4WZ. Tel: 01285 810 811.

26. Dog Warden

The 1990 Environmental Protection Act requires each local authority in the UK to have someone in employment for the collection of stray dogs. Dog Warden is one of the titles most often used for this position, others include; Animal Warden, Dog Control Officer and Animal Welfare Officer.

The precise duties and wages vary greatly between Councils. Below are a few tasks that a dog warden may be required to fulfill:

Stray dogs: Unfortunately, some irresponsible owners allow their dogs to roam and this can cause a wide range of problems and disturbances. A warden will try to return the dog to its home and advise or fine the owner.

Education: Many dog owners benefit from being informed about the law and the need for responsible ownership. Lectures, demonstrations, displays and school talks are vital parts of a Dog Warden's work.

Complaints: This involves the investigation and resolution of complaints about straying, fouling, barking, biting. This must be carried out with tact and compassion but always in a firm enough manner to get an effective outcome.

Assist an injured animal: Injured animals may be encountered through the course of a Dog Warden's work. It is therefore crucial that candidate have first aid knowledge and training about basic veterinary care.

Enforcement: A thorough knowledge of the local and national animal control laws is essential, as is the knowledge and skill to lawfully enforce laws when voluntary compliance can't be obtained. Wardens work closely with the Police, RSPCA and animal welfare organisations.

Register of dogs: By law, a complete and accurate record of dogs lost / found / seized etc, must be maintained. This job therefore requires candidates to have good written skills for record keeping and report writing.

Licensing of animal establishments: There may be involvement with the licensing of Pet Shops, Boarding Kennels, Catteries, etc.

Dog Training: The setting up and running of basic training and husbandry classes may be required.

Specific qualifications are usually not essential, but a good basic education is important as well as some knowledge about dog welfare issues. The Animal Care Welfare and Husbandry Diploma, Diploma in Canine Science, the Rescue Dog Trainer Diploma, Cynology Diploma, Animal Behaviour Diploma, the Professional Pet Care and Veterinary Assistant Diploma, the Advanced Canine Behaviour Diploma and the Advanced Animal Behaviour Diploma are useful qualifications. Candidates must hold a full UK driving licence as they may be required to drive a specially modified vehicle to accommodate any dog, together with specialist equipment that may be necessary to safely handle and contain dogs. Working hours are varied and may include weekends, nights and bank holidays.

Most Dog Wardens have experience with dogs both privately and professionally; confidence in handling dogs other than in a pet capacity can be advantage and animal related work experience can be a big plus. Previous experience with dogs is an advantage.

This can be a rewarding job, but it can often entail dealing with a difficult side of the general public and having a demonstrable ability to do this is important. Experience in law enforcement can, therefore be a huge advantage.

The Dog Warden needs to maintain a professional image so that he or she is both recognisable and accessible. Smart appearance, good use of english, excellent communication skills, the ability to work well alone, demonstrating sound judgement and very importantly, a willingness to learn and use initiative.

Vacancies are normally advertised through local authorities and sometimes through the National Dog Wardens Association. Salaries vary according to region and experience and start from about £14,000 up to £30,000.

Useful contacts:

National Dog Wardens Association (NDWA): Haffield Lodge. Gloucester Road, Corse Staunton, Gloucestershire, GL19 3RA

Find out more about your local Dog Warden service

27. Dog Groomer

Grooming is an important part of a dog's health and well being. Brushing encourages a healthy skin and good growth of a new coat, as it stimulates the blood supply to the skin, removes dead hair and dirt and prevents matting. A regularly groomed dog will be happier, feel more comfortable and have a healthier looking and shinier coat. Therefore, every dog, regardless of coat type, size, breed or age should receive regular grooming. Many owners don't have the time or facilities to bath, groom and/or clip their dogs and some breeds of dogs benefit from professional grooming.

The main job of a dog groomer is to maintain the condition of dogs' coats through bathing, clipping and trimming. Groomers may also be required to clean dog ears, trim nails, bush, blow dry and style coats.

Working as a dog groomer can be very rewarding as grooming can prevent and alleviate suffering. Regular grooming can prevent problems such as excessive shedding and painful mats. It can help identify other problems, for example; sores, fleas lumps, cuts, rashes and bad teeth etc, that might go unnoticed without the hands on attention. Grooming can prevent mats that pull tender skin and lead to hot spots or wounds. Many thousands of dogs and cats are given up for adoption every year due to their owners having allergic reactions. Your work as a Groomer can in some cases help reduce allergic reactions that owners may experience.

You should be manually dexterous, have good hand to eye co-ordination and a good eye for detail. You must be able to handle and control all types of dogs and have patience and confidence to contend with difficulties with the individual temperament of each dog. You need to be gentle and prepared to work calmly and not be rushed. You will need to have a love of working with animals, an understanding of dog behaviour and an interest in learning about hair cutting and styling techniques. You will need to enjoy working with the public, have good communication and customer care skills and be willing to deal with, in some cases, highly demanding dog owners.

The demand for professional groomers is increasing as more people have pets and there is a growing awareness about responsible pet ownership. Career opportunities are varied in this type of animal care and a good dog groomer should never be unemployed. Whilst there are varied career prospects, dog grooming isn't an easy or glamorous career. It involves hard physical work - a job to avoid if you are not physically fit or if you have a bad back as you will need to do a lot of bending, lifting and moving dogs. Be prepared to get dirty and be aware that you may have some unpleasant tasks such as dealing with ticks, fleas, lice and in some cases, severe matting. Most dogs will find a grooming salon to be a potentially threatening environment and they may be fearful – there is always a risk of being bitten and if this happens, remember it is always your fault and not the dog's – never hit or shout at a dog if you are bitten, this is an occupational risk.

Career opportunities as a dog groomer include: working in an animal rescue centre, dog day care centres, mobile grooming vehicles, pet shops, home groomer, boarding kennels, veterinary practices, animal hospitals and working in or owning a grooming salon. If your dream is to run your own dog grooming business or salon, it is advisable to complete a business course as well as a professional dog grooming diploma course. If you are considering setting up your own business, remember that the costs of setting up a grooming salon can be quite high as you will need to buy a variety of grooming equipment including dog baths, clippers, etc. You may also need to consider hiring additional help to run a full appointment diary and to keep your salon open when you are not available. Working as a home groomer can also be fairly lucrative and there are less outlay costs.

Dog grooming should not be undertaken as a career unless you have had some training and, ideally, you should have had some hands on experience working with dogs. Your job as a groomer will be made much easier if you have a natural affinity with dogs and able to read dog body language. Whilst this is something you can receive training on, it is best to gain this type of knowledge from hands on experience. Volunteer to assist a nearby animal charity or a local grooming salon, as this will give you an excellent opportunity to observe the many aspects of a grooming business.

Some people start this career by studying for an NVQ/SVQ in Animal Care (Dog Grooming) at Level 2 or 3. An NVQ/SVQ in Animal Care is also available at level 1, but dog grooming is not available within the qualification at this level. Private courses usually start with three months in the grooming school, followed by work experience for some months, returning to the school to prepare for exams. After at least 18 months' practical experience, Dog Groomers can enrol for the City & Guilds Dog Grooming Certificate - a two-part exam with a written paper and practical element to tests candidates' practical skills on three different dog breeds.

Having NVQs in Animal Care is advantageous as is the Animal Care Welfare and Husbandry Diploma and an Animal Behaviour Diploma.

Useful contacts:

The Pet Care Trust: has a list of centres that offer grooming qualifications Bedford Business Centre, 170 Mile Road, Bedford, MK42 9TW. Tel: 01234 273 933

28. Dog Walker

Professional dog walking services are increasing in popularity in the UK and the number of people setting up their own dog walking businesses has grown considerably in the past few years.

Dog walkers are in particularly high demand in urban areas where dogs are confined in smaller properties and owners are at work all day. To enjoy this type of career, it is important that you are physically fit and that you enjoy walking and exercise.

Typically, dog walkers offer walks of one hour or more and most take several dogs on each walk. Some local authorities have introduced regulations and bylaws that state the maximum number of dogs that may be taken out at any one time; it is important that you are up to date on the latest regulations in your area before starting up this type of business.

Ideally, you should have open spaces near your home that are suitable for off lead walks. It is preferable If you have a few options, such as woodland, park, beaches or fields so that you can vary the areas and prevent boredom for the dogs and yourself!

Your biggest set up costs will be purchasing a vehicle suitable for transporting several dogs at a time and advertising your services. If you run your own business, you will need to take out third party liability and care custody and control insurance. There are franchise business opportunities available and some of these are worth considering.

It is recommended that you request that the dogs in your care are fully vaccinated, insured, micro chipped and that they wear a dog collar with identity tag. In addition, find out about any specific medical problems and ensure that the owner leaves their vet's contact details with you. If you run your own dog boarding business, you will need to take out third party liability and care custody and control Insurance. Registering with your local vet is a good way of advertising your services for free and may result in some business for you from a vet's clients.

Earning rates vary from between £8 - £15 per dog per walk, depending on where you are based. Offering additional services such as boarding or grooming can increase your earning potential and enhance your business.

At last, there is a unique and specialised qualification specifically for this field of work. The Professional Dog Walker Diploma is a recognised and suitable qualification for anyone wanting to work in this area of dog care.

29. Dog Day Care

Dog day care is a homely environment for dogs, ensuring that they receive company, play, exercise and stimulation throughout the day. These types of business are often run from an individuals' home or, sometimes, from a central meeting point where the dogs are dropped off by their owners first thing in the morning.

Dog day care is increasingly in demand by busy dog owners who may be working full time or have other new commitments e.g. a new baby, building work, etc. To make a success of this sort of business, you need to enjoy being around dogs, be physically active, enjoy walking and be creative about ways to keep the dogs in your care occupied and happy.

It is a good idea to get clients to bring their dog's toys and bedding, as this will help them feel more settled. Some dog day care centres have web-cams that allow dog owners to see their dogs during the day - these serve to enhance a business and to attract new customers.

It is recommended that you request that the dogs in your care are fully vaccinated, insured, micro chipped and that they wear a dog collar with identity tag. In addition, find out about any specific medical problems and ensure that the owner leaves their vet's contact details with you.

Dog day care costs between £10 and £25 per day depending on where you are based. Offering additional services such as grooming or boarding can increase your earning potential and enhance your business.

The Canine Science Diploma, Canine Studies Diploma, Dog Home Boarder Diploma, the Animal Behaviour Diploma and the Professional Pet Sitter Diploma are all excellent qualifications. It is also worthwhile considering doing a small business qualification and the Professional Dog Walker Diploma.

Careers with Horses

Most horses in the UK are owned by individuals. Their owners and riders spend over 900 million pounds per year on them; as a result there are a large number of employment possibilities across the equine industry. The largest sector is the racing one. Horse racing is a multi-million pound industry and there are dozens of different roles, including racecourse personnel and betting industry careers, some of which offer excellent salaries.

Although some careers with horses may be better paid than many other types of animal care jobs, you may be required to invest money and time in specialist training. Typically horse care courses are more expensive than other career training in the animal care industry. If you haven't spent time working with or caring for horses, it is worth considering working as a volunteer before embarking on this type of career.

Working around horses is grubby and involves tough physical work. To pursue a career with horses you must enjoy being outdoors in all types of weather as horses need to be exercised and cared for every day. You will need to be physically fit, hard working, have plenty of stamina, able to lift and carry heavy objects and climb up and down out of a saddle. If you are working for a stable yard, you may be required to live on site and it is helpful if you are able to drive as your work may at times involve transporting horses.

Although being able to ride a horse is a useful skill for most careers with horses, it is not essential for all horse jobs. Stud work and some stable jobs may not involve much riding initially; riding and handling can be improved on as the role progresses. However, someone who can correctly ride any horse in any situation is the most sought after employee.

The basic starting point qualifications are the National Vocational Qualification (NVQ) Level 1 or British Horse Society (BHS) Stage 1 and 2. Other relevant courses include a BTEC First Diploma in Horse Care and SQA National Certificate in Equine Studies. After completing these foundations, further qualifications will be specific to the type of equine career you wish to pursue.
There are several online equine courses worth considering, including the Equine Science Diploma, the Equine Behaviour & Psychology Diploma and the Stable Management Diploma.

There are apprenticeships available at different levels:

 UK: http://www.apprenticeships.org.uk
 Scotland: http://www.careers-scotland.org.uk
 Wales: http://www.careerswales.com
 Northern Ireland: http://www.delni.gov.uk.

In this section we have separated the information into the following sub sections:

A. **Horse Racing careers**: Stable Hand, Head Lad/Lass, Travelling Head Lad/Lass, Assistant Trainer, Trainer and Jockey.

B. **Horse Breeding careers:** Stud Hand, Stallion Handler, Stud Groom and Stud Manager.

C. **Other Horse Careers**: Farrier, Saddler, Riding Instructor, Holiday Centre Manager, Mounted Police, Army Mounted Units, Equine Dentist, Equine Veterinary Nurse, Equine Physiotherapist and Equine Rescue Charities.

A: Horse Racing Careers

30. Stable Hand

Stable jobs are the starting point for most careers with horses and to a certain extent, basic stable work remains an element of most careers with horses regardless of how qualified and experienced an individual becomes.

Stable Hands are required at all stables; their work is crucial to the smooth running of any horse business. The welfare of the horses is paramount and it is important that trainees are hard working, passionate and have an affinity with the horses in their care. It is a crucial part of the job to ensure that the horses are well cared for and therefore important that you are able to clean stables to a high standard and that you enjoy taking an interest in the general welfare of the horses in your care.

The daily work of a Stable Hand is physically demanding and involves mucking out stables, tack cleaning, exercising horses, grooming, sweeping and other yard duties. The work is outdoors, in all weathers and involves hard physical labour such as lifting, climbing, and cleaning. There are no set qualifications for this career but having some experience around horses is useful. Stable Hands should be able to ride to a good standard, be prepared to carry out routine jobs, have a general knowledge about horse care and safety and be willing to live on-site if necessary.

Training is offered at the British Racing School and the Northern Racing College. After gaining a few years' experience in the industry a small number of Stable Hands become Apprentice Jockeys (flat racing) or conditional jockeys (jump racing) and some of them go on to be Professional Jockeys. Other Stable Hands may progress to Travelling Head Lad (responsible for the horses and Hands when they travel to meetings), Assistant Head Lad and Head Lad (oversee the work of all the hands and apprentices). Some Jockeys and Head Lads become Assistant Trainers, with experience they may then become Trainers.

31. Head Lad/Lass

This role involves the daily supervision of the stable staff to ensure that the yard is well managed and that it runs smoothly and to schedule. The job demands much responsibility and you will need to be a strong leader with good supervisory skills and be able to work well under pressure. Prior experience working as a Stable Hand or other member of stable staff is crucial as many of these skills are required for this job.

It is not necessary to have formal qualifications and hands-on experience is often more valuable - however, the NVQ Level 3 in Racecourse Care and Management (see qualifications from the British Horse racing Education and Standards Trust) is a useful qualification to have for this role. There are also several online Equine Diploma courses that are worth considering.

You will most probably be required to live on or near the stables and you may be provided with this accommodation as a part of your payment. In addition to your salary and accommodation, you may also receive a share of the pooled prize money when a horse you work with wins a race.

32. Travelling Head Lad/Lass

As this job title implies, this role involves much travelling and may mean working abroad as it involves being responsible for the horses and Stable Hands when they travel to race meetings. The role involves having the overall responsibility for the horses' welfare to ensure that they are in excellent condition (well fed and cared for) when they arrive at the racecourse. Once you arrive at the racecourse, you may be required to assist with declaring the horse, saddling up, assisting the owner and with riding out duties.

In this role, you are also responsible for paperwork, passports, colours, etc - to do this job well, you must be extremely organised, hardworking, reliable and enjoy travelling - you may be required to live on or near the yard and to work long hours. This role is ideally a promotion from Stable Hand as many of these skills and experience are required in this job. You may be required to drive the horse box and must have a Certificate in Equine Transport to do this - it can be gained through The British Racing School.

The horse racing industry has a regulated pay structure that is scaled - the more qualified and experienced you become, the better you are paid - in addition, to your salary, you may also get a share of the pooled prize money.

33. Assistant Trainer

Works closely with the Trainer to ensure that racing and training schedules are adhered to. The role involves having responsibility for the management of stable and senior staff and assisting with the running of the business on a day to day basis. You will be responsible for selecting new bloodstock, entering the horses into races, maintaining the facilities, running an office and you may be required to represent the Trainer at meetings. Experience that can lead to becoming an Assistant Trainer may be gained through stable work, owning and looking after racehorses, or riding as an amateur or professional jockey.

This role demands that you are highly organised, personable and motivated and that you are a good leader with thorough management and training yard experience. It is advisable to have gained the NVQ 3 in Racehorse Care and Management before embarking on this career. There are also several online Equine Diploma courses that are worth considering.

Part of the role involves expanding the Trainers reputation and gaining new clients, there may be some work abroad. If you are aiming to become a Trainer, this is an excellent way of gaining valuable experience.

34. Race Horse Trainer

Trainers are responsible for ensuring that the race horses are fit and able to perform to their best ability in a race. For this role, it is crucial that you are an experienced rider with an in-depth knowledge of the horse racing industry and training. The work involves devising training programmes for individual horses and building up the horses' stamina, fitness and technique.

Most Trainers specialise in either flat (along a track without obstacles) or jump racing (over fences and hurdles). The day to day work with the horses involves; monitoring health, observing performance, managing feeding programmes, managing yard and staff, attracting new owners to the yard and devising training and racing strategies. The Trainer is also responsible for selecting and buying horses and for marketing the business. The job demands excellent business, communication and marketing skills. You must be an excellent communicator and leader with a thorough knowledge of horse welfare and the racing industry.

There are many very early starts, long days and weekend work. Most horse trainers are self employed and it is therefore important to have good business skills. Trainers should have a natural ability to train racehorses and must have thorough experience of horse care. You are required to have a 'Licence to train' and a thorough awareness of the British Horse Racing Authority's Rules of Racing and Orders & Instructions. There are also several online Equine Diploma courses that are worth considering.

An NVQ Level 3 in Racehorse Care and Management is useful, as is a License to train from the British Horse Racing Authority. Trainers are required to attend courses at the British Racing School and the British Horse Racing Authority will expect to see a business plan, professional references, a financial statement that confirms you either have substantial working capital or overdraft and various other documentation. Progress as a trainer involves establishing a strong reputation and building up a client list.

The British Racing School offers one-week training courses in:
Racehorse management - this course gives an insight into horse health, feeding and nutrition, training and fitness, and licensing and racecourse procedures.
Business skills for racehorse trainers - this covers general business skills, business planning, obtaining finance, accounting principles, business law, marketing and media skills
Staff management - this course includes recruiting, employing and managing people, and health and safety obligations.

35. Jockey

Most Jockeys begin their careers as Stable Hands and those with real potential and aptitude are selected to train as jockeys after graduating from a racing school.

Many people aspire to this career as it involves racing horses for a living and can be very lucrative with salaries of over £60,000 for successful race Jockeys. This is a very demanding career and you are required to be extremely fit, committed, highly talented and to have excellent riding and horsemanship skills. You will be required to travel and to compete at very high levels in a competitive environment.

There are two types of jockey; Apprentice Jockey (flat racing) and Conditional Jockeys (jump racing). It is important to have excellent hearing and vision and have quick reaction speeds. Jockeys should be aged 16 to 19 years, weigh no more than 10 stone and to be in good health. As this is an extremely demanding career, most jockeys retire by the age of 40. This work involves long hours and most weekends. Jockeys are required to undergo training at one of two approved centres in the UK, (Newmarket and Doncaster).

Other Horse Racing careers include: Handicappers, Bookmakers, Racing Journalists, Horse Transporters and those employed at the racecourses such as: Racecourse Manager, Ground, Maintenance & Catering Staff.

Horse Racing Careers useful contacts:

British Racing School (BRS): The principal objective of the school is to provide and promote training and education for people employed in the racing industry. The British Racing School, Snailwell Road, Newmarket, Suffolk, CB8 7NU. Tel: 01638 665103

Northern Racing College: is a centre of excellence, offering training. Northern Racing College, The Stables, Rossington Hall, Great North Road, Doncaster DN11 0HN. Tel: 01302 861000

British Horseracing Board: the site has information on many aspects on horseracing   British Horseracing Board, 151 Shaftesbury Avenue, London WC2H 8AL. Tek: 020 7152 0000.

British Horseracing Education and Standards Trust (BHEST): is a government recognised, awarding body for a range of qualifications in the equine industry. BHEST manages a scheme developed to open horse racing to a new, young audience through the use of exciting and informative educational activities based on National Curriculum. BHEST, Suite 16, Unit 8, Kings Court, Willie Snaith Road, Newmarket, Suffolk CB8 7SG. Tel: 01638 560743

Association of British Riding Schools (ABRS): has Britain's longest established riding school approval scheme (since 1954). It is the only organisation solely representing professional riding school proprietors and is thus ideally placed to assist and guide young people seeking careers with horses. ABRS, Queens Chambers, 38-40 Queen Street, Penzance, Cornwall, TR18 4BH, Ph: 01736 369440

National Association of Stable Staff, 74 High Street, Swadlincote, Derbyshire, DE11 8HS.

Professional Jockeys Association (PJA): works to promote, protect and represent the interests of professional jockeys both on and off the racecourse working with regulatory, industry and commercial bodies to secure agreements to the benefit of all and continually working in the best interest of British horseracing. The Professional Jockeys Association (PJA), 39B Kingfisher Court, Hambridge Road, Newbury, RG14 5SJ, Tel: 01635 44102

The Amateur Jockeys Association of Great Britain (AJA): aims to improve the standard and safety of all amateur riders, encourage amateur races under both codes, find sponsors for such events, act on behalf of its members by providing recommendations to the various regulatory and administrative racing bodies, select and finance amateurs to ride abroad, play an important part through its seat on the Industry Committee in the formation of the policy of the British Racing Industry. AJA, Racing Administration, Weatherbys Group Ltd, Sanders Road, Wellingborough, Northants NN8 4BX, Tel: 01933 304778

The Jockey Club: focusing on a portfolio of 14 racecourses and a property & land management company, all profits generated by the Jockey Club's businesses are re-invested back into racing.

B. Horse Breeding Careers:

36. Stud Hand

This career involves being in charge of the management and welfare of several thoroughbred foals and mares. This is hands-on work and includes grooming, exercise, mucking out of stables and assisting with veterinary visits. It also involves the accurate keeping of stud records and livery yard contacts. This career doesn't demand specific qualifications, however, it is useful if you have some riding and horse handing experience. You will need to be dedicated and prepared to work hard in all weathers. There is free relevant training (NVQ Level 2 in Racehorse Care Breeding Option) for all EU citizens aged between 16 and 25, the course includes a residential induction course and a work placement.

37. Stallion Handler

This career involves the responsibility of caring for highly valuable racing stallions. Stallion Handlers are highly experienced and this is a specialist role that some progress to after gaining many years experience as a Stud Hand.

The work is physically demanding and includes being outdoors in all weathers, however it is highly rewarding as the Handlers are able to build up one-to-one relationships with the horses that they may spend many years working alongside. Stallion Handlers need to be strong, fit and calm and prepared to work very long hours and on weekends - particularly during the breeding season.

38. Stud Groom

This is a senior role involving much responsibility for the breeding of horses as well as for the training and management of Stud Hands. It is essential that you have had experience of horses (ideally you should have work experience in the roles of Stud Hand and Stallion Handler), and that you have a thorough knowledge of horse welfare - specifically of the horse breeding industry. You will need to be highly organised, enjoy responsibility and should have prior management experience and enjoy communicating as part of the job involves regular communication with Vets and Farriers.

39. Stud Manager

This is a highly responsible yet varied career and in many cases the Stud Manager is also the Owner of the Stud Farm. This means that the Stud Manager is required to run the business side (accounts, marketing, management), as well as to have ultimate responsibility for the Stud. The day to day work can involve a fair bit of office work but this essential to the promotion of the Stud Farm business.

Horse Breeding Careers useful contacts:
The Thoroughbred Breeders' Association (TBA): is a registered charity and is the only official body representing Thoroughbred Breeders in Great Britain. The TBA has always been actively involved in the broad range of issues affecting its members, all of which have a critical bearing on the health and wealth of British Thoroughbred breeding. TBA, Stanstead House, 8 The Avenue, Newmarket, Suffolk, CB8 9AA. Tel: 01638 661321

The National Pony Society has several qualifications: the Stud Trainee's Certificate, The Stud Assistant's Certificate and the Diploma in Pony Mastership plus NVQ up to level 4.

The National Stud : offers the National Stud Diploma. NVQ Level 2 in Racehorse Care - Breeding Options.

C. Other Horse Careers:

40. Farrier

The work of a Farrier involves the specialist care of horse hooves and horse-shoeing. Farriers must have blacksmith skills as well as a good knowledge of anatomy and physiology of horse feet in order to be able deal with injured and diseased hooves. Whilst most of the work involves hoof trimming and shoeing, farriers are sometimes called upon to make special horse shoes for injured horses or for racing purposes. Farriers are highly skilled and only registered farriers are permitted to practice. Qualification as a farrier involves a four year apprenticeship with an approved practicing farrier as well as an approved college course. Apprentices can gain a diploma upon the successful completion of the course and exams and this will enable you to be eligible for registration.

Useful contacts:

The Farriers Registration Council: is the statutory body for the Farrier profession.

The National Association of Farriers: is the trade union for this trade - protecting the interests of its members and providing free legal services etc for its members.

The Worshipful Company of Farriers (WCF): established in London in 1356 to oversee farriery within the Cities of London and Westminster. It has been responsible for maintaining the standards of farriery through its examination board for more than 100 years.

41. Saddler

Saddlers are highly skilled and creative people. This is a fantastic career for a creative person and once you have qualified, setting up your own business as a Master Saddler is a good business option. The Society of Master Saddlers produces a list of all Master Saddlers and it is advisable to apply directly to a Saddler for an apprenticeship for training.

Useful contacts:

The Society of Master Saddlers: aims to ensure and achieve a high quality of workmanship through setting standards and overseeing the training of the membership's workforce to give their customers a professional and quantified service. It continues its work to carry these standards through build, repair & fit, and to work towards the complete comfort and safety of horse and rider. The Society of Master Saddlers, Green Lane Farm, Stonham, Stowmarket, Suffolk, IP14 5DS, Ph: 01449 711642 repair & fit, and to work towards the complete comfort and safety of horse and rider.

Cambridge & District Saddlery Courses (International) Ltd run a variety of shorter courses throughout the year.

Capel Manor College run a full time one year course.

42. Riding instructor

A Riding Instructor teaches all types, ages and abilities of people to ride horses; either individually or as a group. You will need to have excellent riding skills and be a willing and good teacher. This can be a very rewarding career, the work involves setting up and developing training programmes for a variety of ages and abilities.

There are strict health and safety rules and you will need to ensure these are adhered to. Unless you are working for a large training school with many Stable Hands, your duties may also include grooming, mucking out, tack cleaning, etc. Riding Instructors usually work long hours, often at weekends and in the evenings. Most Riding Instructors are self employed and some run their own riding schools. Most good riding schools insist that instructors have a formal qualification from the British Racing School. These can be gained as an Apprentice, through a full-time or part-time college course, or as a fee-paying student at a riding school.

There are opportunities to progress to senior posts at riding schools, or to other positions of responsibility in the equine industry. Overseas work is possible. Some instructors develop their careers by studying for HNDs, Foundation degrees or degrees in equine studies or related subjects. In the UK the two main training bodies are the Association of British Riding Schools (ABRS) and the British Horse Society (BHS).

43. Horse Riding Holiday Centre Manager

This career involves having responsibility for the running of a horse riding holiday centre, most of which are based in rural areas such as Exmoor, the Lake District and Scotland. The work involves caring for the welfare of horses and ponies and planning activities for holiday guests - ensuring their safety at all times.

As well as being a good horse rider, it is crucial that you enjoy working with all types of people and that you are patient and willing to please your guests. You will need to have some business management skills as you may be required to oversee administration duties and manage staff. This can be very demanding with long hours and much outdoor work. For many jobs, you may be required to live on site and here may be opportunities to work abroad once you have gained experience in the UK. Relevant qualifications include Riding teachers'/instructors' certificates, HNDs and Degrees in Equine Tourism, Equine Studies and Management, and an NVQ/SVQ Level 3 in Horse Care and Management. British Equestrian Tourism (BET) qualifications have been developed for people working in the field. Examinations for the BET management qualification - Riding Holiday Centre Manager, may be taken at various centres throughout the UK. There are also several online Equine Diploma courses that are worth considering.

Useful contacts:
Association of Irish Riding Establishments, 11 Moore Park, Newbridge, County Kildare, Ireland. Tel: 00 353 (0)45 431584.

Riding for the Disabled Association, Lavinia Norfolk House, Avenue R, Stoneleigh Park, Warwickshire CV8 2LY. Tel: 0845 658 1082.

Trekking and Riding Society of Scotland (TRSS), Bruaich-Na-H'Abhainne, Maragowan, Killin, Perthshire FK21 8TN. Tel: 01567 820909.

Wales Trekking and Riding Association, North Barn Glanirfon, Llanwrtyd Wells, Powys LD5 4RR. Tel: 01591 610818.

44. Mounted police

Of the 51 regional police forces in the UK, only approximately 16 still use mounted police. The Metropolitan Police have the largest force, with over 140 officers and 120 horses across London. Their work includes; high visibility patrols, public order duties as well as specific crime initiatives and specialist events, such as trooping the colour. Officers receive extensive training in Surrey to ensure both horse and rider are well equipped to deal with the rigours of policing in the capital.

Mounted Officers play an important part in the community with visits to Schools and various clubs. However, their two main functions are; high visibility patrols (in parks and residential areas), and public order (this includes crowd control at sports matches and public demonstrations).

Useful contact:

Mounted Police (Metropolitan police): Metropolitan Police Service, New Scotland Yard, Broadway, London, SW1H 0BG. Tel: 020 7230 1212

45. Army mounted units

The army has two mounted units: the Kings Troop Royal Horse Artillery and the Household Cavalry Mounted Regiment. Soldiers working for either unit are trained for and may be used in modern combat as well as for British pageantry and ceremonial occasions. There is excellent training and career progression opportunities and skills such as Farriery and Saddlery can be gained.

Useful contacts:

Kings Troop Royal Horse Artillery
Household Cavalry Mounted Unit

46. Equine Dentist

Currently, all advanced equine dental work can only be carried out by a fully qualified vet. However, some of the work such as the removal of tartar and other procedures may be carried out by equine dentistry technicians.

Useful contact:

Equine Dentistry Information:

47. Equine Veterinary Nurse

Equine Veterinary Nurses are employed by some equine practices or veterinary hospitals. The Royal College of Veterinary Surgeons (RCVS) approves workplace training and the qualification takes two years. Our Veterinary Careers guide contains more detailed information on becoming a Veterinary Nurse.

48. Equine Physiotherapist

Equine physiotherapy is in great demand as the racing industry requires physiotherapists to work on site and occasionally to look after horses whilst they are in recovery from racing injury. Equine physiotherapists must first complete training as a human physiotherapist before working with animals. After two years as a Chartered Physiotherapist, practitioners become eligible for certified courses run by The Association of Chartered Physiotherapists in Animal Therapy. After this, training takes place under supervision of a qualified veterinarian where practitioners are able treat a variety of injuries and conditions.

The work of an Equine Physiotherapist involves: treating animals with injuries, investigating mobility problems, preventing recurring injuries and helping to reduce pain. The work is particularly concerned with problems that affect muscles, circulation, bones, the heart system and the lungs. Physiotherapists utilise a variety of techniques including: massage, soft tissue & joint mobilisation, electrotherapy, ultrasound, magnetic field therapy and hydrotherapy. They may also recommend exercise plans to improve an animal's fitness and mobility.

Horses are the most common types of animal referred for physiotherapy. They may be either pets or working animals such as race horses or show jumpers. The work is physically demanding; it requires a high degree of physical fitness, stamina and a strong back as there is likely to be heavy lifting at times. Many Equine Physiotherapists are self employed and run their own businesses - working from home, from local surgeries or travelling to their client's facilities. This means that at times the work may be outdoors or in stable yards in all weathers. Some Equine Physiotherapists work from larger veterinary practices and animal hospitals where they come across a wide variety of cases and may have the opportunity of promotion within the organisation.

A full driving license is usually required, especially if you are self employed and are required to travel to clients premises. Having worked with animals previously is an advantaged as you will need to be patient and experienced in handing different types of animals (some of them large). There is much people interaction; you will need to have good communication skills and be able to build up relationships of trust and respect with clients.

Useful contacts:
Association of Chartered Physiotherapists in Animal Physiotherapy (ACPAT): 21 Woodlands Close, Penenden Heath, Maidstone, Kent ME14 2EX. Tel: 01622 688777.

International Association of Animal Therapists (IAAP): Tyringham Hall, Cuddington, Aylesbury, Buckinghamshire HP18 0AP. Tel: 01844 291526.

Chartered Society of Physiotherapy (CSP): 14 Bedford Row, London, WC1R 4ED. Tel: 020 7306 6666
Royal Veterinary College (RVC): Hawkshead Lane, North Mymms, Hatfield, Herts, AL9 7TA. Tel: 01707 666333
National Association of Veterinary Physiotherapists (NAVP): The association aims to provide a high level of care in assisting the veterinary profession in the rehabilitation of injured animals and also providing means of keeping athletic animals in peak working condition.

49. Equine rescue charity work
There are many equine charities that require a number of employees who not only care for the horses but also have an understanding of the process of rehabilitation.

This link has a list of many equine rescue charities: http://www.horsedata.co.uk/charities.htm

Marine & Aquaria Careers

Introduction

This section covers marine: oceans and freshwater careers, and aquaria: captive marine life careers.

Marine and aquaria career working hours may be unpredictable and you will probably be required to work at weekends and bank holidays. You will need to be physically fit, a competent swimmer, healthy, hard working and have plenty of stamina. Some marine and aquaria careers may require you to live on site. As with all animal related work, it is crucial that you are dedicated, compassionate, committed and that you don't suffer from animal allergies.

Different jobs may include; conducting surveys, monitoring habitats and populations, rehabilitation of sick or injured marine life and the protection and rescue of animals from natural and man-made disasters.

Candidates wishing to pursue a marine or aquaria career should have good problem solving skills and the ability to collect, analyse, and interpret data. In many of these careers, you may be required to be able to teach or explain to others through presentations and reports.

If you haven't spent time working in a marine environment, it is worth considering first working as a volunteer. Several marine rescue organisations run volunteer programmes, work experience placements and some even offer NVQ training courses. All of these opportunities provide excellent ways to gain experience and to improve your employment prospects. A wide range of animal care, conservation, and other positions are available at aquariums. Some positions require a degree in biology, zoology, or a related field, and practical knowledge and hands-on experience. It is worth considering the online Advanced Diploma in Marine Zoology course.

in this section, we have information about the following marine careers: Marine and freshwater biologists, Marine Rescue Officer, Aquarist, Aquarium Supervisor, Aquarium Curator, Naturalist, Herpetologist and Marine Mammal Trainer.

50. Marine and freshwater biologists

Marine biologists work mainly with sea plants and animals. Freshwater biologists work on lakes and rivers or for water companies and environmental agencies researching issues such as pollution concerns and depleted fish stocks resulting from over fishing. These are highly scientific roles and usually require a first degree in the subject or a first degree in biology followed by a higher degree in marine/freshwater biology. However, some scientists suggest that it is better to take a conventional Biology degree and specialise with a Masters or PhD. You must have a good level of competence in chemistry, maths and be computer literate. It is also important to be observant, practical and to enjoy analysing data.

Marine biologists may spend much time working on ships or boats after which they are required to spend time analysing their findings in laboratories and writing reports. Their work involves studying creatures such as plankton, algae, fish larvae and shrimps etc, and understanding how marine organisms function, how they relate to the environment, and to other creatures. Our understanding of such creatures enables us to measure a variety of things including: the impact of global warming, pollution, over-fishing and damage through tourism.

Some marine biologists work in aquarium or zoos that have a marine section. Other employment opportunities exist with research laboratories, environmental agencies, fisheries, water companies, oil companies, commercial fishing companies, coastal authorities and Defra's marine and fisheries department.

The Diploma in Ichthyology is valuable as is the Advanced Diploma in Marine Zoology course

Useful Contacts:

National Oceanography Centre (NOC): The centre, based in Southampton, is the country's focus for oceanography and represents an unparalleled investment in marine and earth sciences and technology in the UK. National Oceanography Centre, Southampton, University of Southampton Waterfront Campus, European Way, Southampton SO14 3ZH. Tel: 023 8059 6666.

Institute of Biology (IOB):works to promote the biological sciences, to foster the public understanding of the life sciences generally, to serve the needs of their members, to enhance the status of the biology profession, and to represent their members and the biology profession as a whole to government and other bodies in the UK and abroad. Institute of Biology
9 Red Lion Court, London, EC4A 3EF. Tel: 020 7936 5900.

Freshwater Biological Association (FBA):promotes freshwater science through innovative research, maintained specialist scientific facilities, a programme of scientific meetings, production of publications, and by providing sound independent scientific opinion. FBA, The Ferry Landing,
Far Sawrey, Ambleside, Cumbria, LA22 0LP.

The Scottish Association for Marine Science (SAMS): is a Scottish charity (est.1884) committed to promoting, delivering and supporting high-quality independent research and education in marine science. SAMS, Dunstaffnage Marine Laboratory, Oban, Argyll, PA37 1QA. Tel: 01631 559000.

Natural Environment Research Council (NERC): funds world-class science in universities and their own research centres that increase knowledge and understanding of the natural world. They are tackling the 21st century's major environmental issues such as climate change, biodiversity and natural hazards. Natural Environment Research Council, Polaris House, North Star Avenue, Swindon, SN2 1EU. Tel: 01793 411500.

The Society for Underwater Technology (SUT): is a multi-disciplinary learned society that brings together organisations and individuals with a common interest in water technology, ocean science and offshore engineering. SUT, 80 Coleman Street, London, EC2R 5BJ. Tel: 020 7382 2601.

Department for Environment, food and rural affairs (Defra) Marine & Fisheries: Defra is the UK custodian of the marine and aquatic environment. Defra, Nobel House,17 Smith Square, London SW1P 3JR.

The Marine Biological Association of the United Kingdom (MBA): is a learned Society and one of the UK's leading marine biological research institutes. Their mission is to promote scientific research into all aspects of life in the sea and to disseminate to the public the knowledge gained. MBA, The Laboratory, Citadel Hill, Plymouth, PL1 2PB, Devon. Tel: 01752 633207.

The Centre for Environment, Fisheries, and Aquaculture Science (Cefas): is an internationally renowned aquatic scientific research and consultancy centre. Cefas aims to be the prime source of high quality science used to conserve and enhance the aquatic environment, promote sustainable management of its natural resources, and protect the public from aquatic contaminants. Cefas, Pakefield Road, Lowestoft, Suffolk, NR33 0HT. Tel: 01502 562244

The Fisheries Research Services (FRS): is an agency of the Scottish Government Marine Directorate (SGMD). FRS provides expert scientific and technical advice to Government on marine and freshwater fisheries, aquaculture and the protection of the aquatic environment. FRS Marine Laboratory, PO Box 101, 375 Victoria Road, Aberdeen, AB11 9DB. Ph: 01224 876544

The International Council for the Exploration of the Sea (ICES): is the organisation that co-ordinates and promotes marine research in the North Atlantic. Scientists working through ICES gather information about the marine ecosystem. As well as filling gaps in existing knowledge, this information is also developed into unbiased, non-political advice.

51. Marine Animal Rescue Officer

Some charitable organisations work to rescue and rehabilitate stranded, sick or injured marine animals – such as dolphin rescue. Their work is particularly important during natural disasters and organisations can require extra help at these times. For this type of career, candidates may require veterinary qualifications or a minimum degree in subjects such as biology or animal behaviour.

It is worth considering the online Advanced Diploma in Marine Zoology course.
This course has a total of twelve modules. It can be studied in two parts and each are independently awarded a Diploma on successful completion. Successful completion of both parts will result in the coveted Advanced Diploma in Marine Zoology.

Here are a few links to these types of organisations – many require volunteers and this is an excellent way of gaining hands on experience, for example the British Divers Marine Life Rescue Group offers rescue training sessions for volunteers. This type of work can be extremely rewarding when successful most of the time yet distressing when a rescue attempt fails - see: http://news.bbc.co.uk/1/hi/england/london/4635874.stm

Useful Contacts:

British Divers Marine Life Rescue (BDMLR): trains over 400 volunteer Marine Mammal Medics a year and has 20 whale rescue pontoons located at strategic points throughout the UK, waiting to help stranded whales and dolphins. Their teams are on standby to respond immediately to any marine disaster or marine mammal stranding anywhere in the UK. BDMLR, Lime House, Regency Close, Uckfield, East Sussex, TN22 1DS. Tel: 01825 765546.

Sea Watch Foundation: is a marine conservation research charity working hard to make sure UK dolphins are protected. PO Box 3688, Chalfont St. Peter, Gerrards Cross, Bucks, SL9 9WE. Tel: 0845 202 3892.

Cetacean Research & Rescue Unit (CRRU): is affiliated with the UK Marine Animal Rescue Coalition (MARC) and providing specialist training in marine mammal rescue for an elite team of professionals, the CRRU operates the only full-time whale and dolphin emergency rescue operation in Scotland. The fully trained team of cetologists and veterinarians are on standby 24 hours a day, throughout the year, with specialist rescue equipment, medical diagnostics and supplies to assist whales and dolphins in trouble.

Marine Mammal Conservancy: works to rescue and rehabilitate marine mammals.

Marine Connection: works globally for the welfare, protection and conservation of all dolphins, whales and porpoises. One of the charity's main objectives is to ensure everyone understands the importance of protecting these marine mammals and their natural habitat - making a positive difference to the current and long term survival of cetaceans worldwide. Marine Connection, Fourth Floor, Charles House, 375 Kensington High Street, London, W14 8QH. Tel: 020 7602 1574.

Marine Animal Rescue Society: is dedicated to the conservation of marine mammals through rescue, rehabilitation, research and education. Marine Animal Rescue Society P.O. Box 833356, Miami, Florida, 33283, USA.

Marine Mammal Centre: "recognise human interdependence with marine mammals and their importance as sentinels of the ocean environment, the health of which is essential for all life. It is our responsibility to use our awareness, compassion and intelligence to foster marine mammal survival and the conservation of their habitat". The Marine Mammal Center, Marin Headlands, 1065 Fort Cronkhite, Sausalito, CA 94965.

52. Aquarist/Fishkeeper

is a popular hands-on, entry level career based in an aquarium environment. It involves having responsibility for the freshwater and marine aquatic systems to ensure that they are well cared for and kept in good conditions. The work requires a lot of cleaning as well as feeding, monitoring animal health and water quality and setting up and maintaining new exhibits. The work also involves observing the behaviour of wild animals in the aquarium to ensure that they are living in as close to natural environment as possible. Aquarists are often responsible for giving tours around the aquarium and conducting research into various marine animals. They may also be responsible for advising on nutrition and assisting with the collection and transport of fish, amphibians and reptiles.

This career requires candidates to be good swimmers and to have an up to date scuba diving qualification. The work is strenuous and may include heavy lifting; it is essential that candidates are physically fit and strong. Candidates must have a good understanding of water chemistry and a general knowledge of fish species. A minimum of a Bachelor of Science degree in biology or a related field is required.

Whist many aquarists work in aquarium environments, some professional aquarists specialise in outdoor fish ponds. For many this means self employment - visiting residential and commercial clients several times per month; analysing water and fish health; changing water, cleaning filters and removing algae and treating sick fish.

Consider the Diploma in Ichthyology for this type of work.

Useful contacts:

UK Aquarist Tropical Fish Forum
Practical Fishkeeping Magazine
Aquarist Handbook

53. Aquarium Supervisor

Is responsible for managing the aquarist team and overseeing the details of daily activities. This work involves recruiting and training new employees and ensuring that the work is carried out efficiently and that high standards of cleanliness are constantly maintained. In addition, the Aquarium Supervisor is in charge of monitoring exhibits and maintaing good stock records of animal food and supplies.

It is crucial that captive animals are well cared for and kept in as close to their natural environment as possible to minimise stress. The Aquarium Supervisor ensures that the aquarium design is suitable for its occupants.

A minimum of two years experience in aquarium related work is required and an educational minimum of a bachelor's degree or the equivalent in biological sciences as well as a scuba diving qualification is essential. It is an advantage to have people management experience or a relevant qualification. The role can include a fair amount of record keeping and paperwork.

54. Aquarium Curator

is responsible for designing and promoting exhibits, overseeing and training of staff and volunteers, implementing husbandry protocols and ensuring that accurate records are maintained. The Curator may also be responsible for acquiring new animal specimens, maintaining accurate records and researching dietary requirements for the aquarium animals. The role can involve responsibility for all animal scientific research programs and assisting with the design and development of animal transportation methods and equipment. Some Curators are involved in the design of new animal exhibits, the management of building contractors and implementation of educational programs. The Curator may be required to travel at short notice and to liaise with other aquarium facilities and zoological professionals around the world

A minimum of a Bachelor of Science degree in biology or a related field is required, as well as people management training and some experience of supervising a team. A scuba diving qualification, thorough knowledge of local marine life and experience in caring for marine animals is essential.

55. Naturalists

are educational specialists, their work involves teach aquarium visitors about marine science and ocean conservation. Naturists specialise in the study of saltwater plants and animals and how they relate to their environment. Their work helps determine how marine ecosystems will cope with changes such as global warming, pollution, pressure from fisheries and damage caused by tourism in sensitive areas. Some aspects of this work can involve field expeditions and school visits.

It is an exciting career for those who are passionate about marine science and can convey enthusiasm in their teaching about the subject. Having a degree in marine science, education or environmental education is a minimum requirement as well as some relevant work experience and some type of teaching qualification or public speaking experience.

56. Herpetologists

A herpetologist studies and provides information about reptiles and amphibians including snakes, lizards, frogs, alligators, turtles and other reptilian and amphibious creatures. The work involves conducting research, observing general behaviour, conducting food supply studies and sometimes even searching for new species.

Herpetologists must be excellent researchers and must enjoy analysing information and producing reports. This includes having good skills of observation and a scientific inclination. Herpetologists working in an aquarium are responsible for caring for the Aquarium's amphibians and reptiles.

Some Herpetologists work to care for the many reptiles and amphibians that are given up by people who wrongly assumed they would make good pets. This is unfortunately a growing problem and there are many charitable organisations requiring expert assistance with these creatures. The Accredited Herpetology Diploma is an unique and excellent qualification for this career as is the Reptile Care, Welfare and First Aid course.

Useful contacts:

Reptile Rescue Organisation listings

Society for the Study of Amphibian and Reptiles (SSAR): is a not-for-profit organisation established to advance research, conservation, and education concerning amphibians and reptiles. It is the largest international herpetological society, and is recognised worldwide.

American Society of Ichthyologists and Herpetologists: is dedicated to the scientific study of fishes, amphibians and reptiles. The primary emphases of the Society are to increase knowledge about these organisms, to disseminate that knowledge through publications, conferences, symposia, and other means, and to encourage and support young scientists who will make future advances in these fields.

57. Marine Mammal Trainer

We have decided to include this career option, even though the authors and publishers are against keeping animals in captivity, (unless it is for recovery from emergency treatment or surgery). However, until legislation prevents the capture and keeping of wild animals, those in captivity do need carers and stimulation to prevent boredom.

Marine Mammal Trainers are sometimes referred to as dolphin trainers and are responsible for training and caring for dolphins, whales, seals, sea lions, walruses and other marine mammals using a training system of positive reinforcement. Training provides environmental enrichment in the form of mental and physical stimulation that is particularly important for captive animals. Trainers are required to be extremely patient and to have a true affinity with animals and a real interest in animal behaviour. It is crucial that they have a good educational background and be confident public speakers. Candidates must have a thorough knowledge of animal biology, behaviour, water chemistry, nutrition, veterinary medicine and marine ecology. Marine Mammal Trainers have a very rewarding career, however, as with most animal care careers, it is not glamorous work and much of a trainer's daily duties involve cleaning, preparing fish, feeding, maintaining records, public education and training. There is much public interaction in this type of work and it is essential that candidates are able to communicate well with people.

Useful contacts:
The International Marine Animal Trainers Association (IMATA): was founded to foster communication, professionalism, and cooperation among those who serve marine mammal science through training, public display, research, husbandry, conservation, and education.

Dolphin Trainer: behind the scenes information about marine mammal training.

The Society for Marine Mammalogy

Alliance of Marine Mammal Parks and Aquariums: is an international association representing marine life parks, aquariums, zoos, research facilities, and professional organisations dedicated to the highest standards of care for marine mammals and to their conservation in the wild through public education, scientific study, and wildlife presentations.

The Association of Zoos and Aquariums (AZA): is a non-profit organisation dedicated to the advancement of accredited zoos and aquariums in the areas of animal care, wildlife conservation, education and science. Association of Zoos and Aquariums, 8403 Colesville Rd, Suite 710, Silver Spring, MD 20910-3314. Tel: 301-562-0777.

European Association for Aquatic Mammals (EAAM): is an organisation of people interested in marine mammals in human care, in a zoological environment or in the wild, and includes veterinarians, biologists, zoo and marine park directors and managers, trainers (husbandry professionals), researchers, students and other persons who devote a significant amount of time to the welfare of marine mammals through research, medical care, training, education, conservation, management and related activities.

58. Marine Veterinary Surgeon

A qualified veterinary surgeon or veterinary student may decide to specialise in marine and aquatic life: MARVET (Marine Veterinary Medicine) is an educational program offering introductory courses in marine animal medicine for veterinary students and veterinarians who would like to become more acquainted with the expanding field of marine animal health and conservation medicine.

Veterinary Careers

A veterinary career invariably requires candidates to undergo tough training and have excellent qualifications. You need to be prepared to train formally and keep up with current veterinary knowledge through Continuing Professional Development (CPD).

Veterinary jobs require candidates to be able to make difficult decisions when dealing with distressing situations; it is important to be caring, sympathetic and genuinely interested in the welfare of animals. In addition, veterinary staff must be able to communicate effectively with people and to keep a level head in emergency situations.

Livestock and wildlife veterinary work may require some tough physical outdoor work and it's advantageous to be physically fit and have plenty of stamina. This could be a difficult career for someone who is squeamish or dislikes the sight of blood, as some aspects of the work can be messy and unpleasant. Often veterinary staff are required to live on site and it is useful if you are able to drive.

As with all animal related work, it is crucial that you are dedicated, committed and that you don't suffer from animal allergies as veterinary jobs are very hands-on. Working hours are unpredictable and varied and you will probably be required to work or be on call at weekends, evenings and bank holidays, as veterinary staff have to provide an emergency service. The Professional Pet Care and Veterinary Assistant Diploma and the Animal Care, Welfare and Husbandry Diploma is an excellent foundation course for many veterinary careers.

In this section, we have information about the following veterinary careers: Veterinary Surgeon (including the State Veterinary Service, Army, Teaching/Research posts, Animal Charities, and Overseas opportunities), Veterinary Nurse, Animal Nursing Assistant, Veterinary Physiotherapist, Veterinary Osteopath, Veterinary Chiropractor, Veterinary Homeopath and Veterinary Receptionist.

59. Veterinary Surgeon

Becoming a vet is a highly popular career choice for those wishing to work with animals. However, this is an extremely tough option as the entrance requirements are high and the number of applications far exceeds the number of available university placements.

To become a vet, you must take a university veterinary degree. There are six universities in the UK that offer Veterinary Science: Bristol, Cambridge, Edinburgh, Glasgow, Liverpool and London (The Royal Veterinary College). The entrance requirements for all of them are A-levels or higher grades AAB in subjects such as chemistry, physics, maths, zoology and biology. The degree course lasts from five to six years.

A vet is responsible for the prevention of disease and for the medical and surgical treatment of animals including domestic pets, zoo animals, farm animals and horses. The work of a vet is varied and may involve: prescribing medicines, acting as an anesthetist, radiographer and surgeon. Carrying out and interpreting diagnostic tests such as x-rays, laboratory work and ultra-sound, vaccinating animals against various forms of disease, euthanasia of old, sick, unwanted or terminally ill animals, caring for in-patient animals, providing documentation for animals travelling abroad, maintaining records, issuing certificates in compliance with current legislation, consulting and pet counselling owners.

A vet needs to be interested in animals and concerned for their welfare, able to handle large animals, be good at science, be able to build up a relationship of trust and respect with clients, be professional and responsible, be prepared to train for a long time and keep up with current veterinary knowledge through continuing professional development (CPD).

As every veterinary surgeon has an obligation to deal with emergencies in any species at any time, the work can at times be stressful with a high level of responsibility. General veterinary practices provide a twenty-four hour service; veterinary surgeons can usually expect to work a rota system and will rarely work a nine to five day. The work environment can vary from a clean, pleasant surgery to owners' homes or outdoors, often in adverse conditions. In rural areas vets may have to travel long distances to remote farms and treat animals in all weathers and sometimes in messy or unpleasant conditions. Vets often work in the presence of animals' owners who may watch them carry out their work and ask questions – having a good bedside manner is essential!

The majority of vets work in private practice, however there are other career options and these include: the state veterinary service, army, teaching/research posts, animal charities, and overseas opportunities. Newly qualified vet salaries start from around £20,000 a year. This may be enhanced by additional allowances for accommodation, a vehicle, fuel for private use, professional fees and Continuing Professional Development (CPD). This can take the average starting package to around £27,000. Experienced vets can earn more than £45,000. Senior partners can earn £60,000 or more depending on the size of practice.

Here's a summary of some career options for vets:

Private Practice: Most practices have two or more vets working in partnership. This is useful to clients who can benefit from having a range of expertise provided by one practice. As this type of work can involve covering emergencies and running evening/weekend surgeries, it is hugely beneficial to have more than one vet available. Private practices are run as businesses and typically a successful surgery makes a minimum of £60k for each partner. If a vet has a particular expertise, they may earn more than this average. Typically urban practices deal mainly with companion animals, i.e. dogs, cats and rabbits and occasionally exotic pets and birds. Rural surgeries usually deal with companion animals as well as livestock and horses. Vets working in private practice can sometimes buy a share in the practice and many set up their own practice after gaining experience.

State Veterinary Service: UK government departments and agencies include the Department for Environment, Food and Rural Affairs (Defra) where vets are employed by the State Veterinary Service. These vets may be required to work in areas of disease control and in areas of animal health and welfare, particularly of livestock. Other agencies include, the Veterinary Laboratories Agency, the Veterinary Field Service (VFS), the Veterinary Medicines Directorate (VMD) and the Meat Hygiene Service (MHS), which is part of the Food Standards Agency.

Military/Army: Vets working for the Royal Army Veterinary Corps (RAVC) are first and foremost military officers. They are required to care for the army's animals – this includes their horses and surveillance dogs. They may be deployed abroad or in the UK and may be required to assist with animal welfare issues in war areas. Each year vacancies arise for RCVS registered veterinary surgeons to join the RAVC on a four-year Short Service Commission (SSC). First appointments normally involve the clinical care of Service dogs and horses within the RAVC units in UK, Germany or Cyprus, and during their SSC the Veterinary Officer will expect to serve in a variety of locations.

Teaching/research: Includes the fields of medical, food and agricultural research work. This type of work may also involve teaching at veterinary universities and conducting research into veterinary problems. The Animal Health Trust is an example of this type of work: "The Animal Health Trust provides specialist veterinary clinical, diagnostic and surgical services and our successes in research have ranged from major breakthroughs in anaesthesia and surgical techniques to the development of vaccines against diseases such as canine distemper and equine influenza. Our scientists and veterinarians, many of whom are world leaders in their field, work alongside bringing together a wide range of expertise for a co-ordinated attack on animal diseases and injuries. By publishing scientific papers, speaking at conferences and talking to other veterinary surgeons about the cases dealt with, this knowledge is passed on to benefit the maximum number of animals".

Animal welfare charities: There are many charities in the UK that employ vets. The Peoples' Dispensary for Sick Animals (PDSA) is one of the larger charities, employing approximately 400 vets nationwide. The RSPCA is also a large vet employer as vets are required to run the Societies' animal hospitals and low cost clinics. Working for an animal charity may mean that you have to settle for a lower salary, however, there is plenty of job satisfaction to compensate.

Overseas opportunities: This work can include improving conditions for zoo animals and assisting with stray dog problems , etc. Voluntary Services Overseas (VSO) and the World Veterinary Service are examples of overseas organisations that have veterinary positions.

Wildlife Veterinary Surgeon: There are often opportunities for vets to work with wildlife, and for veterinary students or those wishing to study for a veterinary career, to gain some useful work experience before embarking on their degree course. Here are some interesting links on this particular career:

Zoo Veterinary Officer

African Wildlife Management and Veterinary Services

Shimongwe Wildlife Veterinary Experience

Veterinary Association for Wildlife Management

Marine Veterinary Surgeon: A qualified veterinary surgeon or veterinary student may decide to specialise in marine and aquatic life:

Veterinarian's Oath:

"Being admitted to the profession of veterinary medicine, I solemnly swear to use my scientific knowledge and skills for the benefit of society through the protection of animal health, the relief of animal suffering, the conservation of animal resources, the promotion of public health, and the advancement of medical knowledge.
I will practice my profession conscientiously, with dignity, and in keeping with the principles of veterinary medical ethics.
I accept as a lifelong obligation the continual improvement of my professional knowledge and competence".

Useful contacts:

Royal College of Veterinary Surgeons (RCVS): the statutory body set up to administer the Veterinary Surgeons Act and is responsible for the education and discipline of the profession): Belgravia House, 62-64 Horseferry Road, London, SW1P 2AF. Tel: 020 7222 2001

British Veterinary Association (BVA): represents the veterinary profession and helps members fulfill their professional roles. 7 Mansfield Street, London, W1G 9NQ

The British Small Animal Veterinary Association (BSAVA): exists to promote high scientific and educational standards of small animal medicine and surgery in practice, teaching and research. Woodrow House, 1 Telford Way, Waterwells Business Park, Quedgeley Gloucestershire, GL2 2AB. Tel: 01452 726700

The Animal Health Trust (AHT): "a charity that has been helping dogs, cats and horses for more than half a century. We provide specialist veterinary clinical, diagnostic and surgical services and our successes in research have ranged from major breakthroughs in anaesthesia and surgical techniques to the development of vaccines against diseases such as canine distemper and equine influenza. Our scientists and veterinarians, many of whom are world leaders in their field, work alongside bringing together a wide range of expertise for a co-ordinated attack on animal diseases and injuries. By publishing scientific papers, speaking at conferences and talking to other veterinary surgeons about the cases dealt with, this knowledge is passed on to benefit the maximum number of animals". Lanwades Park, Kentford, Newmarket, Suffolk, CB8 7UU. Tel: 01638 751000

The Society of Practising Veterinary Surgeons (SPVS): exists to provide advice and information to veterinary surgeons and others actively involved in the management of veterinary practices. The Governor's House, Cape Road, Warwick, Warwickshire, CV34 5DL. Tel: 01926 410454

Royal Army Veterinary Corps (RAVC): Slim Road, Camberley, Surrey, GU15 4NP. Tel: 01276 412782

Worldwide Veterinary Service (WVS): 5 - 7 Castle Street, Cranborne, Dorset, BH21 5PZ UK. Tel: 01725 551123

Volunteering England: Regents Wharf, 8 All Saints Street, London, N1 9RL. Tel: 0845 305 6979

Voluntary Services Overseas (VSO): 317 Putney Bridge Road, London, SW15 2PN. Tel: 020 8780 7200

Defra, State Veterinary Service (Veterinary Laboratories Agency): VLA, New Haw, Addlestone, Surrey KT15 3NB. Tel: 01932 341111

Listings of veterinary schools worldwide can be found at: http://www.animal-job.co.uk/veterinary-schools.html in USA, UK, Africa, South Africa, Australia, New Zealand and Canada.

60. Veterinary Nurse

Anyone wishing to enter training to become a Veterinary Nurse should have 5 <u>GCSEs</u> at grade C or above, or Scottish Standard Grades 1-3, or Scottish Higher Grades A-E. Whatever form of school qualification you have must include English Language and two passes in a physical or biological science (such as Physics, Chemistry or Biology) or mathematics. However, passes in some examinations of a comparable or higher standard may be accepted in place of the usual requirements.

Veterinary Nurses work as part of a veterinary team, to provide medical and surgical nursing care for animals. This popular career broadly involves: hands on nursing care for sick or injured animals, educating owners about pet health and welfare and the carrying out of medical treatments and minor procedures. A veterinary nursing qualification can lead to many different job opportunities in animal welfare.

The duties of a qualified veterinary nurse involve a considerable amount of responsibility. Senior nurses play a key role in the running of a private practice or organisation. Their tasks may include all or some of the following: managing staff, organising workloads for the vets, ensuring the smooth running of the operating theatre, performing minor surgical operations, assisting with surgery, monitoring anaesthesia, running the radiography unit, taking and developing x-rays, overseeing care of in-patients, handling and restraining animals for treatment, administering drugs and medication to sick and injured animals, overseeing the ordering of veterinary supplies, admitting patients, keeping and updating medical records, training students and advising owners on various aspects of pet care.

There are essentially two ways to become a registered veterinary nurse: the vocational route - an NVQ in veterinary nursing, and the higher education route - a BSc degree or Higher National Diploma course.

The NVQ route: this is the more practical option that involves fairly intensive training over a minimum of two years. The training takes place at an RCVS approved training practice where knowledge about treatments and care for a variety of animals is gained in a hands-on way. Some of the tasks during training may seem quite basic e.g. cleaning out kennels. However, the work is usually varied and rewarding and ultimately enables a trainee nurse to gain a better understanding of <u>animal behaviour</u> as well as to develop important skills such as animal handling. You will be continually assessed and have to take formal written exams at the end of each year of study. As well as working as a trainee, you will also be required to attend college for several days a week and continue your studies in the evenings. Your hard work will hopefully result in RCVS National Vocational Qualifications in Veterinary Nursing, levels 2 and 3 and RCVS Certificates in Veterinary Nursing Theory, levels 2 and 3. See the useful contacts below for a list of Veterinary Nurse approved Centres (VNAC) and Royal College of Veterinary Surgeons (RCVS) registered Training Practices. This list is useful to those wishing to find a local centre to request employment as a student veterinary nurse or trainee. As an entrance requirement, you must be 17 years or older and have one of the following: 5 GCSE's grade C incl English Language and 2 science, or have passed the Animal Nursing Assistant qualification In special cases, and at the discretion of the RCVS, you may be accepted without these qualifications - contact the RCVS directly to discuss your situation.

The higher education route: the <u>Higher National Diploma (HND)</u> and the <u>BSc Honours in Veterinary Nursing courses</u> take between 3 and 4 years. These are longer and more academic courses than the NVQ route, however, the qualification can ultimately lead to additional career opportunities such as lecturing, research and the pharmaceutical industry. As an entrance requirement for a BSc Honours in Veterinary Nursing you will need one of the following: <u>2 A Levels,</u> <u>BTEC National Diploma in a science subject</u> or <u>Advanced GNVQs, equivalent qualifications (including the VN Certificate)</u> will also be considered. It is worth noting that you can also apply if you are over 21 and don't have formal qualifications but can show high levels of ability and experience. The course involves practical training (also through Veterinary Nursing Approved Centres – see list below), as well as academic studies and there are usually additional subjects such as practice management/administration.

Once you have successfully completed your veterinary nursing qualifications, you will be eligible to join the RCVS Register of Veterinary Nurses – this allows you to legally practice as a veterinary nurse. Your qualification will mean that you will be awarded a Royal College of Veterinary Surgeons Certificate in Veterinary Nursing.

Career prospects are good for skilled veterinary nurses. There is a strong demand for well-trained animal care professionals and opportunities are open to nurses in a variety of animal care jobs. As a qualified veterinary nurse, there are numerous career options open to you. These include: developing a career as a head nurse in general practice, in a specialised veterinary referral centre, in the equine world, as a veterinary practice manager, in an animal charity/welfare/hospital nursing environment, in academia as a lecturer or researcher, within the pharmaceutical and veterinary supplies industries.

Some experienced nurses choose to do temporary locum work. This can be a good option if you are finding it difficult to find a suitable permanent position and enjoy variety and meeting new people and situations. Salaries for student veterinary nurses start from around £10k, qualified nurses can expect to earn from around £14k and head nurses from around £17k to over £30k depending on experience, qualifications and responsibilities. Some posts are residential and this is reflected in the salary. Salaries may be enhanced if allowances are made for vehicles, fuel and Continuing Professional Development (CPD).

The Professional Pet Care and Veterinary Assistant Diploma course is an ideal starting point for those seeking a career in the veterinary or pet care sector. It covers all the topics in the BVNA Animal Nursing Assistant Course with the exception of the work experience and practical related elements. Unique to this course, you will also gain a good understanding of important Animal Welfare Issues and Animal Law; crucial if you want to make a difference to the welfare of animals. The first part of this course is particularly useful for anyone caring for a range of animals in a professional capacity. The second part is aimed specifically at the veterinary practice assistant. Completion of Part Two will result in a Level 4 qualification.

The Animal Behaviour Diploma is also an excellent qualification for anyone wanting to work in a veterinary capacity with animals as is the Animal Care, Welfare and Husbandry Diploma.

Useful contacts:

British Veterinary Nursing Association (BVNA): 2 Greenway Business Centre, Harlow Business Park, Harlow Essex, CM19 5QE. Tel: 01279 408644.

List of Approved Veterinary Nurse Training Practices: List of Veterinary Nurse approved Centres (VNAC) and Royal College of Veterinary Surgeons registered.

Training/work advice for veterinary nursing in Europe: Veterinary European Transnational Network for Nursing Education and Training.

Veterinary Practice Management Association (VPMA): provides individuals who are involved in the management of veterinary practice with an effective means of communication and interaction with others with similar interests. 76 St John's Road, Kettering, Northants, NN15 5AZ.

61. Animal Nursing Assistant

The role of an Animal Nursing Assistant is crucial in ensuring the smooth running of a veterinary practice. An Animal Nursing Assistant works closely with the animals in veterinary practices or veterinary hospitals, playing the vital role of assisting Veterinary Nurses, Veterinary Surgeons and practice staff.

It is important that you are patient, compassionate and enjoy nursing sick or recovering animals, as well as promoting their health and welfare. The role can include all or some of the following hands-on tasks: feeding, cleaning, handling and general care of animals pre and post operatively, assisting with the day to day running of the practice i.e. reception duties, dealing with clients, assisting in the consulting rooms and preparation of animals and treatment areas.

To become an Animal Nursing Assistant, you must be 16 years or older. No formal qualifications are required and the training usually takes approximately one year. As a first step, you will need to find employment in any veterinary practice – this needs to be for a minimum of 35 hours a week. Once you have gained employment, you are required to enrol with the British Veterinary Nurses Association (BVNA) as a student and register with an Animal Nursing Assistant approved training centre (you can train by correspondence).

The course training includes subjects such as anatomy, first aid, health & hygiene, theatre nursing, animal handling, reception and nutrition. Students are required to undertake examinations that take place in June and to keep a case-log book based on the workplace. Once you have passed the Animal Nursing Assistant (ANA) qualification, you are entitled to carry out duties within a veterinary practice assisting Veterinary Nurses and Veterinary Surgeons, working with animals and helping to care for them. Once you have the ANA qualification, you can also enroll straight onto the NVQ Veterinary Nursing Scheme.

The Professional Pet Care and Veterinary Assistant Diploma course is an ideal starting point for those seeking a career in the veterinary or pet care sector. It covers all the topics in the BVNA Animal Nursing Assistant Course with the exception of the work experience and practical related elements. Unique to this course, you will also gain a good understanding of important Animal Welfare Issues and Animal Law; crucial if you want to make a difference to the welfare of animals. The first part of this course is particularly useful for anyone caring for a range of animals in a professional capacity. The second part is aimed specifically at the veterinary practice assistant. Completion of Part Two will result in a Level 4 qualification.

The Animal Behaviour Diploma is an excellent qualification for anyone wanting to work in a veterinary capacity with animals as is the Animal Care, Welfare and Husbandry Diploma.

Useful contacts:

Animal Nursing Assistant British Veterinary Nursing Association (BVNA): 82 Greenway Business Centre, Harlow Business Park, Harlow Essex, CM19 5QE. Tel: 01279 408644

62. Veterinary Physiotherapist

The work of a Veterinary Physiotherapist involves treating animals with injuries, investigating mobility problems, preventing recurring injuries and helping to reduce pain, The work is particularly concerned with problems that affect muscles, circulation, bones, the heart system and the lungs. Physiotherapists utilise a variety of techniques including: massage, soft tissue & joint mobilisation, electrotherapy, ultrasound, magnetic field therapy and hydrotherapy. They may also recommend exercise plans to improve an animal's fitness and mobility.

Veterinary Physiotherapy is an increasingly popular career choice. The term 'Chartered Physiotherapist,' is protected and can only be used by someone who is trained and qualified as a Member of the Chartered Society of Physiotherapy (MCSP). The qualification is recognised and respected by the veterinary profession and by potential customers. Therefore if you are properly qualified and registered, you are more likely to have patients referred to you. To become a Chartered Physiotherapist, you must first qualify as a human physiotherapist; once you are a member of the Chartered Society of Physiotherapists you can specialise and become a Veterinary or Animal Physiotherapist by completing a postgraduate training run by The Royal Veterinary College (RVC).

Horses and dogs are the most common types of animal referred for physiotherapy. They may be either pets or working animals such as race horses, show jumpers or greyhounds. The work is physically demanding; it requires a high degree of physical fitness, stamina and a strong back as there is likely to be heavy lifting. Many Veterinary Physiotherapists are self employed and run their own businesses - working from home, from local surgeries or travelling to their client's facilities. This means that at times the work may be outdoors or in stable yards in all weathers. Some Veterinary Physiotherapists work from larger veterinary practices and animal hospitals where they come across a wide variety of cases and may have the opportunity of promotion within the organisation.

A full driving licence is usually required, especially if you are self employed and are required to travel to clients premises. You need to be interested in animals and concerned for their welfare. Having worked with animals previously is an advantage as you will need to be patient and experienced in handing different types of animals (some of them large). There is much people interaction; you will need to have good communication skills and be able to build up relationships of trust and respect with clients.

Salaries for newly qualified Animal Physiotherapists start from around £18k. Once you have more experience, you can expect to earn around £25k. Consultants may earn £35k or more. Self-employed animal physiotherapists charge hourly rates that can range from £30 to £70 for an hours' appointment, depending on location and experience.

Useful contacts:

Association of Chartered Physiotherapists in Animal Physiotherapy (ACPAT): 21 Woodlands Close, Penenden Heath, Maidstone, Kent ME14 2EX. Tel: 01622 688777.

International Association of Animal Therapists (IAAP): Tyringham Hall, Cuddington, Aylesbury, Buckinghamshire HP18 0AP. Tel: 01844 291526.

Chartered Society of Physiotherapy (CSP):14 Bedford Row, London, WC1R 4ED. Tel: 020 7306 6666

Royal Veterinary College (RVC): Hawkshead Lane, North Mymms, Herts, AL9 7TA. Tel: 01707 666333

National Association of Veterinary Physiotherapists (NAVP): The association aims to provide a high level of care in assisting the veterinary profession in the rehabilitation of injured animals and also providing means of keeping athletic animals in peak working condition.

63. Veterinary Chiropractor

The purpose of chiropractic treatments is to diagnose and treat mechanical disorders of the spine and musculoskeletal system without the use of drugs or surgery. Veterinary Chiropractors work hands-on with animals, combining traditional human chiropractic with veterinary science, to provide additional treatment options for animals. Various injuries, lameness and hip dysplasia can be treated through chiropractic procedures.

To become a Veterinary Chiropractor, you need to be interested in animals and concerned for their welfare. Having worked with animals previously is an advantage as you will need to be patient and experienced in handing different types of animals. There is much people interaction; you will need to have good communication skills and be able to build up relationships of trust and respect with clients.

In the UK there are only two ways to qualify as a Veterinary Chiropractor, both options are based in Oxfordshire. The first is through the McTimoney College of Chiropractic and the other is through the Oxford College of Chiropractic. Both offer training in Human Chiropractic and provide training in animal manipulative therapy as a separate Post Graduate qualification.

McTimoney College of Chiropractic: emphasises training in the McTimoney method of chiropractic, a gentle, skillful and effective holistic treatment developed by founder, John McTimoney who began teaching his methods in 1972. The College also runs the only University validated post-graduate course in chiropractic for animals in Europe. With expansion of the College in recent years through growing demand, McTimoney chiropractors now represent over one quarter of the UK chiropractic profession. The course is taught over two years, and leads to the award of a MSc Animal Manipulation from the University of Wales.

The MSc Animal Manipulation Course is currently unique in Europe, in that it is the only externally validated course that trains students in Animal Manipulation. The course is designed either for students who already have training in a hands-on therapy (this may include a trained chiropractor, physiotherapist, osteopath or any other fully qualified and suitably experienced practitioner), for those with a BSc degree in Equine or Animal Science or for those who are a member of the Royal College of Veterinary Surgeons. Students from a non-manipulative background will be expected to gain experience in 'hands on' therapies before starting the course. Students who do not have formal training may submit a portfolio of certified experience for consideration.

The course is taught at Masters level and students must be capable of working at this standard. Students who are not chiropractors or osteopaths are required to undertake a course of training in manipulation skills. The programme is open to applicants meeting one of the following criteria (pathway specific): The holding of a professional qualification in Osteopathy, Chiropractic or Physiotherapy, which would qualify the holder for registration with the General Osteopathic Council, General Chiropractic Council or Chartered Institute of Physiotherapists as appropriate. OR: A member of the Royal Veterinary College of Surgeons. OR: The holding of a degree in Animal Science, Equine Science or other University degrees where 80% of the course content includes comparative anatomy, basic physiology and biochemistry.

Mature students over the age of 25 who do not hold formal academic qualifications may apply for this course under the Assessment of Prior Experience and Learning (APEL) system. Those applicants who do not hold a professional qualification in manipulation must successfully complete the College's Access programme. This is to ensure that all entrants to the MSc have the requisite knowledge of science, research, professionalism and manipulation skills on entry to ensure successful completion of the main programme.

Students are taught by specialist veterinary surgeons, and study animal anatomy and the physiology of movement to a level at least on a par with that of veterinary surgeons themselves. Students are assessed partly through coursework and partly through examinations - both practical and theory.

Useful contacts:

The McTimoney College of Chiropractic: Kimber House, 1 Kimber Road, Abingdon, Oxfordshire, OX14 1BZ. Tel: 01235 523336

64. Veterinary Osteopath

Osteopathy involves not only manipulating bones (as in chiropractic treatment), but also the massage of soft tissues and spinal joints to increase circulation and speed recovery. Veterinary osteopathy works on the same principles and theory as human osteopathy, but with specific manipulative procedures for animals. The treatment involves various techniques that work to increase mobility and improve muscle tone and circulation. This can be beneficial for a wide variety of conditions and problems such as lameness, stiffness and various types of injury. Osteopathy is holistic and considers the whole being to find the cause of the problem. Therefore, osteopaths often apply a varied treatment plan and consider diet, exercise and other factors as part of the treatment.

Having worked with animals previously is an advantage, as you will need to be experienced in handing different types of animals. There is much people interaction; you will need to have good communication skills and be able to build up relationships of trust and respect with clients.

Osteopaths undergo a rigorous training of four or more years. Once qualified, some osteopaths choose to specialise in the treatment of animals. Animal training courses vary from short courses to more in-depth post-graduate diploma courses.

The Animal Manipulation (Osteopathic techniques) programme is offered by the McTimoney College of Chiropractic is unique in Europe, in that it is the only University validated masters-level course that trains students in Animal Osteopathic techniques. Developed with the late Anthony Pusey, this programme is designed for qualified osteopaths who wish to transfer their skills to the care of animals.

The course is run in conjunction with Warwickshire College where the first year of the course is undertaken. A wide range of academic subjects are studied as well as an introduction to the philosophy and practice of animal techniques. The second year of the course is conducted at various sites throughout the country where the practical skills are taught under the supervision of a qualified practitioner. The course is semestered over two years and students are required to attend monthly weekend tutorial sessions primarily at Warwickshire College. The course is taught at Masters level and students must be capable of working at this standard.

The McTimoney College of Chiropractic: Kimber House, 1 Kimber Road, Abingdon, Oxfordshire, OX14 1BZ. Tel: 01235 523336

65. Veterinary Homeopath

Homoeopathic vets are fully qualified veterinary surgeons who have chosen to take further training and qualification in the use of homoeopathic medicines. Veterinary homeopathy involves the treatment of an animal as a whole rather than just of a specific complaint. It is an holistic therapy and takes into account factors such as environment, diet, exercise, lifestyle and other symptoms that a patient may be suffering from.

Homeopathy involves a system of medicine that bases its therapeutics on the principle of that of 'like curing like'. It was noted in the late 18th century by the founder of homeopathy, Dr. Samuel Hahnemannm, that if a medicine could cause a group of symptoms in a healthy individual, then, if a sick person was suffering from similar symptoms, the medicine could cure that person.

Remedies used in homeopathy are made from natural substances - mineral, animal or vegetable sources. Homeopathy was first used in animals around 1810, and is now widely available as a treatment that involves no risk of toxic side-effects or stimulation of antibiotic resistance. Laboratory animal research is not required for the development of homeopathic medicines.

In the UK, only courses accredited by the Faculty of Homeopathy are recognised by the British Association of Homeopathic Veterinary Surgeons (BAHVS). A new introductory-level post-graduate exam and qualification has been devised by the Faculty. Further teaching is provided by post-graduate teaching at the Teaching Centres, by the papers given at the Annual Congress of the British Association of Homeopathic Veterinary Surgeons and by papers of the bi-annual congress of the International Association. Neither the Faculty of Homeopathy nor the BAHVS provide teaching in homeopathy for animals to any other than veterinary surgeons, who alone are legally entitled to treat animals (other than one's own animals).

The total course provides a minimum of 120 hours tuition, spread over three years. The course content is structured to exceed the standard required for the post-graduate Faculty Membership examination. Veterinary surgeons who successfully complete the Veterinary Membership examination are awarded the qualification: Veterinary Member of the Faculty of Homeopathy (VetMFHom).

As an entry requirement, Veterinary surgeons must be registered with the Royal College of Veterinary Surgeons or have their qualifications recognised by the RCVS. UK applicants must have a minimum of 12 months' full membership of the RCVS.

Useful contacts:

International Association for Veterinary Homeopathy

British Association of Homeopathic Veterinary Surgeons: Alternative Veterinary Medicine Centre, Chinham House, Stanford in the Vale, Oxfordshire, SN7 8NQ. Tel:1367 710324

British Homeopathic Trust: Hahnemann House, 29 Park Street, West Luton, LU1 3BE. Tel: 0870 444 3950.

66. Veterinary Receptionist

Veterinary receptionists play an important role as part of the team at any veterinary practice, hospital or animal charity. They are responsible for the first impression received by a client (by phone or visit), and they are the interface between the veterinary surgeon, nurses, clients and other veterinary practices or organisations.

Therefore, to consider this career, you need to have excellent communication skills as well as an understanding of routine veterinary treatments. You must be extremely organised, have good administration skills, be calm, positive and be able to give reassurance to a client who may be worried about their pet. In some practices, the receptionist may also be required to process invoices & payments and manage shop stock and orders.

There are several courses that offer excellent training and qualifications. The British Veterinary Nursing Association (BVNA) Animal Nursing Assistant qualification includes a unit entitled 'Finance, Veterinary Reception and Administration'. Candidates can enroll on this course and undertake this specific unit, they do not have to continue to achieve the entire qualification. By undertaking and passing the multiple-choice examination successful candidates will be awarded a Unit of Achievement. If in the future, you want to progress you can then undertake one or all three of the remaining units in order to gain the entire qualification. It is not essential for candidates to be enrolled at college in order to undertake this specific unit, however there are approximately 30 colleges in the United Kingdom who run the Animal Nursing Assistant qualification – see the ANA section of the BVNA website for further information.

The Professional Pet Care and Veterinary Assistant Diploma course is an ideal starting point for those seeking a career in the veterinary or pet care sector. It covers all the topics in the BVNA Animal Nursing Assistant Course with the exception of the work experience and practical related elements. Unique to this course, you will also gain a good understanding of important Animal Welfare Issues and Animal Law; crucial if you want to make a difference to the welfare of animals. The first part of this course is particularly useful for anyone caring for a range of animals in a professional capacity. The second part is aimed specifically at the veterinary practice assistant. Completion of Part Two will result in a Level 4 qualification.

The Reception Skills Course is an online training course that is worth considering - qualifications will greatly improve your chances of employment. The Animal Care, Welfare and Husbandry Diploma is also worth considering.

Useful contacts:

Receptionist Course British Veterinary Nursing Association (BVNA): 82 Greenway Business Centre, Harlow Business Park, Harlow Essex, CM19 5QE. Tel: 01279 408644

Careers with Wildlife

A career working with wildlife requires good communication skills and may involve tough physical outdoor work; for this sort of career, you should enjoy being outdoors in all types of weather. The working hours are unpredictable and varied - you will probably be required to work at weekends and bank holidays. You will need to be physically fit, healthy, hard working, have plenty of stamina and enjoy exercise. Some careers with wildlife, may require you to live on site, to have a driving license and be confident driving off-road vehicles. As with all animal related work, it is crucial that you are dedicated, compassionate, committed and that you don't suffer from animal allergies.

Different jobs may include; conducting wildlife and ecological surveys, monitoring wildlife habitats and populations, protection and rescue of animals from natural and man-made disasters and rehabilitation of sick or injured animals.

Candidates wishing to pursue a career working with wildlife should have good problem solving skills and the ability to collect, analyse and interpret data. Persuasive skills are important when proposing restrictions on land use. Wildlife biologists need to be able to teach and explain wildlife management to others through presentations and reports. This type of work often involves public speaking, training and advising the public, organisations or government on wildlife issues.

There are several excellent training options available for those wishing to pursue a career with wildlife. These include the following Diploma qualifications: Principles of Zoology, Animal Behaviour, Marine Zoology, Ornithology, Birds of Prey, British Wild Mammals, Ecology, Environmental Management and the Conservation Diploma.

If you haven't spent time working with or caring for wildlife, it is worth considering working as a volunteer at a wildlife rescue centre before embarking on a career with wildlife. Many wildlife rescue organisations run volunteer programmes, several offer work experience placements and some even offer NVQ training courses. All of these opportunities provide excellent ways to gain experience and build up your confidence for working around wildlife.

In this career guide, we have information about the following wildlife careers: Wildlife Rehabilitator, Wildlife Biologist, Country Warden/Ranger, Ornithologist, Wildlife/Countryside Conservation Officer, Gamekeeper and Zoologist.

67. Wildlife Rehabilitator

Wildlife rehabilitation involves the temporary care and treatment of injured, sick and orphaned wildlife. Rehabilitation is necessary to improve the chances of survival for sick or injured animals when they are ready to be released back to an appropriate habitat. Wild animals require rehabilitation because of human acts such as road traffic accidents, displacement through destruction of wildlife habitat through construction, poisoning, entanglement in fences, traps, and fishing line, etc. Unfortunately, there has been an increase in the public keeping wildlife as 'pets' and this has resulted in a bigger demand for wildlife rehabilitators who are required to assist when people are unable to properly care for wild animals in a domestic environment.

The work of a wildlife rehabilitator varies considerably and there is no typical job description. The job involves some or all the following: rescuing animals from dangerous situations, transporting wild animals, feeding baby birds or mammals, assisting with fluid therapy and bandaging, providing emergency first aid, supervising staff or volunteers, providing presentations about animals and the environment, cleaning cages, taking calls and advising the public.

This is a challenging, yet extremely rewarding career. Unfortunately, less than half of the animals admitted for wildlife rehabilitation are released; many die or are euthanised for humane reasons. However, this can be extremely rewarding work when animals are successfully rehabilitated and then released to the wild.

The work involves long hours and weekend duties. It can be extremely demanding at times as it takes much time, effort and skill to rehabilitate wildlife correctly. Most recovering animals require intensive treatments and care - for example, baby birds must be fed every 20 minutes during the day! Most rehabilitators learn their skills on the job and gain experience initially through volunteering. However, having a degree in biology or ecology is an advantage and other qualifications such as wildlife management, animal behaviour, ecology and animal nursing are also useful for work in this field.

If you are interested in pursuing a career as a wildlife rehabilitator, it is a good idea to visit wildlife rescue/rehabilitation centres to see first hand what the work involves – assisting as a volunteer is an advisable next step. Candidates for this type of career need to be physically fit and healthy, self motivated, positive, creative thinkers/solution finders, energetic and concerned about wildlife, people & the environment. The work involves cleaning and physically therapy/exercise sessions for the animals in your care - and some of the patients can be large and heavy!

It is crucial that wildlife rehabilitators are able to keep their distance emotionally from the animals they care for. If a bond is formed with a young wild animal, it will lose its instinctive fear of humans and therefore make it difficult or impossible for it to be released back into the wild.

It is advisable to attend wildlife rehabilitation training sessions and conferences, as these provide excellent networking as well as learning opportunities. The National Wildlife Rehabilitators Association (NWRA) sponsors an annual world-class symposium. The International Wildlife Rehabilitation Council (IWRC) offers conferences as well as training.

Useful qualifications include: Animal Care Welfare & Husbandry, Animal Behaviour, Birds of Prey, British Wild Mammals, Ecology, Environmental Management and the Conservation Diploma.

Useful contacts:

International Wildlife Rehabilitation Council: works to preserve and protect through the support of wildlife rehabilitation.

British Wildlife Rehabilitation Council (BWRC): their mission is to promote the welfare of wildlife casualties both whilst in captivity and after release back into the wild, and to ensure that casualties are handled within the framework and spirit of the law. PO Box 8686, Grantham, Lincolnshire NG31 0AG

Tiggywinkles: is the world's busiest wildlife rehabilitation hospital: Aston Road, Haddenham, Aylesbury, Buckinghamshire HP17 8AF Tel: 01844 292292.

Wildlife Rescue League – provides care for wildlife in need, organisation located in Northern Virginia. P.O. Box 704, Falls Church, VA 22040 USA.

68. Wildlife Biologist

Wildlife Biologists have a direct involvement with the well-being of wild animals. Wildlife biologists may specialise in a specific animal area such as wildlife management, wildlife law enforcement, environmental education, natural resources management, environmental biology, conservation biology, or research. Some wildlife biologists work in a more general way in animal management, such as conducting programmes in conservation and management of wildlife populations and their habitats with the aim of problem prevention.

Biologists monitoring wildlife populations and habitats will look for the distribution, size, sex, and age of wildlife. They may determine habitat quality and study the effects of weather, disease, habitat alteration, and animals (including humans) on wildlife populations. Techniques used by biologists in this field include radio tracking, aerial surveys, trapping, marking, and computer modelling.

Some wildlife biologists investigate the impact of land use on wildlife habitats and those specialising in this area conduct workshops and seminars about land use that is compatible with wildlife. Biologists also study the effects of current land use on water, vegetation, and wildlife populations. Pollutants like acid rain, pesticides, and sewage are monitored to determine their effects on the ecological system of the area. Wildlife biologists can make proposals for protecting ecological systems and recommend measures to compensate for affects of land use on wildlife populations and habitat.

Some help make and implement laws and regulations for protecting wildlife. They can make recommendations regarding hunting and trapping regulations and encourage land use and planning that is compatible with wildlife. Those concentrating in this area can set policies and modify regulations to help landowners manage overabundant wildlife species. Researchers study situations similar to a wildlife biologist, but report them in scientific journals or in papers delivered at conferences. They prepare grants and contracts to secure funding for research programs and may supervise students and technicians in field research. The work can be both indoors and outdoors in all weathers, including extended periods away from home. Working with large animals means that candidates need to be physically fit, strong and in good health. There is also some indoor work – this includes nature centres, classrooms, and laboratories.

To enter this field, you will need a minimum of a bachelor's degree in Wildlife Biology, Ecology, Wildlife Management, or Natural Resources Management. In many cases, a master's degree is required. A Ph. D. is needed for research, university teaching, and specialist positions. Problem solving skills and the ability to collect, analyse and interpret data is useful. Persuasive skills are important when proposing restrictions on land use. Wildlife biologists need to be able to teach and explain wildlife management to others through presentations and reports.

Useful qualifications include: <u>Animal Behaviour, Marine Zoology, Birds of Prey, British Wild Mammals, Ecology, Environmental Management and the Conservation Diploma.</u>

Useful contacts:

<u>Countryside Management Association (CMA)</u>: represents professionals engaged in countryside and urban green space management throughout England and Wales. Writtle College, Lordship Road, Writtle, Chelmsford, Essex, CM1 3 RR. Tel: 01245 424116

<u>British Trust for Conservation Volunteers (BTCV)</u>: works to create a more sustainable future by inspiring people and improving places. Sedum House, Mallard Way, Doncaster, DN4 8DB. Tel: 01302 388 883

69. Countryside Warden/Park Ranger

A countryside warden or park ranger works within a designated area of parkland, forest, wetland, common land or in national parks. The work is practical and varied and it includes conducting wildlife surveys, maintaining wildlife habitats - ie, tree planting and pond management, ensuring right of access by maintaining footpaths and bridleways, and educating visitors by providing exhibitions, guided walks and resource centres.

Countryside wardens prevent damage, protect plants and wildlife and ensure that the area is safe for public use. They may also be required to oversee budgets and keep records. To enjoy this type of work, candidates must have a passion for the outdoors and a belief in the importance of caring for places of natural beauty and historical interest.

It is essential to enjoy interacting with people as the work often involves public speaking, as wardens are required to offer advice and information to the public. Countryside wardens need to be physically fit as the work involves a considerable amount of walking, climbing and carrying. Most of the work is conducted outdoors in all weathers. It is essential to have a driving license and to be confident driving off road vehicles. The working hours are varied and normally include evenings and weekends, with holiday seasons being the busiest time for some aspects of the work.

The National Trust offers a training scheme for new wardens - this involves three years of practical training designed to develop theoretical and practical countryside skills. They also offer numerous opportunities for more experienced Wardens to work at one of their 300 properties based in England, Wales and Northern Ireland. Some more experienced wardens are able to specialise in particular areas such as habitat management, fieldwork or education. At the end of the three year scheme, a trainee Countryside Warden will gain an NVQ level 2 & 3 in Environmental Conservation administered by City & Guilds, as well as a wealth of practical skills and knowledge. Coupled with this, are relevant certificates such as the safe use of chainsaws, small tree felling and the use of pesticides.

To be a successful applicant for a job as a countryside warden it is crucial to have relevant experience. The best way to get this is by volunteering with organisations such as: The Wildlife Trusts, National Trust, the Forestry Commission, Groundwork and the British Trust for Conservation Volunteers (BTCV). The BTCV offers a wide variety of courses, some lead to qualifications in environmental subjects relevant to Countryside warden careers – including; species identification, habitat management, coppicing, hedge laying and risk assessment.

Relevant courses at colleges and universities include: City and Guilds NPTC National Certificate in Environmental Conservation. BTEC/SQA National Certificate/Diploma in Countryside Management with options including Water Management, Woodland Management, Rural Tourism, Countryside Interpretation and Habitat Conservation. BTEC/SQA HNC/HND in Environmental Conservation. Foundation degrees in subjects such as Countryside Management and Conservation and Countryside Management. Certificate in Land based Studies (NPTC), NVQ in Environmental Conservation (NPTC).

Degree courses such as BSc in Rural Resource Management, Countryside Management, Rural Environmental Management, Conservation and Environment, or Environmental Studies. The Universities and Colleges Admissions Service (UCAS) have information on colleges and universities offering these degrees. Candidates may be able to work towards NVQ/SVQ levels 2 and 3 in Environmental Conservation (Countryside Management) when employed and you will be able to join the Countryside Management Association (CMA), this will entitle you to professional accreditation, continuing professional development (CPD), training and study days and exchanges, seminars and conferences. Apprenticeships may be available for those under the age of 24. In England these are currently Apprenticeships (level 2) and Advanced Apprenticeships (level 3).

Most countryside rangers and wardens work in the public sector; the main employers are local authority countryside, leisure or recreation departments. The Forestry Commission employs about 300 wildlife rangers. Other employers include the National Trust, Wildlife Trusts and smaller wildlife charities.

Useful contacts:

Wildlife Trusts: dedicated to conserving the full range of the UK's habitats and species. The Kiln, Waterside, Mather Road, Newark, Nottinghamshire, NG24 1WT. Tel: 01636 677711

Forestry Commission: works to protect and expand Britain's forests and woodlands and increase their value to society and the environment. 231 Corstorphine Road, Edinburgh, EH12 7AT. Tel: 0131 334 0303

Groundwork UK: supports communities in need, working with partners to help improve the quality of people's lives, their prospects and potential and the places where they live, work and play. Lockside, 5 Scotland Street, Birmingham, B1 2RR. Tel: 0121 236 8565

The National Trust: care for over 248,000 hectares of countryside in England, Wales and Northern Ireland, plus more than 700 miles of coastline and more than 200 buildings and gardens of outstanding interest and importance. PO Box 39, Warrington, WA5 7WD. Tel: 0870 458 4000

British Trust for Conservation Volunteers (BTCV): works to create a more sustainable future by inspiring people and improving places. Sedum House, Mallard Way, Doncaster, DN4 8DB. Tel: 01302 388 883

70. Ornithologist

An ornithologist studies a type of zoology primarily concerned with the scientific study of birds. Ornithologists are bird specialists who have a strong scientific approach to their work. Their job includes the monitoring and tracking of birds, habitat monitoring and management, studying of populations, bird behaviour, carrying out surveys and research as well as educating the public about the importance of habitat conservation.

Candidates must be passionate about bird observation and conservation and they need to be thorough, analytical, meticulous and pay attention to detail. Many work at observatories and ringing stations where the working hours are variable due to migration cycles. They are sometimes required to work in isolated locations, such as offshore islands and it is therefore important for ornithologists to be able to work alone and to be prepared to travel. The work can be demanding and candidates need to be physically fit, prepared to work outdoors in all weathers, hold a current driving licence and be prepared to drive off road vehicles.

Most people working with birds have a degree or higher degree in countryside or conservation management, ecology, zoology or a related biological science. In addition, it is important that candidates are experienced bird watchers.

The British Trust for Ornithology (BTO) offer bird ringing training. A higher degree or PhD can also be obtained by doing further training through an employer and by conducting a research project. To obtain qualifications in safe bird ringing, candidates need a BTO permit and will need to take the following steps: contact the BTO for a list of bird ringers that are qualified to train others, apply for a trainee permit and do at least two years' training, apply for a 'C' permit which will allow you to ring by yourself. Then after another year and further assessment, students can apply for an 'A' permit

Candidates with an enthusiastic interest in birds but without a scientific background might be able to find work as wardens, education/information officers or in administration. Experience and relevant qualifications in teaching, journalism or administration are needed for jobs in education/information or administrative work. Observatories, ringing stations, nature reserves, some local authorities, charities, wildlife trusts and some private conservation organisations employ ornithologists. There are not many vacancies and competition is high. Most research officers start their careers on a temporary contract as a research student working on a short-term study or project with organisations such as the Royal Society for the Protection of Birds, British Trust For Ornithology (BTO) or the Department for Environment, Food and Rural Affairs.

Useful qualifications include: the Ornithology Diploma as well as the Birds of Prey – Rescue and Rehabilitation Diploma and the British Wild Mammals Diploma.

Useful contacts:
The British Trust for Ornithology (BTO): promotes bird conservation through volunteer based surveys. The Nunnery, Thetford, Norfolk IP24 2PU. Tel: 01842 750050

The American Ornithologists Union (AOU): is devoted to the scientific study of birds. Although the AOU primarily is a professional organisation, its membership of about 4,000 includes many amateurs dedicated to the advancement of ornithological science. Suite 402, 1313 Dolley Madison Blvd, McLean, VA 22101, USA.

Bird Observatories Council: co-ordinates and promotes the work of the Bird Observatories at a national level. A bird observatory's primary purpose is to conduct long-term monitoring of bird populations and migration.

British Ornithologists Union: dedicated to promoting the understanding of avian biology and conservation.

Index to Ornithology: information about wild birds by a professional ornithologist

Birdnet: is provided by the Ornithological Council and provides information for and about ornithology. The site serves professional ornithologists and the general public.

Electronic Ornithology resources

71. Wildlife Conservation Officer

A wildlife conservation officer is involved in the management, improvement and protection of a wildlife or wilderness area. The work can include: managing habitats, environmental impact assessments, field surveys, creating or restoring landscapes and advising landowners and local government on conservation and land issues. Part of the work involves community participation work and can include promoting rights of way, public speaking, guided walks, holding workshops, school visits and developing access (cycle/wheelchair) routes.

Most of the work is outdoors, but there are some office aspects such as writing leaflets, updating records and writing reports. Conservation Officers must be passionate about the countryside and conservation issues, they need to be good communicators and able to educate individuals and groups of visitors. An advanced diploma or masters degree in conservation, ecology, or countryside management is usually necessary.

Competition for vacancies is strong and having practical experience is advantageous when seeking employment – valuable experience can be gained through volunteering. You do not need any set qualifications to be a countryside/conservation officer, but many have degrees or HNDS, so you may find it an advantage to have this type of qualification. Relevant degree subjects include countryside/environmental management, environmental sciences, biology, ecology and geography. Employment prospects can also be enhanced through courses such as those offered by the Field Studies Council and the British Trust for Conservation. Volunteers joining organisations such as the Institute of Ecology and Environmental Management (IEEM) will find it useful for networking opportunities. Conservation Officers are employed by charities, local government and environmental consultancies.

You may find it useful to join professional bodies such as the Institute of Ecology and Environmental Management (IEEM), as this will give you professional recognition, and opportunities for networking.

Useful qualifications include the following Diploma courses: Introduction to Zoology, Birds of Prey, British Wild Mammals, Ecology, Environmental Management and the Conservation Diploma.

Useful contacts:

Natural England: works for people, places and nature to conserve and enhance biodiversity, landscapes and wildlife in rural, urban, coastal and marine areas. Northminster House, Peterborough, PE1 1UA. Tel: 0845 600 3078

Field Studies Council: an environmental education charity committed to helping people understand and be inspired by the natural world. Montford Bridge, Preston, Shrewsbury, Shropshire, SY4 1HW. Tel: 0845 345 4071

Conservation Volunteers Northern Ireland: works to create a better environment where people are valued, included and involved. Beech House, 159 Ravenhill Road, Belfast, BT6 0BP, Ireland. Tel: 028 9064 5169

British Trust for Conservation Volunteers (BTCV): works to create a more sustainable future by inspiring people and improving places. Sedum House, Mallard Way, Potteric Carr, Doncaster, DNL 8DB. Tel: 01302 388888

Woodland Trust: the UK's leading woodland conservation charity. Autumn Park, Dysart Road, Grantham, Lincolnshire, NG31 6LL.

Institute of Ecology and Environmental Management (IEEM): is the professional body that represents and supports ecologists and environmental managers in the UK and abroad. 45 Southgate Street, Winchester, Hampshire, SO23 9EH. Tel: 01962 868626.

72. Gamekeeper

Gamekeepers are usually employed by private country estates/landowners or farms. Tasks include: managing wildlife habitats, training gun dogs, clearing woodland, land management & predator control, breeding & releasing game birds & deer, maintaining equipment & buildings, protecting game from poachers, liaising with authorities on issues regarding wildlife crime such as hare coursing and badger digging/baiting. River keepers (also known as ghillies), protect and manage rivers and streams as habitats for trout and salmon. Many of their tasks are similar to those of a gamekeeper.

The work can include making sure that there is enough game for clients to shoot, so this career may not appeal to everyone. Most of the work is outdoors in all weathers and the job involves weekend work as well as long days. Candidates must be physically fit, hold a current driving licence, have shotgun and firearms certificates, be willing to work on their own initiative and often in isolation. It is important to have practical skills and to be a willing hands-on worker, in some cases carrying out potentially hazardous tasks such as using a chain saw or administering pesticides.

There are few vacancies and whilst there may be training opportunities available on the job, having relevant experience or qualifications is advisable. There are occasionally vacancies for seasonal and contract work and some gamekeepers progress to becoming self-employed contractors.

It may be possible to work towards NVQs/SVQs Levels 2 and 3 or apprenticeships in Game keeping and Wildlife Management. Other relevant qualifications include: City and Guilds National Certificate in Game keeping, BTEC (Edexcel) National Award, Certificate or Diploma in Countryside Management (Game Management). Entry is usually with four GCSEs/S grades (A-C/1-3), equivalent qualifications or appropriate work experience. The National Game Keepers Trust contains a list of colleges offering game keeping courses.

Other relevant courses include: Deer Stalking Certificate offered through the British Deer Society (BDS) and Deer Management Course. Gamekeepers' Refresher Course offered through the Game Conservancy Trust, Wild game meat hygiene certificate offered by the Royal Society for the Promotion of Health (RSPH). Useful qualifications include the following Diploma courses: _ Introduction to Zoology, Birds of Prey, British Wild Mammals, Ecology, Environmental Management and the Conservation Diploma.

Useful contacts:

National Gamekeepers' Organisation (NGO): the national representative body for gamekeepers in England and Wales./ PO Box 107, Bishop Auckland, DL14 9YW. Tel: 01388 665899.

National Gamekeepers Charitable Trust: its founding body was the NGO. The Trust promotes public awareness of the need for sustainable wildlife management in our countryside, and stressing the importance of the conservation work carried out by gamekeepers. It providing ongoing training and education for the game keeping profession to increase competence and best practice. PO Box 3360, Stourbridge, DY7 5YG.

Scottish Game keepers Association (SGA): aims to unite all Scottish Gamekeepers, Stalkers and Ghillies in a strong representative organisation and to promote their professional role in the management of the Scottish environment by publicising their high standards of conduct and highlighting the contribution country sports make to the Scottish rural economy.

Game Conservancy Trust: uses science to promote game and wildlife management as an essential part of nature conservation. Fordingbridge, Hampshire, SP6 1EF. Tel: 01425 652381.

British Deer Society: a charity that works to enable British deer to exist and flourish in today's environment and ensures that their future is secure for generations to come. The Walled Garden, Burgate Manor, Fordingbridge, Hampshire, SP6 1EF. Tel: 01425 655434

73. Zoologist

Zoologists are involved in the scientific study of animals including their anatomy, physiology, classification, distribution, behaviour and ecology. Zoologists work in a wide range of jobs; animal welfare forms one possible aspect and others may include, conservation of endangered species/habitats, disease/pest control and improving livestock and crops. It is usual to specialise in one particular area such as ecology, herpetology, entomology or parasitology and you will normally be required to have a corresponding degree qualification in one or more of these subjects.

Zoologists are required to conduct detailed work accurately and methodically and to be able to analyse and interpret data, and write reports. This career requires candidates to have an aptitude for sciences, particularly biology and chemistry as well as good communication, problem solving and IT skills. To become a zoologist you will need to obtain a degree. Qualifications to study for degree are a minimum of 5 GCSE grades (A-C) and at least 2 A-levels (Biology and Chemistry are the best combination). Having a higher degree (MSc or PhD) will enable candidates a better chance of employment and a PhD is often a requirement for research jobs. NUI Maynooth offers a degree course in biology. Trinity College, Dublin (TCD) offers a degree in science with the option to major in zoology. University College Cork (UCC) has courses in both zoology and animal ecology.

For some jobs, such as conservation and fieldwork, candidates will usually need to gain experience in areas such as scientific data collection and research methods by doing voluntary work. The best way to do this is look for organisations offering volunteer work in a related field.

Working hours and environment vary according to the type of job. Research and higher education jobs usually require normal office hours in a laboratory or classroom. Field researchers may work variable hours, and may for example, be required to work at night if studying nocturnal animals. The work involves spending a lot of time working outside in all weathers. Field researchers work all over the world and in all types of climate.

Employment prospects are varied. A qualified zoologist, could be employed by universities, government research institutions, zoos and wildlife trusts, environmental protection agencies and water authorities. Other jobs include areas such as agriculture, fisheries, biotechnology, chemicals, pharmaceuticals and petroleum. Zoologists can also apply their experience and qualification to other jobs such as management, marketing, sales or scientific journalism.

Useful contacts:

Institute of Zoology : is the research division of the Zoological Society of London (ZSL). It is a government-funded research institute specialising in scientific issues relevant to the conservation of animal species and their habitats. Zoological Society of London, Regents Park, London, NW1 4RY. Tel: 020 7449 6610

Institute of Biology: is the professional body for UK biologists. 9 Red Lion Court, London, EC4A 3EF. Tel: 020 7936 5900

Membership of professional organisations such as those shown above will give you the opportunity for continuing professional development and networking as a zoologist.

74. Wildlife Veterinary Surgeon

There are opportunities for vets to work with wildlife, and for veterinary students or those wishing to study for a veterinary career, to gain some useful work experience before embarking on their degree course. For more information about how to become a vet please see our veterinary careers section.

Useful Contacts:

Zoo Veterinary Officer

African Wildlife Management and Veterinary Services

Shimongwe Wildlife Veterinary Experience

Wildlife Veterinary Investigation Centre

Veterinary Association for Wildlife Management

Careers in Zoos and Safari Parks

With over one hundred million people visiting zoos every year, workers have an excellent opportunity to educate large numbers of people about the need for the conservation of wildlife and the importance of respecting animals. This responsibility assures a varied, interesting and rewarding career. A career working in a zoo requires commitment and hard work and it is worth considering working as a volunteer or pursuing an internship first, as both of these opportunities will provide you with valuable practical experience. The risk of being bitten or scratched exists in all of careers working with animals and it is important to ensure you have sufficient training and that you feel confident being around wild animals before embarking on a career working with them. Having some experience in work such as wildlife rehabilitation is very useful, particularly for any of the hands-on zoo or safari park careers - where having prior experience will greatly improve your employment prospects.

Working directly with wild animals involves tough physical outdoor work; it is crucial that you enjoy being outdoors in all types of weather as all zoos and safari parks have large outdoor areas. You will need to be physically fit, hard working, have plenty of stamina and not be squeamish as some parts of the work can be messy and unpleasant. If you are working in an aquarium type area of a zoo, you need to be a competent swimmer. Depending on the type of organisation and location, you may be required to live on-site and it is useful if you are able to drive. Animal keeper positions are highly competitive and ideally require skilled individuals with a background in a related life science field.

You will need to be able to recognise when animals are unwell or unhappy and be able to pay attention to detail and to health and safety requirements. Confined animals need care twenty four hours a day, seven days a week; therefore the working hours are unpredictable and varied - and you will probably be required to work at weekends.

A bit about zoos:

The world's first zoo, the Zoological Society of London, was established in 1826 in Regents Park, London. The animals were housed in poorly constructed cages and concrete pits. However, nowadays, most zoos have more carefully considered habitats for the animals and many zoos have pioneered breeding programmes to prevent species dying out. The Zoological Federation of Great Britain estimates that twenty percent of zoos actively participate in global conservation strategies for endangered species.

There is statutory legislation and inspections in the UK and this ensures that Britain has a better reputation for zoos than some other EU countries. The UK has taken the lead and campaigned for the adoption of an EU directive to establish minimum standards for zoos. This has led to a far greater focus on conservation and animal welfare issues. Zoos have changed purpose from existing purely for public entertainment to now ensuring that some endangered wild species have a chance of survival. As this emphasis on conservation increases, more zoos are employing specialist zoologists, conservation experts and ecologists. Sadly, not all zoos are forward thinking and unfortunately, many wild animals are still exhibited in appalling conditions with little attention paid to their physical or psychological well being. Unfortunately, many countries still build zoos where wild animals are kept in cramped cages and not cared for properly – however, there is increasing pressure for these places to improve standards and conditions.

Conservation and scientific programs in zoos have become highly technical and specialised. Although practical experience with animals may sometimes be substituted for academic training, most entry-level keeper positions now require a degree qualification. Training in animal science, zoology, marine biology, conservation biology, wildlife management, and animal behaviour is preferred. In addition, it may take several years of hands-on training to fully grasp necessary skills such as animal handling and exotic animal care. Management, research, and conservation positions typically require advanced academic degrees.

The World Association of Zoos and Aquariums (WAZA) works to guide, encourage and support zoos and aquariums in animal care and welfare, environmental education and global conservation. WAZA is the umbrella organisation for the world zoo and aquarium community. Its members include leading zoos and aquariums, and regional and national associations of zoos and aquariums, as well as some affiliate organisations, such as zoo veterinarians or zoo educators, from all around the world.

An organisation called Zoocheck, was set up as an anti-captivity project of the Born Free Foundation, to investigate conditions in zoos, circuses, aquariums and safari parks. In addition, Zoocheck increases awareness of the suffering imposed on zoo animals. Their aims are: "To check, inspect and improve standards in zoos throughout the world, with the ultimate aim of phasing out traditional zoos entirely. To prevent all types of abuse of wild animals, particularly in zoos. To change the attitude of all people towards animals in captivity. To preserve animals in their natural habitat on an international basis. To promote the welfare and conservation of wildlife throughout the world. To canvas, campaign and peacefully persuade zoos, national and local governments and other appropriate bodies to improve animal welfare. To end the importation of animals from the wild"

A bit about Safari Parks (UK):

For those who find the idea of zoos or the confinement of animals to be unappealing, a safari park is another way to see wild animals in the UK. Wildlife Rangers perform a similiar role in safari parks to that of a Zoo keeper - in addition, they ensure that the public are safe and don't leave their vehicles or feed the animals.

Salaries for zoo and safari park staff vary widely depending on the size of the organisation and where it is located - those near main towns or cities generally offer higher salaries. We have listed a variety of careers - not all are found in each organisation and some of the roles are quite specialised with varying duties and responsibilities.

In this career guide, we have information about the following zoo and safari park careers: Zoo keeper, Wildlife Ranger, Zoologist, Habitat designer/zoo horticulturist, Curators, Veterinary team, Registrar, Director of Research and Director of Conservation.

Not all zoo and safari park careers involve work directly with the animals; there are various associated careers, such as Chief Executive Officer, people management, finance/accounting, public relations, marketing, business management, fundraising, gift shop sales, building/construction/maintenance and administration.

75. Zookeeper

Zoos, wildlife/safari parks and special collections are run by zoological societies, charitable trusts, local authorities or private businesses. Zookeepers are responsible for the day-to-day care and welfare of animals kept in these environments. Their primary role is to ensure that these animals are kept physically and psychologically healthy. Zookeepers need to be: enthusiastic about animals, interested in animal biology, patient with both the public and animals, have a pleasant friendly manner and good spoken communication skills. They need to be observant, reliable and punctual, physically fit, safety-conscious, have basic computer skills and a driving license for safari parks. It helps to be interested in animal biology, wildlife habitats, animal behaviour, The following diploma courses will assist with this career: conservation, british wild mammals, Marine Zoology, Introduction to Zoology and the Birds of prey diploma courses.

Keepers carry out tasks such as 'mucking out', cleaning and filling water troughs, replenishing bedding and monitoring temperatures. They are responsible for checking enclosures and may carry out maintenance jobs such as repairing fences. Zookeepers order food and bedding and ensure animals are fed according to their individual needs. They weigh, chop and mix ingredients and may have to provide 'live food', such as locusts and meal worms, or 'dead feed' such as rats or mice. Another important aspect of the work involves observing animals for any signs of injury or illness; if an animal is sick or injured, zookeepers help with care under the direction of a vet. Zookeepers maintain healthcare records and as part of a research project, they may keep detailed records of an animal's activity or behaviour. Keepers answer visitors' questions and may give short talks or presentations. They may train animals for a demonstration, for example training a bird to fly from one place to another. Keepers also make sure visitors do not feed or upset the animals or, particularly in wildlife parks, put themselves in danger by approaching animals too closely. In wildlife parks where animals live in conditions similar to the wild, Keepers will have less contact with the animals. In some cases, Keepers may be involved assisting with the design of new living quarters.

As confined animals are dependent on people to care for them, there is a need for staffing every day of the year, Keepers work on rota systems to cover all periods and more senior Keepers may be on a call-out rota, which could include evenings. Zookeepers may work outside or indoors, depending on the animals they care for. Conditions may be wet, cold, dirty, muddy, hot or humid. Keepers wear a uniform, normally an overall that is supplied by their employer.

As there are approximately only 1,500 people employed in this type of work, entry into this career is highly competitive, and there are many more applicants than vacancies. There are some opportunities to work abroad; some zoos participate in keeper exchange programmes and there may be the chance to participate in work exchange projects in Australia, New Zealand or the USA.

Some zoos require particular qualifications. Others prefer three to five GCSEs/S grades/Intermediate 2s (A-C/1-3/A-C) or equivalent qualifications. English and a science subject may be specified. Acceptable alternative qualifications could be a BTEC First Diploma/City and Guilds (C&G) National Certificate/SQA National Qualification Units in Animal Care. For these, no formal qualifications are needed or a few GCSEs/S grades/Intermediate 1s/2s and preferably some animal experience. A few zoos require a BTEC National Certificate or a Diploma in Animal Care, Welfare and Husbandry or Animal Management/C&G Advanced National Certificate in Animal Care. For these, they usually need four GCSEs/S grades/Intermediate 2s (A-C/1-3/A-C) or other equivalent qualification.

Not all zoos require previous relevant experience, however, as competition for jobs is fierce, it is very useful. It may be possible to start as a trainee at 16 but some employers set a minimum age of 18, especially if they are working with large animals such as elephants. Some people may be able to train on an Apprenticeship. In larger zoos there are prospects of promotion to senior keeper and eventually to Head Keeper.

Experience can be gained by taking part in a volunteer programme or course. Some courses contain practical experience in handling and caring for animals and may include some units relevant to zoo work. Trainees receive practical on-the-job training and experience in different departments of the zoo, with different kinds of animals. Useful training is the Introduction to Zoology Diploma)

Zoological Society of London (ZSL): is a charity devoted to the worldwide conservation of animals and their habitats. Outer Circle, Regent's Park, London, NW1 4RY. Tel: 020 7722 3333

World Association of Zoos and Aquariums (WAZA): is the "umbrella" organisation for the world zoo and aquarium community. Its members include leading zoos and aquariums, and regional and national Associations of zoos and aquariums, as well as some affiliate organisations, such as zoo veterinarians or zoo educators, from all around the world. P O Box 23, CH-3097, Liebefeld-Bern, Switzerland.

Zoocheck was set up as an anti-captivity project of the Born Free Foundation and exists to increase awareness of the suffering imposed on zoo animals and investigate conditions in zoos, circuses, aquariums and safari parks. Born Free Foundation, 3 Grove House, Foundry Lane, Horsham, West Sussex, RH13 5PL. Tel: 01403 240 170

Zoo volunteer scheme: Bristol Zoo Gardens, Clifton, Bristol, Somerset, BS8 3HA. Tel: 0117 970 6176

76. Safari Park Wildlife Ranger (UK)

There are several safari parks in the UK - for example, the Cotswold Wildlife Park, Longleat Safari Park and Woburn Safari Park. Some aspects of the Wildlife Ranger's role are similar to that of a Zoo keeper, but the work is based in a safari park instead of in a zoo. The work is practical and varied and it may also include: conducting wildlife surveys and maintaining wildlife habitats – i.e. tree planting and pond management, educating visitors by providing exhibitions and resource centres. Besides animal care duties, wardens or rangers in safari parks patrol the parks ensuring the public and animals are safe and not causing the animals any distress by driving too close or feeding the animals.

It is essential to enjoy interacting with people, as the work often involves public speaking. Wildlife Rangers need to be physically fit as the work involves a considerable amount of walking, climbing and carrying. Most of the work is conducted outdoors in all weathers. It is essential to have a driving license and to be confident driving off road vehicles. The working hours are varied and normally include evenings and weekends, with holiday seasons being the busiest time for some aspects of the work. To be a successful applicant for a job as a Wildlife Ranger, it is crucial to have relevant experience; the best way to get this is by volunteering.

Relevant training:
The Conservation Diploma is an excellent qualification and study includes the wise use of the earth's resources, so that they can support, or sustain, the generations yet to come.

The Ecology Diploma will provide a detailed explanation on many aspects of the eco-balance in an easy to understand format and help you to understand how all parts of the environment work together.

The Environmental Management Diploma provides specialist knowledge about how we manage our environment and what we need to do to protect it.

In addition, the Introduction to Zoology Diploma, Birds of Prey Diploma and British Wild Mammal Diploma are also useful qualifications.

BTEC/SQA National Certificate/Diploma in Countryside Management with options including Water Management, Woodland Management, Rural Tourism, Countryside Interpretation and Habitat Conservation. BTEC/SQA HNC/HND in Environmental Conservation. Foundation degrees in subjects such as Countryside Management and Conservation and Countryside Management. Certificate in Land based Studies (NPTC), NVQ in Environmental Conservation (NPTC). Degree courses such as BSc in Rural Resource Management, Countryside Management, Rural Environmental Management, Conservation and Environment, or Environmental Studies. The Universities and Colleges Admissions Service (UCAS) have information on colleges and universities offering these degrees.

Candidates may be able to work towards NVQ/SVQ levels 2 and 3 in Environmental Conservation (Countryside Management) when employed. You will also be able to join the Countryside Management Association (CMA), this will entitle you to professional accreditation, continuing professional development (CPD), training and study days and exchanges, seminars and conferences.

Apprenticeships may be available for those under the age of 24. In England these are currently Apprenticeships (level 2) and Advanced Apprenticeships (level 3).

Useful contacts:

The Association of British Wild Animal Keepers (ABWAK): has objectives to: improve co-operation among animal keepers, provide, encourage and organise facilities for the meeting of keepers and wild animals, improve the professional competence of all involved with wild animal husbandry and to support the conservation of wildlife throughout the world.

Federation of Zoological Gardens of Britain and Ireland: Regents Park, London, NW1 4RY. Tel: 020 7586 0230.

77. Habitat designer/zoo horticulturist

Zoo horticulture is a fast growing career as increasingly zoos strive to improve the environment for the animals in their care. Many zoos now strive to create an environment that allows the animals to move freely in re-creations of their natural wild surroundings.

This has a dramatic affect on the natural behaviours of the animals and goes a long way to reduce the stress many species endure in a caged or captive environment. Stress reduction is hugely important in terms of animal welfare. By allowing visitors to see animals in surroundings similar to their natural environments, an awareness of the need for conservation is increased. A career in this type of work is highly stimulating and creative and involves much research into what keeps wild animals happy! Training in biology and/or botany is hugely advantageous and having some experience of building management or architecture is helpful. A qualified habitat designer can seek employment at a zoo, safari park or aquarium. The Introduction to Zoology Diploma, Animal

Behaviour Diploma, Zoology, Marine Biology, Birds of Prey, British Wild Mammals, Ecology and Conservation Diplomas are all useful qualifications for this career.

Useful contacts:

The Association of Zoological Horticulture (AZH): is a non-profit membership organization dedicated to the advancement of zoo horticulture in zoological parks, gardens and aquariums.

78. Curators

In larger zoos, there may be a variety of Zoo Curator career roles as follows:

a) Zoo Curators: are responsible for acquiring animals for the zoo - through captive breeding programmes, from other zoos and from rescue environments. Zoo Curators liaise closely between government agencies and the zoo to ensure that the trade, transport and collection of these animals is done according to government guidelines and rules. The Zoo Curator may be responsible for strategic collection planning and overseeing the micro-management of various sections of the zoo's animal collection; i.c. mammals, birds, fish, reptiles, etc. Some Zoo Curators may be in charge of the various zoological units, a zoo's entire animal collection and animal management staff.

b) Curator of Exhibits: this involves having responsibility for creating exhibits and assisting in the design of graphics.

c) Curator of Horticulture: is responsible for the botanical collection and its application to the animal collection, as well as daily maintenance of the institution's grounds.

d) Curator of Education: plans and implements the Institution's education programs and is responsible for school group and other educational visits and projects.

79. Veterinary Team

The zoo veterinary team Is responsible for animal health, maintaining health records, treating disease, immunisation and dealing with any emergencies that arise. Due to the variety of different species in a zoo, safari park and aquarium, the veterinary team are required to continually train and frequently consult with professional colleagues to get expert opinions. The veterinary team is often responsible for managing diets and nutrition and must be able to handle large animals. Please see the Veterinary Career section for more information about veterinary careers.

80. Registrar

Is in charge of maintaining thorough records about the animal collections. Details such as births, deaths, animal transfer/loan dates, data on offspring from breeding programmes etc, all needs to be carefully recorded. The Registrar is responsible for applying for specific permits and licences to hold or transport animals and is required to work closely with the Curators and government agencies and other zoos or organisations. This role requires attention to detail and involves a considerable amount of reading and on-going learning to keep up to date with government regulations.

81. Director of Conservation

This role includes the overseeing of all the organisation's conservation activities, including field projects. The Director of Conservation is responsible for liaising with government wildlife agencies and other conservation organisations.

Other Animal Related Careers

82. Pet Shops

There are approximately 4,000 pet shops and 600 aquatic centres in the UK, employing over 20,000 people between them. Careers in this line of work involve the option of working for an established pet shop, or of setting up your own business.

There is strong feeling from some animal rescue centres, who have to handle difficult situations with the ever-increasing tide of unwanted animals, that whilst pet shops may be the best places to buy equipment and pet food, they are frequently responsible for people making impulsive decisions about getting a pet. A pet shop is not a good environment to keep, hold or sell animals and there are many sad stories of animals being bred purely for profit and sold to pet shops where they can be bought on impulse by anyone. In many cases, these animals are prone to health problems. Apart from the suffering endured, a sick animal can cause problems for the pet shop owner who has to deal with angry and upset customers as well as having to pay for the animal to be treated and then find another home for it. However, many pet shops do not sell live animals and they provide interesting animal related working environments. This can be a great opportunity to educate people about what animals really need and what to consider before obtaining an animal. Customer care forms a big part of the work and having a detailed knowledge about products sold by the pet shop business is important. Equally, candidates must have good knowledge about specific care requirements for a variety of animals as in many cases, customers rely heavily on pet shops for pet care advice. Other duties include, monitoring stock levels, ordering supplies, dealing with deliveries and using the till. The work can be strenuous and it involves much standing – hours usually include weekend work.

Whilst you do not need any particular qualifications for working in a pet shop, it can be useful if you have retail or customer service experience and it is important to have experience of animal care. The Animal Care, Welfare and Husbandry Diploma is an excellent qualification choice. In addition, the Professional Pet Care and Veterinary Assistant Diploma, Reptile Care, Welare & First Aid course, Rescue Dog Handler Diploma, Professional Kennel Operator Diploma and the Animal Behaviour Diploma all contain useful elements for this career.

Useful Contacts:

The Pet Care Trust: run a Pet Shop Management Course and a Pet Foundation course both have flexible formats where assessments can be taken online. Pet Care Trust, Bedford Business Centre 170 Mile Road, Bedford, MK42 9TW. Tel: 01234 273 933.

Animal Resources: for further information on the possible pit-falls of pet shops that sell live animals

83. Animal Assisted Therapist

This can be a highly rewarding career choice as animal assisted therapy can bring real benefits to people who are ill or disabled. Animals are selected by trained staff on temperament grounds to provide therapeutic visits to hospitals, nursing homes, hospices, special needs schools, prisons, etc.

A career in this type of work involves selecting, training and working directly with animals (typically companion animals such as dogs, cats and rabbits). The animals used for this type of work are selected for their gentle, friendly temperaments - a charity called Pets as Therapy (PAT) is an example of an organisation that utilises therapy dogs. It provides therapeutic visits to hospitals, hospices, nursing and care homes, special needs schools and a variety of other venues. Since it's beginning, over 18,000 dogs have been registered into the PAT scheme.

Today there are currently around 3,500 active PAT visiting dogs and 90 cats at work in the UK. Every week these calm friendly dogs and cats give more than 10,000 people, both young and old, the pleasure and chance to cuddle and talk to them. The bedsides that are visited each year number a staggering half million. There is a strong people element and candidates must enjoy interacting with people and have excellent communication skills as well as animal behavioural experience. There are no formal qualifications for this career and most organisations provide training on the job. The Animal Care, Welfare and Husbandry Diploma and the Animal Behaviour Diploma is a useful qualification for this career.

Useful Contacts:

Society for Companion Animal Studies:

Pets as Therapy: Sick patients often feel isolated and even the most withdrawn seem to open up and let the barriers down when their regular PAT visiting dog is around. These dogs bring everyday life closer and with it all the happy associations for them of home comforts. The constant companionship of an undemanding animal, that gives unconditional love, is often one of the most missed aspects of their lives. PAT was formed to help make this loss more bearable and speed recovery. Pets As Therapy, 3a Grange Farm Cottages, Wycombe Road, Saunderton, Princes Risborough, Bucks, HP27 9NS. Tel: 01844 345 445.

84. Animal Photographer

This is an excellent career choice for those who wish to combine their photographic skills with an animal related career. Animal photos are bought by many places including pet owners, pet magazines, websites, pet charities, etc. There are several career opportunities, such as setting up an animal portrait business, creating a photo library, wildlife/safari photography and running photography courses. Photographers charge between £100 and £1,000 per day depending on experience and skills. You will need to be an excellent communicator, have previous hands-on animal care experience (if working in the companion animal photography sector), and be prepared to work flexible hours in order to be successful. It is most likely that candidates will need to set up their own business and therefore important to have business skills. Competition in this line of work is tough, and candidates must be tenacious and skilled to succeed.

Courses:
Online Photography Course
BA Wildlife Photography degree course
Animal Behaviour Diploma course

85. Pet Taxi Driver

This, along with other general pet care services such as pet sitting, grooming and walking, is a growing industry. This can make an excellent career choice as in many areas, demand for this type of service outweighs supply. Employment possibilities exist through setting up their own business or being hired by a pet taxi company. Pet Taxis may be required for transporting animals to and from vet, groomer, cattery/kennel, pet sitter, airport, etc.

The work involves being responsible for the safe transport of companion animals. You will be required to have a valid driving license and previous driving experience, as well as thorough local road and area knowledge. In addition, you will be required to have animal handling experience. You will be ideally have a recent animal first aid qualification, be physically fit and able to lift animals as necessary, have good organisation and communication skills, pay attention to detail, work well on your own initiative, be resourceful and have good problem solving skills. It is essential that you remain up to date on the latest animal transport legislation. This role requires you to be compassionate and to have a thorough understanding of the needs of animals. You are required to continually consider the animals you are transporting, to ensure that their journey is as stress free as possible. For example: driving with extreme care, stopping regularly for water and exercise breaks, ensuring animals are comfortable and have clean bedding and that their environment is kept at an ideal temperature. Having vehicle maintenance skills will enhance your employment prospects if seeking employment through a pet taxi company. As you may be transporting pet owners as well as their pets, you may be required to hold a people taxi license - your local council will be able to provide you with further information on their requirements on this point.

The Department for Environment, Food and Rural Affairs (Defra) provides advice on transporting pets safely, legally and in comfort - this link will provide you with an insight into the basic requirements.

86. Farm Manager

This is career involves having responsibility for the planning and management of a farm. Depending on the size of the farm, it may include having direct contact with animals. You may be required to supervise with nursing sick animals, milking, feeding, watering, lambing, maintaining hygiene, keeping records, etc. Other duties can include livestock breeding, building maintenance and staff supervision. There are approximately 10,000 farm managers employed in the UK and competition for jobs is high. There has been a tremendous growth in the organic farming sector and this has in turn provided further employment options in an area many regard as taking a more humane approach to animal welfare. The Farm Animal Behaviour Diploma Course is an excellent qualification.

Useful Contacts:

Willing Workers on Organic Farms (WWOOF): International exchange network where you can receive food, lodging and practical experience in exchange for helping with work on organic farms. This is an excellent way to gain experience in organic farming. PO Box 2154, Winslow Buckingham, MK18 3WS, England.

Federation of City Farms and Community Gardens (NFCF): exists to support, represent and promote community-managed farms and gardens across the United Kingdom. The Green House, Hereford Street, Bedminster, Bristol, BS3 4NA. Tel: 0117 923 1800.

"We sometimes wonder why there doesn't seem to be anyone doing anything...then we realise this is why we exist... to do something"

Volunteering with animals

"Never doubt that a small group of thoughtful committed citizens can change the world. Indeed, it is the only thing that ever has" Margaret Mead

There are many different and worthwhile organisations that assist animals in need around the world. By summarising volunteer opportunities by continent, we've made it easy for you to find and make contact with the organisations that you would like to volunteer for.

All of the organisations in this guide work tirelessly to help animals in need. To achieve their aims, they rely on voluntary help. Some welcome volunteers who can only spare a few hours for tasks such as walking dogs for a day or two during their holiday abroad. Other organisations prefer a longer term commitment with a specific project - this type of volunteering may appeal more to those on a gap year.

Whatever your skills or amount of time you have available to offer, there are many animals who will benefit greatly from your offer of volunteering. The opportunities in this guide are exciting and diverse. They include; monitoring wild dolphins, feeding wolves, nursing sick animals, working in a cat houseboat sanctuary, assisting with wildlife recovery and release, attending to injured animals, walking dogs, grooming donkeys, transporting animals for re-homing abroad, caring for orphaned fox cubs, returning stray animals to their colonies after neutering, monitoring turtles and giving distressed animals some tender loving care.

We are working on an on-going basis to ensure that the information in this guide is kept up to date. However, website content can instantly change without notice; if you spot any dead links or discover any new organisations that you feel would benefit from inclusion in this guide, please do let us know.

Before we start, here's a story to help inspire you as you embark on your journey as a volunteer helping animals - it's the Original Starfish Story found in Star Thrower: "One day a man was walking along the beach when he noticed a boy picking something up and gently throwing it into the ocean. Approaching the boy, he asked, 'What are you doing?' The youth replied, 'Throwing starfish back into the ocean. The surf is up and the tide is going out. If I don't throw them back, they'll die.' ' Son,' the man said, 'don't you realize there are miles and miles of beach and hundreds of starfish? You can't make a difference!' After listening politely, the boy bent down, picked up another starfish, and threw it back into the surf. Then, smiling at the man, he said…'I made a difference for that one.'" - naturalist and writer, Loren Eiseley

"The best way to find yourself is to lose yourself in the service of others." - Mahatma Gandhi

Volunteering is a great way to obtain hands on experience and a better understanding of the many different career options open to those wishing to work with animals. Whether you are a school leaver, seeking a career change, or are undecided about whether working within the animal welfare sector is for you, then voluntary work is a great way to find out.

At the same time as giving you the tremendous satisfaction of helping animals in need, your volunteer work can also be an excellent career move. The experience will enable you to gain experience in the specific type of animal care that you aspire to work in.

For many employers, volunteer experience, interest, aptitude and commitment can be more important than initial entry qualifications. Competition for animal care vacancies is tough. It is advisable to be well equipped with as many related skills as possible when seeking employment. Through volunteering, you will acquire many new skills that will help you when applying for jobs or course placements.

It is advisable for anyone wanting to work with animals, from would-be veterinary surgeons to animal care assistants, to do some sort of voluntary work before embarking on their chosen career.

If you are seeking a career change, volunteering can be an excellent way of landing your perfect job, as it is common for volunteers to be offered permanent positions. By enrolling as a volunteer you will gain a much better and invaluable understanding of the work involved.

"I am sometimes asked 'Why do you spend so much of your time and money talking about kindness to animals when there is so much cruelty to men?' I answer: 'I am working at the roots." - George T. Angell

Ten top tips for a positive volunteering experience

1. The range of opportunities is huge and there is a tremendous amount to be learnt on the ground. It is possible to progress quickly if you are reliable, compassionate, committed, patient and willing to learn and develop a thorough understanding of real animal welfare issues. It goes without saying, that to succeed in any career working with animals, you must be hard working, compassionate and genuinely concerned for the welfare and needs of animals.

2. Give careful consideration to what you want to gain from volunteering - new skills, fun, a chance to contribute in a meaningful way to a cause you are passionate about? Also think about what you have to offer - enthusiasm, work skills, life skills, time to spend caring, etc.

3. Whilst volunteering, you will want to enjoy your work and feel that you are making a difference. You are also giving up some of your valuable unpaid time. So choose your volunteer placement carefully and make sure that the placement is the right one for you.

4. Very few animal charities operate in the same way - find out as much as possible about the organisation before you commit to volunteering. Unfortunately, it is not un-common for volunteers to become disillusioned and drop out because they haven't fully understood what the job involves or didn't look into the procedures and policies of the organisation they are volunteering for. An example could be a lack of understanding about an animal rescue centres' destruction policy. Unfortunately, due to the huge numbers of unwanted animals, some shelters are in a position where they have to put healthy animals to sleep because quite simply there is no place to put them. Some people may find this difficult to deal with. Before you start, find out about your chosen organisations' policies on issues you feel strongly about. Make sure you fully understand what they mean, and why a particular policy is in place. If you can't accept the policy, then politely decline to be a volunteer.

5. Arrange to visit the organisations centre or offices and ask to work for a trial day or two before committing yourself. Remember that many tasks may be messy or unpleasant and working with animals is not for the faint hearted or squeamish.

6. Most organisations, especially rescue centres, are extremely busy places. If you work well and do what you are asked to do, you will be appreciated, but don't expect gushing praise and gratitude from the overworked staff! Remember that you are volunteering to help the animals in your care and a wagging tail or loving purr should be reward enough.

7. If you are volunteering for an organisation that you ultimately want to work for, ensure that you make a good impression and keep an ear out for any upcoming job vacancies.

8. Whilst some tasks may be menial and you may feel that you are not learning much, it is important to carry out all tasks with enthusiasm. A job well done will mean that you more likely to land more challenging tasks next time.

9. If you are there to learn, keep your eyes and ears open. Even if you seem stuck with boring jobs you will be amazed at what you can learn from listening and watching others, and from events going on around you.

10. Don't volunteer if you have a big ego. You may be given instruction, by someone younger or less qualified, but don't underestimate the importance of learning the right procedure for what may seem a menial task. Remember that failing to follow instructions properly can put animals lives at risk.

International Organisations

"The greatness of a nation and its moral progress can be judged by the way its animals are treated." - Mahatma Gandhi

Animals' Angels is an internationally operating organisation with permanent teams in Germany, France, Spain, Portugal, Italy, Greece, Poland, Slovenia, Serbia, Romania, Hungary, Canada, the United States of America and Australia. They accompany animals on the way to the slaughterhouses in order to ease their suffering. They fight against every kind of abuse, torture, cruel treatment and exploitation of farm animals. They also work to raise public awareness and informing the public on abuses in the field of animal transportation and slaughtering.

Contact details:
Animals' Angels, Rossertstrasse 8, D-60323 Frankfurt a. Main, Germany.
Tel: +49 (0)69 707 981 70.
www.animals-angels.de/index.php

Brooke Hospital for Animals helps millions of working horses, donkeys and mules and the countless people who depend upon them. Brooke operates in Egypt, India, Jordan and Pakistan, and in Afghanistan, Kenya and Guatemala and aims to deliver a unique blend of direct and very practical veterinary and welfare services through a network of mobile teams and field clinics. With more than 500 staff working in the field, the Brooke is by far the largest charity of its kind. They request that professionally trained vets volunteer directly with the animals and have a variety of projects to choose from.

Contact details:
Brooke Hospital for Animals, 30 Farringdon Street, London, EC4A 4HH, UK
Tel: 0203 012 3456
www.thebrooke.org

Born Free Foundation is an international wildlife charity working with compassion to prevent cruelty, alleviate suffering and encourage everyone to treat all individual animals with respect. Born Free believes wildlife belongs in the wild and is dedicated to the conservation of rare species in their natural habitat, and the phasing out of traditional zoos. They don't offer volunteer roles directly on their conservation projects. However, they ask for assistance with general office duties in their UK office as well as with their Zoo check project. A part of their site acts as a notice board for other conservation/animal jobs voluntary vacancies.

Contact details:
Born Free Foundation, 3 Grove House, Foundry Lane, Horsham, RH13 5PL, UK
Tel: 01403 240 170
www.bornfree.org.uk
info @bornfree.org.uk

Cheetah Conservation Fund Worldwide (CCF) aims to be an internationally recognised centre of excellence in research and education on cheetahs and their eco-systems. CCF works to: create and manage long-term conservation strategies, develop and improve livestock management practices, eliminate the need for ranchers to kill cheetah, conduct conservation education programs for local villagers, ranchers and school children and continue intensive scientific research in cheetah genetics, biology and species survival. CCF has operations in the UK, Namibia, USA, Canada, Kenya, Holland, Japan and South Africa. CCF has programs for general volunteers (working guests), student internships (including Masters & Ph.D. students) and zookeepers. All their volunteer programs require a mandatory donation. However, discounted/subsidised fees are available for student interns and zookeepers, and also for Namibian, South African and Kenyan citizens.

Contact details:
Mail address: Cheetah Conservation Fund UK, Peter Stewart, P.O. Box 151, Godalming, Surrey, GU7 2XW, UK
Tel: +44 (0) 1483 427 526
www.cheetah.org.uk/
ccinfo @iway.na

Care for the Wild Internatio (CWI) this organisation prides itself in their strong track record of getting quick and efficient emergency aid - food, veterinary equipment, medicines and housing through to the animals that need it most. They are a respected international organisation that uses solid scientific research as a basis for its work. Their work includes; protecting wild areas from poachers, rehabilitating sick and injured animals, and providing sanctuary for those animals which can never be returned to the wild. Contact to assist as a volunteer.

Contact details:
The Granary, Tickfold Farm, Kingsfold, West Sussex RH12 3SE, UK
Tel: +44 (0) 1306 627900
Fax: +44 (0) 1306 627901
www.careforthewild.com
info@careforthewild.com

Enkosini Wildlife Sanctuary has offices in South Africa and the USA. The Sanctuary encompasses over 10,000 acres and strives to preserve natural habitat while reintroducing indigenous wildlife onto land they once naturally roamed. Enkosini provides sanctuary and protection for a myriad of African wildlife, many of which would be destroyed if adequate habitat and facilities for their rehabilitation were not available. Volunteers are encouraged to for a minimum of 3 weeks; duties include a variety of tasks in the wildlife sanctuary.

Contact details:
Mail address South Africa: Enkosini Eco Experience, PO Box 1197, Lydenburg 1120, South Africa
Tel: +27 82 442 6773
Skype: enkosini
www.enkosiniecoexperience.com
info@enkosini.com / enkosini@yahoo.com **(please send all correspondence to both email addresses)**

Mail address USA: Enkosini Eco Experience, P.O. Box 15355, Seattle, WA 98115, USA
Tel: +1 206 604 2664
Skype: enkosini
Fax: +1 310 359 0269
www.enkosinicoexperience.com
info@enkosini.com / enkosini@yahoo.com (*please send all correspondence to both email addresses*)

Eleaid Endangered Asian Elephant Conservation charity The EleAid Trustees and management team met while visiting an elephant conservation project in Thailand. They were all deeply moved by their experiences and resolved to work together to increase awareness of the plight of Asia's elephants and to help save the Asian elephant both from extinction and from the appalling conditions in which some of the domesticated elephants live. Contact to assist as a volunteer.

Contact details:
General Enquiries, EleAid, 29 Mill Lane, Clophill, Bedfordshire, MK45 4BX, UK
www.eleaid.com

Friends of Conservation (FOC) is a conservation charity that works with local communities across the world to protect their surrounding wildlife and habitats. FOC works with local partners in the Caribbean, India, Iran, Namibia, Peru, Tanzania, Uganda as well as supporting their field station and programme in the Masai Mara, Kenya. FOC is committed to working with local peoples to develop and promote a balance between their needs and those of the wildlife with which they share their natural habitat and ecosystems. FOC has offices in London UK, Illinois, USA and Nairobi, Kenya. Volunteers are required for a variety of roles.

Contact details:
Friends of Conservation, Kensington Charity Centre, 4th Floor, Charles House, 375 Kensington High Street, London W14 8QH, UK
Tel: 020 7603 5024
focinfo@aol.com
www.friendsofconservation.org.uk

Frontier Want to have the best time of your life while gaining academic qualifications at the same time? Join a Frontier expedition and save endangered wildlife and threatened ecosystems while gaining an A-level. Learn to run expeditions and gain an AS-level. Teach English and get TEFL trained. Whichever you choose, you'll be off the beaten track having adventures beyond anything you've ever imagined! They have projects in Africa, Asia, Fiji & the Pacific Isles, Indonesia, South and Central America, and Nepal.

Contact details:
THE SOCIETY FOR ENVIRONMENTAL EXPLORATION (operating as 'Frontier'),
50-52 Rivington Street, London, EC2A 3QP, UK
Tel: +44 (0) 20 7613 2422
Fax: +44 (0) 20 7613 2992
info@frontier.ac.uk
www.frontier.ac.uk

International Animal Rescue (IAR) aims to come to the aid of suffering animals with hands-on rescue and the provision of short or long term rehabilitation. They have projects around the world and wherever possible they return rescued animals to their natural habitat, but they also provide sanctuary for animals that can no longer survive in the wild. They work with other like minded organisations and government departments to develop sound legislation to protect animals from cruelty and neglect. IAR specialises in providing comprehensive sterilisation and vaccination programmes for stray dogs and cats to control populations and prevent the spread of disease. They aim to produce practical solutions that benefit both animals and people. Volunteers assist with projects abroad and in their UK office.

Contact details:
International Animal Rescue, Lime House Regency Close, Uckfield, East Sussex, TN22 1DS, UK
Tel: +44 (0) 1825 767 688
www.internationalanimalrescue.org
info@internationalanimalrescue.org

Naturenet Conservation Volunteer Groups This list includes many Conservation Volunteer groups who have home pages on the web.

Contact details:
www.naturenet.net
editor@naturenet.net

Project Aware Foundation operates worldwide to conserve underwater environments through education, advocacy and action. Volunteer assistance required.

Contact details:
Project AWARE Foundation **(Americas & Headquarters)**, 30151 Tomas, Suite 200, Rancho Santa Margarita, CA, 92688-2125 USA
Tel: +1 866 80 AWARE (US and Canada) or +1 949 858 7657
Fax: +1 949 267 1221
www.projectaware.org
information@projectaware.org

Contact details:
Project AWARE Foundation **(Asia Pacific)**, Unit 3, 4 Skyline Place, Frenchs Forest, NSW 2086, Australia
Tel: +61 2 9454 2890
Fax: +61 2 9454 2999
www.projectaware.org
information@projectaware.org.au

Contact details:
Project AWARE Foundation **(International)**, Unit 7, St Philips Central, Albert Road, St Philips, Bristol BS2 0PD, Great Britain
Tel: +44 (0)117 300 7313
Fax: +44 (0)117 300 7270
www.projectaware.org
information@projectaware.org.uk

Contact details:
Project AWARE **(Europe)**, Oberwilerstrasse 3, 8442 Hettlingen, Switzerland
Tel: +41 52 243 32 32
Fax: +41 52 243 32 33
www.projectaware.org
info@projectaware.ch

Contact details:
Project AWARE **(Japan)**, 1-20-1 Ebisu-Minami Shibuya-ku, Tokyo 150, Japan
Tel: +81 3 5721 1731
Fax: +81 3 5721 1735
www.projectaware.org
padijpn@padi.co.jp

Society for the Protection of Animals Abroad (SPANA) has a volunteer vet scheme that offers graduate vets the unique opportunity to spend up to three months working in one of their refuges in Morocco. Your time working with them will make a huge difference to the lives of working animals and their owners. Living and working among these fascinating and vibrant communities is a uniquely rewarding experience, but places are limited.

Contact details:
SPANA, 14, John St, London, WC1N 2EB
Tel: +44 (0) 20 7831 3999
www.spana.org
enquiries@spana.org

SOS RHINO is based in the USA and Borneo and is a non-profit, international foundation dedicated to preserving the five rhinoceros species in their natural habitats. Their conservation programs combine research, education, marketing and advocacy, all working collectively to achieve sustainable results. SOS Rhino develops and funds rhino conservation and awareness programs, providing countries with the knowledge and tools to build lasting rhino conservation. They are looking for volunteers interested in saving the Sumatran rhinoceros. Volunteers help collect data, assist with building camp sites, fundraise and help teach english to some of their field staff.

Contact details:
SOS Rhino Borneo Bhd, Lot 15, Block B, 2nd Floor,Visa Light Industrial Center, Mile 5-1/2 Tuaran Road, 88856 Inanam, Sabah, Malaysia
Tel: 60 88 388 405
www.sosrhino.org
info@sosrhino.org

Save China's Tigers has been established to protect and conserve the tiger and other endangered cat species in China, in the knowledge that these are essential for the maintenance of a balanced co-existence with nature. This organisation has charity registration in the UK, USA, and Hong Kong, and field training programs in South Africa. They are small but ambitious and aim to succeed in reversing the fate of the South China Tiger that many consider impossible. They have low overhead and administrative costs and use volunteer resources to achieve big goals. You are welcome to volunteer as member of the team. Your contribution as a volunteer will help them to reduce costs, which means more funds can go to field work. Many of their volunteers help raise awareness and funding through online work, or through being engaged in local representative offices. Others choose to do field work, contact to assist.

Contact details:
Save China's Tigers **(UK)**, 66D Royal Mint Street, London, E1 8LG United Kingdom
Tel: +44 (0) 20 7451 1296
www.savechinastigers.org
info@savechinastigers.org

Contact details:
Save China's Tigers **(US)**, 112 VanWinkle Grove, Berea, KY 40403, United States

Contact details:
Save China's Tigers Limited **(HK)**, P.O.Box 98322, Tsimshatsui Post Office, Kowloon, Hong Kong
Tel: +852 2525 8786

Contact details:
Save China's Tigers **(Beijing)**, P.O.Box 1928, Chinese Forestry Academy, 100091 Beijing, China
Tel: +86 0 106286 6588

Contact details:
Save China's Tigers **(SA)**, LAOHU Valley Reserve, Philippolis, Free State, South Africa

Sea Shepherd Conservation Society is committed to the eradication of pirate whaling, poaching, shark finning, unlawful habitat destruction, and violations of established laws in the World's oceans. To that end, Sea Shepherd assists national and international bodies in the enforcement of international law under authority of the United Nations World Charter for Nature. Information on volunteering (both at sea and on shore) is on their website.

Contact details:
Mail address USA - International Headquarters, PO Box 2616, Friday Harbor WA 98250, USA
Tel: +1-360-370-5650   Fax: +1-360-370-5651
info@seashepherd.org

Contact details:
Sea Shepherd **UK**, Argyle House, 1 Dee Road, Richmond-Upon-Thames, Surrey, TW9 2JN
uk@seashepherd.org

Contact details:
Australia - Suite 7, 288 Brunswick Street, Fitzroy, VIC 3065
Tel: + 61 3 9445 0323
australia@seashepherd.org
Australia Business Number (ABN): 38123339499

Contact details:
Brazil - Instituto Sea Shepherd Brasil, Caixa Postal 17.501, Porto Alegre, RS, CEP 91010-972
www.seashepherd.org.br
seashepherd@seashepherd.org.br

Contact details:
Mail address Canada: P.O. Box 48446, Vancouver, B.C. V7X 1A2
Tel: 604-688-SEAL (7325)
canada@seashepherd.org

Contact details:
Mail address Europe – P.O. Box 58055, 1040 HB Amsterdam, The Nethetherlands
europe@seashepherd.org

Contact details:
Mail address Belgium - PO Box 65, 1840 Londerzeel   belgium@seashepherd.nl

Contact details:
France - Sea Shepherd France, 22 rue Boulard, 75014 Paris, FRANCE
France@seashepherd.org
www.seashepherd.fr

Contact details:
Galapagos/Ecuador - Sea Shepherd Galpagos, Av Charles Darwin Y Floreana, Oficina PB, Puerto Ayora, Santa Cruz, Galapagos, Ecuador
Tel: +593-97984645
galapagos@seashepherd.org

Contact details:
Singapore/Asia - Block 503 #02-237, Pasir Ris St. 52, Singapore 510503
Tel: 65-9 684 0950   grant@seashepherd.org

Trees for the Future is an organisation that has been the steward of planting trees throughout the world since the early 1970's. Through a people to people action plan, they restore tree cover to the world's most degraded lands. Planting trees helps keep people productive on their lands, preserving their traditional livelihoods and cultures for generations to come.

Contact details:
Mail address: Trees for the Future, PO Box 7027, Silver Spring, MD 20907
Tel: 1-800-643-0001
www.treesftf.org/
info@treesftf.org

Vets Beyond Borders is a not-for-profit, incorporated organisation established by volunteer vets. They help to set-up and run animal welfare programmes in developing communities, and co-ordinate veterinary volunteer work on projects throughout the region.

Contact details:
Mail address: Vets Beyond Borders Secretariat, PO Box 576, CROWS NEST NSW
Tel: 1585+61 2 9431 8616

Wildlife Vets International. The mission of Wildlife Vets International is to apply specialist veterinary expertise and experience to saving rare and endangered wildlife.

Contact details:
Wildlife Vets International, Keighley Business Centre, South Street, Keighley, Yorkshire, BD21 1AG.
Tel: +44(0)1535 661 298
Fax:+44(0)1535 690 433
info@wildlifevetsinternational.org

Worldwide Veterinary Service (WVS) WVS seek to alleviate suffering and improve the welfare and moral perception of animals worldwide by: co-ordinating teams of volunteers to assist the work of animal welfare organisations in all countries, supplying medicines, equipment and advice where they are needed most, providing sustainable input, building long term relationships and leading education programmes to the benefit of local animal and human populations, promoting and conducting research in all matters relating to animal welfare.

Contact details:
14 Wimborne Street, Cranborne, Dorset, BH21 5PP, UK
Tel: 01725 551123   www.wvs.org.uk/   info@wvs.org.uk

"Kindness and compassion toward all living things is the mark of a civilised society." - Cesar Chavez

AFRICA

"Think occasionally of the suffering of which you spare yourself the sight." - Albert Schweitzer

African Conservation Trust works to conduct environmental, cultural and heritage conservation projects as well as provide a means for these projects to become self funding through active participation by the public. This gives ordinary people a chance to make a positive and real contribution to environmental, cultural and heritage conservation by funding and participating as volunteers. Further information on volunteer projects is on their website.

Contact details:
Mail address: African Conservation Trust, P.O.Box 310, Link Hills, 3652, South Africa
Tel: +27-31-7675044
Fax: +27-86-5117594
www.projectafrica.com
E-mail: info@projectafrica.com

African Conservation Experience exists to: give volunteers the opportunity to experience conservation work in Southern Africa and to provide financial support and information exchange for conservation projects in Southern Africa. They offer a variety of voluntary animal jobs and opportunities throughout Africa ranging from dolphin research, game capture and wildlife veterinary work.

Contact details:
African Conservation Experience, Unit 1, Manor Farm, Churchend Lane, Charfield, Wotton-Under-Edge, Gloucestershire, GL12 8LJ
Tel: 0845 5200 888
www.conservationafrica.net

Amara Conservation aims to conserve, protect and restore viable ecosystems in Africa, and to provide conservation education to African communities. They believe that conservation and education are seamlessly intertwined, and that to achieve sustainable results with the preservation of the vast ecosystems of Kenya & East Africa, assistance must be offered to the people, as this is their land, and their future. Contact to assist with voluntary work.

Contact details:
Mail address: Amara Conservation Ltd, P.O.Box 24393, Karen 00502, Nairobi, **Kenya**
Attn: L Bergemann
www.amaraconservation.org

Contact details:
Amara Conservation Ltd, 1531 Packard #12, Ann Arbor, MI 48104, **USA**
Attn: J Haney
Tel: (734) 761 5357
www.amaraconservation.org

Contact details:
Amara **UK** Trust, 70 Dyne Road, Garden Flat, London, NW6 7DS
Attn: Heidi Bergemann – Chairman and Trustee
Tel: +44 207 372 2648
www.amaraconservation.org

Bushmeat Project be warned that this is a site with graphic, disturbing images cleverly designed to spur viewers onto action. The Bushmeat Project has been established to support partnerships that will help the people of equatorial Africa to protect the region's vital ecosystems and vibrant societies. The program is a long-term effort to provide economic and social incentive and to enable the expansion of capacity in the conservation arena. A primary theme of the Bushmeat Project has been the attempt to convert "poachers to protectors". They appreciate voluntary help – "whatever you can give -- ideas, volunteer talent, encouragement, or donations -- will be welcome and appreciated".

Contact details:
Mail address: Biosynergy Institute / Bushmeat Project, PO Box 3430, Palos Verdes, California 90274
Tel: 310 377-0317
Fax: 310 377-0315
Biosynergy Retreat Center – Tel: 909 767-1220
hq@biosynergy.org
www.bushmeat.net/

East African Wildlife Society (EAWLS) works to promote conservation and the wise use of wildlife and the environment in East Africa. In order to achieve this mission, EAWLS has been proactive in advocacy, facilitation of conservation education, promotion of conservation activities and the facilitation of field projects. The Society has a volunteer scheme designed to provide graduates with an opportunity to develop their experience and skills in conservation activities. Support and advice is given in developing skills useful to further employment within the field of conservation and environment protection. Volunteers work to a defined job description and work plan.

Contact details:
Mail address: East African Wildlife Society, P.O. Box 20110, Nairobi, Kenya
Tel: +2542.574145 or 574171
Fax: +2542.746868
www.eawildlife.org

Nile Basin Initiative provides a strategic framework for environmentally sustainable development of the Nile River Basin and supports basin wide environmental action projects. Volunteer placements advertised when available.

Contact details:
Mail address: Gedion Asfaw, P.O. Box 2891, House No 2, Plot 15, Al-Jamhorva Street, Khartoum, Sudan
Tel: +249 183 784232
Fax: +249 183 784248
gasfaw@nilebasin.org **or** info@nilebasin.org
www.nilebasin.org/

Society for the Protection of Animals Abroad (SPANA) has 19 veterinary centres and 20 mobile clinics and treats over 370,000 animals each year throughout North and West Africa and the Middle East. Efforts are concentrated wherever animals are mistreated, neglected or struggling to survive without proper care. SPANA also works in remote desert communities, where qualified vets are few and far between and offers a longer-term solution to improving the health and welfare of working animals. SPANA responds immediately to crises, such as when a natural disaster strikes or at a time of civil unrest or war. Their emergency programmes dispatch help whenever and wherever animals are in distress. SPANA has animal job volunteer opportunities in the African countries where they operate.

Contact details:
SPANA, 14, John St, London, WC1N 2EB
Tel: +44 (0) 20 7831 3999
www.spana.org
enquiries@spana.org

Botswana
Botswana SPCA (BSPCA) takes in all unwanted, stray and abused dogs and cats, provides veterinary treatment and tries to find homes for them. All dogs and cats are sterilised before being re-homed from the shelter so that BSPCA pets do not contribute to the pool of unwanted animals. The BSPCA is available to handle rescue/cruelty issues of other animals. They require volunteer assistance with walking, feeding, grooming, cleaning and general animal care.

Contact details:
Tel: +267 3500621
bspca@info.bw
www.spca.org.bw/

Cheetah Conservation Botswana Botswana has one of the last free-ranging populations of cheetah in the world. Sadly, cheetahs are now Africa's most endangered large cat - despite being listed as a species threatened with extinction by the Convention on International Trade in Endangered Species (CITES). Cheetah Conservation Botswana has been set up as a long term monitoring project, incorporating practical conservation, scientific research and community participation. Volunteers are required to assist with research work.

Contact details:
Cheetah Conservation Botswana, Mokolodi Nature Reserve, Private Bag 0457, Gaborone, Botswana
Tel/Fax: 00 (267) 3500613
info@cheetahbotswana.com or cheetah@mokolodi.com
www.cheetahbotswana.com

Living With Elephants (LWE), Botswana is dedicated to relieving conflict between the African Elephant and human populations in Botswana. They do this by identifying sources of conflict, developing strategies for resolution and offering educational programs that encourage a harmonious relationship between elephants and people. LWE believes that extensive participation and commitment by the communities is a requirement for success. They are currently looking for animal jobs volunteers to assist with elephant handling, environmental education, fundraising, art promotion, marketing, freelance writing and business management.

Contact details:
Mail address: Living With Elephants Foundation, P.O. Box 66, Maun, Botswana
Tel/Fax: +267 68 63 198 (Botswana)
contact@livingwithelephants.org
www.livingwithelephants.org/

Mokolodi Nature Reserve, Botswana is a nationally recognised educational, conservation and tourist facility. The Reserve is home to a diversity of flora and fauna and also houses one of two wild animal orphanages in Botswana. These and other wildlife and nature conservation projects on the Reserve are utilised in formulating a comprehensive environmental education programme for thousands of school children. Income from tourism and the sustainable use of wildlife and natural resources is used to subsidise the conservation projects and the environmental education programme. As a result of this intimate relationship with the village, the local community has a strong sense of ownership over the Reserve. Mokolodi has had many famous visitors and Alexander McCall Smith mentions the park in his book, Blue Shoes and Happiness. Volunteers provide a vital role at the Park, influencing all aspects of its operation from conservation to marketing, catering to maintenance. They are currently looking for volunteers to assist with marketing, IT, photography, journalism, animal sanctuary permaculture, ranger conservation, general labour & maintenance, catering, hosting and office assistant.

Contact details:
Mokolodi Nature Reserve, Private Bag 0457, Gaborone, Botswana
Tel: (267) 3161955 or (267) 3161956
Fax: (267) 3165488
information@mokolodi.com www.mokolodi.com/

Cameroon

In Defense of Animals (IDA), Cameroon is making a difference for orphaned chimpanzees and waging a strong campaign against the illegal killing of Cameroon's great apes. In the rain forests of Cameroon, the number of wild, free-living chimpanzees is dwindling at an alarming rate. The slaughtered chimpanzees are not the only victims of the illegal trade in bush meat. The orphans – infants, juveniles and adults – are victims as well. Visits to remote jungle villages and urban markets often include the sight of dejected orphans listlessly pining for their dead mothers. Visitors to roadside zoos and resort hotels are often shocked at the sight of adult chimpanzees – the grown-up orphans – tethered to the ground by short, heavy chains, or caged behind bars for a lifetime. IDA needs volunteers to assist for six months or more at their Sanaga-Yong Chimpanzee Rescue Center located on the edge of the forest near a remote village in Cameroon to assist with animal jobs.

Contact details:
700 SW 126th Avenue, Beaverton, OR 97005
Tel: 503 643 8302
Fax: 503 520 1195
kimber@ida-africa.org www.ida-africa.org

Last Great Ape Organisation (LAGA), Cameroon aims to create an effective deterrent factor for wildlife crimes in Cameroon. They work with government to deter dealers in meat and products of endangered species and to educate the public about gives the severity of the bush meat trade. LAGA is looking for hard working volunteers who have experience of working/living in Africa and are willing to do animal jobs.

Contact details:
LAGA, The Last Great Ape Organization, Vallee Nlongkak, Yaounde, Cameroon
Tel: +237-99651803
lastgreatape@yahoo.com or ofir@LAGA-enforcement.org
www.laga-enforcement.org/

Cameroon Wildlife Aid Fund (CWAF) aims to ensure that Cameroon's primates have a healthy future. Working with the government, local communities and other ecological groups around the world, CWAF aims to show people the amazing diversity of wildlife in Cameroon. CWAF operates two sites in Cameroon in co-operation with the Cameroon Ministry of Environment and Protection of the Nature: the Mefou National Park and the Mvog-betsi zoo. CWAF offers a limited number of self-funded volunteer posts to enthusiastic people aged over 21 with an interest in primate conservation and Africa. The maximum placement is 3 months and the minimum is one month. All their volunteers are based at the forest site where the accommodation is very basic, it is very hot and humid and they expect volunteers to work very hard, so it's not for the faint hearted!

Contact details:
CWAF, Yaounde Cameroon, B.P 20072 Yaounde
Tel: (+237) 22 20 75 79 **or** (+237) 99 51 30 73
CWAFCAMEROON@YAHOO.CO.UK
www.cwaf.org/

Côte d'Ivoire (Ivory Coast)

Monde Animal En Passion (MAEP) fights against wild and companion animal suffering in the Côte d'Ivoire region. MAEP runs petitions, media awareness, education, etc to assist animals at risk. They request that volunteers become members of MAEP first.

Contact details:
BP 1281, Abidjan, Côte d'Ivoire
Tel: +225 07885796
panimale@africaanimal.org
www.africaanimal.org/panimale/index.fr.php

Democratic Republic of Congo

Friends of Animals in Congo (AAC) their principal aim is to protect the Bonobos. This is achieved through ensuring confiscation of the bonobos for sale on the markets of Kinshasa, providing medical and psychological attention to confiscated bonobos and providing a suitable exercise area suitable to enable them to readapt when released. Contact to assist.

Contact details:
bonoboducongo.free.fr/us/frameus.htm

HELP Project, Congo The organisations' founder started the project by rescuing chimpanzees from miserable conditions in the Pointe Noire zoo. They now care for chimpanzees displaced by poaching/illegal traffic, or seized by the Congolese authorities. They work to reintegrate the chimpanzees into their natural environment. They also work with the Congolese authorities in their fight against the poaching and encourage the local communities to conserve the natural environment. They welcome volunteers over the age of 20, to stay for a minimum period of 3 months. Work includes chimpanzee care, veterinary projects, mechanic work, plantations & gardening projects, construction, etc.

Contact details:
www.help-primates.org/

Egypt

Society for the Protection of Animal rights in Egypt (SPARE) founded in 2001, is the first animal welfare organization in Egypt to address the situation of all animals. SPARE has grown to include 60 dog kennels, a cat shelter for 25 cats, a donkey sanctuary & day clinic, a dedicated clinic for spay and neuter operations, and plans are underway for a donkey mobile clinic. SPARE also developed as an animal advocacy organisation, and now its members work on issues related to animal welfare in all of Egypt, including: fighting to improve conditions at the Cairo zoo, working to stop the growing "private zoos" that are the latest fashion in Egypt, campaigning to get the government to stop poisoning and shooting animals, lobbying for new Animal Protection Law, exposing the conditions in the Egyptian slaughterhouses and pressuring the government to improve the standards, educating the public on animal kindness and specifically on the need to spay and neuter companion animals. Volunteers are required to assist with a wide variety of animal job tasks.

Contact details:
S.P.A.R.E.,Shobramant, Sakkara, Egypt
Tel: +20 2 338 13855
www.sparelives.org

Ethiopa

Homeless Animals Protection Society (HAPS), Ethiopia promotes the welfare of homeless animals and is working to promote a mobile animal health post. Contact to assist practically as a volunteer.

Contact details:
Mail address: Homeless Animals Protection Society, P.O. Box 2495, Addis Ababa, Ethiopia
Tel: 251- 11- 654 47 56
www.an-group.org/x_haps.htm
info@haps-eth.org.et

Gambia

Chimpanzee Rehabilitation Trust (CRT), Gambia has been working since 1969 to give orphaned chimpanzees the opportunity to grow up free and independent in their natural environment, rather than leaving them to their all too frequent fates as sad captives in a human world, or worse, as substitute humans in a laboratory. They are now the longest running chimpanzee rehabilitation project in Africa.

Contact details:
David Marsden, 32 Grosvenor Place South, Cheltenham, **United Kingdom**, GL52 2RX
Tel: ++44 (0) 1242 269 799
Fax: +44 (0) 1306 627901
chimpgambia@gmail.com
www.chimprehab.com/

Contact details:
Hanne Bray, Ahornvaenget 21, DK-7800 Skive, **Denmark**
Tel: +45 97 54 54 85
bray@mail.dk
www.chimprehab.com/

Contact details:
Hendrik-Jan and Ineke van den Berg, Voorsburgstraat 17, 3634 AV Loenersloot, **Netherlands**
Tel: +31 (0)294 290 0300
bergvdhj@hetnet.nl
www.chimprehab.com/

Contact details:
Mrs Kerstin Norrman, Björnbärsvägen 16, S-260 40 Viken, **Sweden**
Tel: +46 (0)42 237 304
mossen@home.se
www.chimprehab.com/

GambiCats, Gambia

Assists stray cats in need in the Gambia by providing neutering and veterinary assistance.

Contact details:
Mail address: Dodou F Bojang, Coordinator, P O Box 2874, Sere Kunda, **The Gambia**
Tel: (00 220) 9900756

Contact details:
Peter and Francis Miller, Trustees, Parc Llwyd, Aberporth, Cardigan, SA43 2DU, **UK**
Tel: (00 44) 01239 810595
Fax: (00 44) 01239 811193
www.GambiCats.org.uk/
gambicats@aol.com

Gambia Horse and Donkey Trust was established to reduce rural poverty by increasing productivity of working horses and donkeys through animal welfare and management education. Many thousands of working horses and donkeys in the Gambia are suffering appalling treatment simply through their carers' lack of knowledge. The Gambia Horse and Donkey Trust alleviate these problems by: educating the farming community, training extension workers, liaising with appropriate agricultural agencies and providing hospital and mobile treatment facilities. At the moment, they only taking on long term volunteers and short term professional teams of vets. This is because the Centre is approximately eight hours away from the coast over very bad roads and it is a long and tiring journey for anyone coming for only two weeks. However, they would welcome voluntary help in the UK with fundraising and administration and are particularly in need of pony and cob size head collars / bridles and 4" and 4.5" bits to alleviate suffering.

Contact details:
Brewery Arms Cottage, Stane Street, Ockley, Surrey RH5 5TH
Tel: 01306 627568
www.gambiahorseanddonkey.org.uk/

Kenya

Africa Network for Animal Welfare (ANAW), Kenya works together with communities and other animal welfare stakeholders in promoting humane treatment of farm, wild and companion animals in Africa through compassion, care, appreciation and protection. Volunteers are required to assist with many aspects of their work.

Contact details:
Mail address: Africa Network for Animal Welfare, P.O. Box 3731-00506, Nairobi, KENYA
Tel: +254-20-606-510
Fax: +254-20-609-691
www.anaw.org/
info@anaw.org

Colobus Trust, Kenya is a conservation organisation working to promote the conservation, preservation and protection of primates - particularly the Angolan Colobus monkey and its habitat on the South Coast of Kenya. Other activities include forest protection and restoration, public awareness, community education and various aspects of primate welfare. Volunteer vacancy information is kept up to date on their website.

Contact details:
Mail address: WAKULUZU: Friends of The Colobus Trust Ltd., Plot 75, Beach Road, P.O. Box 5380, 80401, Diani Beach, Kenya
Tel/Fax: + 254 (0) 711 479 453
www.colobustrust.org
info@colobustrust.org

David Sheldrick Wildlife Trust, Kenya is a small, flexible charity established in memory of a famous Naturalist, David Leslie William Sheldrick MBE, the founder Warden of Tsavo East National Park in Kenya. The Trust has played an extremely significant role in Kenya's conservation effort, speaking out on controversial issues and stepping in unobtrusively and rapidly o bridge a gap or meet a shortfall that jeopardises wildlife during times of Governmental economic constraints.

Contact details:
Mail address: The David Sheldrick Wildlife Trust, P.O. Box 15555, Mbagathi, 00503, NAIROBI, **KENYA**
Tel: +254 (0) 202 301 396 or+254 (0) 20 891 996
Fax: +254 (0) 20 890 053
www.sheldrickwildlifetrust.org/
rc-h@africaonline.co.ke

Contact details:
The David Sheldrick Wildlife Trust, Unit 19, Brook Willow Farm, Woodlands Road, Leatherhead, KT22 0AN, **UK**
Tel: +44 (0)1372 844 608
www.sheldrickwildlifetrust.org/
infouk@sheldrickwildlifetrust.org

Contact details:
U.S. Friends of The David Sheldrick Wildlife Trust, One Indiana Square, Suite 2800, Indianapolis, Indiana 46204-2079, **USA**
Tel: (317) 238 6380
Fax: (317) 636 1507
www.sheldrickwildlifetrust.org/
kfenley@sheldrickwildlifetrust.org

Gallmann Africa Conservancy Foundation, Kenya was established with the specific purpose of creating an environment where development and conservation work together, complimenting each other harmoniously, the Foundation aims to prove that Africa can survive through ecological, educational, creative and sustainable use of its natural resources. The Foundation's programs are primarily dedicated and its international outreach focused on wildlife protection, the environmental education of youth, community service and the preservation of traditional skills. There is an online volunteer application form on their website.

Contact details:
Mail address: The Gallmann Africa Conservancy Foundation, P.O.Box 63704, 00619 Nairobi, Kenya, East Africa
www.gallmannkenya.org/
info@gallmannkenya.org

Kenya SPCA is the only charitable organisation in Kenya that deals with companion animals. They work to rescue, care for and re-home animals and also run an educational programme. Contact to volunteer.

Contact details:
Mail address: KSPCA, P.O.Box 24203-00502, Nairobi, Kenya
Tel: +254-20-882500 or 890806
www.kspca-kenya.org
jules@kspca-kenya.org

Local Ocean Trust (LOT), Kenya is a marine conservation organisation committed to the protection of the Kenyan marine environment through hands-on conservation, research, education, campaigning and community development. The involvement of local communities is an essential part of the project with the aim of making it sustainable for the future. LOT aims for stakeholders to embark on wise and sustainable use of Kenyan marine resources and for sea turtle populations, as an indicator species of marine health, to show signs of recovery. Volunteers are required to assist this busy team and training is provided.

Contact details:
Mail address: Nelly Kadogai (Volunteer Coordinator), Local Ocean Trust, P.O.Box 125, Watamu, Kenya
www.watamuturtles.com
volunteering@watamuturtles.com/

Youth For Conservation, Kenya was established by young Kenyans concerned about the future of their county's wildlife heritage. Besides protecting Kenya's wildlife, the organisation is nationally and internationally recognised in conservation programs, community involvement and environmental education. Their main activities involve community conservation education, animal welfare campaigns, de-snaring and afforestation programs. Voluntary work includes research, education, hands on animal welfare, proposal writing, accounting, editing, writing and analyzing legal documents, reporting, artwork, website updating and maintenance, ecotourism, journalism, de-snaring and afforestation.

Contact details:
Mail address: P.O. Box 27689 Nyayo Stadium, NAIROBI 00506, Kenya
Tel: +254-020-606479
Fax: +254-020-606478
www.youthforconservation.org
info@youthforconservation.org

Madagascar

Animal SOS Madagascar works to rescue, care for and re-home animals in need. Contact to assist as a volunteer.

Contact details:
Lot II N ABA Analamahitsy, Antananarivo 101, BP: 6231, Fiadanana, Madagascar
Tel: (+261) 20 22 415 45
Fax: (+261) 20 22 490 76
www.animalsos-mada.com
animalsos@sssm.mg

Duke Lemur Centre (DLC), Madagascar promotes research and understanding of prosimians and their natural habitat as a means of advancing the frontiers of knowledge, to contribute to the educational development of future leaders in international scholarship and conservation and to enhance the human condition by stimulating intellectual growth and sustaining global biodiversity. They require volunteers to assist with day to day operations.

Contact details:
Andres Katz, Staff Specialist, Madagascar Programs, Duke Lemur Center, Durham, NC 27705
www.lemur.duke.edu
askatz@duke.edu

Madagascar Fauna Group (MFG) is an international consortium of zoos and that related organisations pool their talents and resources to work together in one of the world's most endangered places. Madagascar is legendary for its levels of biodiversity and endemism but unfortunately, the island is now home to fragmented populations, burned forests, vast stretches of unpalatable grasslands, people struggling to survive, and rivers of red topsoil. The MFG offers volunteers the opportunity to serve as Voluntary Rangers at Parc Ivoloina, assisting in the upkeep, monitoring and patrolling of the park – a full job description is available on their website.

Contact details:
Madagascar Fauna Group, c/o Saint Louis Zoo, 1 Government Drive, St Louis MO 63110, USA
www.savethelemur.org

Malawi

Project African Wilderness (PAW), Malawi is an organisation formed to protect and restore the Mwabvi Wildlife Reserve in Southern Malawi. Its aim is to work with local people and the Government of Malawi and integrate social, economic and environmental solutions to create a sustainable future for the reserve and improve local community livelihoods. PAW is not only a conservation project – money raised is put into the development of projects (and infrastructure) that will benefit the local people of Mwabvi and allow them to take control of their own livelihoods through businesses and education relating to eco-tourism. Volunteers can assist in their UK office as well as with hands on work in Malawi.

Contact details:
Project African Wilderness **(UK)**, Studio 2M, Beehive Mill, Jersey Street, Ancoats, Manchester M4 6JG
Tel: 0161 228 1689
www.projectafricanwilderness.org
pawadmin@projectafricanwilderness.org

Wildlife Action Group, Malawi works in nature conservation and management in Malawi and has influence towards a positive trend in the management of Malawi's dwindling flora and fauna by initiating a new approach in Forest- and Wildlife management. The organisation welcomes volunteers.

Contact details:
Mail address: Wildlife Action Group Malawi, P.O. Box 282 post net Crossroads, Lilongwe, Malawi
Tel: +265 (0)1 972 649
www.wag-malawi.org
Thuma Forest Reserve:thuma@wag-malawi.org

Mauritania

Association for the Humane Treatment of Animals in (ATHAM) works against poverty by demonstrating the value of working animals; works against zoonotic disease such as rabies through vaccination and reduces the number of stray animals through neutering. ATHAM provides free medical treatment to the large population of poorly cared for working donkeys through a mobile and stationary clinic and works with the donkey owners to educate them on the proper care of their animals. Contact to volunteer.

Contact details:
288, Rue 42-100 (Rue Abdallaye), BP 222, Nouakchott, Mauritania
Tel: +222 525 2660 ext 4519
Fax: +222 525 3583
Michelle_Dnnlly@yahoo.com

Mauritius

Protection of Animals Welfare Society (PAWS) works to make Mauritius a better place for animals. Founded in July 1999 by a small group of animal lovers who were very troubled by the terrible condition of domestic and stray dogs and cats on the island. They were also distressed by the population's ignorance in matters of pet care, and the lack of aid provided when they sought help. Volunteers are required to assist with animal jobs veterinary work, fundraising, field work and education.

Contact details:
PAWS Refuge, Domaine Rivière la Chaux, Beau Vallon, Mahébourg, Mauritius
Tel: +230 631 2304
Fax: +230 631 2296
www.pawsmauritius.org
info@pawsmauritius.org

Contact details:
PAWS Animal Care Clinic, 2nd West Lane, Floréal, Mauritius
Tel: +230 686 3121
www.pawsmauritius.org

Morocco

American Fondouk Animal Hospital, Morocco works to provide free veterinary care, guidance on proper nutrition and handling, and compassionate care for the animals of Morocco and their owners. The Fondouk strives to better the lives of all Moroccan animals, particularly working animals and the families who depend on their labour. Contact to assist.

Contact details:
The American Fondouk, B.P. 2048, Fez (V.N.) Morocco
Tel: 011-212-(0)35-93-1953
www.mspca.org/americanfondouk
dennee@menara.ma.

Namibia

Namib Desert Environmental Education Trust (NaDEET) is a non-profit organisation aimed to empower Namibians to make decisions for a sustainable future. They aim to provide a non-profit environmental education service for the learners and educators of Namibia based in the beauty and magic of the Namib Desert, to build capacity and know-how at all levels of the environmental education sector and to engage in education, advocacy and awareness of the critical role of sustainable living in a desert environment. The organisation invites school, youth and educator groups to participate in a unique hands-on, experiential environmental learning programme and offer internships.

Contact details:
Mail address: NaDEET, P.O.Box 31017, Pioneerspark, Windhoek, NAMIBIA
Tel: +264 (0)63-693 012
Fax: +264 (0)63-693 013
www.nadeet.org
admin@nadeet.org

Rare and Endangered Species Trust (REST), Namibia works to initiate and support the scientific and practical study of rare and endangered species in Namibia and to help develop and facilitate solutions to community, national and international problems with these species. Contact directly for information about their animal jobs volunteer programme.

Contact details:
Mail address: REST, P.O. Box 178, Otjiwarongo, Namibia 9000
Tel: 00264 67 306226
www.restafrica.org
Rest@Principia.edu

SPCA Windhoek, Namibia strives to be a safe haven for all strays and works to prevent abuse to all animals and to teach respect for animals to the public. Volunteers are required to assist in a variety of ways and training is provided.

Contact details:
Tel: 061-238654
Fax: 061-225715
www.spcawindhoek.org.na
spcawhk@mweb.com.na

Nigeria

Centre for Education, Research and Conservation of Primates and Nature (CERCOPAN), Nigeria has established an international research and education centre for the study of non-human primates, biodiversity research, forest management and conservation in is a non-profit, non-government organisation based in Cross River State, Nigeria. Cross River State's tropical rain forest north of Calabar. CERCOPAN accepts both long term supported volunteers, and short term volunteers who are self supporting (3 months or less). Apart from animal husbandry and wildlife rehabilitation, volunteers can assist with environmental education, fundraising, veterinary nursing, biology, engineering, mechanics, and building, welding, and construction.

Contact details:
CERCOPAN, 4 Ishie Lane, Hepo 826, Calabar,Cross River State, NIGERIA
Tel: +234 (0) 706 494 9572
www.cercopan.org
info@cercopan.org

Society for the Welfare of Animals Protection (SWAP), Nigeria works to improve the status and welfare of animals in Nigeria. The organisation believes that all animals should be treated with respect and compassion and that all animals have a right to existence as much as humans do - clean water, good shelter, veterinary care etc. Contact to help as a volunteer.

Contact details:
Mail address: Society for the Welfare of Animals Protection, P.O. Box 18, Benin City, Nigeria
Tel: +2347037087977, 08061253444
www.swap-nigeria.org
info@swap-nigeria.org

Seychelles

Seychelles SPCA works to assist organisations throughout the Seychelles with the prevention of cruelty to and protection of animals. Assists the community with a re-homing service for unwanted and abandoned animals. Co-operates with the relevant authorities towards finding a solution to the stray animal population in the Seychelles. Contact to assist.

Contact details:
Mail address: SPCA International, P.O. Box 8682, New York, NY 10001
www.spcai.org

South Africa

APES, South Africa aims to treat and assist all forms of wildlife or companion animals that are sick, injured or orphaned. Any sick or injured wild animal that recovers is returned to its natural habitat within the shortest time possible. Any domestic animal that has been assisted is returned to the owner without charge, or though a donation. Those animals who do not recover enough to be released are homed in the best way as to allow them as natural life as is possible, avoiding zoo type environments. APES is a unique destination for volunteers, back-packers and wildlife enthusiasts seeking enviro-experience and eco-tourism opportunities in Southern Africa. Volunteers gain hands-on animal jobs experience within a working primate sanctuary & rehabilitation centre and also have the opportunity to broaden their experience by visiting a host of associated animal welfare centres in the region.

Contact details:
Mail address: Apes, P.O. Box 443, Greytown 3250, Kwazulu/Natal South Africa
Tel (Local): 072-306-5664 Tel (Int): 027-72 306 5664
Fax: c/o 033-413 1933 Fax (Int): c/o 027-33-4131933
www.apes.org.za
apes1@gom.co.za

Animal Anti-Cruelty League, South Africa has been protecting and caring for animals since 1956. It is South Africa's second largest independent animal welfare organisation, relying entirely on the generosity and goodwill of the animal-loving public for financial support. They get involved with all aspects of animal welfare - providing shelter for abandoned animals, promoting an efficient adoption programme and prosecuting animal cruelty.

Contact details:
Mail address: P.O. Box 634, Rosettenville, 2130
Tel: (011) 435 0672
Fax: (011) 435 0693
www.aacl.co.za
pro@aacl.org.za

Contact details:
Head Office mail address: P.O. Box 7 Rosettenville 2130
Tel: (011) 435 0672
Fax: (011) 435 0693
www.aacl.co.za
jhb@aacl.org.za

Animal Trust Organisation, South Africa runs a virtual adoption centre which has an overview of homeless animals from various animal welfare organisations. The organisation goes to underprivileged areas to educate and aid families in taking care of their animals. The organisation recommends organisations that need volunteer help.

Contact details:
www.theanimaltrust.org
kelly@theanimaltrust.org
lisa@theanimaltrust.org

Animal Rescue Society, Cape Town, South Africa is a companion animal rescue organisation located near Cape Town. Their goal is to provide animal health care and sterilisation to the local impoverished communities along with running an adoption program for abandoned stray animals. Volunteer work here takes on many roles from feeding and caring for the many animals to working closely with staff as they go out into the local informal settlements to collect, return and vaccinate animals. There is also the opportunity to work along side the resident vet, who requires assistance daily. This work is not for the faint hearted, contact directly to assist with animal jobs volunteering.

Contact details:
Tel: 0113 205 4620
www.i-to-i.com/volunteer-projects/work-with-animals-south-africa.html

Animal Welfare Society of Stellenbosch, South Africa aims towards a community where animals have a good quality of life and are kept as close to their natural environment as possible. This Society opposes the inhumane practise of companion animals being indefinitely caged without proper daily physical and mental stimulation. Their practical work involves neutering, confiscation of animals at risk and campaigning against indiscriminate breeders. Volunteers receive training from a team of animal behaviourists and assist in a practical way with animal jobs.

Contact details:
Mail address: Animal Welfare Society of South Africa, Devon Valley Road, Stellenbosch 7600, P.O. Box 90, Stellenbosch 7599
Tel: +27 (0)21 886 4901**(volunteering) or** 021 886 4901 **(main office)**
Fax: 086 545 7083
www.aws-stb.co.za

Border Collie Rescue, South Africa works to assist and re-home Border Collies and to educate the public about the breed. They need volunteer help with fundraising and fostering.

Contact details:
Tel: 0824129969 (Irene Thompson)
www.bordercollierescue.co.za
mwmoz@mweb.co.za **or** karen.grey@absamail.co.za

Centre for Animal Rehabilitation and Education (CARE), South Africa is a wildlife rehabilitation facility in Phalaborwa, South Africa bordering the Kruger Park. CARE is dedicated to the care, welfare, rehabilitation and protection of injured and orphaned indigenous wild animals. The centre specialises in the care of chacma baboons, actively pursuing their rescue, rehabilitation and release. CARE accepts a limited number of volunteers to assist in the daily running of the centre, and in the rehabilitation programme. CARE favours volunteers with experience in dealing directly with animals or those who have previously held animal jobs.

Contact details:
Mail address: C.A.R.E Johannesburg, P.O.Box 986, Fourways 2055, South Africa
Tel: +27 (11) 468 3553
www.primatecare.org.za
info@primatecare.org.za

Cart Horse Protection Association, South Africa to provide static and mobile clinic services, support, education and training to under developed communities living on the Cape Flats who use horses and carts to collect scrap metal as a means of generating an income for themselves and their families. Contact to assist.

Contact details:
Mail address: Cart Horse Protection Association, P.O.Box 846, Eppindust, 7475
Tel: 021 535 3435
Fax: 021 535 3434
www.carthorse.org.za
info@carthorse.org.za

Campaign Against Canned Hunting, South Africa sadly, some lions are bred in captivity simply to become living targets for so called 'hunters' who pay large fees to shoot a trophy. This organisation is dedicated to getting all trophy hunting banned in South Africa. Contact to assist with animal jobs volunteering duties.

www.cannedlion.org

Cape of Good Hope SPCA is the founding Society of the SPCA movement and animal welfare in South Africa. They strive to provide caring treatment and comfortable shelter, and to protect the rights of animals, birds, reptiles and the creatures of the ocean by actively promoting a love and respect for all. This SPCA runs an animal hospital and mobile clinic that operates in informal settlements around Cape Town. Their Inspectorate team handles over 700 cases per month. Volunteers helping the Inspectorate assist with their administration or making pre and post adoption home checks. The wildlife section cares for abandoned and ill wildlife, including tortoises, crows, goats, peacocks, geese, squirrels, etc. The Horse Care Unit has volunteers to assist with cleaning stables and general care of horses. The Education Unit educates school children about pet care, animal rights and the SPCA. The Education Officer visits schools throughout the Greater Cape Town area and gives tours of the SPCA to school children and these animal jobs are also assisted by volunteers.

Contact details:
Mail address: Cape of Good Hope, P.O.Box 3, Plumstead, Cape Town, 7800
Tel: +27 21 700-4140
www.spca-ct.co.za
enquiries@spca-ct.co.za

Centre For Rehabilitation of Wildlife (CROW), South Africa is situated in Yellowwood Park, Durban, South Africa. It is a wildlife hospital that cares for the injured and orphaned wild animals and birds and is considered to be one of the leading rehabilitation centres in South Africa. The organisation is committed to the rescue, rehabilitation and release of orphaned and injured wildlife, and believes in action and education with regard to the protection of all natural resources. CROW have a very active volunteer program and are delighted to welcome local and international volunteers. They have a volunteer house that accommodates up to 8 volunteers at a time, and costs R160 per person per day (inclusive of meals). CROW has over 300 animals in its care at any one time – ranging from birds to monkeys and reptiles and requires help with rescues, nursing, feeding and releases.

Contact details:
Mail address: The Centre for Rehabilitation of Wildlife (CROW), P.O. Box 53007, Yellowwood Park 4011 Durban, Kwa-Zulu Natal, South Africa.
2 Coedmore Avenue, Yellowwood Park, Durban
Tel: +27 (31) 462 1127
Fax: +27 (31) 462-9700
www.crowkzn.co.za
info@crowkzn.co.za

Community Led Animal Welfare (CLAW), South Africa works in deprived areas to assist animals and educate their owners. During the clinic, the volunteers and a veterinarian tend to approximately 200 animals. CLAW depends on it's volunteers and say they need people who are sympathetic to their cause and who want to make a stand against animal cruelty and neglect.

Contact details:
Mail address: Claw South Africa, P.O.Box 546, Florida, 1710 South Africa
Tel: 011 763 1638
Fax: 011 672 1604
www.claw-sa.org
clawsouthafrica@gmail.com

Daktari Wildlife Orphanage, South Africa aims to give people with disabilities, the opportunity to experience the care of orphaned animals. The goal of the organisation is to improve the quality of life of people and orphaned animals. Volunteers are required to assist with animal care, marketing, education and other practical animal jobs.

Contact details:
Mail address: Michele & Ian Merrifield, Bona Ingwe Farm, Harmony bloc 81 (P.O.Box 1599), Hoedspruit, Limpopo, South Africa 1380
Tel: (+27) (0) 82 656 2969
www.daktaribushschool.org
info@daktaribushschool.org

Domestic Animal Rescue Group (DARG), South Africa is a non-profit organisation that rescues, cares for and re-homes abused, neglected and abandoned cats and dogs. It is their vision to be a leading example of animal sheltering in South Africa. Contact to assist as a volunteer with jobs at their animal shelter.

Contact details:
DARG, Main Road, Hout Bay
Tel: (021) 790 0383 or (021) 790 2050
www.darg.org.za info@darg.org.za

Durban and Coast SPCA, South Africa is dedicated to the Prevention of Cruelty to Animals. The Society exposes perpetrators of cruelty, enforces the animal protection act and promotes responsibility, care and compassion for all animals. As Durban's official pound, they provide shelter to strays and are committed to placing animals in caring homes. They also provide local underprivileged communities with low cost veterinary services. This SPCA is heavily reliant upon volunteers: from walking dogs and collecting pet food to assisting in their bookshop, fundraising and cleaning kennels.

Contact details:
Durban & Coast SPCA, CNR Willowfield Crescent & Inanda Road, Springfield Park
Tel: 031-579 6500
Fax: 031-579 4351
www.spcadbn.org.za
info@spcadbn.org.za

The Emma Animal Rescue Society (TEARS,) South Africa is based in Fish Hoek, South Africa and was formed as the suffering of animals in poorer communities in South Africa has reached horrific proportions; the SPCA and other Animal Welfare organisations are simply overwhelmed and cannot cope. TEARS is in the business of "hands-on, grass-roots upliftment. They aim to teach children to have compassion for animals as studies have shown that where traumatised or brutalised children are taught to care for something more helpless than themselves, the cycle of abuse can be broken. TEARS requires volunteers to assist with all types of animal jobs.

Contact details:
Mail address: TEARS, P.O.Box 22376, Fish Hoek, Cape Town 7974
Tel: 021 785 4482
Fax: 021 785 4354
www.tears.org.za
tears@tears.org.za

FreeMe, South Africa is a rehabilitation centre for indigenous wildlife that aims to rescue, rehabilitate and release indigenous wildlife onto carefully chosen reserves and conservancies. FreeMe strives to promote a responsible attitude to wildlife and the environment through education programmes, newsletters, publicity and advice. Volunteers continuously learn new skills and knowledge through contact with similar organisations and experts in the field. Almost all of the work at FreeMe is done by volunteers, ranging from feeding, cleaning and nursing patients in the clinic to raising funds, fixing plumbing, building cages ... whatever your talent, FreeMe can use it!

Contact details:
Mail address: Box 1666, Cramerview, 2060 South Africa
Street Address: Rietfontein Nature Reserve, Holkam Road, Paulshof, Johannesburg, South Africa
Tel: (011) 807-6993
Fax: (011) 807-6814
www.freemewildlife.org.za
info@freeme.org.za

Harnas Wildlife Foundation, South Africa was previously a family run cattle farm - today it is a charitable organisation dedicated to save endangered wild animals in Namibia. Harnas aims to establish a game reserve for orphaned wild animals. Harnas also aims to assist the local Bushman tribes who are in desperate need of medical/health care assistance. Volunteers are called "working guests" and there is further information and application form on their website.

Contact details:
Harnas, Arebush 48, Windhoek, Namibia
Tel: +264 (811) 40 33 22
www.harnas.org
bookings@harnas.org **(volunteering)**

Highveld Horse Care Unit, South Africa is the largest equine welfare organisation in the Southern hemisphere. They have an Inspectorate team who deal with the problems of illegal slaughter, security horses, bush racing and general complaints. Volunteers are required to assist with fundraising and with some horse care duties on weekends.

Contact details:
Mail address: Highveld Horse Care Unit, P.O.Box 20, Randvaal, 1873
Street Address: Highveld Farm, Portion 42, Maanhaarjakkels Street, Valley Settlements, Meyerton
Tel: 016 360 9900
Fax: 016 360 9901
www.horsecare.org.za
info@horsecare.org.za

Kitten Action, South Africa is a project of the animal rights group, Justice for Animals. Kitten Action was launched in 1997 to rescue abandoned and unwanted kittens. Since their inception, they have rescued over two thousand kittens. They operate a spay and return policy and have a sanctuary which cares for 40 adults and 60 kittens. Volunteers are asked to assist with their fostering programme.

Contact details:
Mail address: KITTEN ACTION, P.O.Box 755, Kloof, 3640
Tel: +27 (31) 764 3845
www.kittenaction.org.za
info@kittenaction.org.za

Karoo Animal Protection Society (KAPS) is the only organisation providing a mobile welfare service for animals (dogs, cats and livestock) in the deprived areas of the Little Karoo in rural South Africa. KAPS offers free welfare services on a daily basis into areas of need. This is all done on a voluntary basis and there are no paid staff. They have an excellent success rate and have transformed the communities where they operate. They are grateful for all practical voluntary assistance.

Contact details:
Mail address: KAPS, P.O.Box 134, Barrydale 6750, South Africa
Tel/Fax: 028 572 1717 (overseas +27 28 572 1717)
www.kaps.org.za
info@kaps.org.za

Monkeyland, Plettenberg Bay, South Africa this unique primate sanctuary is currently the top eco-tourism attraction on the Garden Route. Monkeyland has captured the hearts of visitors in its efforts to rehabilitate and free previously caged primates. The sanctuary cares for several species of primates who are not caged. Animal jobs volunteer opportunities are numerous.

Contact details:
Mail address: P.O. Box 1190, Plettenberg Bay, 6600
Tel: +27 (0) 44 534 8906
Fax: +27 (0) 44 534 8907
www.monkeyland.co.za
info@monkeyland.co.za

Sondela Wildlife Animal Centre, South Africa offers volunteer opportunities for candidates who complete any of their game capture course. Staying on afterwards as a volunteer entitles you to a 15 % reduction in your course fees. The Game Capture School is the first comprehensive school in South Africa offering courses that focus on the theoretical and practical aspects of all forms of wildlife conservation and education. Supporting the education and practice of wildlife handling and care, their courses are aimed at minimising animal stress and mortalities. The School offers six courses in African wildlife conservation and management. Courses enable candidates to: work in their wildlife hospital, learn about conservation medicine, learn humane methods of capture and translocation of game, learn to dart wild animals from a helicopter. Their website has comprehensive, up to date information.

Contact details:
Mail address: P.O. Box 1637, Mookgophong, South Africa, 0560
Tel: +27 (0)14 743 3051
www.gamecapture.info
info@gamecapture.info

South African Foundation for the Conservation of Coastal Birds (SANCCOB) is a non-profit sea bird rehabilitation centre based in Cape Town, South Africa. SANCCOB aims to conserve and protect South Africa's sea birds, especially threatened species. The organisation rehabilitates ill, injured, oiled and orphaned sea birds on a daily basis, prepares for and manages the rehabilitation of sea birds during a major oil spill, raises awareness about conservation through environmental education and collaborates on research projects SANCCOB has treated more than 83 000 sea birds throughout the last 37 years and cannot achieve it's objectives without the assistance of volunteers to assist with animal jobs.

Contact details:
Mail address: P.O. Box 11116, Bloubergrandt, 7443, South Africa
Street Address: 22 Pentz Drive, Table View, 7441, South Africa
Tel: (+27 21) 557 6155
Fax: (+27 21) 557 8804
www.sanccob.co.za

SanWild Wildlife Trust, South Africa it's objectives are a combination of acquiring habitat and saving individual wild animals in need of help. All land acquired through fundraising efforts fall under the auspices of the SanWild Wildlife Trust and are protected in perpetuity. Their goal is to establish a 15,000 hectare sanctuary and the vision is to ultimately incorporate adjoining farmlands to form an ecologically viable wildlife reserve to protect a unique wilderness area. Long term volunteering opportunities do arise and these are specifically mentioned on the website. SanWild volunteers are automatically entitled to a Free "Big 5" training course.

Contact details:
Mail address: The SanWild Wildlife Trust, P.O. Box 418, Letsitele, 0885, South Africa
Tel: +27 (15) 318 7900
Fax: +27 (0) 15 318 7901
www.sanwild.com
sanwild@pixie.co.za

Sunnydale Animal Sterilisation and Health Association (SASHA), South Africa works to assist animals in need by running neutering, education and awareness projects. Contact to assist.

Contact details:
59 Francolin Road, Sunnydale, 7975
Tel/Fax: (021) 785 4748
www.businesssa-westerncape.co.za/sasha/home.html
sashapets@gmail.com

South African Guide Dogs Association requires volunteers to assist with puppy socialising and fostering.

Contact details:
The South African Guide-Dogs Association for the Blind, 126 Wroxham Road, Rietfontein, Sandton 2191
Tel: 011 705 3513/4 **or** 087 754 9295
Fax: 086 506 3364
www.guidedog.org.za
info@guidedog.org.za

Wolf Sanctuary, Tsitsikamma, South Africa supports the survival of the wolf around the world by providing a sanctuary and natural habitat for wolves and emphasising the importance of not removing animals from their natural domain. There is a volunteer application form and further information on their website.

Contact details:
Mail address: The Lupus Foundation, P.O. Box 44890, Claremont, 7735
Tel: +27 21 6575859
Fax: +27 21 6717909
www.wolfsa.org.za
info@wolfsa.org.za

White Shark Research Institute, South Africa is dedicated to the conservation of the world's greatest predator and the preservation of it's environment. The organisation collects data on the white shark and assists in management programmes for the ensured survival of the species. As it is not possible to ensure survival of a hated species, they aim to change negative public attitude towards sharks through awareness and education. The organisation requests that volunteers first complete a 14 day student educational programme as offered by them before volunteering to assist the projects.

Contact details:
Mail address: P.O. Box 50775, V & A Waterfront, Cape Town 8001, South Africa
Tel: (021) 5529794
Fax: (021) 5529795
www.whiteshark.co.za
info@whiteshark.co.za

Sierra Leone

Tacugama Chimpanzee Sanctuary, Sierra Leone is committed to the rescue and rehabilitation of orphaned and abandoned chimpanzees in the hills of the Western Forest of Sierra Leone. The chimps enjoy a semi-wild life within the 100 acre reserve. The sanctuary aims to encourage effective local law enforcement agencies to take positive action against the trading of chimpanzees and other endangered species, to integrate orphaned chimpanzees into social groups with a view to gradually rehabilitating them into a semi-wild environment, to provide an educational, research and leisure facility to increase public awareness on the plight of Sierra Leone's chimpanzee population by attracting visitors. They aim to reintroduce wild-born rehabilitated chimpanzees into protected habitats. They value volunteer help and advertise specific volunteer vacancies on their website.

Contact details:
Mail address: Tacugama Chimpanzee Sanctuary, P.O. Box 469, Freetown, Sierra Leone
Tel: +232-76-611211 **or** +232-33-548572
www.tacugama.com
info@tacugama.com
volunteer@tacugama.com

Tanzania

Dar Animal Haven, Tanzania was created by a group of concerned individuals, who believe that the plight of animals in Tanzania is severely neglected and urgently needs attention. In a country where infrastructure is lacking in many areas and poverty is widespread, almost no attention is paid to the welfare of animals. This organisation works to rescue, neuter and care for animals in need. They also run an education project. Contact to assist.

Contact details:
Mail address: P.O. Box 105395, Msasani, Dar es Salaam, Tanzania
Tel: +255 784 438 278
Fax: +255 22 260 0772
www.daranimalhaven.org info@daranimalhaven.org

Tanzania Animals Protection Organisation (TAPO) this organisation works to protect all animals in Tanzania from torture, cruelty, abuse and disease. To respect all animals as living beings. Contact to assist.

Contact details:
Mail address: TAPO, P.O. Box 62921, Dar Es Salaam, Tanzania
Tel: +255 0746 027419
http://tanzania-animals-protection-org.blogspot.com
tap_org@yahoo.com

Zambia

Chipembele Wildlife Education Centre, Zambia is a fun, interactive and contemporary learning facility for Zambian children. It focuses its programmes on wildlife, the environment and conservation issues. Contact to assist.

Contact details:
Mail address: Steve & Anna Tolan, Chipembele Wildlife Education Trust, P.O. Box 67, Mfuwe, Zambia
Tel: +260 216 246108
www.chipembele.org
info@chipembele.org

Kansanka Trust, Zambia was formed to bring effective management to Kasanka National Park and thereby protect the flora and fauna in as natural a state as possible. By developing infrastructure and tourism the aim is to make the Park self-sustaining and bring benefits to the local community. The Trust promotes education and research in wildlife conservation and supports rural development schemes in the adjacent community. Kasanka relies heavily on voluntary assistance.

Contact details:
Mail address: The Park Manager, Kasanka Trust Ltd., P.O.Box 850073, Serenje, Zambia
www.kasanka.com

Munda Wanga Trust, Zambia works to protect natural heritage through education and conservation. They run an environmental education centre, wildlife sanctuary and botanical gardens. Volunteers are welcome to assist in a variety of ways.

Contact details:
Mail address: Plot 175, Kafue Road, Chilanga, P.O. Box 350068, Chilanga, Lusaka, Zambia
Tel: +260 (0)21 1278 614
Fax: +260 (0)21 1278 529
www.mundawanga.com
mundawanga@iconnect.zm

Zimbabwe

African Dogs, Zimbabwe aims to conserve and increase the range and numbers of African hunting dogs in Zimbabwe. Volunteers are involved on a day to day basis and experience first hand the reality of operating a conservation project in the African wilderness. They operate predominantly in the areas around Hwange National Park, located in the far west of Zimbabwe. Volunteers assist with rehabilitation, fieldwork, education and wildlife work – see the website for more information.

Chipangali Wildlife Orphanage, Zimbabwe is a haven for wild animals which have little hope for survival in the wild – creatures which have been orphaned, abandoned, injured, born in captivity or brought up unsuccessfully as pets. It is often the last refuge for those brought in sick or injured, and increasingly it is a sanctuary for confiscated animals. Chipangali has been featured in countless documentaries and is now world renowned for it's pioneering work and is famed as one of Africa's largest and most successful wildlife rehabilitation/release centres. Volunteers are requested to commit to a minimum four week placement; three weeks will be spent at the orphanage itself and one week at either Hwange or Matopos National Park where they conduct leopard and cheetah research. A week is spent working on each of the orphanage's three major sections (carnivores, black rhinos and primates). Volunteers may be given the task of helping to hand rear any orphans brought into Chipangali and monitoring any sick and injured animal in the nursery.

Contact details:
Mail address: Chipangali Wildlife Orphanage, P.O. Box 1057, Bulawayo, Zimbabwe
Tel: +263-9-287739/287740
Fax: +263-9-287741
www.chipangali.com
info@chipangali.com

Spotted Hyaena Research, Zimbabwe the rapid decline of populations outside conservation areas due to persecution and habitat loss makes hyaenas increasingly dependent on the continued existence of protected areas. As Hwange National Park holds around 20% of the hyaena population of the country in one protected area, it is a very important stronghold for the species. This organisation welcomes volunteers.

"I have always held firmly to the thought that each one of us can do a little to bring some portion of misery to an end." - Albert Schweitzer

ASIA

ACTAsia is a non-profit organisation set up by experienced animal protectionists to develop sustainable and professional animal advocates in Asia. They work to build the capacity of local organisations and people working in the field of animal protection, we can secure a better future for animals in Asia. They provide detailed training on animal issues and sustainable activism to potential and current animal protectionists. Their mission is: "To make lasting improvements for animals in Asia by developing professional animal protectionists in Asia". They are currently looking for volunteers to help with their work in China.

Contact details:
Mail address: ACTAsia for Animals, P.O. Box 1264, High Wycombe, HP10 8WL, UK
Tel: +44 20 8123 0226
www.actasia.org
info@actasia.org

Animal Asia Foundation (AAF) is a Hong Kong-based government-registered animal welfare charity, it also has charitable status in UK, USA, Germany, China and Australia. The AAF is devoted to the needs of wild, domesticated and endangered species throughout the Asian continent. The mission of the AAF is to improve the lives of all animals in Asia, end cruelty and restore respect for animals Asia-wide. They currently have volunteer vacancies at their Bear Rescue Centre in China.

Contact details:
Hong Kong Head Office, 10/F, Kai Tak, Commercial Building 317-319 Des Voeux Road, Central Sheung, Hong Kong
Mail address: Hong Kong Post Box, P.O. Box 374, General Post Office, Hong Kong
Tel: +852 2791 2225
Fax: +852 2791 2320
www.animalsasia.org
info@animalsasia.org

Frontier Want to have the best time of your life while gaining academic qualifications at the same time? Join a Frontier expedition and save endangered wildlife and threatened ecosystems while gaining an A-level. Learn to run expeditions and gain an AS-level. Teach English and get TEFL trained. Whichever you choose, you'll be off the beaten track having adventures beyond anything you've ever imagined! They have projects in Africa, Asia, Fiji & the Pacific Isles, Indonesia, South and Central America, and Nepal.

Contact details:
Tel: 020 7613 2422
www.frontier.ac.uk

Jane Goodall Institute (JGI) works to increase primate habitat conservation, increase awareness of, support for and training in issues related to our relationship with each other, the environment and other animals (leading to behavior change), expand non-invasive research programs on chimpanzees and other primates, promote activities that ensure the well-being of chimpanzees, other primates and animal welfare activities in general. The Jane Goodall Institute advances the power of individuals to take informed and compassionate action to improve the environment of all living things. To assist as a volunteer with one of their many projects worldwide, see their website for further information.

Contact details:
The Jane Goodall Institute-**USA Headquarters,** 4245 North Fairfax Drive, Suite 600
Arlington, VA 22203
Tel: (703) 682-9220
Fax: (703) 682-9312
www.janegoodall.org

Borneo
KalaweitGibbon Rehabilitation Project, Borneo works for the conservation and rescue of gibbons. They fight the illegal trade and illegal possession of gibbons by confiscations in cooperation with the Indonesian forestry department. Currently, Kalaweit takes care of 240 gibbons and siamangs in Borneo and Sumatra. They require voluntary assistance with a number of projects.

Contact details:
www.kalaweit.org

Save The Orangutan, Borneo one of the rehabilitation centres, Wanariset, is situated in the forest and sanctuary project, Samboja Lestari. They are transforming 2,000 hectares of grass land into tropical rain forest. The area houses islands for orangutans, a sun bear sanctuary and an organic garden. Get involved by staying in the Samboja Lodge.

Contact details:
International Website: www.savetheorangutan.org

UK Contact details:
Tel: 08456 521 528
www.savetheorangutan.org.uk

China
Beijing Human and Animal Environmental Education Center (BHAEEC) aims to alert and educate the public about animal protection, to nurse and find homes for wounded and homeless animals and to spread knowledge about animals. BHAEEC could not survive without the help of dedicated, committed volunteers - fill out their online application form to apply to volunteer.

Contact details:
Mail address: Mail Box 100070-182, Beijing, the PRC, 100070
www.animalschina.org   info@animalschina.org

CatsZone, China works to enhance the welfare of cats through rescue, care and education. Contact to assist with fostering and other volunteer duties.

Contact details:
5-1-202 Jia Shang Xin Cun, Hangzhou City, Zhejiang Province, P.R. 310000, China (PRC)
Tel: +86 571 87972361
Fax: +86 571 88316253
www.catszone.ngo.cn
info@CatsZone.ngo.cn

Second Chance Animal Aid (SCAA), Shanghai is a private, non-profit organisation committed to protecting and improving the health and welfare of companion animals through education, health care, advocacy, outreach, adoption and the promotion of foster care as an alternative approach to traditional shelters. The organisation believes that every companion animal should have a safe, healthy life in a loving home. Contact to volunteer in their shelter with animal care duties, education, fundraising and more.

Contact details:
www.scaashanghai.org
volunteer@scaashanghai.org

Hong Kong

Companion Animal Federation, Hong Kong works to rescue, care for and re-home companion animals in Hong Kong. Volunteers contribute to their activities – contact directly to assist.

Contact details:
Mail address: P.O. Box No 75, Tuen Mun Central Post Office
Tel: (852) 2146 4383
Fax: (852) 2369 8183
www.hkcaf.org
caf@hkcaf.org

Conservancy Association, Hong Kong is a non-government environmental organisation in Hong Kong. Dedicated to the protection of the environment and the conservation of natural and cultural heritage, their mission is to ensure that Hong Kong shoulders her regional and global environmental responsibilities. They achieve this by advocating appropriate policies, monitoring government action, promoting environmental education and taking a lead in community participation.

Contact details:
www.conservancy.org.hk
cahk@cahk.org.hk

Hong Kong Alleycat Watch assists street cats with injuries and newborn kittens needing urgent medical care. The organisation doesn't have a shelter and is reliant on foster carers to help look after cats in need – get in touch to assist as a volunteer with fostering and their trap, neuter and return project.

Contact details:
www.hkalleycats.com/
Athenaho@netvigator.com

Laboratory Animal Defenders, Hong Kong exists to discourage the use of animals in education and scientific procedures. Their mission is to work towards abolition of all animal experimentation in Hong Kong. They are working to pass legislation for the welfare of laboratory animals and eventual elimination of animal experimentation in Hong Kong. Contact directly to assist.

Contact details:
www.lad.org.hk/

Lamma Animal Welfare Centre (LAWC) works to rescue and find homes for abandoned and abused animals and educate individuals and the public in responsible pet ownership. They work with the SPCA to promote the Spay Bus to provide low cost neutering of dogs and cats and to trap, neuter, release Lamma's colonies of street cats. Contact to join their comprehensive volunteer programme.

Contact details:
www.lammaanimals.org/
info@lammaanimals.org

Lamma Animal Protection, Hong Kong exists to help animals in distress on Lamma Island, Hong Kong and to bring about conditions whereby every animal has a good home. Volunteers assist by organising events, walking dogs, bottle-feeding motherless puppies and kittens, matching shelter pets with the right prospective adopters, answering phones, and fostering newborn orphaned pets – contact to get involved.

Contact details:
www.lap.org.hk/
jen@lap.org.hk

India

Animal Welfare Society, Hyderbad, India is an organisation with 24 hrs emergency veterinary aid and a rescue facility. They conduct over 700 sterilisations each month. Their efforts on public awareness are well appreciated by the public as well as authorities and they welcome volunteers to assist in a variety of ways.

Contact details:
Plot no. 238, Vet n Pet, Kamalapuri Colony, Srinagar Colony, Hyderabad 500073, Andhra Pradesh, India
Tel: +91-040-65539535, 237 38 237
www.animalwelfaresociety.in
vetnpet@yahoo.com

Animal Aid Unlimited, Rajasthan, India is a charitable organisation devoted to achieving a paradigm shift in support of animal rights in India. Animal Aid brings relief to suffering animals - through their 20 skillful staff and compassionate volunteers from all over the world, they are able to treat about 100 animals every day. Volunteers needed to assist in a hands-on way.

Contact details:
Tel: 09352511435 or 09950531639
www.animalaidunlimited.com
info@animalaidunlimited.com

Anand Chhaaya (Shelter of Happiness), India was set up in 1997 with the primary aim to control the stray dog population through neutering. The organisation is unique in that it is against restraint or lassoing stray animals (as this causes stress, pain and trauma), instead it has staff and volunteers who befriend the animals in order to capture them for neutering/treatments. It has been highly successful, has a well equipped clinic in Koramangala and also runs an animal shelter located at Bellandur village that accommodates abandoned dogs and pups that are taken care of till they are rehabilitated. Compassion and affection to all animals is the aim of this organisation. Contact to assist as a volunteer.

Azam for Animals, India conduct a variety of activities to help animals in the north east of India – volunteer to assist their work.

Contact details:
107/C, Railway Colony, New Guwahati – 781021, Assam, India
Tel: +91-94350-48481
www.freewebs.com/azamsiddiqui/
azamsiddiqui@animail.net or azam24x7@gmail.com

Animal India Trust operates an Animal Birth Control and Anti-Rabies Vaccination programme for street and stray dogs and cats in Delhi. They provide assistance to any injured or sick animal found on the streets as well as free medical treatment to pets of the economically disadvantaged and placement of orphaned street puppies and kittens into loving homes. Animal India Trust is commited to the education of the public provides regarding pet and stray animal welfare. Volunteer to assist with re-homing, walking, cleaning, education and more.

Contact details:
Animal India Trust, Jal Vihar (Near Jal Vihar Bus Terminal), Lagpat Nagar I, New Delhi 110024
Tel: +00 91 11 55669924
Fax: +00 91 11 29810390
www.animalindiatrust.com
animalindiatrust@yahoo.com

Animal Aid Society (AAS), India is based in Udaipur, Rajasthan, India. Their mission is to bring relief to suffering animals and their 16 staff and volunteers from all over the world enable them to treat about 100 animals every day. Contact to assist their volunteer programme.

Contact details:
In USA:-
Animal Aid Unlimited, 6900 37th Ave SW, Seattle, WA 98126 USA
www.animalaidunlimited.com
info@animalaidunlimited.com

In India:-
Tel: 09352511435 or 09950531639

Asha Foundation Animal Care Centre offers free treatment to the stray animals and birds, provides shelter to sick and injured animals, aims to prevent cruelty through spreading awareness about animals and birds. Contact to assist as a volunteer.

Contact details:
Office address: C-182, Ashok, Nagar, Opp ISRO Satelite, Ahmedabad 380015 (Guj.), India
Shelter address: Beside Lalgaebi Ashram, Hathijan, Ahmedabad
Tel: +91-9824037521
www.ashafoundationindia.org

Beauty Without Cruelty (BWC), India is involved in the investigation of cruelty-free products and processes (no animal ingredients, not tested on animals) and investigates the activities of establishments that use animals. They have a volunteer programme and online application form.

Contact details:
4 Prince of Wales Drive, Wanowrie, Pune 411 040
Tel: (020) 2686 1166
Fax: (020) 2686 1420
www.bwcindia.org
admin@bwcindia.org

Blue Cross of India was established to alleviate the suffering of animals. It has grown from small beginnings to become one of India's largest animal welfare organisations, running active animal welfare, animal rights and humane education programmes. Volunteers assist with a variety of activities including dog walking, transport, fundraising, etc.

Contact details:
Blue Cross of India, 1 Eldams Road, Chennai – 600 018, India
Tel: +91-44-22354959/22300666/22300655
Fax: +91 44 2250 1801
www.bluecrossofindia.org
bluecrossofindia@gmail.com

Circle of Animal Lovers, India the organisation offers food to 100s of stray animals every day. They also collect sick, injured animals from the road, treat them either in their mobile clinic or take them to their shelter home for treatment. Neutering is their major activity and they have been successful in reducing stray-animal population. Contact to assist as a volunteer with a variety of activities.

Contact details:
Circle of Animal Lovers (Regd.), E-67 DDA Flats, Saket, New Delhi – 110017, India
Tel: 26531419/26511569
www.circleofanimallovers.org
info@circleofanimallovers.org

Compassion Unlimited Plus Action (CUPA), Bangalore, India operates a wide variety of animal care activities ranging from, animal therapy programmes, animal hospital, cruelty cases, education & awareness, neutering, re-homing, wildlife rescue & rehabilitation etc. They have a comprehensive volunteer programme which allows volunteers to assist in many aspects of their work.

Contact details:
CUPA-Bangalore, India
www.cupabangalore.org
cupablr@gmail.com

Friendicoes SECA, India Animal rescue is one of the most important parts of this organisations work. Every day on an average their five ambulances rescue over 100 animals-cats, dogs, birds, camels, horses, donkeys, monkeys etc. They also run a shelter, spay and neuter programme and education projects. Volunteers are encouraged to spend as much time as they can at the city shelter and also at their country sanctuary. Creating awareness about neutering and vaccinations, grooming, cuddling and playing with the puppies and kittens, taking them for walks, cleaning, feeding, etc comprises the main part of the hands-on work that volunteers can do. There is also fundraising and campaigning work for volunteers.

Contact details:
271 & 273 Defence Colony, Flyover Market, New Delhi - 110024
Tel: +91 11 24314787 **or** +91 11 24320707
www.friendicoes.org
info@friendicoes.org

Goa SPCA has the following aims: "To provide shelter and medical facilities to all animals in need, by virtue of age, infirmity, injury, abuse or calamity. To spread awareness about prevention of cruelty to animals through workshops, the media, and other teaching and promotional aids. To appoint inspectors to investigate cruelty to animals". To help set up and assist other animal welfare organisations in the State of Goa in carrying out their charge. Contact to assist.

Contact details:
www.goaspca.org
lynn@goaspca.org

Help In Suffering (HIS), Rajasthan, India has three animal shelters; the original shelter, founded in l980, on two acres of land in south Jaipur, a second shelter provided by the Municipality to conduct an ABC programme in northern Jaipur, and a shelter in Kalimpong (West Bengal). A specialised Camel Rescue Centre is being built at Bassi and is the first of its kind in India. Six separate projects are conducted, each headed by a vet. The teams leave base to head out into the city and nearby villages each day. Kalimpong is a town in the foothills of the Himalayas surrounded by small rural villages. The shelter there employs about ten staff and has one rescue vehicle. Contact to assist as a volunteer.

Contact details:
Help in Suffering, Maharani Farm, Durgapura, Jaipur, Rajasthan 302018, India
Tel: +91 141 3245673 **or** +91 141 2760012
www.his-india.in
office@his-india.in

Hope and Animal Trust, India has the following aims: "To reduce the stray dog population and eradicate rabies through vaccination, sterilisation, and adoption programs. To provide veterinary care and emergency aid for the animals in the local communities. To promote animal welfare through education programmes in schools and villages. To help the local population out of poverty by promoting humane income-generating activities through the management and care of farm animals. To set up a joint old age home, orphanage and animal shelter together, to give love, affection and companionship to each other". Contact to assist.

Contact details:
HOPE & Animal Trust, C/o Mr S P Singh, House # 21, Road # 1, Mandir Marg, Birsa Nagar, Birsa Chowk, Ranchi-834 003, Jharkhand, India
Tel: +91-9431725769 or +91-9431171929
www.hopeandanimal.org
hopeandanimal@gmail.com

Indian Project for Animals and Nature (IPAN), India is a non-governmental organisation which works to reduce and prevent cruelty towards animals, to promote the health of domestic and wild animals, to protect the environment and by so doing improve the livelihood of people depending on their well-being and balance. They welcome volunteers, see website for further information.

Contact details:
Hill View Farm Animal Refuge, Mavanalla, Masinagudi post, 643223 Nilgiris, Tamil Nadu, India
Tel: +91 (0)423 2526158
www.indiapan.org
ipannilgiris@gmail.com

In Defence of Animals (IDA), India works to assist animals in need in India. They have a wide variety of projects including; animal rescue, care, neutering, campaigning, education, mobile clinics and more. Contact to assist.

Contact details:
IDA, 7, Shanti Kuni, 124, Hindu Colony, 5th Lane, Dadar, Mumbai-400 014, India
Tel: 91-22-2414 2195/2414 3412/3268 1417
www.idaindia.org
info@idaindia.org

Jeevashram, New Delhi, India exists promote kindness and prevent or suppress cruelty to animals. To successfully implement the above objectives it has set up an animal shelter with excellent medical facilities in Rajokri. This facility includes kennels, cattery, operating facilities, mobile dispensary,etc. They are currently looking for volunteer vets to assist their work.

Contact details:
Jeevashram Animal Shelter Village Rajokri, New Delhi - 110038
Tel: 25064114/25063696/25064118
Fax: 41667272
www.jeevashram.org
vetvinodsharma@gmail.com **or** jeevashram@gmail.com

Karuna Animal Welfare Association, Bangalore, India was established in the year 1888 as 'Bangalore Society for the Prevention of Cruelty to Animals'. The name of the organisation has changed to 'Karuna Animal Welfare Association of Karnataka'. They have a wide variety of activities and are assisted by volunteers – contact for more information.

Contact details:
Kasturba Road, Bangalore-560 001
Tel: +91-080- 22860205
www.karunaanimalwelfare.org
contact@karunaanimalwelfare.org

Marwar Trust, India is committed to eliminating rabies in India. Adhering to the World Health Organisation's (WHO) rabies control guidelines and standards, the Marwar Trust believes in supporting and building the country's local capacity for controlling canine rabies, while promoting the highest standards of animal welfare. This organisation has a large number of volunteer jobs, visit their website for further information.

Contact details:
Wg Cdr Baldev Singh (Retd), The Marwar Animal Protection Trust, 32 Abhaygarh, Ratanada, Jodhpur – 342011, India
Tel: +98 291 19615
www.marwartrust.org
kdoyle@marwartrust.org

MAITRI Centre, Leprocy Animal Care Programme, India runs a shelter for stray animals and assists with surgery, sterilisation and education. Volunteers are required to assist their shelter.

Contact details:
Mail address: Adriana Ferranti – Director, MAITRI Leprosy Prevention, Treatment & Rehabilitation Centre, P.O. Box 32, Bodhgaya, Gaya Distt, Bihar 824 231, India
Tel: (91) 631 2200841
Fax: (91) 631 2201946
http://fpmt.org/maitri/animals.asp
ferranti@ndc.vsnl.net.in

People for Animals, Bangalore, India is a non-profit conservation organisation working for the rescue and rehabilitation of urban wildlife. To date, four thousand mammals, avians and reptiles have been treated back to health in the hospice, and rehabilitated back to their natural habitats. This organisation has a large number of volunteer jobs, visit their website for further information.

Contact details:
People for Animals Survey no. 67, Uttarahalli Road Kengeri, Bangalore 560 060
Tel: +91-80-2860 4767/+91-80-2860 3986/+91-80-2273 3350
Fax: +91-80-2860 3986
www.pfa-bangalore.org
info@pfa-bangalore.org

Tree of Life for Animals, India has several aims: to create a rabies free environment, to create an environment where stray animals can be free of suffering, to assist rural people with veterinary help and to provide a mobile veterinary unit for use in remote areas. They are on the lookout for volunteers – particularly for vets to help their work.

Contact details:
Address in India: Tree of Life for Animals, Kharekhari Village, Nr Foy Sagar, Ajmer, Rajasthan, India
Tel: 0091 9829 786362
Volunteer Postal Address: The Tree of Life for Animals, Creative Media Centre, 45 Robertson Street, Hastings, East Sussex, TN34 1HL, United Kingdom
http://tolfa.org.uk/
volunteers@tolfa.org.uk

Visakha SPCA, Pradesh, India has one of the most comprehensive animal shelters in India: dogs and cats, cattle and birds, and wildlife that was being illegally kept to be sold dead or alive. They also have an eco-friendly, 100% organic farming and renewable energy projects to run, plus medical facilities for the animals! One of their most important projects is their animal birth control program (ABC) for dogs and cats. Recently, due to heightened publicity about dog bites, the public's tolerance for any trouble with the street dogs has decreased. Consequently, Visakha SPCA wants to go full tilt to spay/neuter/vaccinate 10,000 street or community dogs: fewer dogs means fewer bites -- and fewer dogs put down. The organisation needs help to accomplish this and to show the public that the problem is under control so the authorities don't have to start killing street dogs again en-masse. There is an urgent call for veterinary volunteers; their new mobile camps require skilled veterinary help and they need ongoing teams to assist in these surgeries.

Contact details:
Visakha Society for Protection and Care of Animals, 26-15-200, Main Road, Visakhapatnam, Andhra Pradesh, India 530-001
Tel: 91-891-2716124
http://vspca.org
info@vspca.org

Welfare of Stray Dogs, India is a Mumbai-based organisation working to eradicate rabies and control the street dog population in a humane, scientific way. Since 1989 they have been carrying out a mass sterilisation programme for stray dogs, volunteers are crucial to their worthwhile work.

Contact details:
Administrative Office: The Welfare of Stray Dogs, C/o Akanksha, Voltas House "C", T B Kadam Marg, Chinchpokli, Mumbai 400 033.
Tel: +91 22 23733433 **(weekdays 10am – 5pm)** +91 22 23891070 **(at other times)**
www.wsdindia.org
wsdindia@gmail.com

Indonesia

Bali Animal Welfare Association (BAWA) is a not-for-profit charity registered in Indonesia. Its mandate is to relieve suffering, control the population and improve the health of Bali's street dogs while educating the local population in animal welfare. BAWA supports a fully staffed clinic near Ubud, a 24 hour animal ambulance, a mobile sterilization clinic, an education program, a puppy adoption program, plus a continually expanding range of community programs. Contact to assist as a volunteer.

Contact details:
BAWA Headquarters, Jalan Monkey Forest 100X, Ubud, Bali, Indonesia
Tel: +62 (0) 361 977217 **or** 081 1389004
www.bawabali.com
info@bawabali.com

Bali Street Dog Foundation, Bali works to assist street dogs in a variety of ways. This organisation has done a huge amount of work to assist animals affected by the Tsunami. To assist as a volunteer, see more information on their website.

Contact details:
Yudisthira, J1. Tukad Balian #170, Renon, Bali
Tel: +62 361 270864
Fax: +62 361 282105
www.yamp.com/balidogs/volunteer.htm
BaliDogs@ix.netcom.com

Japan

All Life In Viable Environment (ALIVE), Japan There are over 10,000 animal breeders and dealers in Japan. ALIVE has been investigating those who keep animals in bad conditions and campaigning for the tightening of regulations in order to put them out of business. The revision of the Japanese Animal Welfare Law in 2005 has made it mandatory for an animal dealer to register with the appropriate authority but it is still hard to sweep off unscrupulous dealers. They are currently campaigning for the next revision, with which we hope that the sale of live animals at stores will be banned and further restriction will be placed on animal dealers changing registration to licensing. Contact to assist.

Contact details:
ALIVE, 5-18-10-102, Honkomagome, Bunkyo-ku, Tokyo, 113-0021, Japan
Tel: +81-3-5978-6272
Fax: +81-3-5978-6273
www.alive-net.net/english

Animal Refuge Kansai, Japan is a non-profit, non-governmental private organisation with the aim of forming a network of people who love animals, believe in sharing their lives with them, and who work actively to rescue them from suffering. The organisation welcomes volunteers and requires help at their shelter with all types of animal care work. They provide accommodation for those who are willing to assist for more than one day.

Contact details:
595 Noma Ohara, Nose-cho, Toyono-gun, Osaka-fu 563-0131, Japan
Tel: +81 727 37 0712
http://arkbark.tripod.com
ark@arkbark.net

Japan Wildlife Conservation Society (JWCS) exists to conserve wildlife by establishing coexisting relationships between human beings and wildlife. They aim to create a more environmentally aware culture that is interested in conserving the natural environment. Contact to assist as a volunteer.

Contact details:
Japan Wildlife Conservation Society (JWCS), Suehiro Bldg.5F, 2-5-4 Toranomon, Minato-ku, Tokyo 105-0001, Japan
Tel/Fax: +81 3 2595 1171
www.jwcs.org
info@jwcs.org

Okinawan-American Animal Rescue Society, Japan works to rescue, care for, neuter and re-home animals. Voluntary help required

Contact details:
www.oaars.org
oaarsvolunteers@gmail.com

Korea

Korea Animal Rights Advocates is a campaigning organisation working to prevent all types of cruelty to animals. Contact to assist.

Contact details:
101 White-Vill, 208-43 Budam-Dong, Jongno-Gu, SEOUL, 110-817
Tel: 02-3482-0999 (Intl.dial 82 first)
Fax: 02-3482-8835 (Intl.dial 82 first)
http://animalrightskorea.org

Malaysia

Ipoh SPCA rescue, cares for and re-homes animals. Contact to assist.

Contact details:
ISPCA, Lot 38642, 4 ½ Mile Stone, Jalan Gopeng, 31300 Ipoh
Tel: 016-5608905
www.aramisdesign.com/ispca

LASSie (Langkawi Animal Shelter and Sanctuary Foundation), Malaysia. is set-up to receive, rehabilitate and care for neglected, abused and needy animals. The organization also runs the Langkawi Island Animal Clinic - a charity project aimed at the sterilization of the stray cat population. Both are non profit ventures, staffed by volunteers and aimed at improving the lives of unwanted animals.

Contact details:
www.langkawilassie.org.my
info@LangkawiLASSie.org.my

Malaysian National Animal Welfare Foundation (MNAWF) aims to promote a caring Malaysian society through creating awareness and a balanced approach to animal welfare for the well being of animal and mankind. The organisation works to generate awareness and responsibility of all residents in Malaysia on animal welfare as part of the policy towards the creation of a caring Malaysian society. Volunteers are asked to help their work.

Contact details:
Malaysian National Animal Welfare Foundation, Wisma Medivet, 8, Jalan Tun Razak, 50400 Kuala Lumpur, Malaysia
Tel: 6(03) 40435113/40432420
Fax: 6(03) 4041 3660
http://mnawf.org.my/how.html
secretary@mnawf.org.my

PAWS Malaysia works to rescue, care for and re-home companion animals. They are requesting help from volunteers.

SPCA Penang aims to prevent the unnecessary suffering of animals and to ensure responsible pet ownership. Hence the Society acts to prevent cruelty to animals and promotes kindness towards them by fostering public interest. This SPCA patrols the State investigating complaints of cruelty and neglect; visits markets and all the areas where animals may be at risk, collects unwanted animals for adoption and provides transport to pet owners who find difficulty in sending their pets to the veterinary clinic for vaccinations and treatment. They also provide treatment to sick and injured animals though their clinic. They require volunteer help with fostering.

Contact details:
Society For The Prevention Cruelty to Animals, Jalan Jeti, Jelutong 11600, Penang, Malaysia
Tel: (604) 2816559
www.spca-penang.net

SPCA, Sarawak their mission is to act as an advocate on behalf of animals and as an enforcer of their rights; to provide for the well-being of the animals of the State of Sarawak who are abandoned, injured, subjected to unfair or cruel treatment, or otherwise in need; to cultivate in the people of our community an awareness of the animals whose world we share; to promote a bond of mutual assistance between people and animals; and to instill respect for and appreciation of all living things. They welcome volunteers to assist their work.

Contact details:
Mail address: The Sarawak Society for the Prevention of Cruelty to Animals (SSPCA), Lot 1787 Blk No. 233, 6 1/2 Mile Penrissen Road, P.O. Box 2415, 93748 Kuching, Sarawak
Tel: 082-618 200
Fax: 082-616 500
www.sspca.sarawak.com.my
sarawakspca@gmail.com

SPCA, Selangor The aim of the SPCA is to protect defenseless animals and to alleviate their suffering. Established in 1958, the SPCA provides temporary shelter to unwanted animals in Selangor and the Federal Territory. These include mainly cats, dogs, rabbits, hamsters, guinea pigs … usually pets that are no longer desired by their owners. From here, they try to re-home as many as possible but with more than 1,100 animals arriving every month (reaching some 13,000 annually), the shelter is constantly challenged by a shortage of space and limited funds.

Contact details:
SPCA Selangor, Jalan Kerja Air Lama, 68000 Ampang, Selangor
Tel: 03-42565312/42535179
Fax: 03-42528382
www.spca.org.my
enquiries@spca.org.my
spca@streamyx.com

Nepal

AnimalNEPAL.org, Kathmandu, Nepal believes that through awareness raising and practical interventions widespread animal cruelty can be gradually reduced, and that Nepal can ultimately become a model country for animal welfare in the region. Contact to assist as a volunteer.

Contact details:
Mail address: Animal Nepal c/o Saathi Nepal Ekantakuna, Patan P.O. Box 7770, c/o Saathi Nepal, Kathmandu, Nepal
Tel: ++977 9841-334537
www.animalnepal.org
animalnepal@gmail.com

Kathmandu Animal Treatment Centre (KAT) is a non-profit registered charitable organisation dedicated to the humane management of street dogs in Kathmandu, Nepal. The Centre's mission is to create within the Kathmandu Valley a dog friendly, rabies-free, non-breeding street dog population through an Animal Birth Control (ABC) program. KAT uses humane and effective methods to control the stray dog population of Kathmandu Valley. Contact to assist as a volunteer.

Contact details:
Kathmandu Animal Treatment Centre, Chapali Gaon, Budanilkantha, GP Box 8975, EPC 4120, Kathmandu, Nepal
Tel: +977 1 4373169
Fax: +44 (0) 1306 627901
www.katcentre.org.np
katcentre@wlink.com.np

UK Contact details:
Chris Richardson, Turn Lee Barn, Cottonstones, Sowerby Bridge, HX6 3EX UK
Tel: +44 (0) 1422 823591
Chris@turnleebarn.co.uk

Society for Animal Welfare and Management (SAWM), Nepal is established as a non-profitable social organisation for the welfare and management of domestic,farm and wild animals. Contact to assist.

Contact details:
Mail address: Society for Animal Welfare and Management (SAWM Nepal), Baneshwor, Kathmandu, Nepal Post Box 8973, NPC 284
Tel: 977-1-4785518
www.sawmnepal.org.np
info@sawmnepal.com.np

Team for Nature and Wildlife (TNW), Nepal is a not for profit making non-governmental organisation of Nepalese young people. TNW Nepal aims to contribute towards environmental conservation, community empowerment and sustainable rural development with the involvement and empowerment of young people.

Contact details:
Mail address: Team for Nature and Wildlife (TNW), Baneshwor, Kathmandu, Nepal P.O. Box No 7403
Tel: +0977 1 2313933
www.tnwnepal.org
info@tnwnepal.org

Philippines

Animal Welfare Coalition (AWC), Philippines is an alliance of animal welfare advocates and non-government organisations founded in response to the overwhelming need to share resources, establish common goals, minimise expenditure and represent a dominant voice in animal welfare. The organisation advocates for animal welfare and implementation of existing laws, regulations and policies. They rescue, shelter and provide emergency veterinary care and lobby for interest of better laws, rules and regulations covering other animal welfare issues.

Contact details:
Animal Welfare Coalition (AWC), 2F Dacon Building, 2281 Pasong Tamo Extension, 1231 Makati City, Metro Manila, Philippines
Tel: (632)867-4506
Fax: (632)816-7182
www.animalwelfare.com.ph
animalwelfarecoalition@animalwelfare.com.ph

Compassion and Responsibility to Animals (CARA), Philippines have helped and volunteered at the Makati Dog Pound for many years and have recently been successful in reaching a Memorandum of Agreement with the Makati City Hall and the Dog Pound for a better and more humanely managed facility. Many CARA members volunteer the use of their homes to house stray animals. A volunteer form can be downloaded from their website.

Contact details:
www.caraphil.org
infocaraphil@yahoo.com

MyZoo Volunteer Group, Philippines aims to transform zoos in general into effective educational institutions that inspire action towards the conservation of biodiversity; improve the image, facilities and programs of different zoos; and to strengthen links to communities vital to the preservation of endemic species. Download volunteer form to get involved.

Contact details:
Temporary Office Address: 100 Selecta Drive, A Bonifacio Ave., Balintawak Quezon City, Philippines 1106
Tel: +(63) 2 364-2469
Fax: +(63) 2 364-4684
www.myzoofoundation.org
info@MyZooFoundation.org

Sri Lanka

Blue Paw Trust, Sri Lanka works to develop a better environment for animals by focusing on the stray population. The organisation also cares for accident victim, builds awareness at national level to educate the general public on how to take care of animals better.

Contact details:
The Bluepaw Trust, 421/5 Malalsekera, Mawatha, Colombo 07
Tel: 011 2 599799
Fax: 011 2 599800
www.petvetclinic.org/bluepaw/home_bluepaw.htm
bluepaw@petvetclinic.org

Millennium Elephant Foundation (MEF), Sri Lanka is situated on a 15 acre estate known as Samaragiri which has a holding capacity for 10-15 female elephants. In an effort to increase awareness and generate the funds needed for the maintenance and care of the elephants, they actively welcome visitors. International volunteers play an important role contributing to the daily running of the charity. They welcome volunteers from all over the world, with all kinds of skills and interests.

Contact details:
The Millennium Elephant Foundation, Randenyia, Hiriwadunna, Kegalle, Sri Lanka
Tel: (+94) (0)3522 65377 or 66572
Fax: (+94) (0)3522 66572
www.eureka.lk/elefound/
Elefound@sltnet.lk

Tsunami Animal Memorial Trust, Sri Lanka while the devastation brought by the tsunami is no longer front page news, the recovery process will take years. This organisation is dedicated to reducing rabies and dog bites in the disaster zone and refugee camps of Sri Lanka through the combination of vaccinations and neutering. They are currently looking for volunteer veterinary help.

Contact details:
Tsunami Animal-People Alliance, 352/1 Vidyaloka Mawatha, Yowun Pedesa, Hokandara South, Sri Lanka
www.tsunami-animal.org
info@tsunami-animal.org

Singapore

Action for Singapore Dogs (ASD) aims to fulfill their mission through various activities and programs including rescuing, fostering and re-homing of stray and abandoned dogs, advocating neutering as a means of controlling the stray population, heightening public awareness of the responsibilities involved in pet ownership and highlighting the plight of local dogs. They are requesting voluntary assistance with their projects.

Contact details:
Tel: 6100-2737
www.asdsingapore.com
info@asdsingapore.com

Animal Concerns Research and Education Society (ACRES), Singapore has run a number of campaigns both in Singapore and throughout Asia on many different issues and for many different species, all to improve animal welfare and work towards the eradication of animal abuse. The organisation aims to: foster respect and compassion for all animals, improve the living conditions and welfare of animals in captivity, educate people on lifestyle choices which do not involve the abuse of animals and which are environment-friendly. They rely on volunteers to assist their work.

Contact details:
ACRES Wildlife Rescue Centre (AWRC), 91 Jalan Lekar,Singapore 698917
Tel: (+65) 6892 9821
Fax: (+65) 6892 9721
www.acres.org.sg
info@acres.org.sg
volunteer@acres.org.sg

Cat Welfare Society is a charity, run almost entirely by volunteers, whose aim is to improve the welfare of stray cats in Singapore through neutering rather than destruction. They have a comprehensive volunteer programme, contact to assist.

Contact details:
Mail address: Orchard Road, P.O. Box 65, Singapore 912303
www.catwelfare.org
volunteer@catwelfare.org **or** info@catwelfare.org

House Rabbit Socety (HRSS), Singapore was established by a group of concerned volunteers to address the problem of unwanted rabbits in Singapore and to improve rabbits' lives through owner education. They are seeking volunteer foster carers.

Contact details:
www.hrss.net
information@hrss.net.

Singapore SPCA works to rescue, care for and re-home animals in need. They require volunteers to assist in a variety of ways.

Contact details:
31 Mount Vernon Road, S(368054)
www.spca.org.sg
volunteer@spca.org.sg

Taiwan

Animals Taiwan are a volunteer group dedicated to improving the livelihood and treatment of animals in Taiwan. They aim to find solutions for the problem of pet overpopulation through educational activities, adoption efforts and outreach programs. To assist as a volunteer, see more information on their website.

Contact details:
Tel: Taiwan 02-2833-8820
Fax: Taiwan 0943-315-403
www.animalstaiwan.org
volunteer@animalstaiwan.org **or** inquiries@animalstaiwan.org

Thailand

Care for Dogs, Thailand works to reduce the overpopulation of street- and temple dogs. This is achieved through education, neutering, rescuing and offering medical assistance. Assistance required by volunteers.

Contact details:
12 Moo 11, Wiang Dong, Nam Prae, Hang Dong, Chiang Mai 50230, Thailand
Tel: 0847 52 52 55
www.carefordogs.org
contact@carefordogs.org

Elephant Kingdom Nature Park, Thailand works to ensure the safety and well being of the animals under its care. The organisation works to ensure to assist in the survival of the Asian Elephant and improve the quality of life of these magnificent animals and the local indigenous communities, so that future generations can share a vibrant and sustainable world. Volunteers required to assist.

Contact details:
Mail address in Thailand: Elephant Nature Foundation, 1 Ratmakka Road, T. Phra Sing, A. Muang, Chiang Mai, Thailand 50200
Tel: +66-53-272-855
www.elephantnaturefoundation.org

Contact details:
Mail address in UK: Elephant Nature Foundation UK, Hilltop, Windmill Hill, Shere Road, West Horsley, Surrey KT24 6EJ
www.elephantnaturefoundation.org
info@elephantnaturefoundation.org

Koh Phangan Animal Care (PAC), Thailand aim to greatly improve the quality of life of PhaNgan's animals by providing emergency relief and nursing care for illnesses and injuries, while controlling the population growth through the much more humane method of neutering. They also hope to eradicate (or at least minimise) the rabies virus from this island. Volunteers required to assist their work.

Contact details:
Mail address: Phangan Animal Care, P.O. Box 70, Thong-Sala, Koh Phangan, Surat Thani, Thailand
Centre address: PhaNgan Animal Centre, 14/1 Moo 4, Woktum, Koh PhaNgan, Suratthani 84280, Thailand
Tel: (0066) 898757513 (International) or 0898757513 (within Thailand)
http://pacthailand.org
info@pacthailand.org

Phuket Animal Welfare Society (PAWS), Thailand is a licensed animal welfare charity that is well known amongst the local community. They provide fixed and mobile clinics that are available to neuter and assist animals. They require voluntary help, particularly from vets.

Contact details:
http://phuketdir.com/paws
info@phuket-animal-welfare.com

Soi Cat And Dog (SCAD), Bangkok, Thailand was established in 2002 as a not-for-profit organisation with realistic goals: to reduce the number and improve the lives of Bangkok's strays and, in so doing, create a happier and healthier environment for all to enjoy. The organisation involves residents and local businesses in neighbourhoods affected by large numbers of strays, working with locals to tackle the problem at community level using humane and effective methods. SCAD provides appropriate information on the benefits of animal birth control, shares the knowledge required to be responsible pet owners and hopes to kindle in people the belief that showing kindness to all the animals that share our world has far better consequences for humankind than apathy or cruelty. They require the following voluntary help: Translators (Thai/English), Educational assistants (Thai and English speakers, Window dressers (for ReTails Store), Event planners, Dog trainers, Electricians/Builders/Painters/Plumbers/Architects/Gardeners. Contact for further information.

Contact details:
SCAD c/o ReTails Too, 289 Pridi Phanomyong Soi 42, Sukhumvit 71, Prakanong, Wattana, Bangkok 10110
Tel: +66 (0) 2713 3354
www.scadbangkok.org
info@scadbangkok.org

Soi Dog Foundation, Thailand aims to reduce the number of unwanted dogs and cats and to better the lives and living conditions of the street and stray dogs and feral cats in Thailand, currently focused on the island of Phuket. Contact to assist as a volunteer.

Contact details:
Mail address: Soi Dog Foundation, c/o John Dalley, 57/61 Moo 4, Srisoonthorn Road, Cherngtalay, Amphur Talang, Phuket, 83110, Thailand
Shelter address: 167/9 Moo4, Soi Mai Khao 10, Tambon Mai Khao, Amphur Talang, Phuket 83110
www.soidog.org

Thai Animal Rescue Foundation takes it's name from two dogs - Noi & Star rescued from the island of Koh Tao, Thailand. On this island there is no RSPCA, no PDSA, no animal's shelters, no sanctuaries, no medical care of any kind for the animal population. Ravaged by mange, hungry and often abused, many of them don't survive. Volunteers urgently required.

Contact details:
Koh Tao Animal Clinic (Thailand)
Tel: +66 (0)8 10 90 53 72
www.kohtaoanimalclinic.org

Contact details:
UK: Noistar Thai Animal Rescue Foundation, Stable House, 1A Westfield Place, Clifton, Bristol, UK BS8 4AY
www.kohtaoanimalclinic.org

Thai Animal Guardians Association (TAGA), Thailand aims to protect animals, promote kindness, and relieve animal suffering. They have three major areas of work: animal rescue (for animals in need of emergency relief); animal clinic (a less expensive alternative for pet owners, providing treatment to animals); and mobile clinic (providing neutering and spaying services to animal lovers to control the population of strays). Other work includes campaigns against elephants entering cities and dog skin and meat trade. Volunteer application form can be found on their website.

Contact details:
Thai Animal Guardians Association, 45 Moo 4, Sukrapiban 3 Rd., Saphansoong, Bangkok, Thailand 10240
Tel: +66 2 728 1658 (International) or (02) 728 1658 (Thailand)
Tel/Fax: (02) 373-2886
www.thaiaga.org
thaiaga@hotmail.com **or** thaiaga@gmail.com **or** roger2@truemail.co.th

Thai Society for the Conservation of Wild Animals, Thailand welcomes volunteers with a veterinary background who are able to assist with both wild animals and stray dogs. Biologists and zoologists are asked to conduct fieldwork towards wildlife conservation and/or behavioural studies. To volunteer, contact the organisation with a bit of information about yourself including the timeframe that you are available to assist.

Contact details:
Thai Society for the Conservation of Wild Animals, 517 Soi Ratchata Phan, Rajaprarop Road, Makkasan, Bangkok 10400 Thailand
Tel: 02+2480405
Fax: 02+248-0403
www.tscwa.org
info@tscwa.org

Wildlife Friends of Thailand works to rescue wild animals from places where they are maltreated and/or neglected, and help them to spend the rest of their lives in a sanctuary as close to the natural environment as possible with the best possible care. Educate people about animal cruelty and prevent hunting and promote conservation. Volunteers required.

Contact details:
108 Moo 6, Tha Mai Ruak, 76130 Thailand
Tel: 032-458135
www.wfft.org

Wild Animal Rescue Foundation, Thailand has become one of Thailand's leading advocates for nature conservation. Currently WAR operates four different wildlife sanctuaries that are focused on providing appropriate housing and care for animals placed under their protection. Many of the animals in WAR's care, including gibbons, macaques, bears and tigers are former pets that have been maltreated, or have grown too big and unmanageable for their owners. WAR's goal is to rehabilitate these animals wherever possible and return them to the wild. However many animals are too disabled or have been too traumatised to be able survive on their own. For these animals, the long-term care offered in the sanctuaries is their only hope of survival. Volunteers required.

Contact details:
Bangkok office: 65/1 3rd Floor, Sukhumvit 55, Klongton, Wattana, Bangkok 10110
Tel: +6627129715, 7129515
Fax: + 662 7129778
www.warthai.org
war@warthai.org **or** volunteer@warthai.org

Contact details:
Phuket Office: 104/3 M.3 Paklock, Talang, Phuket 83110
Tel/Fax: +6676 260491, + 6676 260492
www.warthai.org
grp@warthai.org **or** volunteer@warthai.org

Contact details:
Ranong Office: 15/1 M.1 Kumpuan, Suksumran Subdistrict, Ranong 83150
Tel: +6677 870 247
www.warthai.org
wared@warthai.org **or** volunteer@warthai.org

Contact details:
Chiang Mai Office: 218 Group 3, Tambon Thadua, Doi Tao District, ChaingMai 50260
Tel/Fax: +66 53 833 119
www.warthai.org
warf_reforst@warthai.org **or** volunteer@warthai.org

Contact details:
Lopburi Office: 24 Prayakumjud Rd. Tambon Tha Hin, Muang District, Lopburi
volunteer@warthai.org

Vietnam

Education for Nature Vietnam (ENV) their mission is to foster greater understanding amongst the Vietnamese public about environmental issues of local, national and global significance, ranging from protection of wildlife and natural ecosystems to climate change. They highlight the need to protect Vietnam's rich natural heritage and the living world, and also encourage greater public participation in achieving this important and challenging task. They need volunteer assistance to stop wildlife crimes.

Contact details:
Mail address: Education for Nature – Vietnam N5. IF1, Lane 192 Thai Thinh Street, Dong Da District, Ha Noi, P.O.Box 222, Hanoi
Tel/Fax: (84 4) 3514-8850
www.envietnam.org env@fpt.vn

Endangered Primate Rescue Centre (EPRC), Vietnam is based at Cuc Phuong National Park and is dedicated to the rescue, rehabilitation, research and conservation of the endangered primates of Vietnam. Volunteering at the EPRC gives you a unique opportunity to directly help endangered wildlife whilst experiencing Vietnam.

Contact details:
Endangered Primate Resue Center, Cuc Phuong National Park, Nho Quan District, Ninh Binh Province, Vietnam
Tel: 0084 30 848 002
Fax: 0084 30 848 088
www.primatecenter.org
t.nadler@mail.hut.edu.vn

Wildlife at Risk (WAR), Vietnam is dedicated to the long-term conservation of Vietnam's threatened biodiversity. It aims to reduce the pressure on Vietnam's wildlife by helping to build local capacity to implement legislation, raise environmental awareness and develop alternatives to the unsustainable expoloitation of Vietnam's natural resources. The WAR sponsored Cu Chi Rescue Centre always has a need for volunteers with relevant skills, particularly qualified vets or those with experience of animal husbandry. They also need volunteers for other jobs at the centre, including maintenance, cleaning and helping with visitors. WAR has joined forces with Hanoi-based Education For Nature - Vietnam (ENV) to wage a nationwide, long-term campaign against the illegal wildlife trade. ENV has a well-established network of volunteers who help to monitor and combat the wildlife trade. WAR is actively recruiting volunteers on ENV's behalf in Ho Chi Minh City and the southern provinces. Every crime that volunteers report will be pursued with the relevant law enforcement agency. In other words, your volunteer activities will have an immediate and direct impact. To get involved, visit their website and complete their volunteer application form.

Contact details:
202/10 Nguyen Xi Street, Ward 26, Binh Thanh Dist, Ho Chi Minh City, Vietnam.
Tel: (84) (8) 3899 7314/3899 7315
Fax: (84) (8) 3899 7316
www.wildlifeatrisk.org
info@wildlifeatrisk.org

"A man is truly ethical only when he obeys the compulsion to help all life which he is able to assist, and shrinks from injuring anything that lives." - Albert Schweitzer

MIDDLE EAST

"I hold that the more helpless a creature, the more entitled it is to protection by man from the cruelty of man" - Mahatma Gandhi

Bahrain

Bahrain SPCA aims to: "Foster a public sentiment of kindness to animals and to oppose and prevent cruelty to them. Provide food, shelter & medical assistance to all abandoned animals and those in need of care. Successfully home all healthy animals coming through the Sanctuary. Encourage the spaying and neutering of all animals in Bahrain, both owned and stray. Discourage and oppose the import & breeding of animals, particularly for financial gain". Contact to volunteer to assist at their sanctuary.

Contact details:
Mail address: P.O. Box 26666, Manama, Bahrain
Tel: +973 17 591 231
www.bspca.org
info@bspca.info **or** catsdogs@baleco.com.bh

Israel

Israel Cat Lovers' Society, Israel runs a neutering programme for stray cats, provides veterinary assistance where necessary, rescues and cares for cats in need, runs a education and advocacy project. Contact to assist.

Contact details:
www.isracat.org.il

Safe Haven for Donkeys in the Holy Land (SHADH), Israel exists to promote the importance of basic welfare of donkeys, and wherever possible to teach compassion to achieve long-term changes for the better. They organisation has neutering programmes and ensures that any animal found abandoned on highways is safely transported to the rescue centre, where they are guaranteed to live free from the burdens of toil, stress and suffering, until they can be re-homed. Voluntary help required.

Contact details:
UK: The Old Dairy, Springfield Farm, Lewes Road, Scaynes Hill, Haywards Heath, West Sussex, RH17 7NG
Tel: 01444 831177
Fax: +44 (01444) 831172
www.safehaven4donkeys.org
info@safehaven4donkeys.org

Spay Israel is affiliated with Spay USA, an American organization dedicated to providing affordable spaying and neutering services throughout the USA. Today, over 8,000 vets take part in the American network. The organisation shares the belief that spaying and neutering is the only form of humane animal population control. Contact to assist as a volunteer.

Contact details:
Tel: 03-577-4007
www.spayisrael.org.il

Kuwait

PAWS-Kuwait are an active group of local and international volunteers committed to protecting animal welfare in Kuwait. PAWS aim in forming, in early 2004, was to open Kuwait's first officially licensed shelter for injured, lost or abandoned animals. Until PAWS formed, little was being done to address the issue of stray, abandoned and injured animals in our country. Volunteers are needed to assist in many ways including fostering.

Contact details:
www.paws-kuwait.org

Lebanon

Beirut for the Ethical Treatment of Animals (BETA) works to assist the animals in Beirut with rescue, care, neutering and more. Contact to assist as a volunteer.

Contact details:
Tel: (961) 70 248765
www.betalebanon.org
volunteer@betalebanon.org

Homeless Dogs and Cats Society, Lebanon assists companion animals with shelter and medical care – they are requesting voluntary assistance with their work.

Contact details:
www.hcds.5u.com
homeless_cd_society@hotmail.com

Pro Animals Lebanon works to rescue, care, re-home, neuter and educate. Contact to get involved as a volunteer.

Contact details:
Tel: 70 223 808
www.animalslebanon.org
contact@animalslebanon.org

Oman

Animal Rescue Centre (ARC), Oman is run by a group of Omani Nationals and International volunteers who work with abandoned, stray and injured animals from the streets of Muscat. They are a non profit group with the aim to reduce the number of stray animals through their catch/neuter an release programme. They also try and re-home abandoned animals left on the streets. Contact to assist as a volunteer.

Contact details:
http://animal.rescueme.org/om

Saudi Arabia

Peoples Animal Welfare Society, Saudi Arabia is a group of volunteers dedicated to helping homeless animals in the Eastern Province of Saudi Arabia. Their goals are to reduce the population of unwanted animals, provide care as needed to support the health and welfare of homeless animals and promote responsible pet guardianship. They have a comprehensive volunteer programme and volunteer job descriptions.

Contact details:
www.saudipaws.com
paws@saudipaws.com

United Arab Emirates

Feline Friends of Abu-Dhabi helps cats in the United Arab Emirates. Volunteers rescue and re-home stray cats and kittens; promote the control of street cats by neutering and provide care and relief to sick and injured cats and kittens. Download a volunteer form from their website.

Contact details:
Tel: Abu Dhabi 050 582-2916
www.felinefriendsuae.com
info@felinefriendsuae.com

Feline Friends of Dubai is staffed by volunteers who all have one common goal - to bring relief and care to the feral/stray, domestic and abandoned feline population in the United Arab Emirates. The group's aims can be summarised as follows: "To provide care and relief to sick and injured cats and kittens. To rescue from the streets tame and abandoned cats and kittens and foster them until good, loving and permanent homes can be found. To promote the control of the feral and domestic cat population within the Emirates by following a programme of spaying and neutering. To provide guidance and support for cat owners and to encourage responsible care and ownership. To encourage and educate the public to care and respect the cat population whether they are domestic or stray, via publications, animal related events and visits to schools". They require volunteer help with fostering, fundraising, etc - contact to assist.

Contact details:
www.felinefriendsdubai.com
volunteers@felinefriendsdubai.com **or** info@felinefriendsdubai.com

K9 Friends, United Arab Emirates As a result of the formation of K9 Friends in 1989, thousands of dogs have been homed. In addition to this, they have funded veterinary treatment, reunited lost dogs with their owners and have been instrumental in homing an incalculable number dogs, as well as offering counsel to dog owners and rescuers. At the same time, they have raised awareness of the plight of dogs in the U.A.E. through a variety of ways. Volunteers are required to assist in numerous ways.

Contact details:
K9 Friends, P.O. Box 72741, Dubai, United Arab Emirates
Tel: +971- 4- 8858031
Fax: +971-4-8858952
www.k9friends.com
info@k9friends.com

"Animals are reliable, many full of love, true in their affections, predictable in their actions, grateful and loyal. Difficult standards for people to live up to." - Alfred A. Montapert

AUSTRALASIA

"The basis of all animal rights should be the Golden Rule: we should treat them as we would wish them to treat us, were any other species in our dominant position." - Christine Stevens

Cook Islands

Esther Honey Foundation (EHF), Cook Islands works to bring compassionate and affordable veterinary and education services to South Pacific Island companion animals in need. EHF supports the only veterinary clinic for the Cook Islands' thousands of companion animals. Volunteers required and accommodation may be provided in exchange for volunteer services.

Contact details:
www.estherhoney.org   info@estherhoney.org

Fiji Islands

SPCA Fiji believes that all animals are equally deserving of our compassionate consideration, whether domesticated or wild animal. They need volunteer help with animal care, maintenance, cleaning, fundraising and more.

Contact details:
Mail address: P.O. Box 14216, Suva, Fiji Islands
Tel: +679 3301266/3304632
Fax: +679 3315234
www.spcafiji.org.fj   spca@connect.com.fj

Guam

Guam Animals in Need (GAIN) their charitable purposes include the prevention of cruelty to animals, education of the public concerning animal welfare, and the implementation and enforcement of good laws pertaining to animals. They need volunteers to help at their shelter with walking, playing, feeding, grooming, etc.

Contact details:
Mail address: P.O. Box 22365, GMF Guam 96921
Street address: Chalan Setbisio, Marine Corps Drive, Yigo
www.guamanimals.org/index.html   guamanimals@yahoo.com

Papua New Guinea

Papua New Guinea RSPCA is a charitable organisation committed to the promotion of the welfare of "all creatures great and small" in Papua New Guinea through: The prevention of cruelty to all animals. The promotion of responsible ownership and management of all animals.

Contact details:
Mail address: RSPCA of PNG, RSPCA Veterinary Clinic, Membership Secretary, P.O. Box 111, Port Moresby, NCD, Papua New Guinea
Tel: +675 325 2363
Fax: +675 325 6833
www.rspca.org.pg

New Zealand

Animal Rights Legal Advocacy Network (ARLAN) is New Zealand's premier animal law organisation. Made up of more than 100 legal professionals from around the country, ARLAN works to promote and protect the interests of those who cannot speak for themselves. ARLAN campaigns and launches legal actions aimed to improve the law relating to animals and win them the legal protections they deserve. They rely heavily on their network of volunteers but, due to the nature of their work, you must be a legal professional or law student to assist as a volunteer.

Contact details:
Mail address: P.O. Box 6065, Wellesley Street, Auckland, New Zealand
www.arlan.org.nz
contact@arlan.org.nz

Auckland Cat Rescue (ACR) was established in response to the enormous problem of stray and unwanted cats and kittens in Auckland. They endeavour to operate as an organisation that promotes animal welfare, and runs low cost neutering campaigns. They require volunteer help with bookkeeping and fundraising.

natasha@aucklandcatrescue.org

Cats in Need Trust, Auckland this is an organisation that rescues cats and kittens that are unwanted, abandoned, or abused. All cats that leave the cattery are spayed or neutered, wormed, and vaccinated. Volunteers are particularly needed for evenings and weekends. Jobs include cleaning, preparing food and playing with the cats and kittens helps socialise them and keep them happy.

Contact details:
Tel: 09 276 9960 or 027 426 4372
catsnjammas@maxnet.co.nz
www.catsinneedtrust.org.nz

Cats Protection League, Wellington is a purely voluntary New Zealand charity devoted solely to the welfare of cats. Their objectives are: to rescue stray and unwanted cats and kittens, rehabilitate and re-home them where possible, to inform the public on the care of cats and kittens and to encourage the neutering of all cats. The organisation requires voluntary help with cat trapping, fostering, transport, fundraising, etc.

Contact details:
Tel: 0064 4 3899 668
www.cpl-wellington.org.nz
catsprotectionleaguewgtn@hotmail.com

Chained Dog Awareness Society of NZ (CDANZ) was formed to "make people aware of what is going on right under your noses in our neighbourhood all over this country in increasing numbers to dogs who are permanently chained/tethered and for whom life is a living hell". Their aim is to inform the general public about the cruelty of long-term chaining or incarceration of dogs and to alleviate the animals' suffering where possible through education and support of their existing owners. The organisation requires help with a wide variety of volunteer jobs - contact to assist.

Contact details:
www.petsonthenet.co.nz/cdanz.htm
CHAINEDDOG@GMAIL.COM

Dogwatch Sanctuary Trust, Christchurch cares for abandoned dogs who have not been re-homed from the Pound. They take over the legal ownership of these dogs and they are cared for by volunteers at their purpose built Adoption Centre until they are re-homed. The organisation is currently looking for volunteers to help on week days - volunteers must be confident with dogs.

Contact details:
230 Dyers Road, Bromley, Christchurch 8062
Tel: (03) 981 4708
www.dogwatch.co.nz
info@dogwatch.co.nz

Donkey and Mule Protection Trust exists to inform the public and to protect and rehabilitate and re-home donkeys and mules in need. Contact to assist as a volunteer with their fostering project.

Contact details:
www.donkey-mule-trust.org.nz

Greyhounds as Pets (GAP) is an independent charitable trust established by Greyhound Racing New Zealand to find pet homes for retired racing greyhounds. Due to misconceptions about the breed, greyhounds are generally not considered when choosing a pet, and while many racing owners try to re-home their dogs, there is a definite lack of good homes. GAP aims to find loving homes for as many ex-racers as possible and is working to inform the public about the true and wonderful nature of greyhounds! Contact to assist with fostering and more.

Contact details:
Mail address: P.O. Box 48-217, Silverstream, Upper Hutt 5142
Tel: 04 528 0460
www.greyhoundsaspets.org.nz
jacqui@greyhoundsaspets.org.nz

Greymouth Branch of the RNZSPCA RNZSPCA stands for the Royal New Zealand Society for the Prevention of Cruelty to Animals. It is a voluntary organisation that, through its district branches, provides help to animals and owners 24 hours a day, seven days a week. The organisation requires volunteers to assist in a variety of ways.

Mail address: Greymouth SPCA, P.O. Box 32, 34 Gresson Street, Greymouth 7801
Tel: 0-3-768 5223
greyspca@xtra.co.nz

Global Volunteer Network, Lower Hutt The aim of New Zealand program is twofold; first they provide volunteer assistance to conservation groups and conservation projects within New Zealand. In return they offer volunteers a unique and diverse experience that will expose them to many aspects of NZ conservation. Volunteers form an integral part of habitat restoration, wildlife monitoring and environmental/conservation research projects. More information available on their website.

Contact details:
Mail address: Global Volunteer Network Ltd., P.O. Box 30-968, Lower Hutt, New Zealand
Street address: Level 2, 105 High Street, Lower Hutt, New Zealand
Tel: +64 4 920 1451
Fax: +64 4 920 1456
www.globalvolunteernetwork.org
info@volunteer.org.nz

Hearing Dogs for Deaf People, NZ specially trained Hearing Dogs provide valuable services to deaf and hearing-impaired people in much the same way as guide dogs for blind people. In 1998 Hearing Dogs for Deaf People New Zealand was formally established and incorporated as a charitable trust. Previously no organisation for training and placing these dogs existed in New Zealand. Hearing Dogs for Deaf People have the same access rights as Guide Dogs for the blind - they are allowed into all public places, including food premises. Contact to assist as a volunteer with socialising dogs and doing public talks.

Contact details:
Mail address: P.O. Box 8117, New Plymouth 4342, New Zealand
Tel: (06) 769 5000
Fax: (06) 769 5400
www.hearingdogs.org.nz
info@hearingdogs.org.nz

Auckland SPCA Horse Welfare Auxilliary Inc was founded to prevent the ill treatment of horses exported to Europe for slaughter. It has grown to become one of the world's leading international equine welfare charities. ILPH was established in New Zealand in 1990 to act as an equine lobby group and equine welfare watchdog. Volunteers assist with fundraising etc.

Contact details:
Mail address: P.O. Box 10-368, Te Rapa, Hamilton, New Zealand
Tel: 07-849-0678
Fax: 07-849-9034
www.horsetalk.co.nz/ilph/
ilphnz@xtra.co.nz

Karori Wildlife Sanctuary, Karori has over 400 volunteers assisting their work - it is one of the largest volunteer organisations in Wellington. The Sanctuary simply would not exist and not be the success it currently is without the dedication and immeasurable hours put in by the community organisations and individuals involved. Volunteering at the Sanctuary is extremely rewarding and offers the ability to learn new skills in a sociable environment. Tasks are varied and range from: fence monitoring, bird feeding and weeding through to office support, boat skippering and guiding.

Contact details:
Mail address: Karori Sanctuary Trust, P.O. Box 9267, Marion Square, Wellington 6141, New Zealand
Tel: +64 4 920 9200
Fax: +64 4 920 9000
www.sanctuary.org.nz

Lonely Miaow Association, Auckland is dedicated to the rescue and care of stray and abandoned cats and kittens in the greater Auckland area. Every day they receive calls about injured, starving and lonely cats and kittens. Volunteers are required to assist the organisation in a number of ways.

Contact details:
Mail address: P.O. Box 125 138, St Heliers, Auckland 1740
Tel: 09 575 9760
www.lonelymiaow.co.nz
info@lonelymiaow.co.nz

Project Jonah this organisation has pioneered rescue techniques, and shares this technology and expertise with the rest of the world. Much of their work comes from a practical 'let's just do it' approach. At the heart of Project Jonah is a passionate belief that caring about marine mammals is simply the right thing to do. They are reliant on volunteers to assist with a variety of tasks including, beach litter clean-ups, raising awareness, developing campaigns, assisting with administration. They also require volunteers to work as Marine Mammal Medics - contact to get involved.

Contact details:
Mail address: P.O. Box 8376, Symonds Street, Auckland, 1150
Tel: 09 302 3106
Fax: 09 376 4544
www.projectjonah.org.nz
info@projectjonah.org.nz

Save Animals From Experiments (SAFE), Auckland continues to be at the forefront of exposing animal abuse within New Zealand and around the globe. In 1932, an anti-vivisection organisation called The Auckland Branch of the British Union for the Abolition of Vivisection was formed in Auckland, New Zealand. The focus of the group broadened to incorporate other practices and eventually, in 1978, a name change was made and Save Animals From Experiments was launched. Contact to assist as a volunteer.

Contact details:
Christchurch Office: Level 1, 145 Armagh Street, Christchurch, New Zealand
Mail address: PO Box 13 366, Christchurch, New Zealand
Tel: +64 3 379 9711
Fax: +64 3 379 9711
www.safe.org.nz
safe@safe.org.nz

Contact details:
Auckland Office: Maranatha Building, Room 3, 63 Great North Road, Ponsonby
Mail address: P.O. Box 5750, Wellesley Street, Auckland, New Zealand
Tel: +64 9 361 5646
Fax: +64 9 361 5644
www.safe.org.nz
auckland@safe.org.nz

Contact details:
Wellington Office: Trades Hall, Room 11, Level 1, 126 Vivian Street, Wellington, New Zealand
Mail address: P.O. Box 6442, Wellington, New Zealand
Tel: +64 4 802 4460
Fax: +64 4 802 4460
www.safe.org.nz
wellington@safe.org.nz

SPCA Otago The main objective of the SPCA is perhaps contained in its motto - "we speak for those who cannot speak for themselves". They aim to promote kindness to animals and prevent or suppress cruelty to them. This organisation desperately requires more volunteers - contact to assist.

Contact details:
OTAGO S.P.C.A, 1 Torridon Street, Opoho, Dunedin
Tel: (03) 473 8252
www.petpals.co.nz
spca@petpals.co.nz

SPCA Auckland works to encourage the humane treatment of all animals and to prevent cruelty that may be inflicted on them. They require volunteers to assist with the over 20,000 animals that they assist each year.

Contact details:
Mail address: P.O. Box 43221, Mangere, Manukau 2153, New Zealand
Street address: Auckland Animal Village, 50 Westney Road, Mangere South, Manukau 2022, New Zealand
Tel: 09 2567300
Fax: 09 2567314
www.spca.org.nz
volunteer_coordinator@spca.org.nz **or** info@spca.org.nz

SPCA Wellington is an animal welfare charity consisting of two animals shelters. Volunteer work involves many duties. Washing bedding is just one of the many duties that our volunteers carry out. As well as shelter work we aim to improve the welfare of all animals, and actively campaign against certain issues such as factory farming practices.

Contact details:
Newtown Animal Centre
Mail address: P.O. Box 7069, Newtown, Wellington 6242, New Zealand
Street address: 305 Mansfield Street, Newtown, Wellington 6021, New Zealand
Fax: 04 389 5577
www.wellingtonspca.org.nz

Contact details:
Waikanae Animal Centre
Mail address: P.O. Box 250, Waikanae 5250, New Zealand
Street address: Main Road North, Waikanae, New Zealand
Tel: 04 293 4292
Fax: 04 293 7588
www.wellingtonspca.org.nz

SPCA Nelson works to investigate and deal with complaints of cruelty and neglect, uphold the laws relating to the treatment of animals and take prosecutions where necessary, give sanctuary to animals in distress, re-home suitable animals where possible, ensure that animals which cannot be kept alive for whatever reason are humanely euthanised, assist with public education and promote responsible pet ownership. The organisation requires volunteers for a variety of jobs including driving the ambulance and deal with the public.

Contact details:
Mail address: 379 Waimea Road, P.O. Box 50, Nelson
Tel: (03) 547 7171
Fax: (03) 547 7959
www.nelsonspca.org.nz
info@nelsonspa.co.nz

SPCA Wairarapa provides a twenty four hour, seven day a week rescue service for injured and unclaimed animals. They provide shelter, care and re-homing for lost, abandoned and unwanted pets. They also investigate claims of cruelty. Contact to assist as a volunteer.

Contact details:
299 Ngaumutawa Road, Masterton
Tel: 377 1912
Fax: 377 1298
www.spcawairarapa.org.nz
spca@spcawairarapa.org.nz

SPCA Waikato, Hamilton aims to advance the welfare of all animals in New Zealand by: "Preventing Cruelty to Animals, Alleviating suffering of animals, Promoting their policies through education and advocacy". They urgently require volunteer help with a variety of tasks including; walking, cleaning, feeding, fostering - contact to assist.

Contact details:
219 Ellis Street, Frankton, Hamilton
Tel: (07) 847 4868
Fax: (07) 846 9221
www.waikato.spca.net.nz
manager.spca@xtra.co.nz **or** admin.spca@xtra.co.nz

SPCA Taupo works to assist animals in need in Taupo. They require volunteers to assist in a variety of ways including at their animal hospital - contact for further information.

Contact details:
Taupo SPCA Animal Centre, 131 Centennial Drive, P.O. Box 493, Taupo, New Zealand
Tel: 07 378 4396/07 378 0825
Fax: 07 378 0827
www.spcataupo.org.nz
info@spcataupo.org.nz

SPCA Te Awamutu provides help to animals and owners 24 hours a day, seven days a week. They investigate and deal with complaints of cruelty and neglect; uphold the laws relating to the treatment of animals and take prosecutions where necessary. They provide sanctuary to animals in distress, re-home animals and assist with public education and promote responsible pet ownership. Contact to assist with volunteering.

Contact details:
Mail address: Care Shelter, Te Awamutu, P.O. Box 386
Street address: 229 Bruce Berquist Drive, Te Awamutu
Tel: 07 871 5222
www.teawamutu.net/spca

SPCA Whangarei the area this organisation covers stretches all the way north to Towai, south to Te Hana, and west to Tangiteroria. Around 3,000 animals are brought to this centre each year and each year they investigate around 400 animal abuse complaints. They rely on volunteers to assist with their work.

Contact details:
Mail address: Whangarei SPCA, P.O. Box 564, Whangarei, New Zealand
Street address: 143 Kioreroa Road, Whangarei, Northland, New Zealand
Tel: (Area Code 0140) (09) 438 9161
Fax: 09 430 0887
www.whangareispca.co.nz

SPCA Marlborough assists companion animals and needs volunteering help with walking, fostering animals, cleaning, fundraising and more - contact to assist.

Contact details:
Mail address: Foxes Island Road, P.O. Box 115, Renwick, Marlborough
Tel: 03 572 9156
Fax: 03 572 9456
www.spcamarlborough.com
marlspca@xtra.co.nz

SPCA Fielding and Districts needs voluntary staff to assist with attend to the needs of animals in the Feilding and Districts area 24 hours a day, 7 days a week, 365 days a year. Contact to assist with a variety of animals.

Contact details:
Tel: (06) 3236407
www.spcafeilding.org.nz
spca.feilding@inspire.net.nz

SPCA Canterbury works to "speak out for those that cannot speak for themselves". The animal shelter cares for dogs, cats, rabbits, sheep and horses. Contact to assist as a volunteer.

Contact details:
Mail address: SPCA Canterbury, P.O. Box 16880, Hornby, Christchurch 8441
www.spcacanterbury.org.nz

Save Animals from Exploitation (SAFE), Christchurch continues to be at the forefront of exposing animal abuse within New Zealand and around the globe. Public awareness campaigns and political lobbying are the main means used to help expose and question the use of animals in cruel and needless experiments. To volunteer for this organisation, see further details on their website.

Contact details:
Christchurch Office, Level 1, 145 Armagh Street, Christchurch, New Zealand
Mail address: P.O. Box 13 366, Christchurch, New Zealand
Tel: +64 3 379 9711
Fax: +64 3 379 9711
www.safe.org.nz
sacha@safe.org.nz

Contact details:
Auckland Office, Marantha Building, Room 3, 63 Great North Road, Ponsonby
Mail address: P.O. Box 5750, Wellesley Street, Auckland, New Zealand
Tel: +64 9 361 5646
Fax: +64 9 361 5644
www.safe.org.nz
auckland@safe.org.nz

Contact details:
Wellington Office, Trades Hall, Room 11, Level 1, 126 Vivian Street, Wellington, New Zealand
Mail address: P.O. Box 6442, Wellington, New Zealand
Tel: +64 4 802 4460
Fax: +64 4 802 4460
www.safe.org.nz
wellington@safe.org.nz

Upper Hut Animal Rescue Society works to show kindness and justice to all living creatures, to assist sick, wounded and homeless animals and to assist in the spaying of animals. Contact to get involved with their work as a volunteer.

Contact details:
Upper Hutt Animal Rescue Society, 4 Kings Charles Dr, Kingsley Heights, Upper Hutt, 5018
Tel: (04) 526-2672
www.animalrescue.org.nz
animalrescue@xtra.co.nz

World Wildlife Fund (WWF) NZ WWF-New Zealand, with the help of the Tindall Foundation, supports groups around the country who are taking action for their environment through habitat protection projects. They have a list of some of those projects on their website. Please contact them to see what volunteering vacancies they have available.

Contact details:
Mail address: WWF-New Zealand, P.O. Box 6237, Marion Square, Wellington 6141
Tel: 0800 4357 993
Fax: 04 499 2954
www.wwf.org.nz

Contact details:
WWF New Zealand, Wellington, The Treehouse Botanic Garden, Glenmore Street, Wellington, New Zealand
Tel: +64 4 499 2930/+64 4 499 2954
www.wwf.org.nz

World Society for the Protection of Animals, NZ WSPA's work is focused on four priority animal welfare areas: Companion animals - responsible pet ownership, humane stray management and preventing cruelty. Commercial exploitation of wildlife - intensive farming and cruel management and killing of wild animals for food or products. Farm animals - intensive farming, long distance transportation and slaughter of domestic animals for food. Disaster relief for animals - providing care to animals in distress from man-made or natural disasters. They require voluntary assistance in their Auckland office.

Contact details:
Tel: 0800 500 9772
www.wspa.org.nz

"The soul is the same in all living creatures, although the body of each is different." – Hippocrates

Australia

"Animals cannot speak, but can you and I not speak for them and represent them? Let us all feel their silent cry of agony and let us all help that cry to be heard in the world." - Rukmini DeviArundale

Act, Rescue, Foster (ARF), Canberra aims to save and improve the lives of dogs through the rescuing and re-homing of unwanted dogs, educating the community about responsible dog companionship and working with local pounds to help achieve, develop and implement minimum destruction policies and procedures. Volunteers can assist with fostering, transportation, marketing, etc.

Contact details:
Mail address: ACT Rescue and Foster (ARF) Inc., PO Box 1308, Woden, 2606
www.fosterdogs.org
info@fosterdogs.org

Animal Rights and Rescue (ARRG) New South Wales is a no kill, foster care, self funding group that cares for animals in need. They currently require volunteer foster carers.

Contact details:
Mail address: Animal Rights and Rescue Group Inc., P.O. Box 987, Lismore NSW 2480
Tel: 02 6622 1881
Fax: 02 6622 1881
www.animalrights.org.au
nonkill@animalrights.org.au

Animal Welfare League (AWL) Queensland cares for over 10,000 stray and abandoned companion animals every year and re-homes animals at the highest rate in Australia. They are non government funded and rely on volunteers for assistance.

Contact details:
Coombabah Rehoming Centre, Shelter Road, Coombabah
Tel: 07 5509 9000
Fax: 07 5594 0131
www.awlqld.com.au
volunteering@awlqld.com.au

Contact details:
Stapylton Rehoming Centre, Rossmans Road, Stapylton
Tel: 07 3807 3782
Fax: 07 3807 0580
www.awlqld.com.au
volunteering@awlqld.com.au

Animal Welfare League (AWL) of South Australia receives no government funding to pay for operating costs and therefore rely upon the support of volunteers, we would not be able to achieve our important work. The League was originally built by Volunteers and as such they recognise the importance of their continued contribution.

Contact details:
Street address: Wingfield, 1-19 Cormack Road, Wingfield, SA 5013
Tel: (08) 8348 1300
Fax: (08) 8268 9545
www.animalwelfare.com.au
wecare@animalwelfare.com.au

Animal Aid, Victoria (VAAT) is an Animal Welfare organisation dedicated to the care of all lost, unwanted and abused animals, and is bound by the Code of Practice for Animal Shelters. Voluntary animal jobs are described on their website.

Contact details:
Mail address: P.O. Box 34, Coldstream VIC 3770, Australia
Street address: 35 Killara Road, Coldstream VIC 3770, Australia
Tel: (03) 9739 0300
www.animalaid.org.au
enquiries@animalaid.org.au or kblizzard@animalaid.org.au

Animals Australia is Australia's largest and most dynamic national animal protection organisation, representing some 40 member societies. The organisation believes that we can create a better world for all through promoting kindness to animals. Their goal is to significantly and permanently improve the welfare of all animals in Australia. Contact to assist as a volunteer.

Contact details:
Animals Australia, 37 O'Connell Street, North Melbourne, Victoria 3051, Australia
Tel: (613) 9329 6333 / Tel: (Freecall Australia 1800 888 584)
Fax: (613) 9329 6441
www.animalsaustralia.org
enquiries@animalsaustralia.org

Australian Animal Protection Society (AAPS) works for the aid, assistance, protection and welfare of all animals. Although most animals in their care are dogs and cats, they accept all animals including native animals, farm animals, birds, ferrets, mice, rabbits and other domesticated animals. They have an active volunteer programme and rely on volunteers to assist with a variety of tasks.

Contact details:
The Australian Animal Protection Society, 10 Homeleigh Road, Keysborough 3173, Victoria, Australia
Tel: 03 9798 8415 or 9798 8044
Fax: 03 9769 0317
www.aaps.org.au

Australian Orangutan Project exists to ensure the survival of both Sumatran and Bornean orangutan species in their natural habitat and promote the welfare of all orangutans. The project raises awareness of the need to preserve orangutan populations in their natural habitat and the intrinsic value of individual orangutans. There are few paid staff and the organisation is reliant on voluntary assistance.

Contact details:
Mail address: Australian Orangutan Project, P.O. Box 1414, South Perth, Western Australia, 6951
www.orangutan.org.au
help@orangutan.org.au

Bali Street Dogs Fund works to raise awareness of the plight of the dogs in Bali. Their policy is "Healing not Killing" and they work hard to treat and neuter as many dogs as possible on the island. They have recently implemented a volunteer vet programme that involves qualified vets assisting their work in Bali in a practical way.

Contact details:
Mail address (Sydney):
P.O. Box 1844, Bondi Junction, NSW 1355
Tel: 61 2 9371 5141
www.balistreetdogs.org.au
info@balistreetdogs.org.au

Contact details:
Mail address (Melbourne):
P.O. Box 1382, Kensington, VIC 3031
Tel: 61 3 9376 4817
www.balistreetdogs.org.au
info@balistreetdogs.org.au

Cat Protection Society, NSW believes that every cat deserves a responsible home. They work to protect and enhance the welfare of cats, educate the public about responsible cat ownership and to encourage community understanding of the issues surrounding the care and management of cats. Volunteers can assist in their Newtown adoption centre or with other areas of their work – there is a download volunteer application form.

Contact details:
103, Enmore Road, Newtown, NSW 2042
Tel: (Welfare Office) 02 9519 7201 or (Adoption Centre) 02 9557 4818
Fax: 02 9557 8052
www.catprotection.org.au
info@catprotection.org.au

<u>Darling Range Wildlife Centre, Perth</u> this group cares for sick, injured or orphaned wildlife with the goal of rehabilitation and successful return to the natural environment. Volunteers assist with the hands on care of animals.

Contact details:
Mail address: P.O. Box 732, Gosnells, WA 6990
www.darlingrangewildlife.com.au
volunteers@darlingrangewildlife.com.au

<u>DoggieRescue.com, Sydney</u> are a registered no kill animal rescue charity committed to rescuing neglected, abused and abandoned dogs from the death rows of Sydney pounds, and finding them loving homes. Job descriptions for volunteers are listed on their website.

Contact details:
Ingleside Shelter, 2 McCowan Road, Cnr Bloodwood Road, Ingleside
Mail address: 8 Chiltern Road, Ingleside, NSW 2101
Tel: 02 9486 3133
Fax: 02 9486 3136
www.doggierescue.com
admin@doggierescue.com

Contact details:
Petbarn Alexandria, Corner of Harley Street & McEvoy Street, Alexandria, NSW
www.doggierescue.com
mepcoles@bigpond.com

Contact details:
Petbarn Chatswood, Unit 3, 372 Eastern Valley Way, Chatswood, NSW
www.doggierescue.com
mepcoles@bigpond.com

<u>Dogs' Homes of Tasmania (TCDL)</u> is a non-profit organisation caring for Tasmania's stray, lost and abandoned dogs. Contact to assist as a volunteer with a variety of tasks at their rescue centres.

Contact details:
Mail address: **Hobart Dogs' Home**, P.O. Box 7, Lindisfarne, Tas 7015
Street address: **Hobart Dogs' Home**, 101 Scotts Road, Risdon Vale, 7016
Tel: (03) 6243 5177
www.dogshomesoftas.com.au

Contact details:
Mail address: **Burnie Dogs' Home**, P.O. Box 78, Burnie Tas 7320
Street address: **Burnie Dogs' Home**, Stowport Road, Stowport 7321
Tel: (03) 6431 6199
www.dogshomesoftas.com.au

Contact details:
Mail address: **Devonport Dogs' Home**, P.O. Box 698, Quoiba, Tas 7310
Street address: **Devonport Dogs' Home**, Spreton Park Racecourse, Spreton 7310
Tel: (03) 6427 2178
www.dogshomesoftas.com.au

For Australian Wildlife Needing Aid (FAWNA), NSW is a volunteer wildlife rescue and rehabilitation service for injured and orphaned native wildlife operating on the mid north coast of NSW. They strive to rehabilitate native wildlife for return to their natural environment, to relocate native wildlife which is under threat or causing distress to the public into a natural habitat for that species, to train volunteer members to carry out the rescue and care of native wildlife and encourage protection of the environment and to review policies and initiate actions in pursuit of its objectives and aims.

Contact details:
Mail address: F.A.W.N.A. (NSW) Inc., Box 218 P.O., Wauchope, NSW, 2446
www.fawna.org.au
fawna.nsw.inc@gmail.com

Free the Bears Fund, Stirling WA aims to protect, preserve and enrich the lives of bears throughout the world. They seek to achieve this by funding and facilitating conservation and rehabilitation projects, through preservation and reservation of areas of natural habitat with the aim of conserving bio-diversity and by encouraging harmonious and respectful animal-human relationships by facilitating profitable and sustainable alternatives to the illegal wildlife trade. They require volunteers to assist their work.

Contact details:
Mail address:
Head Office,Western Australia: Free The Bears Fund Inc., P.O. Box 1393, Osborne Park, DC WA 6916
Office address: 5A, Laga Court, Stirling, Western Australia
Tel: (08) 9244 1096/(Int'l: +61 8 9244 1096)
Fax: (08) 9244 4649/(Int'l: +61 8 9244 4649)
www.freethebears.org.au
info@freethebears.org.au

Friends of the Pound, NSW works to save animals from destruction and improve conditions at the pound. They also encourage responsible pet ownership such as de-sexing and micro-chipping. Volunteers assist with fostering and other hands on tasks.

Contact details:
Mail address: P.O. Box 260, Murwillumbah, NSW 2484
www.friendsofthepound.com
leola.robbo@yahoo.com
friendsofthepound@gmail.com

Good Samaritan Donkey Sanctuary Inc (GSDS) is dedicated to helping needy donkeys enjoy a very healthy, happy life. They offer donkeys a safe haven while they recover from ill treatment — which is all too often deliberate. GSDS is dedicated to providing professional and intensive care for injured and traumatised donkeys while also creating a refuge for these orphaned, abandoned, starved and unwanted creatures. Contact to assist.

Contact details:
Mail address: Clarence Town Post Office, Clarence Town, NSW 2321
Tel: +61 (02) 4996 5596
www.donkeyrescue.org.au
admin@donkeyrescue.org.au

Help for Wildlife, Victoria offers a 24 hour state wide emergency service to members of the public who seek advice or information about caring for wildlife. All operators are highly trained and familiar with wildlife emergencies. They are the largest provider of wildlife help within Victoria, handling over 18,000 calls annually. Their site contains information on wildlife caring and about volunteering to assist animals and wildlife. They offer to help volunteers to find their closest animal shelter in need of voluntary help.

Contact details:
Mail address: P.O.Box 181, Coldstream 3770, VIC Australia
Tel: 0417 380 687
www.helpforwildlife.com
helpforwildlife@bigpond.com

Horse Rescue Australia, NSW and is devoted to the care and rehabilitation of horses that have been abused, abandoned or neglected. They have assisted over 1,400 horses - the vast majority placed into new homes. By supporting the new owners and not allowing horses to be sold on, they are able to assure that they will never return to the condition in which we found them. The organisation requires volunteers to help with feeding, grooming, property maintenance, administration, etc.

Contact details:
Mail address: Horse Rescue Australia Inc., P.O.Box 234, North Richmond, NSW, 2754
Business address: 539 Kurmond Road, Freemans Reach, NSW
www.horserescue.com.au
info@horserescue.com.au **(preferred method of contact)**

Humane Society International (HSI) Australia, NSW seeks to create a humane and sustainable world, through education, advocacy and empowerment. They aim to relieve animal suffering; to prevent animal cruelty, abuse, neglect and exploitation and to protect wild animals and their environments. HSI Australia requires volunteer help with research and administration (click through from the 'how you can help' button on the left hand side).

Contact details:
Mail address: P.O.Box 439, Avalon, NSW, 2107
Tel: (61) (2) 9973 1728
Fax: (61) (2) 9973 1729
www.hsi.org.au
admin@hsi.org.au

Kanyana Wildlife Rehabilitation Centre, Gooseberry Hill, WA is committed to the protection and welfare of native wildlife. Kanyana is run entirely by volunteers from the local community, with the generous support of local businesses. It takes over 100 volunteers to cover two shifts per day, every day of the year. The day-to-day activities of the volunteers provide for all of the needs of the animals and the operation of the centre. Specific tasks include nursing and feeding sick and injured birds and animals, cleaning and maintenance, administration and public education. They have a comprehensive volunteer programme with more information on their website.

Contact details:
Kanyana Wildlife Rehabilitation Centre (Inc)., 120 Gilchrist Road, Lesmurdie, Western Australia 6076
Tel: (08) 9291 39000 (Int'l 61 8 9291 3900)
Fax: (08) 9291 0384 (Int'l 61 8 9291 0384)
www.kanyanawildlife.org.au
kanyanawildlife@kanyanawildlife.org.au

Lost Dogs Home, Melbourne is Australia's largest animal shelter, offering the community a wide variety of animal welfare services and rescuing 10,000 dogs and 7,000 cats per year. Their mission is: "To serve the community and enhance the welfare of dogs and cats by alleviating animal suffering and reducing the number of lost, injured and unwanted animals." Information about volunteering can be found on their website.

Contact details:
2 Gracie Street, North Melbourne, Vic 3051
Tel: (03) 9329 2755 (Country code +61)
Fax: (03) 9326 5293 (Country code +61)
http://dogshome.com
info@dogshome.com

NSW Animal Rescue has a no kill policy and is staffed by volunteers. They care for small breed, special needs animals. They offer boarding of animals for owners who are elderly, in hospital, nursing homes and refuges. We are able to assist with the care of the animals by providing practical assistance, food, medications and veterinary treatment. In addition, they rescue animals from pounds and shelters in Sydney, NSW. The organisation welcomes new volunteers and particularly needs foster carers.

Contact details:
Mail address: NSW Animal Rescue Inc., P.O. Box 156, Bringelly, NSW 2556
Tel: (02) 4774 9999 (Int'l +61 2 4774 9999)
www.nswar.org.au
admin@nswar.org.au

Oceania Project, NSW is a not-for-profit, research and information organisation dedicated to raising awareness about Cetacea (Whales, Dolphins and Porpoises) and the Ocean Environment. They are asking for participants for their Internship Program aboard the Annual Whale Research Expedition.

Contact details:
Mail address: The Oceania Project, P.O. Box 646, Byron Bay, NSW, 2481, Australia
Tel: +61 (2) 6685 8128
www.oceania.org.au
trish.wally@oceania.org.au

Organisation for the Rescue and Research of Cetaceans in Australia (ORRCA), NSW is the most experienced and successful whale rescue organisation in Australia. Every year ORRCA trains many members of government agencies (including the Department of Environment and Climate Change) and ORRCA Members in marine mammal rescue. They are also involved with the protection and welfare of seals, sea lions, dolphins and dugongs. Every year ORRCA volunteers spend many hours protecting hauled out seals and monitoring other marine mammals. They also work with Government Authorities and other groups with marine mammal rehabilitation and release. Contact to assist as a volunteer.

Contact details:
Mail address: GPO Box 315, Gosford, New South Wales, 2250, Australia
Tel: +61 2 9415 3333
www.orrca.org.au
orrca@orrca.org.au

Paws and Claws, Port Douglas is a small homeless animal society that requires volunteers to assist in a variety of practical ways – see website for more details.

Contact details:
Lot 1, Captain Cook Highway, Craiglie (via Port Douglas), Far North Queensland, 4877
Tel: (07) 4098 5721
www.pawsandclaws.org.au
pawsandc@pawsandclaws.org.au

Paws 'n Hooves, Sydney their main objective is to save animals from certain death in various pounds and shelters in Sydney and surrounding areas. Animals rescued from "death row" are taken to their foster carers' homes where they are treated like any family pet, until such time as a new and loving home can be found for them. They require volunteer assistance with fostering, driving, promotions, etc.

Contact details:
Tel: 02 9835 1055
www.pawsnhooves.net
lewis@pawsnhooves.net

PAWS Welfare, NSW comprises a small group of self-funded rescuers and volunteer foster carers and walkers whose primary aim is to help lost, abandoned or pound animals in NSW, Australia. Their idea is to feature photos and stories on their website about animals from Pounds and therefore save a life without the "emotional trauma" of visiting the Pound in person as an adopter. They require volunteers to assist with fostering, etc.

Contact details:
www.paws.com.au
mail@paws.com.au

RSPCA Australia has the following objectives: "To prevent cruelty to animals by ensuring the enforcement of existing laws at federal and state level. To procure the passage of such amending or new legislation as is necessary for the protection of animals. To develop and promote policies for the humane treatment of animals that reflect contemporary values and scientific knowledge. To educate the community with regard to the humane treatment of animals. To engage with relevant stakeholders to improve animal welfare. To sustain an intelligent public opinion regarding animal welfare. To operate facilities for the care and protection of animals". Volunteers are an integral part of all levels of RSPCA operations - from National and State Councils to the occasional gardener and everything in between. They assist in many ways including caring for animals in the Shelters, assisting with administrative tasks and helping out in Opportunity Shops. Many more help out with special events, fundraising and promotions that take place throughout the year.

Contact details:
Mail address: **RSPCA Australia Inc.**, P.O. Box 265, Deakin West ACT 2600, Australia
Tel: 02 6282 8300
Fax: 02 6282 8311
www.rspca.org.au

RSPCA, Victoria
Contact details:
Tel: 03 9224 2222
www.rspcavic.org
volunteer@rspcavic.org.au

RSPCA South Australia, Adelaide

Contact details:
Head Office: 172 Morphett Street, Adelaide S.A. 5000
Mail address: G.P.O. Box 2122, Adelaide S.A. 5001
Tel: (08) 8231 6931
Fax: (08) 8231 6201
www.rspcasa.asn.au

Contact details:
Shelter address: 25 Mayer Road, Lonsdale S.A. 5160
Tel: (08) 8382 0888
Fax: (08) 8326 2410
www.rspcasa.asn.au

RSPCA, Queensland
Contact details:
RSPCA Fairfield Shelter/RSPCA QLD Head Office, 301 Fairfield Road, Fairfield, 4103
Tel: (07) 3426 9915
http://volunteering.rspcaqld.org.au
volunteering@rspcaqld.org.au

RSPCA, NSW

Contact details:
Mail address: RSPCA NSW, P.O. Box 34, Yagoona, NSW 2199
Tel: 02 9770 7555
www.rspcansw.org.au

Are all non-government community based animal welfare organisations. Volunteers are a crucial component of the successful day-to- day running of the RSPCA. The RSPCA recognises that people choose to volunteer for many reasons. Reliability, commitment and a concern for animal welfare are essential ingredients to an enjoyable volunteer experience at the RSPCA. Up to 1,000 volunteers work state-wide in Australia. Such a strong volunteer presence reflects community concern for community needs and ensures that a strong culture of animal welfare is maintained. The RSPCA recognises that people choose to volunteer for many reasons. Contact to assist.

Save Foundation of Australia is committed to saving the endangered species of Africa from extinction. Founded in 1987, the organisation has a broad range of activities, with a particular focus on the African black rhinoceros and Zimbabwe. Voluntary assistance is appreciated by the organisation.

Contact details:
Head Office: SAVE FOUNDATION of Australia (Inc.),229 Oxford St, Leederville, Western Australia, 6007
Tel: (+61) (0) 8 9444 6550
Fax: (+61) (0) 8 9444 9270
www.savefoundation.org.au
save@savefoundation.org.au

Contact details:
New South Wales Branch: SAVE FOUNDATION of Australia (Inc.) (New South Wales Branch, c/o Dee Williamson, 24 Parklands Avenue, Lane Cove, NSW 2066
Tel: (+61) (0) 2 9997 1828
www.thesavefoundation.org.au
theafricanqueen@bigpond.com

Save a Dog Scheme, Victoria is controlled and operated by volunteers with the help of paid staff. It operates as a registered animal shelter and combines this with foster care in the community. Each dog is neutered, vaccinated, wormed, microchipped, vet-checked and temperament-assessed prior to adoption. Save-A-Dog Scheme is a "coal-face" organisation, which saves hundreds of dogs each year and which seeks, by example, to provide a better way of treating non-human animals.

Contact details:
Mail address: Save-A-Dog Scheme Inc., Central Park P.O. Box 2325, East Malvern VIC 3145
Shelter Address: 36 Weir Street, Glen Iris, VIC Australia
Tel: Tel: (03) 9824 7928 or 0418 389 810
www.saveadog.org.au
admin@saveadog.org.au

Silvery Gibbon Project, WA works to assist and conserve the Silvery Gibbon in Western Australia, contact to assist with voluntary work.

Contact details:
Mail address: The Silvery Gibbon Project, P.O. Box 335, Como WA 6952, Australia
Tel: 0438 992 325 or 0403 431 103
www.silvery.org.au
SGP@silvery.org.au

Sydney Pet Rescue and Adoption Inc has the following aims: "To rescue and re-home companion animals from death row in pounds, and other homeless animals. To short circuit the surrender process, and thus reduce the number of animals reaching death row, by providing owners with viable alternatives to surrender, including: short term emergency foster care, assistance with locating pet friendly accommodation and assistance with re-homing. To educate the public on responsible pet ownership, and their rights and responsibilities under the Companion Animals Act, the Prevention of Cruelty to Animals Act, and other relevant legislation. To promote an understanding of the valuable role companion animals play in the lives of individuals and the community. To promote the prevention of cruelty to animals". Volunteer to help with transport, adoptions, fostering and more.

Contact details:
Mail address: Sydney Pet Rescue & Adoption, P.O. Box 1169, Menai Central, NSW, 2234
Tel: (02) 9519 3331
www.freewebs.com/sydneypetrescueandadoption
david@sydneypetrescue.com.au

Sydney Dogs and Cats Home their goal is to prevent the unnecessary euthanasia of healthy, loving cats and dogs and find them new homes that will last a lifetime. They urgently need volunteers who are available weekday mornings on a regular basis to come and walk the dogs and/or spend a little time with their cats.

Contact details:
77 Edward Street Carlton, NSW, 2218
Tel: (02) 9587 9611
Fax: (02) 9588 9569
www.sydneydogsandcatshome.org
SDCH@sydneydogsandcatshome.org

Swan Animal Haven, WA rescues and cares for abandoned dogs until compassionate homes can be found. They advocate the sterilisation of all dogs and hope they won't need to exist as a result. Information on volunteering animal jobs are on their website.

Contact details:
Swan Animal Haven, Kalamunda Road, South Guildford Western Australia 6055
Tel: 08 9279 8485 (11am-3pm)
www.swananimalhaven.asn.au

Vets Beyond Borders, NSW is an Australian based, not-for-profit, incorporated organisation established by volunteer vets. Vetcharity helps set-up and run animal welfare programmes in developing communities of the Asia-Pacific region, and coordinates veterinary volunteer work on projects throughout the region.

Contact details:
Mail address: Vets Beyond Borders Secretariat, P.O. Box 576, Crows Nest NSW 1585
Tel: +61 2 80033691
Fax: +61 2 92614033
www.vetsbeyondborders.org
secretariat@vetsbeyondborders.org.au

Victorian Animal Aid Trust caring for animals and encouraging people to be more active with their pets are the main drivers behind the Animal Aid program. The organisation says that humans need to understand the plight of animals at risk, and learn how they can change the situation. They have a comprehensive volunteering programme - contact to assist.

Contact details:
Mail address: *P.O. Box 34, Coldstream, VIC 3770, Australia*
Street address: 35 Killara Road, Coldstream, VIC 3770, Australia
Tel: (03) 9739 0300
www.animalaid.org.au
enquiries@animalaid.org.au or kblizzard@animalaid.org.au www.animalaid.com.au

Wildcare Australia is the registered trading name of the Australian Koala Hospital Association Incorporated. Their primary aims and objectives are: To provide a high standard of rescue, care, rehabilitation for sick, injured, orphaned and displaced native fauna for successful release into the natural environment. For the protection and enhancement of the environment by providing quality care in Queensland for sick, injured, orphaned and displaced native Australian wildlife. The conservation of native fauna and their habitat Australia-wide, including research on the biology and medicine of native fauna is also of primary concern. To provide extensive and up to date training for wildlife volunteers in all aspects of wildlife care – please see their website for comprehensive information on voluntary animal jobs.

Contact details:
www.wildcare.org.au
enquiries@wildcare.org.au

Wildlife Victoria works to assist wildlife in need in Victoria. Volunteers are required to assist with manning their phone line, driving, rescuing, transport, campaigning and animal care jobs.

Contact details:
Volunteer Information Officer, Wildlife Victoria, 3 / 288 Brunswick Street, Fitzroy 3065
Tel: 9445 0310
www.wildlifevictoria.org.au
volunteer@wildlifevictoria.org.au

Wildlife Information and Rescue Service (WIRES), NSW has established a network of hundreds of volunteer who rescue, rehabilitate and release sick, injured or orphaned native animals. Each year they receive over 100,000 phone calls and rescue over 56,000 native animals from injured bluetongues to orphaned wombats. Their website contains comprehensive information about volunteering.

Contact details:
Mail address: WIRES, P.O. Box 260, Forestville, NSW, 2087
Tel: (02) 8977 3333
Fax: (02) 8977 3399
www.wires.org.au
info@wires.org.au

World League for the Protection of Animals (WLPA), NSW is committed to promoting the well being and rights of all animals throughout the world, both native and non-native. They receive no government subsidies and is staffed primarily by volunteers.

Contact details:
Mail address: The World League for Protection of Animals, P.O. Box 211, Gladesville, NSW 2111, Australia
Street address: The World League for Protection of Animals, 1-2/201 Victoria Road, Gladesville, NSW 2111, Australia
Tel: +612 9817 4892
Fax: +612 9817 4509
www.wlpa.org
admin@wlpa.org

Young Animal Protection Society, Queensland cares for homeless and unwanted dogs and cats in the Cairns area. The overall goal of the organisation is to provide a service aiming at excellence to the Cairns and surrounding district in the area of animal welfare. Volunteers are required to assist them in numerous ways.

Contact details:
Mail address: Young Animal Protection Society Inc.,Post Office Box 233, Smithfield, Cairns, North Queensland, Australia 4878
Located: Lot 2 McGregor Road, Smithfield, Cairns
Tel/Fax: (07) 4057 6373
www.yaps.org.au
pets@yaps.org.au

"Animals do feel like us, also joy, love, fear and pain but they cannot grasp the spoken word. It is our obligation to take their part and continue to resist the people who profit by them, who slaughter them and who torture them." - Denis de Rougement

EUROPE

"If man is not to stifle human feelings, he must practice kindness to animals, for He who is cruel to animals becomes hard also in his dealings with men. We can judge the heart of a man by his treatment of animals." - Immanuel Kant

Armenia

Eurasia CPO, Armenia works to protect the stray animals and combat cruel attitude towards them. The organisation actively endorses the implementation of trap, neuter, return as a state program. Contact to volunteer.

Contact details:
Apt. 1, 6 Leningradyan str., Yerevan, Republic of Armenia
Tel: (374 10) 38 00 01
Tel/Fax: (374 10) 39 03 22
www.eurasia-cpo.com
eurasia7am@yahoo.com

Belarus

Centre of Animal Protection (Feniks), Belarus was established in 1995, they have a shelter with over 80 animals and assist with mini shelters. The organisation supports neutering and education. Contact to assist their work.

Contact details:
246022. Gomel, Pobeda St., 2
Tel: 375-232-71-35-50 or 375-232-77-50-88
feniks-gomel.iatp.by/about-us-eng.htm
katya_petro@tut.by

Bulgaria

Animal Welfare Foundation, Bulgaria this organisation seeks to instill compassion in Bulgarian people for animals. They are currently concentrating on the problem of the excessive pet breeding in households, impulsive acquiring of kittens and puppies and the unrestricted movements of animals. Contact to assist.

Bosnia

ARKA, Bosnia is the society for the protection and welfare of animals. This organisation works in a variety of ways to assist animals in need. Contact to assist.

Contact details:
ARKA, Poslovni blok "Delta" Bulevar mira BB, 76100 Brčko Distrikt BiH
Tel: +387 49 233 430
www.arka.org.ba
arka@eunet.yu **or** arka@spinter.net

Stichting Dierenopvang Bosnië works to assist the many animals in great need in Bosnia. They require volunteer assistance with fostering animals and general assistance with their work.

Contact details:
Mail address: Foundation Dierenopvang Bosnia, PO Box 3147, Dordrecht 3301 DC
Giro 94 74 694
Tel: 06-46198579
www.hondenopvang.com
info@hondenopvang.com

Croatia

Animal Friends Croatia was founded with the purpose of promoting the protection and animal rights and presenting vegetarianism as an ethical, ecological, and healthy way of living. They require volunteer assistance in a variety of ways.

Contact details:
Animal Friends Croatia/Prijatelji zivotinja/Gajeva 47, 10000 Zagreb, Croatia
Tel: ++ 385 1 4920226
www.prijatelji-zivotinja.hr
prijatelji-zivotinja@inet.hr

Society Life, Croatia is a non governmental, non profitable organisation that works for the respect and care of animals. It stands for protecting the rights and general well-being of all animals based on foundations of contemporary achievement of civilised society.The organisation rescues and re-homes animals and has various animal welfare campaigns. Contact to assist as a volunteer.

Contact details:
Gornjodravska obala 84, 31000 Osijek, Croatia
Tel: +385 (0)31 283-445
Fax: + 385 (0)31 284-415
www.zivot.hr
zivot@zivot.hr

Cyprus

Animal Responsibility, Cypress, (ARC) this organisation aims to be the voice of all animals: captive animals, wild creatures, animals used in farming, experiments etc. Contact to assist as a volunteer.

Contact details:
Mail address: ARC, P.O. Box 56986, 3311 Limassol, Cyprus
www.animalscyprus.org
arc.kivotos@cytanet.com.cy

Malcolm Cat, Cypress is helping to make a difference for cats in need in Cypress. This organisation requests voluntary assistance in a variety of ways at their sanctuary.

Contact details:
Mail address: MCPS Calendars, Malcolm Cat Protection Society, P.O. Box 53759, Limassol, Cyprus
Tel: +357 25 952622
www.malcolmcat.org
catsanctuary@hotmail.com

British Forces Animal Rehoming Centre (BARC), Cyprus this organisation is RSPCA associated and is run by a small group of volunteers bonded by a desire to improve the welfare of the cats and dogs owned by members of BFC. Volunteers required to assist with building maintenance, walking, feeding and cleaning duties - contact to assist.

Contact details:
Mail address: Building 720, Norfolk Hill, Episkopi, BFPO 53
Tel: +357 25 963733
Fax: 25 963733
www.barc-cyprus.org
barc_admin@cytanet.com.cy

Spaying and Neutering Feral Cats of Limassol (Catsnip), Cyprus is run by a small group of animal lovers who got together in Limassol Cyprus to trap, neuter and return feral cats. Since forming in June 2006 they have concentrated on colonies with four or more cats. Contact to assist as a volunteer.

Contact details:
Tel from UK: 00357 25 933672
Tel in Cyprus: 25 933672
www.catsnip.co.uk
cat-snip@hotmail.com

Cyprus Association for the Protection and Care of Animals (CAPCA), Cyprus This organisation cares for over 150 dogs at any one time. They need volunteers to assist their charity shops and animal shelter - help required with cleaning, dog walking, playing with animals, feeding etc.

Contact details:
Tel: +357 99683775
www.dogscyprus.org/PAWS/index.php

Cyprus Donkey Sanctuary today there are more than 100 donkeys in the care of this sanctuary. They are all no longer wanted as machines have largely replaced them in the fields and vineyards, or, their owners are too elderly to look after them any more. The donkeys are collected or brought to the sanctuary from villages all over Cyprus. In addition to their sanctuary, they also operate an outreach programme that goes to villages where there are working donkeys. On a selected day, the donkeys are gathered and with the mobile clinic they provide vaccinations, medication for worms and parasites, treatment for feet and teeth, a general medical examination, medication and advice. Contact to assist.

Contact details:
Friends of the Cyprus Donkey, 4772 Vouni Village, Limassol District, Cyprus
Tel: 357 25 944 151
Fax: 357 25 942582
www.windowoncyprus.com/friends_of_the_cyprus_donkey.htm

Nicosia Dog Shelter, Cyprus works hard to help dogs in need and ensure that the dogs in their care live as comfortably as possible at the shelter. They offer a vital rescue service in the Nicosia and Larnaca area believe animal welfare is greatly improved through education and encourage people and schools to visit the shelter. They have a fantastic policy that is never to refuse help for any reason. Contact to assist as a volunteer and assist with walking, feeding and caring.

Contact details:
Nicosia Dog Shelter & Rescue Service, 30C, Germanou Patron Street, Engomi, Nicosia 2414, Cyprus
Tel: 22357005
www.dogshelter.org.cy
nicosiadogshelter@gmail.com

Paphiakos and CCP Animal Welfare, Cyprus this organisation has many services including; veterinary clinic, 24 hour emergency service, shelter, boarding, re-homing, education projects etc. Contact to assist in a variety of roles.

Contact details:
12 Dedalos Building, Kato Paphos, Paphos, 8049, Cyprus
Tel: 00357 26946461
Fax: 00357 26222236
www.cyprusanimalwelfare.com
info@cyprusanimalwelfare.com

Denmark

Galgos in Need Project, Denmark works in Denmark to find homes for Galgos that have been abandoned and abused in Spain. The organisation puts pressure on the Spanish government, in that hope that legislative changes will be made so that the atrocities against the dogs can be stopped. Contact to assist.

Contact details:
www.galgo-sos.dk

Estonia

Pets, Estonia works to assist abandoned animals through offering veterinary assistance, food and care as needed. Contact to assist their work.

Contact details:
Mail address: PK 630, 12601 Tallinn, Estonia
Tel: +372 58 012 597
www.pets.ee
lara@pets.ee

Estonian Society for the Protection of Animals (ELS) is a non-profit association with a mission to improve animal welfare and prevent animal abuse. This mission is carried out by helping the animals directly, raising public awareness, educating people on the subject, animal protection control and being engaged in legislative drafting. The organisation relies on volunteers, contact to assist.

Contact details:
Tel: +372 52 67 117
www.loomakaitse.ee
info@loomakaitse.ee

Finland

Animalia - Federation for the Protection of Animals, Finland is Finland's largest animal protection organisation - working to promote the welfare and the rights of animals. The organisation opposes any treatment of animals that inhibits their natural behaviour or causes them pain and distress. Animalia campaigns and lobbies for better legislation and on solving animal protection problems related to animal experimentation, the conditions of farm animals, and fur farming. Contact to assist.

Contact details:
Animalia ry, Porvoonkatu 53, 00520
Tel: (09) 720 65 90
www.animalia.fi
Animal@animalia.fi

Pro Animals, Finland has neutering programmes, local educational campaigns and a therapy dog programme. Their current challenge is to build animal rescue center to Tg-Jiu with a veterinary clinic, education and international volunteer programme, etc. Their aim is to help the local people achieve the knowledge to take care of the wellfare of society without the support of third party. Contact to assist as a volunteer.

Contact details:
www.proanimalsfinland.net
pr@pafiry.net

Finish Federation for Animal Welfare Associations (SEY), Finland is an animal welfare federation that has been working for better animal welfare since 1901. The Federation is built upon the idea of respect for the individual animal and the promotion of animal welfare. The federation is working to protect all animals in the best possible way from pain, suffering, anxiety, harm and fear. The federation wants to influence the political decision-making process so that all these animal welfare issues are taken into consideration. SEY does practical animal welfare work through animal inspection work and information. Contact to assist as a volunteer.

Contact details:
Sey Suomen Eläinsuojeluyhdistysten Liitto Ry, Kotkankatu 9, 00510 Helsinki
Tel: 0207 528 420
Fax: (09) 877 1206
www.sey.fi
sey@sey.fi

France

Brigitte Bardot Foundation, France works directly on the field with animal rescue, veterinary help, stray cat sterilisation campaigns, etc. It also intervenes at the judicial level, with the help of inspectors spread out all over France. Abroad, the Foundation created a sanctuary for bears in Bulgaria and set up a clinic for East European countries. To develop its work, the Brigitte Bardot Foundation has created a network of voluntary delegates and inspectors who extend the Foundation's work. They welcome volunteers to help them in their struggle for animal protection can become a voluntary delegate or inspector for the Brigitte Bardot Foundation. Each one of these voluntary jobs requires a very demanding personal involvement - contact if you are able to assist.

Contact details:
Foundation Brigitte Bardot, 28 rue Vineuse, 75116 Paris
Tel: 33 (0)1 45 05 14 60
Fax: 33 (0)1 45 05 14 80
www.fondationbrigittebardot.fr

L'Ecole du Chat de Bordeaux, France this organisation neuters feral cats and takes care of kittens and cats. All of their cats are in foster families which means that they rely on people and due to shortages of foster homes, it is often hard to take care of all the nice cats that they find. Last year, they spayed and neutered 880 cats in Bordeaux and the whole region. Contact if you can assist.

Contact details:
www.ecole-du-chat-bordeaux.com
mimigau@yahoo.fr **or** benevolat.ecoleduchat@gmail.com (volunteers)

Les Quatre Pattes/PAWS Aid for Animals in Distress, St Martin their work entails sterilising and finding good homes for the island animals. They find as many good homes on the island as possible, but unfortunately there are simply not enough good homes on the island to keep up with the overpopulation of animals. They do not presently have a shelter, nor any form of government aid on either side of the island. Volunteers can assist in the following ways: Become a Foster Home - they have no shelter on the island and are in need of people available to help foster dogs and/or pups. Volunteer to transport a pup - If you are animal lovers and visiting the island and would like to volunteer to escort puppies or dogs to Seattle, Detroit, Hartford, Boston or JFK please contact this organisation three to four weeks before arriving. There would be no cost to you and they would have a volunteer meet you at your airport back home who will take the pups to their new foster home for adoption. Visit their website for further information.

Contact details:
Local address: Les Quatre Pattes/PAWS, C/o The Mailbox – Suite 2427, Palapa Center – Bldg. 30, Unit A, Airport Blvd., St Maarten, N.A. **or** Les Quatre Pattes/PAWS, 9 Lot, Terres Basses, 97150 Saint Martin
www.sxmpaws.org

Contact details:
From the United States or Canada:
Les Quatre Pattes/PAWS, C/o The Mailbox – Suite 2427, P.O. Box 523882, Miami, FL 33152-3382
www.sxmpaws.org

New European Distressed Donkey Initiative (NEDDI), France offers care and safety to donkeys at risk from neglect, cruelty or maltreatment. They work to rehabilitate rescued donkeys, by offering all necessary veterinary care, suitable diet & rest. Contact to assist.

Contact details:
Donkey Home/Sanctuary: (UK & N. France) La Ferme du Village, 107 rue de la Place, Questrecques, Boulogne sur Mer, 62830, France
Tel: (00 33) (0) 321 87 42 30
Fax: (00 33) (0) 321 87 43 88
www.neddi.org
info@neddi.demon.co.uk

Contact details:
Mail address: UK Office: P.O. Box 56. Wadebridge, Cornwall, PL27 9BJ
Tel: (00 44) (0)1208 816640
www.neddi.org
info@neddi.demon.co.uk

Georgia

Animal Rights Committee (ARC), Georgia is a non-profit organisation based in Tbilisi, Georgia. Their mission is to alleviate animal suffering and promote animal rights and cruelty-free living in Georgia. The organisation relies on volunteer assistance.

Contact details:
Tel: +995 (8)77 469197
Fax: +995 32 251501
www.animalrights.ge/eng
arc@animalrights.ge

Greece

Agni Animal Welfare Fund (AAWF), Corfu is run by a small group of individuals working to improve the life of animals on Corfu, set up in association with Agni Travel in order that friends and visitors can make donations to help theislands stray animals. Contact to assist as a volunteer.

Contact details:
Tel: **(UK)** 0044 (0) 1737 845434 **or (UK)** 0044 (0) 0115 972 6625
Tel: **(CORFU)** 0030 26630 91780
www.agni-animal-welfare-fund.com
info@agni-animal-welfare-fund.com

Animal Care Samos, Greece As in any other part of Greece, stray dogs and cats are still a problem on Samos. They mostly live in the mountains close to the villages or army camps, in summertime they usually come down to the major touistic areas to search for food. Many of these animals carry diseases or are otherwise ill. This organisation is looking for volunteers who have some experience of animal handling, are not squeamish about ticks or rats, are able to deal with sick or injured animals and are willing to work hard. They are also looking for volunteer vets. The shelter is fairly isolated and modest accommodation and some food is provided. They say: "although it may be nicer to be on Samos in summertime our dogs need food and care all year round!". Contact to assist.

Contact details:
Mail address: Animal Care Samos, P.O. Box 102, GR-83100, Vathi, Samos
www.animalcaresamos.com

ARCTUROS, Greece was founded in 1992 in order to put an end in the phenomenon of the 'dancing bear' which was at the time a common sight around Greece. Since then ARCTUROS has been actively working for the conservation of large carnivores both in Greece and around the Balkans. Through applied research it gathers information that allows dynamic intervention in cases where important habitats are threatened or destroyed by large technical works such as roads, dams, quarries, etc. The activities of ARCTUROS depend highly on volunteers. Many people both participate in their programmes each year gaining valuable experience in a variety of conservation programmes. The volunteers mainly participate in the following areas: assistance in public awareness campaigns and fieldwork and research programmes. Contact to assist.

Contact details:
Maria Styliadou, ARCTUROS' Environmental Centre, Aetos Florinas 530 75
Tel/Fax: +30 23860 41500
www.arcturos.gr
mstyliadou@arcturos.gr

ARGOS Animal Welfare Society, Greece was formed in 1996 by animal lovers who decided to unite their forces to ease the suffering of the thousands of stray animals in Thessaloniki and suburbs. The organisation assists with neutering and recovery of sick animals. Contact to offer voluntary assistance with transportation, public relations, adoptions and animal care.

Contact details:
Mail address: ARGOS Animal Welfare Society, P.O. Box 11052, Thessaloniki, Greece
Tel: +306944748968
www.argosgr.org
info@argosgr.org

CIDAG, Greece This coalition of Greek and Foreign animal welfare/rights groups was launched in June 2002 with the objective to lobby the Greek Government, EU politicians and MEP's to solve the problem of the ever-increasing stray dog and cat population in Greece by: implementing a nation-wide spay, neuter, release and identification program; an educational program on responsible pet ownership and enforcing existing animal protection laws. All CIDAG members run trap-neuter-release programs. Volunteers are really rare in Greece, so any voluntary help is extremely valuable - please contact to assist.

Contact details:
www.argosgr.org/cidag

Corfu Donkey Rescue (CDR) this organisation aims to give; "the old; a safe and happy retirement, the sick; a chance of cure, the injured; the chance of recovery, the abused; the chance of regaining trust and hope, and the abandoned; the feeling of security again". This organisation welcomes volunteers to assist with their practical animal care work. They operate a comprehensive volunteering and gap year programmes.

Contact details:
Mail address: Corfu Donkey Rescue, Box 5210, Liapades, Corfu 49083, Greece
www.corfu-donkeys.com
judyquin@otenet.gr

Corfu Animal Rescue Establishment (CARE) operates a very successful castrating and neutering programme to diminish the hundreds of unwanted puppies on the Island. Contact to assist as a volunteer.

Contact details:
Corfu Care Shelter, Perouladis, Near Sidari
Tel: 00 (30) 6972072155 (Greece)
www.carecorfu.com
enquiries@carecorfu.com

Contact details:
London Office: 111 Cheyne Walk, London SW10 0DJ
Tel: 020 7376 3600 (UK)

Corfudogs, Greece is run by a small group of people dedicated to helping abused and unwanted animals on the island of Corfu. This organisation was set up to help the plight of the unwanted animals that are abandoned on the streets throughout Greece. The organisation helps stray dogs and then works to find them good homes in Germany, Austria, Sweden and Holland. They require volunteer help with their rescue work. They also require volunteers to assist by accompany dogs on chartered flights form Corfu to Germany. You are not requried to pay - just to check in with the dogs at the airport and claim them at the destination where one of the Corfudogs colleagues will be waiting to collect them at the airport. Contact to assist.

Contact details:
www.corfudogs.org

Cretan Animal Welfare Group (CAWG), Greece works to assist needy animals in Corfu. They assist sick, needy and elderly animals and also run a subsidised neutering project, a donkey project and cat cafes. They require voluntary help with transporting animals, feeding, walking, campaigning etc. Contact to help.

Contact details:
http://cretananimalwelfare.org
info@CretanAnimalWelfare.org

Cretan Cat-a-list, Greece this organisation is committed to helping animals in need - particularly feral, sick, needy and un-neutered cats. Their priority is to reduce numbers through their neutering project. Contact to assist as a volunteer.

Contact details:
Cretan Cat a List, c/o Jayne Butler, 74100 Pengalahori, Rethymno, Crete, Greece
Tel: 0030 28310 72138
www.cretancatalist.eu
jayb@otenet.gr

Friends of Animals, Athens, Greece run a shelter caring for over 40 dogs. They also offer vaccinations, neutering, veterinary attention and a feeding service for feral animals or for those who need help feeding their pets. Contact to assist as a volunteer.

Contact details:
Friends of Animals, C/o Kiki Karathanassi, Adanon 10 – 14341, Nea Filadelphia, Athens, Greece
Tel: 694-494-9741
Fax: 210-258-5296
www.friendsofanimals-nf.com

Friends of Animals, Rethymnon, Greece works for the rescue, care and re-homing of animals through a network of voluntary foster carers. Contact to assist their work as a volunteer.

Contact details:
www.animals.rethymnon.org

Friends of Animals in Mykonos, Greece are a group of local residents who are concerned about the health and welfare of the stray animal population in Mykonos. One of their primary aims is to control the cat and dog overpopulation problem. As well as a sterilisation programme, the organisation also offers veterinary aid to those sick and injured and they have set up feeding programs to help the animals survive the lean winter month. In addition, they arrange adoption to good homes as often as possible and have successfully placed many animals throughout Europe and North America. Although most of their strays are cats and dogs, we help any animal in distress and have on occasion lent a hand to a flamingo, pelican, turtles, ducks and owls. Contact to offer your assistance.

Contact details:
Tel: (+30) 6955 582372-3-4
www.mykonosanimals.com
info@mykonosanimals.com

Greek Animal Welfare Fund (GAWF), Greece this organisation provides Greek animal protection societies with project funding, expert assistance, training and practical help, including assistance with neutering campaigns. Over the past twenty years, GAWF has provided more than a million pounds (sterling) towards animal welfare work in Greece. GAWF is currently helping around 80 animal protection groups with expertise, equipment and financial help. They also actively support several wildlife groups with literature, equipment, training and expert visits (including wildlife veterinarian). In this way, GAWF extends its work beyond that which we could achieve directly themselves and, most importantly, equips national societies on the mainland and in the islands to carry on and develop vital welfare work in their own country. Contact to assist as a volunteer.

Contact details:
www.gawf.org.uk

Hellenic Ornithological Society, Greece is the only Greek non-governmental body exclusively concerned with the protection of wild birds and their habitats in Greece. Contact to assist as a volunteer with a variety of field projects.

Contact details:
Headquarters: Hellenic Ornithological Society, Vas. Irakleiou 24, GR-106 82, Athens, Greece,
Tel/Fax: +30 210 8227937, +30 210 8228704
www.ornithologiki.gr
info@ornithologiki.gr

Hellenic Society for the Protection of Nature (HSPN), Greece has been instrumental in the creation of most Greek National Parks, Ramsar wetlands and many other protected areas. It has also played a leading role in the efforts to protect endangered species. Today, it is active along four axes: environmental education, nature protection programme, environmental intervention, general Public awareness. To carry out its mission, it relies on an extensive network of volunteers. Contact to help.

Contact details:
Greek Society for the Protection of Nature, Nike 20, 105 57 Athens
Tel: 210 3224944 **or** 210 3314563
Fax: 210 3225285
www.eepf.gr
info@eepf.gr

Hellenic Wildlife Hospital, Greece assists between 3,000 to 4,500 wild animals from all over Greece every year. Its' main premises are on the island of Aigina, but it also operates through a vast network of volunteers, collaborating organisations, first aid stations and departments covering the whole country. It is the first wildlife rehabilitation centre founded in Greece to obtain an official licence from the Greek State to possess, treat and release all species of indigenous wildlife. Volunteers at the HWH actively take part in the necessary everyday care of the animals in rehabilitation which includes feeding, cleaning up cages, taking part in adapting cages for new animals. Contact to help.

Contact details:
Hellenic Wildlife Hospital, 18010 Panchia Rachi, Aegina island, Greece
Tel: (+30) 22970 28267
Fax: (+30) 22970 31338
www.ekpazp.gr
ekpaz@ekpazp.gr

Kefalonia Animal Trust, Greece provides the following projects; a neutering program for strays and ferals on both Kefalonia and Ithaki (Ithaca), the treatment of sick and injured animals (with veterinary assistance, when needed), provision of fostering where appropriate and the provision of winter feeding for strays. The organisation also funds neutering and treatment where appropriate and re-home animals in Greece, Germany and the UK. Contact to help as a volunteer.

Contact details:
Mail address: P.O. Box 142, Argostoli, Kefalonia, Greece, 28100
www.kefalonia-animal-trust.org
helpoffers@kefalonia-animal-trust.org

Lesvos Animal Welfare Society, Greece was formed in 1995 by people who love and care for homeless animals. They don't run a shelter but instead arrange neutering, veterinary care and rehabilitation for animals in need it the town of Mytilene and also in villages when help is requested.The organisation is also active with other animal welfare issues such as: slaughtering, animal transportation, circuses, poisoning of animals, etc. Contact to assist as a volunteer.

Contact details:
Tel:(0251) 47710/43580/46897
Fax: (0251) 40060
www.lesvos-animal-ws.ndo.co.uk

Nine Lives Greece is a group of volunteers who take care of a 90-strong colony of cats that live in two adjacent parks in central Athens. The cats are dumped there when their owners go on holidays, move house, have babies, get divorced or simply get bored of their pets. The cats are in danger, mainly from dogs, but also from fast cars on the surrounding roads, poisoning and other cruelties.This group provides food, neutering and medical treatment for all of the cats as necessary. Contact to assist as a volunteer with feeding, transport, adoption, campaigns and more.

Contact details:
www.ninelivesgreece.com
ninelivesgreece@gmail.com

Paros Animal Welfare Society (PAWS), Greece this organisation aims to re-home every unwanted dog, to control the populations of stray cats and to improve the quality of life of animals on Paros Island. Volunteers are needed to transport dogs and cats from Paros to Santorini and Myconos from where most of the charter-flights to re-homing destinations leave. Anyone interested in being involved with this re-homing team and ready to make a trip from: Paros to Santorini or Myconos with 2 or 3 dogs/cats, OR, travelling from Myconos, Santorini or Athens to Frankfurt, Dusseldorf or Stuttgart, OR, anyone traveling from Frankfurt or Dusseldorf to Paros, Santorini, Myconos or Athens, if you can assist please make contact with this organisation.

Contact details:
Tel: +30 22840 28291
www.paws.gr

Skiathos Dog Shelter, Greece has been operational since 1995 and have re-homed over 1,000 dogs and cats. Contact to assist this shelter as a volunteer - they even welcome volunteers who are only able to help by walking a few dogs for a day or two whilst on holiday in Skiathos.

Contact details:
www.skiathosdogshelter.com

Skopelos - Caring for Animals and Nature (SCAN), Greece provides feeding, neutering and veterinary treatment for animals in need, contact to assist as a volunteer.

Contact details:
Mail address: SCANSKOPELOS.ORG., P.O. Box 46, 37003, Skopelos, Greece
www.scanskopelos.org
info@scanskopelos.org

Society for the Protection of Stray Animals (SPAZ), Greece has no office, no clinic, nor any animal shelter. Their members work on the street, neutering cats and dogs and providing medical care in their own homes. They also produce educational brochures, lobbies and campaigns for animal rights, and networks with animal welfare groups all over the country. Become a member and assist as a volunteer.

Contact details:
Mail address: PO Box 70213, Glyfada, Athens, Greece 166-10
www.spazgreece.org
spazgreece@hotmail.co.uk

Voice of the Cats Alliance, Greece provides food, veterinary care, advice, neutering and does some campaigning work for the stray cats in North East Crete. Volunteers can assist with the many tasks.

Contact details:
Elounda, Crete
Tel: +30 6944 807727
vswain@miaow.info
www.miaow.info

Contact details:
Rethymno, Crete
Tel: +30 28310 72433
jayb@otenet.gr
www.miaow.info

Contact details:
Germany
Tel: +49 163 769 8262
john.heaton@arcor.de
www.miaow.info

Contact details:
Holland
Tel: +31 65 88 16 853
info@dierenhulpkreta.nl
www.miaow.info

Hungary

Minisa Society for Animal Protection, Hungary works to assist animals in need in Hungary. They have a variety of animals at their shelter including: dogs, cats, horses, pigs, goats, grey cattle, a buffalo, rackajuh (that is a Hungarian variety of sheep), a donkey, fowls, small animals and birds. Contact to assist the shelter as a volunteer.

Contact details:
Mail address: 7601 P
Misina Nature and Animal Protection Association, 7691 P
Tel/Fax: 06-20-217-3653 or 72/337-035
www.misina.hu/english_page.php
misina@t-online.hu

The White Cross, Budapest, Hungary Hungary has a terrible stray animal program (some estimates as high as 2 million cats and dogs) and there are no real state organisations to deal with this issue. This is a small, non profit animal protection organisation run entirely by volunteers in Budapest since 1991. They seek to make it easy for people to adopt and keep the loving, affectionate stray cats and dogs that come their way. The organisation has recently began a legal advocacy program to help enforce Hungary's 1998 animal protection law. They provide advice and help to citizens wishing to take action against people who have committed cruel acts to animals. Contact to help as a volunteer.

Contact details:
Tel: (1) 303-5694
Fax: (1) 453-24-69
www.feherkeresztliga.hu
feherkereszt@feherkeresztliga.hu

Ireland

Assisi Animal Sanctuary, Ireland was founded in 1995 to provide rescue and long term care for abused, neglected and abandoned small domestic animals. At any given time the Sanctuary is home to over 200 animals including dogs, cats, rabbits and guinea pigs. A few cats and dogs are permanent residents, all other animals await new homes, contact to assist with work at the Sanctuary.

Contact details:
1 Old Bangor Road, Conlig, Newtownards, County Down BT23 7PU
Tel: (028) 9181 2622
www.assisi-ni.org
info@assisi-ni.org

Blue Cross Animal Welfare Society, Ireland is dedicated to the needs of sick and injured animals. The charity is recognised as one of Ireland's foremost welfare organisations and has treated well over half a million sick animals since its foundation in 1945. Annually, up to 10,000 pets are treated and vaccinated and restored to full health at their mobile clinics and arising from our referrals to private practice. Today, there are ten mobile clinic locations in operation. All clinics are operated in the evenings by dedicated teams of volunteers, including drivers, veterinary surgeons and helpers. Contact to assist.

Contact details:
The Irish Blue Cross, 15A, Goldenbridge Ind Est., Tyrconnell Road, Inchicore, Dublin 8
Tel: 01 416 3030
Fax: 01 416 3035
www.bluecross.ie
info@bluecross.ie

Cats Aid Dublin, Ireland has the following aims: to rescue, rehabilitate and find good homes for unwanted cats on the explicit understanding that no health-recoverable cat taken in by Cats' Aid will be destroyed. They value the education of the general public in the care of cats with particular emphasis on the importance of spaying and neutering. Volunteers are required to assist with the use special purpose-built traps are used to catch cats who need veterinary attention or neutering. This helps reduce the overpopulation of stray cats and promote better health and quality of life.

Contact details:
Mail address: PO Box 2874, Ballsbridge, Dublin 4
Tel: (01) 6683529
www.catsaid.org
catsaid@gmail.com

Dog Rescue, Ireland is dedicated to rescuing and re-homing unwanted, abandoned Irish Greyhounds and dogs. The organisation believes that every dog has a right to life and states that no healthy dog will ever be destroyed while under 'Dog Rescue' care. Dog Rescue plays a huge part in rescuing Irish greyhounds, both ex-racer and other. These would otherwise be destroyed. These greyhounds are re-homed throughout Ireland, the United Kingdom and the United States as domestic pets. Contact to assist as a volunteer with fundraising, fostering or animal transport

Contact details:
Mail address: Dog Rescue Ireland, P.O. Box 4734, Dublin 1
Tel: +353 862171628/ Tel (inside Ireland) 0862171628
www.dogrescueireland.com
Berniew@esatclear.ie

Dogs Aid Animal Sanctuary, Ireland has a no destruction policy, and as a result the sanctuary is a permanent home for many dogs that are "too old or too bold" to be re-homed. From time to time they also take care of other animals including rabbits, bats, birds, foxes, feral cats, hedgehogs etc. Dogs Aid is entirely staffed by volunteers and entirely funded by public donations. The sanctuary aims to give the animals as normal a life as possible until they get re-homed - they spend most of the day playing in the grounds of the sanctuary rather than being cooped up in runs. Dogs Aid always needs volunteers for feeding, cleaning, walking, play and fundraising.

Contact details:
Tel: 087 2944310
www.dogsaid.ie
info@DogsAid.ie

Friends of Animals, Ireland works to assist animals in need. The dogs don't stay in cages but instead live as a group. Please contact to assist as a volunteer with dog walking, grooming and bathing, cleaning, DIY or fundraising.

Contact details:
Friends of Animals Rescue Centre, Greenpeace Cottage, Cullionbeg, Mullingar, Co. Westmeath
Tel: 044 93 42205
www.friendsofanimalsmullingar.com
info@friendsofanimalsmullingar.com **or** mary@friendsofanimalsmullingar.com

Galway SPCA, Ireland has been in Galway for roughly twenty years. The organisation has a shelter in Heathlawn , Killimor, Co. Galway and a shop offices and cattery in Galway City. They now also have a full time field inspector covering Galway city and county. They daily strive to improve the welfare of all animals both locally and international through education, assistance and advice. Volunteers are urgently needed, please contact to assist.

Contact details:
Galway Society for the Prevention of Cruelty to Animals, 2a Augustine Street, Galway
Tel: 091 563631
www.galway-spca.com
gspca@eircom.net

Leitrim Animal Welfare, Ireland is one of the largest rescue centres in Ireland, housing up to 100 dogs at any one time at their Drumkeerin base in North Co. Leitrim. Contact to offer your assistance as a volunteer.

Contact details:
Leitrim Animal Welfare, Drumkeerin, Co Leitrim
Tel/Fax: 071-9648300
www.leitrimanimals.com
leitrimawt@eircom.net

Irish Society for the Prevention of Cruelty to Animals (ISPCA) Their mission is that through education, legislation and ongoing support for their 26 affiliated societies they can Prevent Cruelty to All Animals. Local SPCAs throughout the country are constantly in need of volunteers - to help out at kennels and clinics, to assist in re-homing an animal, maybe fostering an animal while waiting for a good home, and to run and support fundraising events. Click here for information on each local SPCA in Ireland.

Contact details:
ISPCA Head Office: National Animal Centre, Derryglogher Lodge, Keenagh, Co. Longford, Ireland
Tel: 043 33 250 35
Fax: 043 33 250 24
www.ispca.ie
info@iscpc.ie

Limerick Animal Welfare, Ireland aims to promote the humane treatment of all animals, working towards a more compassionate Society. They believe in educating young people about responsible pet ownership and regularly give talks to primary and secondary schools. In this way they hope to educate and inform the animal owners of tomorrow and encourage them to make kindness and respect for all animals a way of life. They neuter all animals before re-homing and never to destroy an animal unless it is so ill that we cannot alleviate its suffering. Contact to assist as a volunteer.

Contact details:
Tel: 063 91110 or 087 6371044
www.limerickanimalwelfare.ie
limerickanimalwelfarequeries@gmail.com

Peoples Animal Welfare Society (PAWS), Ireland assists animals in need through neutering, veterinary treatments and re-homing. Contact to assist as a volunteer with dog walking, feeding, cleaning, fostering and transport.

Contact details:
PAWS Animal Rescue, Mullinahone, County Tipperary, Ireland
Tel: 052 9153507
www.paws.ie
pawsanimalrescue@eircom.net

Rainbow Re-homing Centre, Ireland works to assist hundreds of unwanted and abandoned dogs and cats. The centre is run by a dedicated group of volunteers and animal lovers. The organisation relies on these volunteers to feed and walk the dogs, clean out the pens and runs and deal with enquiries and visitors. Some volunteers provide additional support by helping to maintain the premises, building pens, securing the property and fostering timid or very young animals.

Contact details:
Rainbow Rehoming Centre, Ballygudden Road, Eglinton, Co. Derry BT47 3AF
Tel: 028 7181 2882 (dial 048 if ringing from RoI)
www.rainbowrehoming.com
rainbowrehoming@gmail.com

West Cork Animal Welfare Group, Ireland works to promote and encourage the welfare and protection of animals. They provide shelter and treatment for neglected, abandoned, unwanted and abused animals until they are ready to be re-homed. Visit schools to educate and advise, promote the benefits of vaccinations and investigate reports of cruelty. They have a non destruction policy. Contact to assist as a volunteer.

Contact details:
Mail address: West Cork Animal Welfare Group, P.O. Box 4, Clonakilty, Co. Cork, Ireland
Tel: 086 8500131 **or** 086 3862714
www.westcorkanimals.com
info@westcorkanimals.com

Italy

Bottlenose Dolphin Research Institute (BDRI) Sardinia, Italy is dedicated to the conservation of Bottlenose Dolphins and marine environment through education and research. BDRI members seek to contribute to the understanding and conservation of dolphins, expand the public awareness and concern for the marine environment, and add to the knowledge base of bottlenose dolphins through the sharing of collected field data.

Contact details:
Bottlenose Dolphin Research Institute BDRI, Via A. Diaz 4. Golfo Aranci 07020, Oblia – Tempio, Sardinia, Italy
Tel: +39 0789 183 1197 or +39 338 469 5878
www.thebdri.com
info@thebdri.com

ENPA National Board for Animal Protection, Italy was established in 1871, this organisation manages animal rescue organisations, rescues injured animals, promotes school education projects about pet care and has an inspectorate who prosecute those who abuse animals. Contact to assist as a volunteer.

Contact details:
Head Office: Via Attilio Regolo, 27, 00192 Rome
Tel: +39 (0)6.3242873 or +39 (0)6.3242874
Fax: +39 (0)6.3221000
www.enpa.it
enpa@enpa.it
international@enpa.it

International Organisation for Animal Protection (OIPA), Italy is an International Confederation of associations for the animal protection and for the defence of animal rights all over the world. OIPA is a Non Governmental Organisation affiliated to the UN Department of Public Information since 1992. The Organisation's purpose consists in the defence of animal rights and in the defence of the animals from every kind of mistreatment. Contact to assist.

Contact details:
OIPA – via Passerini 18–1–20162 Milano, Italy
www.oipa.org
info@oipa.org

Roman Cat Sanctuary, Italy this organisation shelters anywhere from 250 to 300 abandoned cats in Rome. They are an international group of volunteers who work together to raise the quality of life of Rome's abandoned cats. Volunteers aer crucial to this organisation - there is a lot of work to be done, please contact to assist.

Contact details:
Tel: +39 06 454 25240
www.romancats.com
torreargentina@tiscali.it **or** torreargentina@catsdb.com

Kosovo

Kosovo Dog Shelter, Kosovo the shelter exists to provide a safe, clean and humane refuge for the stray dogs of Kosovo. There are tens of thousands of stray dogs in Kosovo and unfortunately it is just not possible to provide sanctuary to all. The shelter can comfortably house approximately one hundred dogs. Healthy dogs suitable for adoption are vaccinated, treated for internal and external parasites, sterilised, tattooed and made available to home. They remain indefinitely at the shelter until they are successfully re-homed. Healthy dogs not suitable for adoption are treated as above and released to safe areas. The shelter is also a valuable education tool as it serves to show members of the public how dogs should be treated and cared for. Contact to assist as a volunteer.

Contact details:
Kosovo Shelter and Coaching Centre for Stray Dogs, Rexhep Luci 6/8, 10000 Prishtina
Tel: +377 (44) 126439 **or** +377 (44) 199061
www.kosovodogshelter.eu
qkstqe@hotmail.com

Malta

The Island Sanctuary, Malta has been in operation for over 20 years, catering for the needs of stray and abandoned dogs in Malta. Volunteers are needed to assist with walking, cleaning, feeding, grooming and fundraising at this shelter, please contact to help.

Contact details:
The Island Sanctuary, Fort Tas-Silg, Delimara, Marsaxlokk
Tel: (Malta) 21659895
www.islandsanctuary.com.mt
info@islandsanctuary.com.mt

Noahs Ark, Malta this is the only animal sanctuary in the north of the island. Volunteers are urgently required to help this shelter with cleaning, walking, feeding etc - please contact to assist.

Contact details:
Tel: (Malta) 79730900.
www.noahsarkmalta.org
fabio@noahsarkmalta.org

Society for the Prevention of Cruelty to Animals (SPCA), Malta promotes kindness to animals and attempts to prevent all forms of cruelty to all animals. The SPCA is interested in ensuring that any legislation that affects, or is likely to affect, the welfare of animals is promoted or opposed accordingly. This organisation works to care for an re-home abandoned pets, raise awareness of animal treatment and cruelty and assist animals in need. Volunteers are required to assist with DIY jobs and driving - contact to volunteer.

Contact details:
SPCA Malta, Triq L-Argotti, Floriana, Malta
Tel: (+356) 2123 4431
Fax: (+356) 2123 0486
www.spcamalta.org
home@SPCAMalta.org

Netherlands

AAP, Netherlands is a European sanctuary for exotic animals, it is based in Almere in the Netherlands The animals that end up with AAP often come from illegal trade, research laboratories, circuses, illegal zoos or directly from private people. The foundation specialises in hosting apes and monkeys. Other small exotic mammals can also find a shelter there, including raccoons, skunks and prairie dogs. The organisation requires voluntary help with hands-on animal assistance.

Contact details:
Mail address: P.O. Box 50313, 1305 AH Almere
Street address: Kemphaanpad 1, 1358 AC Almere
Tel: +31 (036)-5238787
Fax: +31 (036)-5384240
www.aap.nl
info@aap.nl

Animal Medical Care Foundation (AMCF), Netherlands works to support animal refuges and shelters worldwide with medicine, medical equipment and other care products. Contact to assist as a volunteer.

Contact details:
Animal Medical Care Foundation, Postbus 34, 5100 AA Dongen the Netherlands / Nederland
Tel: (00) 33 (0)386787442
Fax: (00) 33 (0)426236883
www.animalmedicalcarefoundation.com
info@amcf.nl

Cat Boat, Netherlands this is the only animal sanctuary in the Netherlands that literally floats. A refuge for stray and abandoned cats which, thanks to its unique location on a houseboat in Amsterdam's picturesque canal belt, has become a world-famous tourist attraction.a modern and professional sanctuary assisting hundreds of cats.

Contact details:
The Cat Boat, Singel 38.G, 1015 AB Amsterdam, The Netherlands
Tel: 020 6258794
www.poezenboot.nl
depoezenboot@gmail.com

Foundation for World Animals, Netherlands this organisation works to prevent the suffering of animals in developing countries and to treat wounded, ill treated and neglected animals.They are aiming to set up international laws for animal protection and to develop a universal declaration for animal welfare. Contact to assist as a volunteer.

Contact details:
Foundation for World Animals, Beukenlaan 236, 6823 MK ARNHEM
Tel: +31 (0)26 379 379 7
www.world-animals.org
email@world-animals.org **or** wouterdeboer@mail.com (volunteers)

Norway

Animal Protection Bergen, Norway was established in 1862 and is the oldest, independent animal protection organisation in Norway. Their main objective is to rescue, rehabilitate and re-home animals in distress. The centre accommodates between 30 - 60 cats at any given time. They also run a number of cat feeding stations for wild, stray cats and through our network of foster homes and help animals in need of special attention. Contact to help as a volunteer.

Contact details:
Dyrebeskyttelsen Bergen, Postboks 92, 5804 Bergen, Norway
Tel: (+47) 55 56 09 60
www.dyrebeskyttelsen-bergen.no
post@dyrebeskyttelsen-bergen.no

Norwegian Animal Protection Alliance, Norway is a national membership organisation that collaborates with animal welfare and animal rights organisations in Norway and abroad.his organisation is run on a voluntary basis.

Contact details:
Norwegian Animal Protection Alliance (Dyrevernalliansen) Brenneriveien 7, 0182 Oslo, NORWAY
Tel: (+47) 22 20 16 50
Fax: (+47) 22 20 60 39
www.dyrevern.no
post@dyrevern.no

Poland

Association for Nature (WOLF), Poland is a non-profit organisation, dedicated to conservation of mammals, particularly carnivores, and their habitats. Their mission is to protect endangered species and preserve their habitats. They are aiming to become a centre of excellence in research and education on carnivores and their habitats, working to achieve best practice in their conservation and management in Poland and abroad. Individuals interested in mammal ecology and conservation are invited to volunteer to assist them in the study of wolves, lynx, medium size carnivores and bats. Volunteers should be able to stay for at least two months, during which time you will carry out fieldwork involving spending days (and sometimes nights) in the mountains. Duties may include: searching for and collecting/recording different evidences of carnivore species e.g. tracks, scats, scent-marking; snow-tracking in the winter season and conducting transects through the forest in the vegetation season; observation of animal dens and searching for new dens, etc. Contact to assist.

Contact details:
Mail address: Association for Nature "Wolf" - Twardorzeczka 229, 34-324 Lipowa, Poland
Tel: +48 606 110046 **or** +48 604 625228
www.polishwolf.org.pl
sdnwilk@vp.pl **or** robert.myslajek@gmail.com

Portugal

Animais de Rua, Portugal this project does not have a physical space of its own. Instead, their work consists of capturing and neutering of stray animals and then returning them to their familiar grounds. Contact to assist as a volunteer with driving, trapping and fostering animals.

Contact details:
www.animaisderua.org
geral@animaisderua.org

Amigos dos Gatos do Algarve (AGA), Portugal
aim is to relieve the suffering of feral and stray cats in the Algarve, and to educate the public in their care and welfare. Volunteers assist in a variety of ways including the trap, neuter and return of animals.

Contact details:
A.G.A.,The Animal Charity Shop, Loja A5, Ed. Isamar, Av.Sá Carneiro, 8200 Montechoro Albufeira, Algarve Portugal
Tel: (00351) 289-514218
www.agalgarve.com
agalgarve@hotmail.co.uk

Grupo Lobo, Portugal is an independent non-profit organisation founded in 1985 working toward the conservation of the wolf and the wolves' habitat in Portugal, where the wolf population has been declining fast for many decades. Their Volunteers' Programme is intended for people who want to help conserve and protect one of nature's most beautiful and mysterious creatures the Iberian wolf. Volunteer duties include feeding and checking water supplies for the wolves, prevention of fires and monitoring the health and well-being of the wolves. Contact to assist.

Contact details:
Departamento de Biologia Animal . Faculdade de Ciências de Lisboa, Bloco C2., Campo Grande, 1749-016 Lisboa. Portugal
Tel: 217 500 073
Fax: 217 500 073
http://lobo.fc.ul.pt
globo@fc.ul.pt

Lagos Animal Protection Society (LAPS), Portugal they were the first sanctuary to be established in the Algarve (1980). Their work entails the rescue of domestic animals, birds, wildlife, plus an ongoing programme of sterilisation. Contact to assist as a volunteer.

Contact details:
Lagos Animal Protection Society (LAPS), Monte Ruivo, Odiaxere, 8600 Lagos, Algarve, Portugal
Tel: (00351) 282 687 334
www.laps.iperium.com
laps@sapo.pt

Romania

Help Labus, Romania is a non profit organisation working for the protection of animals, particularly the stray dogs in the town hall pound in Galati. Taking care of almost 800 dogs from the town hall shelters is not an easy task and they rely on voluntary help. Contact to assist with walking, grooming, feeding and transporting animals.

Contact details:
Str. Al. Cernat nr.15-19, bl. M5A, ap. 21, Galati, 800084, Romania
Tel: 0040724305053/0040751024562
www.help-labus.ro
help_labus@yahoo.com

Pro Animals, Romania works to assist all types of animals through rescue, neutering, re-homing and education projects. This organisation welcomes volunteers to assist with dog walking, cleaning, socialising, feeding, grooming, etc - contact to volunteer.

Contact details:
Carmena Serbanoiu - president
www.proanimals.ro/en
office@proanimal.ro

Contact details:
Patricia Paraschiv – vice-president
www.proanimals.ro/en
proanimals@xnet.ro

Romanian League in Defense of Animals (ROLDA), Romania is an international group operating in the Galati area. They work to improve the living conditions of strays through neutering and where possible, re-homing. Contact to assist.

Contact details:
ROLDA Romania, 16 Feroviarilor Str.,Bl C2,ap.18, Galati, Romania, 800563
www.rolda.org
rolda@care2.com

SPCA Romania works to prevent the abusive and cruel treatment of animals. The major principles guiding SPCA work are some of the six considerations in the preamble of the Universal Declaration of Animal Rights. Contact to assist.

Contact details:
www.spca.ro
spca_halmageanu@yahoo.com
office@spca.ro

White Fang Foundation for Animal Protection, Romania works to assist animals in need through neutering, re-homing and education. Contact to assist at their shelter with animal care, administration and education.

Contact details:
8, Carol Davila Street, Sector 5, Bucharest, Romania
Tel: (004) 021 – 410 05 91
www.platinumnet.ro/white_fang
fundatia_coltalb@yahoo.com

Russia

VITA Animal Rights Centre, Russia works at government level to introduce the animal welfare laws in Russia. They campaign against cruelties to animals by lobbying organisations, carrying out peaceful actions and spreading publications through the media. Contact to volunteer.

Contact details:
www.vita.org.ru
vita@vita.org.ru

Serbia

Cats Protection Sanctuary (Zenka), Serbia works to rescue and neuter stray and unwanted cats and kittens and, when and where possible, to re-home them to selected homes. They encourage the neutering of all cats and also disseminate information and educational resources to promote the cat welfare message. 'Zenka' Cats sanctuary has a strict non-euthanasia policy, cats and kittens are looked after until loving new homes are found. Contact to assist.

Contact details:
Sibnicka 10, 11210 Beograd, Serbia & Montenegro
Tel: +381 13 353-272
www.cathouse.bravehost.com
ljubica@panet.co.yu

Society for the Welfare of Homeless Animals, Serbia this is a registered no kill shelter that works to assist stray dogs and cats - contact to assist as a volunteer.

Contact details:
http://serbiananimalsvoice.wordpress.com

Spain

Abandoned Animals , Spain gives abandoned and maltreated animals refuge and protection and then rehabilitates and re-homes them. They assist dogs and cats and also ferrets, owls, goats, iguanas, pigeons, a piglet and even a young wild boar whose mother was killed during a hunt. They aim to return these to their natural habitat as quickly as possible, and even look for caring homes for non protected species such as goats. This organisation requires volunteers to assist with fostering, transport and more.

Contact details:
Tel: (0034) 696280319, Spanish and English
www.aaahelps.com
info@aaahelps.com

National Association of Animal Lovers (Asociación Nacional Amigos de los Animales - ANAA), Spain is a non profit making organisation, founded in 1992 in Madrid, Spain, in response to the high number of abandoned and mistreated animals in this country, and the government's lack of attention to the issue, limited only to the recollection and destruction of strays, making little effort to solve the problem in a humane and effective manner. This organisation has a comprehensive volunteering programme, contact to assist.

Contact details:
A.N.A.A., Apartado de Correos 197, 28140 Fuente el Saz de Jarama, Madrid (España)
www.anaaweb.org
voluntarios@anaaweb.org

APAP Alcala, Spain this shelter and adoption centre is managed by a team of volunteers; they work to make this animal protection centre a decent shelter, where the animals feel protected, are fed, have a clean place, where they get veterinary assistance, training, exercise and a lot of love, while they wait to be re-homed. Continue to assist as a volunteer.

Contact details:
www.apap-alcala.org
apap@apap-alcala.org

Asociacion Pro-Animales, Spain works to assist animals in need through rescue, care and re-homing. The organisation also offers veterinary help and assist other shelters and pounds. Contact to help as a volunteer.

Contact details:
www.proanimalesmallorca.org
asociacion@proanimalesmallorca.org

Centro Canino Internacional, Spain is now in its third decade of fighting for animal rights and helping to protect and care for abandoned and unwanted pets from all over Mallorca, but principally from the south-west and Palma city. They have saved thousands of dogs, cats, horses and donkeys from either neglect or physical cruelty. The organisation welcomes volunteers to assist with everything from dog walking, adoption counseling, humane education visits to schools, fundraising, animal assisted therapy or general office support.

Contact details:
Mail address: Apartado de Correos no 307, 07080 Palma de Mallorca, Illes Balears, España
Tel: (+34) 971 261 149
Fax: (+34) 689 500 521
www.centrocaninointernacional.org
centrocanino@centrocaninointernacional.org

Costa Blanca Feral Cat Trust, Spain arc working to reduce the feral and abandoned cat population with T.N.R. (Trap, Neuter and Return). Please contact to assist as a volunteer with the jobs of trapping cats and with transport.

Contact details:
Vera Davis, 13 Stansted Way, Frinton-on-Sea, Essex C013 0BG
Tel: 01255 679040 (UK)
www.feralcattrust.org.uk
vera1@feralcattrust.org.uk

Defensa Derechos Animal (Defending Animal Rights), Spain was the first Spanish NGO devoted to the defence and well-being of animals in general. The organisation works to: denounce the abuse and ill treatment of animals, promote and participate in drawing up appropriate legal standards, pressurise through acts of protest or vindication, information and awareness campaigns, preparing and publishing educational programmes and editing publications and awareness material. Contact to assist as a volunteer.

Contact details:
ADDA - Association Defending Animal Rights, c/o Bailén 164 Bajos, 08037 Barcelona
Tel: 93 459 1601
www.addaong.org
adda@addaong.org

El Refugio Del Burrito (The Donkey Sanctuary), Spain is a registered Spanish Association primarily concerned with the welfare of donkeys and mules. For many years they have been involved with rescue cases in Spain and have now established a refuge North of Malaga. They are a subsidiary of The Donkey Sanctuary in Southern England. The organisation is based in Fuente De Piedra, where they provide a safe haven with wonderful facilities for some of the many donkeys and mules that have faced such a hard life. They also investigate cases of neglect and cruelty and lobby for improved legislation for donkeys and mules in Spain and the rest of Europe. Contact to assist as a volunteer with caring for the donkeys.

Contact details:
El Refugio del Burrito, Apartado 25, 29520 Fuente De Piedra, Málaga, Spain
Tel: (00 34) 952 735 077
Fax: (00 34) 952 735 400
www.elrefugiodelburrito.com
info@elrefugiodelburrito.com

Fund for the Protection of Wild Animals FAPAS, Spain is a NGO, whose underlying objective is nature conservation. It works at a national level within Spain although the main part of its work involves the protection of endangered wildlife species in the Cantabrian mountain range. FAPAS has a network of volunteers who collaborate in the association's activities, contact to assist.

Contact details:
La Pereda s/n 33509 - LLanes - Asturias-España
Tel: 985401264
Fax: 985402794
www.fapas.es

Mona Foundation for Primate Welfare, Spain was set up to end the exploitation of primates in captivity. The foundation has established a sanctuary near Girona in Spain, which provides a home where rescued chimpanzees and other primates can live in a natural environment and where people can be inspired to understand and respect wild animals. This organisation depends heavily on volunteer helpers to continue its work. Volunteer keepers stay for six months at the project and take part in all aspects of caring for the primates. This includes, collecting and preparing food, cleaning indoor quarters, maintaining structures in the outdoor enclosure, organising enrichment activities, feeding primates and collecting data on the re-socialisation of primates. Once volunteers have gained two or three months experience at the project they will take on a considerable degree of responsibility in the daily care of primates. Other duties undertaken by volunteers include gardening, attending to visitors and helping at fundraising events. Contact to assist.

Contact details:
www.mona-uk.org

Nerja Donkey Sanctuary, Spain is run by volunteers dedicated to rescuing, caring for and protecting donkeys, mules and horses. They have along the way given refuge to many other animals from countless dogs to goats, pigs, chickens, cats, turkeys and many more. Contact if you can volunteer to assist with cleaning, dog and donkey grooming, walking, maintenance or transport.

Contact details:
Apartado de Correos 414, Nerja, 29780, Malaga, Spain
Tel: (+34) 664 558 133
www.nerjadonkeysanctuary.com
admin@donkeyaid.com

Peoples Animal Welfare Society (PAWS), Spain aims to provide shelter, care and compassion to animals who are lost or abandoned. They need voluntary assistance with dog walking, grooming, cleaning, maintenance and more - contact to assist.

Contact details:
Mail address: Paws at Box 627, Mojácar Playa, 04638, Almería, Spain
Tel: (+34) 678 490 217 or (+34) 678 490 217 **(volunteers)**
pawsenquiries@gmail.com **or** y.tromp@hotmail.co **(volunteers)**

SOS Animals, Spain works to help give the stray dogs and cats of the Costa del Sol a chance to lead full and active lives. This organisation assists with the rescue, care and re-homing of stray dogs and cats, contact to volunteer.

Contact details:
Tel: +34 626 351 881
www.sos-animals.org
info@sos-animals.org

Sociedad Protectora de Animales de Roquetas de Mar (SPAR), Spain is an animal welfare charity based in Roquetas de Mar in the province of Almeria, southern Spain that works to assist the homeless cats and dogs in Spain. To continue their vital work, this organisation is dependent on volunteers to assist in all aspects of running the sanctuary. Their volunteers help with feeding the animals, cleaning, construction, welcoming visitors, administration, etc.

Contact details:
Tel: La Mojonera - (+34) 950 520358 (Spanish/German/Dutch/English) or (+34) 950 334683
Fax: (+34) 950 520358
www.tuspain.com/spar/
sanctuary@tuspain.com

Scooby Shelter, Spain is a leading association in Spain that deals with the rescue of Galgos (Spanish Greyhounds). It is also the largest shelter in the country for all sorts of rescued animals. Tens of thousands of Galgos are bred annually in Spain in the hope of producing the national coursing champion. It was an annual tradition to kill Galgos by hanging them en-masse in the pine forests at the end of the coursing season. Scooby also takes in ducks, geese, battery hens, sheep, goats, pigs, ponies, and more. They welcome volunteers from all over the world to assist with: the preparing of food, feeding the dogs, cleaning the paddocks, providing the dogs with attention, and the many other jobs that come with working at a shelter.

Contact details:
Scooby, C/ San Francisco nº 3, 47400 Medina del Campo, (Valladolid), España
Tel: +34 983 48 10 65
Fax: +34 983 83 75 79
www.scoobymedina.org
info@scoobymedina.com

Sweden

Baltic Animal Care, Sweden is a non-profit organisation not affiliated with any political or religious organisation. Their aim is to improve animal welfare and we try to contribute to a development of veterinary medicine in east Europe. They support those who work at animal shelters in Latvia, Poland, Romania and Russia. Cats and dogs are their first priority. Contact to assist.

Contact details:
Mail address: Baltic Animal Care, Djurskydd i Östeuropa, Box 34171, 100 26 Stockholm, Sweden
Tel: +46 8 579 33 165
www.djurskyddiost.se
info@djurskyddiost.se **or** monica.ohlsson@zurich.se

Turkey

Friends of Fethiya Animals Association, Turkey assists with the rescue and care of stray animals. They are operating the first successful Neuter and Return program to control street dogs and cats in Turkey. As the program expands it could become the catalyst for changing the attitudes of animal care and control. Contact to assist as a volunteer.

Haykod Animal Sanctuary, Turkey rescues, cares for and re-homes animals. This is a large sanctuary working hard to make a difference for the animals in need in the area. Contact to assist as a volunteer.

Contact details:
Hayvanları Koruma Derneği, 35. Sokak, No. 10 Bahçelievler, 06500, ANKARA
Tel: Ankara 0312-215 15 55/0312-222 26 22
Fax: +44 (0) 1306 627901
www.haykod.org
info@haykod.org

Ukraine

Kiev City Society for the Protection of Animals, Ukraine works to establish a network of shelters for homeless animals and a comprehensive neutering programme. Volunteers are required to assist their work in a variety of ways.

Contact details:
213 Lenina Street, Urban Village, Gostomel
Tel: Ukraine 241 0435
www.animalprotect.org
ask@animalprotect.org

United Kingdom

"I looked at all the caged animals in the shelter...the cast-offs of human society. I saw in their eyes love and hope, fear and dread, sadness and betrayal. And I was angry. "God," I said, "this is terrible! Why don't you do something?" God was silent for a moment and then He spoke softly. I have done something," He replied. "I created you." - The Animals' Savior Copyright Jim Willis 1999

Advocates for Animals has a vision where all animals live their natural lives free from exploitation and abuse. Advocates for Animals works to secure respect for all animals, by overcoming exploitation and abuse, and inspiring a more compassionate society. They effect positive change for animals through high profile campaigns, political lobbying, investigations and public education. The organisation tries to match your skills & experience with the role you are given, sometimes it's all hands-on-deck for general work and at other times they have more specific opportunities available.

Contact details:
10 Queensferry Street, Edinburgh EH2 4PG
Tel: 0131 225 6039
www.onekind.org

Animal Defenders International (ADI) works to educate, create awareness, and promote the interest of humanity in the cause of justice, and the suppression of all forms of cruelty to animals; wherever possible to alleviate suffering, and to conserve and protect animals and the environment. Contact to assist.

Contact details:
Animal Defenders International, Millbank Tower, Millbank, London SW1P 4QP, UK
Tel: +44 (0) 20 7630 3340
Fax: +44 (0) 20 7828 2179
www.ad-international.org
info@ad-international.org

Animals in Distress, West Country undertakes to care for and nurture any unwanted domestic pet that is brought to them, providing it is suitable for re-homing and there is accommodation available at the Rescue Centre. They provide shelter, food, exercise and veterinary care for the animals in their care. Volunteers are required to help at their charity shop and at the shelter.

Contact details:
Head Office, 102 Reddenhill Road, Babbacombe, Torquay, Devon TQ1 3NT
Tel: 01803 312603
www.animalsindistress.uk.com

Animal Protection Agency (APA) is the UK organisation committed to ceasing the trade in wildlife for pets. Perhaps unbelievably, it is still legal in Britain to sell wild animals captured from other countries. The majority of wild-trapped animals die from the stress and disease that is associated with every stage of their harrowing journey. Next to habitat destruction, collection of animals for the pet trade is the main reason for the decline in many species. Attempts to regulate and control the trade have globally failed. The problem is getting worse, and time is running out! Contact to assist with campaigning and fundraising.

Contact details:
Animal Protection Agency, Brighton Media Centre,68 Middle Street, Brighton, BN1 1AL
Tel: +44 (0) 1273 674253
Fax: +44 (0) 1273 674927
http://apa.org.uk/
info@apa.org.uk

Ashbourne Animal Welfare was established in 1988 and is dedicated to the rescue and re-homing of stray and unwanted cats and dogs. They provide neutering and veterinary care before re-homing. Volunteer assistance required.

Contact details:
Wyaston Road, Ashbourne, Derbyshire DE6 1NB
Tel: 01335 300494 or 01335 300825
www.ashbourneanimalwelfare.org
ashbourneanimalwelfare@yahoo.co.uk

Animal Aid is the UK's largest animal rights group and one of the longest established in the world, having been founded in 1977. They campaign peacefully against all forms of animal abuse and promote a cruelty-free lifestyle. They investigate and expose animal cruelty, and our undercover investigations and other evidence are often used by the media to bring these issues to public attention. Contact to assist as a volunteer.

Contact details:
The Old Chapel, Bradford Street, Tonbridge, Kent TN9 1AW
Tel: +44 (0)1732 364546
Fax: +44 (0)1732 366533
www.animalaid.org.uk
info@animalaid.org.uk

Animal Accident Rescue Unit (AARU) is a Nottinghamshire based charity run by volunteers that is committed to rescuing animals by providing a transport service for sick and injured animals and birds and re-homing where possible. Contact to assist as a volunteer.

Contact details:
Mail address: Animal Accident Rescue Unit, P.O.Box 5414, Nottingham, NG14 5DT
www.animalaccident.org.uk
admin@aaru.org.uk

Animal Care Lancaster works to look after stray dogs and cats in the Lancaster area, visit the volunteer section of their website for further information about volunteering at their shelter.

Contact details:
Animal Care, Blea Tarn Road, Scotforth, Lancaster LA2 0RD
Tel: 01524 65495
www.animalcare-lancaster.co.uk
admin@animalcare-lancaster.co.uk

Animals in Need aims to alleviate animal suffering by attending to animal casualties in the Northamptonshire area. This is a rescue organisation run solely by volunteers; they attend both domestic and wild animals, and in 1999 were asked by Northamptonshire Police to work with them attending road traffic accidents and out of hours emergencies. Contact to assist as a volunteer.

Contact details:
Mail address: Animals In Need, P.O.Box 145, Northampton, Northamptonshire NN1 3AQ
Street Address: Pine Tree Farm, London Road, Little Irchester, Northants, NN8 2EH
Tel: 01933 278080
www.animals-in-need.org
admin@animals-in-need.org

Animal Protection Trust (APT) was formed in 1984 in response to local need for caring action to help unwanted, abandoned and ill treated animals, and was registered as a charity shortly afterwards. Its main function is the rescue and re-homing of unwanted domestic animals, providing the rehabilitation and veterinary treatment needed by so many who come into our care. No animal, domestic or wild, is refused help; those they cannot care for are referred to other rescue organisations who can help. Contact to assist as a volunteer.

Contact details:
Animal Protection Trust, Coldlands Farm, Haroldslea, Horley, Surrey RH6 9PJ
Tel: 01737 221280
www.animalprotectiontrust.org.uk

Animal Rescue Charity (ARC) their aim is to provide a safe haven (sanctuary) for neglected, unwanted and abandoned animals and wherever possible to treat and re-habilitate all animals including wildlife; sanctuary as we see it being a place of protection; a refuge. They are affectionately known as 'the small charity with a big heart'. They need volunteers for driving, dog walking, animal care and more.

Contact details:
Animal Rescue Charity, Foxdells Lane, Rye Street, Bishop's Stortford, Hertfordshire CM23 2HD
Tel: 01279 501547
www.animalrescuecharity.org.uk

Bat Conservation Trust (BCT) works on a number of levels to create a better world for bats. Volunteers are at the very heart of bat conservation in the UK - volunteer to count bats for the National Bat Monitoring Programme, or join the dedicated out of hours volunteers to keep the Bat Helpline running during our peak summer season - this directly saves the lives of bats and protects their roosts. Or, with the appropriate training, you could be one of the many Natural England volunteer bat workers who provide free roost visits to householders who have bats in their home to offer advice and support.

Contact details:
Bat Conservation Trust, 15 Cloisters House, 8 Battersea Park Road, London SW8 4BG UK
Tel: 020 7627 2629
Fax: 020 7627 2628
www.bats.org.uk
enquiries@bats.org.uk

Battersea Dogs & Cats Home has been rescuing lost and unwanted dogs since 1860 and cats since 1883. The organisation works to rescue, rehabilitate, re-unite and re-home dogs and cats. They have rescue centres in Battersea London, Windsor and Brands Hatch. Volunteers required.

Contact details:
Battersea, London, 4 Battersea Park Road, London SW8 4AA
Tel: 020 7622 3626
www.battersea.org.uk

Contact details:
Battersea, Old Windsor, Priest Hill, Old Windsor, Windsor, Berkshire SL4 2JN
Tel: 01784 432929

Contact details:
Battersea, Brands Hatch, Crowhurst Lane, Ash, Brands Hatch, Kent TN15 7HH
Tel: 01474 874994

Birmingham Nature Centre is situated 2 miles south of Birmingham City Centre and covers over six acres. Range of habitats includes woodland, wetland, farm and gardens and there are representatives from all the major groups of the world's animal kingdom. There are over 130 different species. Volunteers required.

Contact details:
Birmingham Nature Centre, Pershore Road, Birmingham, B5 7RL
Tel: 0121 472 7775
Fax: 0121 471 4997
www.birmingham.gov.uk/naturecentre
nature.centre@birmingham.gov.uk

Birmingham Dogs Home has been rescuing, re-uniting and re-homing stray, neglected and unwanted dogs from all over the West Midlands area for over 100 years. Contact to volunteer.

Contact details:
Birmingham Dogs Home, New Bartholomew Street, Digbeth, Birmingham, B5 5QS
Tel: 0121 643 5211
www.birminghamdogshome.org.uk

Contact details:
Sunnyside Kennels, Dark Lane, Coven, Wolverhampton, South Staffs, WV10 7NP
Tel: 01902 790618

Blue Cross aims to: "ensure the welfare of animals by providing practical care, highlight the benefits of companionship between animals and people and promote a sense of respect and responsibility towards animals in the community. The organisation provides support to the nation's pets and their owners by: treating pets whose owners cannot afford private veterinary treatment, finding permanent homes for unwanted or abandoned animals and educating the public in responsible animal ownership". Volunteers required.

Contact details:
Shilton Road, Burford, OXON, OX18 4PF
Tel: 01993 822651
Fax: 01993 823083
www.bluecross.org.uk
info@bluecross.org.uk

Bristol Dogs and Cats Home founded in 1887, the Home has grown in size and many improvements have been made to house a variety of animals. What started as a shelter just for dogs, now accommodates cats, rabbits, ferrets, birds and other small animals. Volunteers required to help with dogs walking.

Contact details:
Bristol Dogs & Cats Home, 50 Albert Road, St Philips, Bristol, BS2 0XW
Tel: 0117 9714197 (Admin Office) **or** 0117 9776043 (Bristol Dogs & Cats Home)
www.rspca-bristoldogsandcatshome.org.uk

Brighton Greyhound Owners Association are an independent charity who work alongside the national Retired Greyhound Trust and other local welfare organisations to ensure all greyhounds have a happy retirement. Voluntary help is required at their kennels – see bottom of their home page for further information.

Contact details:
Mail address: Brighton & Hove RGT, Eastridge Bungalow, Wineham Lane, Bolney, West Sussex, RH17 5SD
Tel: 01444 881788
Fax: 01444 881788
http://brighton.retiredgreyhounds.co.uk

Bransby Home of Rest for Horses provides safe permanent refuge to horses, ponies, donkeys and mules. Bransby has taken over 800 animals into care since it was founded in 1968 and registered as a charity. There are currently over 280 rescued animals at the Home as well as over 140 placed on their foster scheme. They require volunteers to assist with their fostering programme.

Contact details:
Bransby Home of Rest for Horses, Bransby, Saxilby, Lincoln, LN1 2PH
Tel: (01427) 788464
Fax: (01427) 787657
www.bransbyhorses.co.uk
mail@bransbyhorses.co.uk

Bath Cats and Dogs Home works to shelter and care for unwanted animals in the Bath; North East Somerset and West Wiltshire areas, until they are successfully re-homed. The organisation recognises the valuable and unique contributions volunteers can make to its work and aims to maximise the opportunities for volunteer involvement at all levels of the organisation and in shaping and delivering the organisational objectives. There are a variety of voluntary roles available.

Contact details:
Bath Cats and Dogs Home, The Avenue, Claverton Down, Bath, BA2 7AZ
Tel: 01225 787321
www.bathcatsanddogshome.org.uk

Cetacean Research and Rescue Unit (CRRU), NE Scotland is dedicated to the conservation and protection of whales, dolphins and porpoises in Scottish waters through scientific investigation, environmental education, and the provision of professional, veterinary assistance to sick, stranded and injured individuals. Volunteers required.

Contact details:
Mail address: Cetacean Research & Rescue Unit (CRRU), P.O.Box 11307, Banff, AB45 3WB, Scotland
Tel: +44 (0) 1261 851 696
http://crru.org.uk
info@crru.org.uk

Cat and Rabbit Rescue Centre (CRRC) believe animals deserve compassion, respect and consideration. That prevention of unwanted animals through the promotion of neutering and education, and the humane control of feral colonies is required, and no healthy animal should be destroyed if a responsible home cannot be found. Contact to assist as a volunteer.

Contact details:
The Cat & Rabbit Rescue Centre, Holborow Lodge, Chalder Lane, Sidlesham, Chichester, West Sussex, PO20 7RJ
Tel: 01243 641409
www.crrc.co.uk
info@crrc.co.uk

Celia Hammond Trust, London provides care and refuge for feral cats and kittens and for those animals which on the basis of age, temperament or appearance would not normally be taken in elsewhere. The organisation strives to: promote the welfare of animals through example and education, provide low cost treatment in their clinics for sick/injured animals, provide low cost neuter/vaccination clinics, operate a rescue service for animals, both domestic and feral in emergency situations, provide long and short-term sanctuary accommodation and re-homing facilities for rescued animals and to investigate complaints of cruelty and neglect and to take appropriate action. Volunteers required.

Contact details:
Head Office and Charity Shop: Celia Hammond Animal Trust,High Street, Wadhurst, East Sussex, TN5 6AG
Tel: 01892 783367
Fax: 01892 784882
www.celiahammond.org
headoffice@celiahammond.org **or** info@celiahammond.org

Contact details:
East Sussex – Greenacres Sanctuary: Animal Sanctuary & Rescue Centre, Greenacres, Stubb Lane, Brede, Near Hastings, East Sussex
Tel: 01424 882198
www.celiahammond.org
brede@celiahammond.org

Cat Survival Trust acts as a rescue organisation for "unwanted" cats from zoos and other collections. It currently cares for about 40 cats at its headquarters in Hertfordshire, England, many of which are rescued animals. This organisation relies on voluntary help - contact to assist.

Contact details:
The Cat Survival Trust, The Centre, Codicote Road, Welwyn, Herts, AL6 9TU
Tel: +44 (0)1438 716873
Fax: +44 (0)1438 717535
www.catsurvivaltrust.org
cattrust@aol.com

CottonTails Rabbit Rescue, Wiltshire works to rescue and re-home rabbits and guinea pigs in the UK. They also run education projects and require volunteers to assist their work.

Contact details:
Sherbourne House, 47 Station Road, Westbury, Wiltshire, BA13 3JW
Tel: 01373 864222
www.cottontails-rescue.org.uk

Colchester Cat Rescue is an independent local cat rescue charity covering Colchester and the surrounding area. They assist cats in need and provide neutering, microchipping, re-homing, etc. Contact to assist as a volunteer.

Contact details:
Colchester Cat Rescue, "Lyndhurst" Bromley Road, Colchester, Essex, CO7 7SF
Tel: 01206 864284
www.colchestercatrescue.org.uk
mail@colchestercatrescue.org.uk

Crescent Cat Rescue, Essex has been caring for cats for over 20 years. They require voluntary help in a number of ways - contact for more information.

Contact details:
www.crescentcatrescue.org.uk

Cats Protection (CP) was formed in 1927, Cats Protection (CP) has grown to become the UK's leading feline welfare charity. They now care for and find new homes for around 60,000 cats and kittens every year, through a network of 29 Adoption Centres and 260 voluntary-run Branches. They also provide an array of cat care information and promote the benefits of neutering for a happier pet and distribute education packs to a third of schools in the UK. Volunteers required.

Contact details:
National Cat Centre, Chelwood Gate, Haywards Heath, Sussex, RH17 7TT
Tel: 08707 708 649
www.cats.org.uk
helpline@cats.org.uk

Chilterns Dog Rescue Society cares for and re-homes dogs in need. They have a non destruction policy and provide training and support. Contact to assist with dog walking as a volunteer.

Contact details:
Bromley Heights, St Leonards Road, Chivery, Nr Tring, Hertfordshire HP23 6LD
Tel: 01296 623885
Answerphone: 01494 791467
www.cdrs.btinternet.co.uk/

Dorset Animal Workers Group, Dorset is a rescue organisation local to the Poole/Bournemouth area. They take in local dogs as well as those from rescues based in Ireland. Contact to assist as a volunteer.

Contact details:
Tel: 01202 380467 or 01202 428868
www.sithean.com/dawgdogs/
helengriffiths2110@hotmail.co.uk

Diana Brimblecom Animal Rescue Centre (DBARC), Berkshire assists and provides shelter for a variety of animals in need in the Berkshire area. Contact to assist as a volunteer.

Contact details:
Diana Brimblecombe Animal Rescue Centre, Nelsons Lane, Hurst, Nr Wokingham, Berkshire, RG10 0RR
Tel: 0118 9341122
Fax: 0118 9706762
www.dbarc.org.uk

Destitute Animal Shelter, Bolton has a non-destruction policy and are committed to reducing the unwanted dog and cat problem in Bolton by neutering every animal they re-home. They deal with over 2,000 animals per year, either reuniting them with their owners or finding them new homes. Volunteer assistance required.

Contact details:
The Destitute Animal Shelter, Northolt Drive, Bolton, UK
Tel: 01204 526486
www.animalshelter.org.uk

Drifters Reach Cat Refuge, Newcastle are an independent cat rescue and re-homing operation run on a voluntary basis. Their aim is to help stray, abandoned or abused cats along with those whose owners are no longer in a position to keep them. Drifters Reach is not intended to be a permanent sanctuary, but is aimed at providing a safe and caring environment for the cats while they are assessed and found a good permanent new home. Contact to help as a volunteer.

Contact details:
Drifters Reach Cat Refuge, 4 Dipton Avenue, Newcastle-upon-Tyne NE4 8DT
Tel: 0191 273 1827
www.driftersreach.org.uk/
admin@driftersreach.org.uk

Dolphin Care UK, Yorkshire works to stop the needless killing of dolphins. They require volunteers to assist with dolphin spotting.

Contact details:
Dolphin Care UK, 343 Cottingham Road, Hull, East Yorkshire HU5 4AS
Tel (mobile throughout day until 18:00):07761 109895
www.dolphincareuk.org/

Dogs Trust was founded in 1891, and formerly known as the NCDL. The organisation has always campaigned on dog-welfare related issues to ensure a safe and happy future for our four-legged friends. They have numerous sites around the country and volunteers are required.

Contact details:
Head Office mail address: Dogs Trust, 17 Wakley Street, London, EC1V 7RQ
Tel: 0207 837 0006
www.dogstrust.org.uk
info@careforthewild.com

David Shepherd Wildlife Foundation (DSWF) is an adaptable and flexible, non-bureaucratic organisation responding promptly to conservation threats by supporting trusted, reputable individuals and organisations operating in the field. Lean on administration but generous on funding, DSWF supports a range of innovative, vital and far-reaching projects throughout Africa and Asia, achieving real results for wildlife survival. They require voluntary assistance at their offices in Guildford.

Contact details:
David Shepherd Wildlife Foundation, 61 Smithbrook Kilns, Cranleigh, Surrey GU6 8JJ
Tel: 01483 272323/267924
Fax: 01483 272427
www.davidshepherd.org
dswf@davidshepherd.org

Eden Animal Rescue, Cumbria works to prevent cruelty to animals and relieve the suffering and distress of all animals in need of care and attention. They also arrange for the provision of good homes for the animals in their care. Contact to assist as a volunteer.

Contact details:
The Eden Animal Rescue Centre, Hardendale Shap, Cumbria CA10 3LQ
Tel: 01931 716 114
www.edenanimalrescue.org.uk/
admin@edenanimalrescue.org.uk

Foal Farm Animal Rescue Centre, Kent aims to take in as many sick, distressed and unwanted animals as possible and restore them to health and happiness. The animals are kept on a 26 acre farm where they are neutered, microchipped, vaccinated and given any other medical assistance necessary. Contact to assist as a volunteer with cleaning, maintenance, dog walking, cat fussing, home vetting, etc.

Contact details:
Foal Farm Animal Rescue Centre Jail Lane Biggin Hill Kent TN16 3AX
Tel: 01 959 572 386
www.foalfarm.org.uk
info@foalfarm.org.uk **or** volunteering@foalfarm.org.uk

Feline Cat Rescue, Luton works to help unwanted and abandoned cats find good homes, they also assist with neutering and veterinary care. Contact to assist with fostering.

Contact details:
Tel: (Barbara) 01582 732347 (All enquiries)
www.felinecatrescue.org.uk

Faith Animal Rescue, Norfolk provides a rescue, rehabilitation and re-homing service for abandoned, ill-treated and unwanted animals. The organisation cares for them in social accommodation, wherever possible with communal exercise areas. Contact to volunteer.

Contact details:
F.A.I.T.H. Animal Rescue, Stubb Road, Hickling, Norfolk NR12 0BW
Tel: 01692 598 312
www.faithanimalrescue.co.uk

Folly Wildlife Rescue, Kent has thousands of injured, orphaned or sick animals and birds admitted annually to their centre where they receive expert care and veterinary treatment. Most have been the victims of human activity. They specialise in the hand-rearing of mammals and birds and many are eventually returned to the wild. Their education programme, conducted through leaflets and talks, aims to reduce the number of incidents occurring. Contact to assist as a volunteer.

Contact details:
Folly Wildlife Rescue, Folly Cottage, Danegate, Eridge Green, Tunbridge Wells, Kent TN3 9JB
Tel: 01892 750865
Fax: 01892 750337
www.follywildliferescue.org.uk

Fen Bank Greyhound Sanctuary , Lincolnshire takes in Greyhounds of all ages from all over the United Kingdom, provides refuge and re-homes them. Contact to assist as a volunteer.

Contact details:
The Farmhouse, Fen Bank, Friskney, Lincolnshire PE22 8PS
Tel: 01754 820593
Tel/Fax: 01472 822979
www.fenbankgreyhounds.co.uk

Greenwich Cats Protection, London requires voluntary help with fostering and caring for cats in need.

Contact details:
Tel: (Volunteering Greenwich Branch) 020 8853 8666
www.greenwich.cats.org.uk

Great Dane Adoption Society, Lincolnshire Since 2000, over 700 dogs have been helped to find new, loving homes by the society which has over 600 members and over 200 home checkers and drivers. On average the Society homes between 12-15 dogs per month. They require volunteer help with fostering, home checking and transport.

Contact details:
Laurels Farmhouse, East Fen Lane, New Leake, Lincolnshire PE22 8JQ
Tel: 0870 7874691
Fax: 0870 7874691
www.danes.org.uk
information@danes.org.uk

Greyhound Compassion UK Greyhounds are exploited around the world for racing and coursing. At least 40 000 greyhounds are bred annually in Great Britain & Ireland to supply Europe. It is estimated that at least 20 000 are killed and 10 000 "retire" each year from racing at an average age of 2.5 yrs in the British Isles. Rescued greyhounds make wonderful pets and Greyhound Compassion operates a re-homing initiative from Devon, South West England. To assist with volunteering, see their website.

Contact details:
www.greyhoundcompassion.com
info@greyhoundcompassion.com

Green Fields Rescue, Berkshire work to rescue and re-home rabbits and guinea pigs and state that "we are not here to judge people who bring their animals into our rescue or re-home animals from our rescue. As long as you are acting in the best interests of the animal, then you are ok with us". Contact to help as a volunteer.

Contact details:
Green Fields Rescue, 29 Beedon Drive, Easthampstead Grange, Bracknell, Berkshire RG12 8GJ
Tel: 01344 488208
www.greenfieldsrescue.co.uk
contact@greenfieldsrescue.co.uk

Gables Farm Dogs' and Cats' Home, Cornwall founded in 1907, the organisation now looks after some 2,000 cats and dogs every year. They enforce a strict non-euthanasia policy and are committed to providing the best environment possible. Volunteers needed.

Contact details:
Gables Farm Dogs' & Cats' Home, 204 Merafield Road, Plymouth PL7 1UQ
Tel: 01752 331602
Fax: 01752 331604
www.gablesfarm.org.uk
info@gablesfarm.org.uk

Hereford and Worcester Animal Rescue is a small charity dedicated to the re-homing of stray, abandoned and unwanted dogs. Contact to assist as a volunteer.

Contact details:
Tel: 01568 760033
www.hwanimalrescue.org

Hebridean Whale and Dolphin Trust (HWDT) is dedicated to the conservation of Scotland's whales, dolphins, and porpoises and the Hebridean marine environment through education, research and working with Hebridean communities. Volunteers required.

Contact details:
Hebridean Whale & Dolphin Trust, 28 Main Street, Tobermory, Isle of Mull, Scotland, PA75 6NU
Tel: +44 (0) 1688 302 620
Fax: +44 (0) 1688 302 728
www.whaledolphintrust.co.uk
info@hwdt.org **or** volunteercoordinator@hwdt.org

Hawk and Owl Trust is dedicated to conserving owls and other birds of prey in the wild. They are also dedicated to conserving the places where owls and other wild birds of prey nest and feed and therefore, they also support many associated species - from field voles to skylarks, dragonflies to grass snakes - in a whole variety of habitats. Contact to assist with: conservation fieldwork, survey, practical expertise, such as making nest boxes.

Contact details:
Mail address: Hawk and Owl Trust, PO Box 400, Bishops Lydeard, Taunton TA4 3WH
Tel: 0844 984 2824
www.hawkandowl.org

Holly Hedge Sanctuary, Bristol works to assist companion animals in need in a variety of ways. Volunteers required to assist their work.

Contact details:
Holly Hedge Animal Sanctuary, Wild Country Lane, Barrow Gurney, Bristol BS48 3SE
Tel: 01275 474719
www.hollyhedge.org.uk
info@hollyhedge.org.uk

Horse and Pony Protection Association (HAPPA), Lancashire is one of the oldest and most respected equine welfare charities. Founded in 1937 to help fight against the transportation of large horses to the continent for slaughter, HAPPA continues to play a major role in all aspects of equine welfare. Volunteer assistance required.

Contact details:
HAPPA, Taylor Building, Shores Hey Farm, Black House Lane, Halifax Road, Briercliffe, Nr Burnley, Lancashire BB10 3QU
Tel: 01282 455992
www.happa.org.uk

Hyndburn Stray Dogs in Need, Lancashire this organisation assists stray dogs in need through rescue, care and re-homing. Voluntary assistance requested.

Contact details:
Tel: 01254 875990
www.hyndburnstraydogsinneed.co.uk

HorseWorld, Bristol is a charity that specialises in rescuing, rehabilitating and re-homing. There are lots of ways you can get involved, and you don't necessarily need specialised skills or experience, contact to assist. horses, ponies and donkeys in need.

Contact details:
Headquarters: HorseWorld, Delmar Hall, Keynes Farm, Staunton Lane, Whitchurch, Bristol BS14 0QL
Tel: 01275 832425
Fax: 01275 836909
Visitor Centre: HorseWorld, Staunton Manor Farm, Staunton Lane, Whitchurch, Bristol, BS14 0QJ
Tel 01275 540173/Tel: 01275 893039 **(Volunteer coordinator)**
Fax: 01275 540119
www.horseworld.org.uk

Hessilhead Wildlife Rescue Trust cares for Scotland's injured and orphaned wildlife. Volunteers needed for feeding, cleaning, caring for and monitoring patients. Resident volunteers stay in cabins on the site.

Contact details:
Hessilhead Wildlife Rescue Trust, Gateside, Beith, Scotland KA15 1HT
Tel: 01505 502415 (+44 1505 502415 international)
www.hessilhead.org.uk
info@hessilhead.org.uk

HULA - Home for Unwanted and Lost Animals, Milton Keynes operates from a 17 acre site which provides sanctuary for dogs, cats, rabbits, and other domestic animals until new homes can be found. They also have a number of resident animals including Goats, Pigs, Sheep, Cows, Ponies, and a Donkey who are permanently retired. Volunteers required to assist with fundraising, dog walking, animal care and general maintenance.

Contact details:
HULA Animal Rescue, Glebe Farm, Salford Road, Aspley Guise, Milton Keynes MK17 8HZ
Tel: 01908 584000
Fax: 01908 282020
www.hularescue.org
hularescue@tiscali.co.uk

Island Farm Donkey Sanctuary, Oxfordshire this organisation is a registered charity which cares for and protects abused and ill-treated donkeys and other animals. Volunteer assistance required.

Contact details:
Island Farm Donkey Sanctuary, Old Didcot Road, Brightwell-Cum-Sotwell, Wallingford, Oxfordshire OX10 0SW
Tel: 01491 833938
Fax: 01491 833938
www.donkeyrescue.org.uk
mail@donkeyrescue.org.uk

Jersey Society for the Prevention of Cruelty to Animals (JSPCA) was founded in 1868 with the intention of attempting to change public attitudes towards animals. Their mission is to prevent cruelty, promote knowledge, and, provide for aged, sick, lost and unwanted animals. To assist, complete the online volunteer application form on their website.

Contact details:
JSPCA Animals' Shelter, 89 St. Saviours Road, St. Helier, Jersey JE2 4GJ
Tel: (01534) 724331
Fax: (01534) 871797
www.jspca.org.je
info@jspca.org.je

Lothian Cat Rescue (LCR) is a registered charity formed in 1978 to help cats and kittens that have been abandoned, ill-treated, neglected or are unwanted for whatever reason.

Contact details:
Brewers Bush, Cockpen Road, Bonnyrigg, EH19 3JH
Tel: 01875 821025
www.lothiancatrescue.org
lothiancatrescue@live.co.uk

League Against Cruel Sports was established in 1924, and works to end cruelty to animals in the name of sport. The organisation welcomes voluntary help. Volunteers in the West Country would primarily help with monitoring hunts. A cool head and an ability to use a video camera are definite advantages. There are also opportunities to help with practical maintenance on a League sanctuary, contact to assist.

Contact details:
Mail address: League Against Cruel Sports, New Sparling House, Holloway Hill
Godalming, Surrey GU7 1QZ
Tel: 01483 524 250
www.league.org.uk
info@league.org.uk

Lancashire Cat Rescue aims to rescue and re-home stray, injured, sick or unwanted cats and kittens. This organisation cares for about 25 cats at a time and concentrates on quality of care rather than quantity of animals. They require voluntary assistance with fundraising.

Contact details:
Lancashire Cat Rescue, 33 New Lane, Penwortham, Preston, Lancashire PR1 9JH UK
Tel: 01772 750263
www.lancatrescue.co.uk
info@lancatrescue.co.uk

Llys Nini RSPCA, Swansea Wales is a self-financing organisation committed to providing animal welfare services in its area. The Branch is affiliated to the national RSPCA, but receives no automatic funding from it. Volunteer help required.

Contact details:
Llys Nini Animal Center, Penllergaer, Swansea SA4 9WB
Tel: 01792 229435
www.rspca.org.uk
info@rspca-llysini.org.uk

Lluest Horse and Pony Trust, Wales is a 40 acre farm rescue centre that works to assist horses and ponys in need of care and re-homing. They require volunteers to assist their work.

Contact details:
Lluest Horse and Pony Trust, Beili Bedw Farm, Llanddeusant, Llangadog, Carms SA19 9TG
Tel: 01550 740661
www.lluesthorseandponytrust.co.uk
lluestmanager@hotmail.co.uk

Leicester Animal Aid (LAA) is an animal charity that provides unwanted and homeless dogs and cats with immediate shelter, sanctuary, food and health care and the opportunity for permanent and safe re-homing with responsible and loving pet owners. Comprehensive volunteer job descriptions available.

Contact details:
The Huncote Pet Rescue Centre, Elmwood Farm, Forest Road, Huncote, Leicester LE9 3LE
Tel: 01455 888257
Fax: 01455 888550
www.leicesteranimalaid.org.uk

Labrador Lifeline Trust operates in Hampshire, Surrey, Berkshire, Middlesex and Lincolnshire. The organisation keeps in contact with the dog for the remainder of its life and will not supply dogs for working purposes, as the majority are already well-loved family pets and would not adapt to living outside. Contact to assist as a volunteer.

Contact details:
1 Street End, Elvetham, Hook, Hampshire, RG27 8BD
Tel: 01252 849560
www.labrador-lifeline.co.uk
selabres@btconnect.com

Marjorie Nash Cat Rescue, Buckinghamshire is a small charity in Buckinghamshire operated entirely by volunteers. Their 'motto' is that they always respond even when the National Charities have declined to help. They have a shortage of fosterers who can look after cats and kittens while they are convalescing or waiting for a new home.

Contact details:
The Marjorie Nash Cat Rescue, 31 Snowdrop Way, Widmer End, High Wycombe, Bucks HP13 6HP
Tel: 01494 715345
www.communigate.co.uk/bucks/mncr

Manx SPCA, Isle of Man promotes animal welfare throughout the Isle of Man. Every year, an average of 1,500 animals and birds are admitted to the sanctuary ranging from domestic pets such as dogs, cats and rabbits to wild birds such as seagulls and swans. The Society has successfully raised money for a specialised area to care for and treat injured or sick baby seals.
They require volunteers to assist at their shelter with dog walking and building maintenance.

Contact details:
Manx SPCA, Ard Jerkyll, East Foxdale Road, Eairy, IM4 3HL Isle of Man
Tel: 01624 851672/01624 852923
mspca@manx.net

Mammal Society, Southampton works to protect British mammals, halt the decline of threatened species, and advise on all issues affecting British Mammals. They study mammals, identify the problems they face and promote conservation and other policies based on sound science. The Mammal Society relies on volunteers to take part in mammal recording and survey work. It is only with voluntary help that they can continue. Contact to assist this project in your area.

Contact details:
The Mammal Society, 3 The Carronades, New Road, Southampton SO14 0AA
Tel: 023 80237874
www.mammal.org.uk
enquiries@mammal.org.uk

Mid Sussex Happy Breed Dog Rescue aims to protect dogs from ill-usage, cruelty and suffering and, in particular to provide kennelling and subsequent new homes for the dogs who have been lost or maltreated or are unwanted or abandoned, to provide veterinary treatment for dogs in the care of the Society and to educate the public to a sense of moral responsibility towards dogs and to encourage kindness towards them. Volunteer help required.

Contact details:
Mail address: PO Box 126, Burgess Hill, Sussex RH15 0SL
Tel: 01444 239005 or 01273 843897
www.happybreed.co.uk
carole@happybreed.co.uk **or** linda@happybreed.co.uk

Mare and Foal Sanctuary, Devon was established in 1988 and has rescued hundreds of horses throughout the UK and successfully re-homed them in safe, knowledgeable and loving homes. They are asking for voluntary help in their stables; with the mucking out, grooming and general welfare of the horses.

Contact details:
Honeysuckle Farm, Haccombe With Coombe, Newton Abbot, Devon TQ12 4SA UK
Tel: 01626 355969 (International +44 1626 355969)
Fax: 01626 355959
www.mareandfoal.org
office@mareandfoal.org

Margaret Green Foundation Trust (MGFT), Dorset specialises in animal care for all types of animals: cats, dogs, horses, rabbits, guinea pigs, birds, and even Doris a pot-bellied pig! With so many animals in need of care, their three sanctuaries are always busy, finding loving homes for our animal friends, welcoming new animals and looking after the permanent residents in their care. Volunteers are essential to their work.

Contact details:
Church Knowle:
Animal Sanctuary and Visitor Centre, Church Knowle, Wareham, Dorset BH20 5NQ, UK.
Tel: 01929 480474
www.animalsanctuaryuk.com
ck@margaretgreenanimalrescue.org.uk

Contact details:
Lincoln Farm:
Lincoln Farm Animal Rescue & Rehoming Centre, Bere Road, Winterborne Kingston, Blandford, Dorset DT11 9BP, UK
Tel: 01929 471340
www.animalsanctuaryuk.com
lf@margaretgreenanimalrescue.org.uk

Contact details:
Wingletang:
Wingletang Animal Rescue & Rehoming Centre, Brentor Road, Heathfield, Tavistock, Devon PL19 0LF, UK.
Tel: 01822 810215
wt@margaretgreenanimalrescue.org.uk

Marine Connection, London works for the welfare and conservation of all cetaceans and aims to secure a safer future for dolphins, whales and porpoises through education, campaigning and research, the Marine Connection raises awareness and minimises threats in order to make a positive difference to the current and long term protection of cetaceans worldwide. They need voluntary assistance with fundraising and with field research.

Contact details:
Mail address: Marine Connection, PO Box 2404, London W2 3WG
Tel: 07931 366352
www.marineconnection.org
info@marineconnection.org

Mayhew Animal Home, London has a vision of a world where all companion animals are wanted. They aim to set the standards in animal welfare. The Mayhew offers a wide variety of community services providing advice, care and assistance to animals and their carers whatever their circumstances and strives to tackle the companion animal welfare crisis from every possible angle. They require voluntary assistance with a variety of roles, some hands on with animals and other jobs involve assisting with administration and fundraising.

Contact details:
The Mayhew Animal Home, Trenmar Gardens, Kensal Green, London NW10 6BJ
Tel: 020 8969 0178 **or** 020 8968 2346 **(volunteers)**
Fax: 020 8964 3221
www.mayhewanimalhome.org
info@mayhewanimalhome.org **or** volunteering@mayhewanimalhome.org

The Moggery, Bristol aims to provide an all round solution for local cat problems. Their work includes: finding a new home for the loved pet of an elderly local resident entering a nursing home, trapping and neutering a feral colony, caring for a family of sick / abandoned kittens, re-homing an unwanted litter of kittens and providing assisted neutering. Voluntary assistance required.

Contact details:
Tel: 0117 924 3128
www.themoggeryrehomingcentre.co.uk

Nine Lives Cat Rescue, Hampshire exists to help elderly cats in need of care. Contact to assist as a volunteer.

Contact details:
Newtown Road, Sherfield English Hants, Romsey, Hampshire SO51 6JY
Tel: 01794 340743 (10am-5pm)
www.nine-lives.org.uk
cats@nine-lives.org.uk

National Seal Sanctuary, Cornwall based in Cornwall, are a rescue, rehabilitation, and release centre for seals. Last season they rescued over 40 pups – contact to assist as a volunteer or for information about internships.

Contact details:
Work Placement Coordinator, National Seal Sanctuary, Gweek, Nr Helston, Cornwall TR12 6UG
Tel: 01326 221361
www.sealsanctuary.co.uk
seals@sealsanctuary.co.uk

National Animal Welfare Trust (NAWT) aims for the provision of care and shelter for stray, neglected and unwanted animals of all kinds; the protection of animals of all kinds from ill-usage, cruelty and suffering; and in particular, to rescue and provide care and shelter for stray, neglected and unwanted animals of all kinds and find suitable homes for any such animals. Contact to volunteer.

Contact details:
Head Office: Tyler's Way, Watford-By-Pass, Watford, Hertfordshire WD25 8WT
Tel: 020 8950 0177 (0900 to 1700 Mon-Fri)
Fax: 020 8420 4454
www.nawt.org.uk
watford@nawt.org.uk

National Fox Welfare Society (NFWS), Northants works to assist injured and sick foxes in need. Contact to assist as a volunteer with the rescue, care and fostering of foxes.

Contact details:
NFWS, 135 Higham Road, Rushden, Northants, NN10 6DS
www.nfws.org.uk

North Clwyd Animal Rescue (NCAR) works to rescue, care for and re-home animals in this area. They require volunteers to assist by fostering animals.

Contact details:
North Clwyd Animal Rescue, Maes Gwyn, Glan yr Afon Road, Trelogan, Nr. Holywell, Flintshire CH8 9BD
Tel: 01745 560546
www.ncar.org.uk
reception@ncar.org.uk **or** owain@ncar.org.uk **or** nickyowen@ncar.org.uk

Orangutan Foundation UK exists to undertake conservation and promote the understanding of the wild orangutan's natural habitat and tropical rain forests of Borneo and Sumatra and works to promote the long-term study of wild orangutan behaviour, evolution, ecology and biology. Voluntary assistance required in their London office.

Contact details:
Orangutan Foundation, 7 Kent Terrace, London NW1 4RP
Tel: +44 (0)207 724 2912
Fax: +44 (0)207 706 2613
www.orangutan.org.uk

Original Cat Action Trust, Devon is the pioneer society for feral cats. Feral cats are domestic cats living wild, either because they and their descendants have strayed from home or more commonly because they are unwanted and have been abandoned. The Original Cat Action Trust does a lot of excellent trapping and neutering work and urgently needs dedicated people to start up new branches all around the country to help feral cats. Contact to assist as a volunteer.

Contact details:
The Original Cat Action Trust, Kingsmill Partnership, 75 Park Lane, Croydon, Surrey CR9 1XS
Tel: 01726 824284 or 07968 344427
www.catactiontrust.org.uk
info@catactiontrust.org.uk

Paws for Kids, Bolton was started by a group of women who recognised that there is a gap in the provision of services to women and their families who were escaping from violent homes. While refuges could accommodate women and their children, they could not take in any pets belonging to the family. Animals had to be either left behind to suffer at the hands of the violent man, given away to someone else or even put down. Often women remain in a violent relationship rather than have to abandon their pets to a violent fate or give them away permanently. Paws for Kids fostering service offers some peace of mind for women and their children, knowing their pets are safe while they await re-housing from a refuge. Volunteers required and training is provided.

Contact details:
Mail address: Paws for Kids, P O Box 329, Bolton BL6 7WA
Tel: 01204 394 842
www.pawsforkids.org.uk
petfostering@pawsforkids.org.uk **or** safehaven@pawsforkids.org.uk

Peoples Dispensary for Sick Animals (PDSA) works to care for the pets of needy people by providing free veterinary services to their sick and injured animals and promoting responsible pet ownership. They are the largest private employer of fully qualified veterinary surgeons and veterinary nurses in Europe. PDSA is non-campaigning, and non-political. Volunteers required.

Contact details:
Mail address: PDSA National Volunteering Centre, Unit 8/9 City Business Centre, Hyde Street, Winchester, Hampshire SO23 7TA
Tel: 0800 854 194
www.pdsa.org.uk

People's Trust for Endangered Species (PTES) takes on a whole range of projects for endangered and threatened species and their habitats all over the world, as well as in the UK. This work varies enormously from project to project and includes research into conservation problems or practical conservation work in the field. They are currently looking for enthusiastic volunteers in eight UK counties: Herefordshire, Gloucestershire, Worcestershire, Cambridgeshire, Cumbria, Devon, Essex and Kent to carry out orchard surveys.

Contact details:
People's Trust for Endangered Species, 15 Cloisters House, 8 Battersea Park Road, London SW8 4BG
Tel: 020 7498 4533
Fax: 020 7498 4459
www.ptes.org
enquiries@ptes.org

Pet Rescue UK is a voluntary organisation aspiring to find suitable everlasting homes for mistreated and unwanted animals throughout the UK. They arrange foster homes and ensure micro-chipping, neutering, home visits, etc. Pet Rescue UK was also created to bring attention to all the animals that are in need of a new home, or transport to get there, or a place to stay until a new home is found, etc. Pet Rescue UK helps create a link between rescues, fosterers, transport and animals in need and also helps other rescues. Contact to assist in a voluntary capacity.

Contact details:
Mail address: Pet Rescue UK, P O Box 138, South Shields NE34 8WY
www.pet-rescue.org.uk

People and Dogs Society (PADS) aims to improve life for dogs by helping owners with problems and promoting responsible dog ownership. PADS is run entirely by volunteers, contact to assist.

Contact details:
People And Dogs Society (PADS), Longwood, Carleton Close, Pontefract, West Yorkshire WF8 3NB
Tel: 0845 269 0093
www.padsonline.org
pads@padsonline.org.uk

Royal Society for the Provention of Cruelty to Animals (RSPCA) has a vision of a world in which all humans respect and live in harmony with all other members of the animal kingdom. Their mission is to prevent cruelty, promote kindness to and alleviate suffering of animals. Volunteers required to fulfill many different roles at their branches throughout the country.

Contact details:
RSPCA Enquiries Service, Wilberforce Way, Southwater, Horsham, West Sussex RH13 9RS
Tel: 0300 1234 555
Fax: 0303 123 0100
www.rspca.org.uk

Retired Greyhound Trust (RGT) is a national charity dedicated to finding homes for greyhounds at the end of their racing careers. It was set up in 1975 and since then has re-homed almost 40,000 greyhounds. There are 70 branches of the Trust based right across the UK, from the Isle of Skye to Jersey. Volunteers required to fulfill many different roles at their branches throughout the country.

Contact details:
RGT Head Office: Park House, Park Terrace, Worcester Park, Surrey KT4 7JZ
Tel: 0844 8268424
Fax: 0844 8268425
www.retiredgreyhounds.co.uk

Re-homing Animal Telephone Service (RATS) doesn't have a shelter and relies on help from volunteer foster carers. The group aims to re-home animals into loving, secure homes so that they can live out the remainder of their lives happily. Whilst in their care, every animal will receive any necessary veterinary treatment required and it is our policy never to have a healthy animal put to sleep. Volunteer help required.

Contact details:
www.rats-animalrescue.co.uk
info.rats@gmail.com

Royal Society for the Protection of Birds (RSPB) was founded in 1889 and since then has grown into Europe's largest wildlife conservation charity with more than a million members. From its initial stance against the trade in wild birds' plumage, the issues which the Society tackles have grown hugely in number and size. Voluntary job vacancies advertised.

Contact details:
UK Headquarters – The Lodge, Sandy, Bedfordshire SG19 2DL
Tel: 01767 680551
www.rspb.org.uk
volunteers@rspb.org.uk

Raystede Animal Welfare Centre, Sussex aims to prevent and relieve cruelty to animals and to protect them from unnecessary suffering. Over 1,500 unwanted and abandoned animals arrive at the centre annually. Dogs, cats and other companion animals are found new caring homes while others remain in Raystede's care for the rest of their days. Visit their site for a volunteer application form and more information about volunteering.

Contact details:
Raystede Animal Welfare, Ringmer, East Sussex, BN8 5AJ
Tel: (01825) 840252
Fax: (01825) 840995
www.raystede.org
info@raystede.org

Rabbit Welfare Association and Fund (RWAF) works to improve the lives of domestic rabbits across the UK through education and communication by making people realise that rabbits are intelligent creatures that need space, exercise, companionship and stimulation and are not to be bought on a whim. This organisation is run by volunteers and welcomes assistance.

Contact details:
Mail address: Rabbit Welfare Association & Fund, P O Box 603, Horsham, West Sussex RH13 5WL
Tel: 0844 324 6090
www.houserabbit.co.uk

Stokenchurch Dog Rescue, Buckinghamshire was originally formed by local residents in 1963 to save the lives of stray and unwanted dogs as well as those impounded by the Police. The organisation currently has kennelling facilities for 60 dogs and aims to re-home all the dogs that come in to them. Contact to assist as a volunteer.

Contact details:
Tower Farm, Oxford Road, Stokenchurch, Bucks, HP14 3TD
Tel: 01494 482695
www.stokenchurchdogrescue.co.uk

Siamese Cat Rescue UK are a registered charity, looking after the welfare of Siamese cats. They operate a rescue and re-homing service and foster unwanted cats. Voluntary assistance required with home visits.

Contact details:
www.siameserescue.org.uk

Sea Watch Foundation, Buckinghamshire is a national charity, dedicated to the conservation and protection of whales, dolphins & porpoises in British & Irish waters. Through its continuous programme of research and monitoring, Sea Watch provides invaluable information on changes to the status and distribution of cetacean populations and the condition of their habitats. This is used to raise awareness of any issues and prompt environmental change to help conserve & protect these mysterious creatures. Contact to assist as a volunteer.

Contact details:
Mail address: Sea Watch Foundation, PO Box 3688, Chalfont St Peter, Gerrards Cross SL9 9WE
Tel: 0845 202 3892
www.seawatchfoundation.org.uk
info@seawatchfoundation.org.uk

Seal Group, Cornwall was set up to monitor the presence (or absence) of seals in a north coast colony. Contact to assist as a volunteer.

Contact details:
Tel: Sue Sayer on 01736 754562
www.suesseals.eclipse.co.uk
ssayer@suesseals.eclipse.co.uk

Scottish Society for the Prevention of Cruelty to Animals (SSPCA) was established in 1839 to prevent cruelty to animals and promote kindness and humanity in their treatment, the Scottish Society for the Prevention of Cruelty to Animals is Scotland's leading animal welfare charity. Today, its work is as necessary as ever. The Scottish SPCA is a reporting agency for the enforcement of animal protection laws. Volunteers required.

Contact details:
Scottish SPCA, Kingseat Road, Halbeath, Dunfermline KY11 8RY
Tel: 03000 999 999
www.scottishspca.org

Second Chance Animal Trust (SCAT), Norfolk finds homes for cats, dogs and all manner of animals. Veterinary and home checks are part of the service. Contact to assist as a volunteer.

Contact details:
www.oldies.org.uk
oldies@oldies.org.uk

St Francis Persian Rescue, Yorkshire is a small independent cat rescue charity based in North Yorkshire. They specialise in the rescue and re-homing of Persian and other long-haired breeds of cat. Contact to assist.

Contact details:
St Francis Persian Rescue, St Francis Cottage, Thornborough, Bedale DL8 2RQ
Tel: 01677 470 344 or 01924 826 149
www.stfrancisrescue.co.uk

Secret World Wildlife Rescue is now the only 24/7 wildlife rescue centre in the South West, annually caring for over 4,000 sick, injured and orphaned animals. The aim of their rescue and rehabilitation work is always to return the animals to the wild whenever possible, and the organisation believes in always giving an animal the best possible care. They have a team of around 400 dedicated volunteers who assist in a number of ways. This ranges from performing animal care duties, cleaning animal enclosures or maintenance, through to picking up injured animals and bringing them to Secret World, and many jobs in between - contact to assist.

Contact details:
New Road, East Huntspill, Highbridge, Somerset, TA9 3PZ, UK
Tel: (44) (01278) 783250
www.secretworld.org

Safe House for Unwanted Animals (SHUA), Cardiff is a charity involved in emergency rescue, rehabilitation and re-homing of kittens & cats in Cardiff and the Vale area. Volunteers required to assist with cat trapping, fostering, etc.

Contact details:
Hayes House, Hayes Road, Sully, Cardiff CF64 5SE UK
www.shua.org.uk
contact@shua.org.uk

Tiggywinkles Wildlife Hospital is the world's busiest wildlife hospital and cares for sick & injured hedgehogs, badgers, wild birds, foxes, even reptiles & amphibians. They are a specialist hospital, using all available veterinary welfare skills, dedicated to rescuing and rehabilitating all species of British wildlife. Volunteers required.

Contact details:
Tiggywinkles, Aston Road, Haddenham, Aylesbury, Buckinghamshire HP17 8AF
Tel: 01844 292292
Fax: 01844 292640
www.sttiggywinkles.org.uk
mail@sttiggywinkles.org.uk

Thornberry Animal Sanctuary, Sheffield is a medium sized animal sanctuary that operates a strict no kill policy and helps dogs and cats in need of rescue and care. The organisation requires voluntary help.

Contact details:
Thornberry Animal Sanctuary, The Stables, Todwick Road, North Anston, Sheffield, South Yorkshire, S25 3SE
Tel: 01909 564399
www.thornberry-animal-sanctuary.org
tasadmin@hotmail.co.uk

Twinkle Trust Animal Aid are a small UK registered charity dedicated to helping feral or neglected cats abroad. Their primary role is to humanely control the feral cat population through treatment and sterilisation. They need voluntary help with cat sterilisation trips in Fuerteventura.

Contact details:
Mail address: Twinkle Trust Animal Aid, P.O. Box 3080, South Croydon, CR2 6GX
www.twinkletrust.org
twinkletrust@aol.com

Vale Wildlife Rescue offers help to thousands of these casualties every year by treating them and where possible release them back in to the wild. They are on call 24 hours a day, every single day of the year. Volunteers required to assist in the wildlife hospital with a variety of tasks.

Contact details:
Vale Wildlife Hospital & Rehabilitation Centre, Station Road, Beckford, Nr Tewksbury, Gloucestershire GL20 7AN
Tel: 01386 882288
Fax: 01386 882299
www.valewildlife.org.uk
info@valewildlife.org.uk

<u>Weirfield Wildlife Hospital, Lincolnshire</u> helps wildlife and provides first aid, primary and secondary care followed by recuperation, rehabilitation and eventual release back into the wild. All care is provided on a voluntary basis – contact to assist.

Contact details:
Tel: 01522 530428
www.weirfield.co.uk
mail@weirfield.co.uk

<u>Wildlives Wildlife Rescue and Rehabilitation Centre, Essex</u> works to provide treatment and care for sick, injured and orphaned wildlife with the ultimate aim of rehabilitating them back into the wild. The organisation works to create public awareness of wildlife and all issues relating to the benefit of wildlife. Voluntary help required.

Contact details:
Wildlives Rescue and Rehabilitation Centre East Anglia, 'Catkins' Frating Road, Thorrington, Colchester, Essex CO7 8HT
Tel: 01206 251174
Fax: 01206 251174
www.wildlives.org.uk

<u>Waggy Tails Rescue</u> is based near Poole and Bournemouth. They have a non destruction policy and rescue and re-home dogs that have been abandoned, neglected, mistreated, orphaned or otherwise need a new, loving home. They work with foster homes, so dogs are rarely placed in kennels – contact to assist as a volunteer.

Contact details:
69 Cobham Road, Ferndown Industrial Estate, Wimborne, Dorset BH21 7QE
Tel: 01202 875000
www.waggytails.org.uk

<u>Wiccaweys</u> is a non profit making organisation who are dedicated to the welfare of Border Collies & Working Sheepdogs. They have rescued, rehabilitated and re-homed hundreds of Border Collies, many of whom would have otherwise been put to sleep. Contact to assist as a volunteer.

Contact details:
Tel: 07905 203254 - 10am & 7pm, Monday – Friday, 10am & 4pm, Saturday - Sunday
www.wiccaweys.co.uk
wiccaweys@aol.com

Wood Green Animal Shelters has been rescuing and re-homing animals since 1924. The charity has two sanctuaries – in London and Cambridge and takes in over 6,000 animals a year. Volunteers required.

Contact details:
Godmanchester Shelter (HQ):
King's Bush Farm, London Road, Godmanchester, Cambs PE29 2NH
Tel: 0844 248 8181
Fax: 01480 832815
www.woodgreen.org.uk
info@woodgreen.org.uk

Contact details:
London Shelter:
601 Lordship Lane, Wood Green, London N22 5LG
Tel: 0844 248 8181
Fax: 0208 889 0245
www.woodgreen.org.uk
info@woodgreen.org.uk

Contact details:
Heydon Shelter:
Highway Cottage, Heydon, Herts SG8 8PN
Tel: 0844 248 8181
Fax: 01763 838824
www.woodgreen.org.uk
info@woodgreen.org.uk

Woodside Animal Sanctuary, Devon assists a variety of animals in need through their neutering and re-homing programmes. Contact to assist this organisation as a volunteer.

Contact details:
www.theonly.net/woodside/about.htm

Willows Animals, Scotland aims to take animals that are unsuitable for re-homing elsewhere and that have been rejected by other organisations. Willows helps people as well as animals through Animal Assisted Therapy (AAT) programs. These programs offer people who find it therapeutic, the chance to interact with the animals and help with their care and upkeep. The animal contact coupled with the good atmosphere here has proved to be a great help to people in need of some friendly support. Volunteer help requested.

Contact details:
Willows Animal Sanctuary, Mrs Kate Robinson, Lambhill, New Pitsligo Fraserburgh, AB43 6NY
Tel: 01771 653112
www.willowsanimals.com
kate@willowsanimals.com

Wellcat Cat Rescue, Birmingham is a small charity dedicated to caring for and re-homing cats. Volunteers required.

Contact details:
30 Quinton Road West, Quinton, Birmingham B32 2QD
Tel: 0121 426 5594
www.wellcat.org.uk
wellcatwoman@blueyonder.co.uk

World of Owls, UK works to ensure the survival of owls throughout the world. They aim to achieve this by rescue, conservation, education, research and restoration of their natural habitat. Volunteer helpers required.

Contact details:
World of Owls Centre, Randalstown Forest, County Antrim, BT41 3LE
Tel/Fax: 028 94 472 307
www.worldofowls.com
admin@worldofowls.com

World Association for Transport Animal Welfare and Studies (TAWS) started as an informal group of vets who wanted to use their specialist knowledge to improve the long term health, welfare and management of draught and transport animals. Their work spans four continents, contact to assist.

Contact details:
World Association for Transport Animal Welfare and Studies, Hardwick Court Farm, Hardwick Lane, Chertsey, Surrey, KT16 0AD, United Kingdom
Tel: 01932 564366 / (+44 1932 564366)
Fax: 01932 567837 / (+44 1932 567837)
www.taws.org
info@taws.org

Yorkshire Swan Rescue Hospital was set up in early 2006 to rescue, rehabilitate and release sick and injured swans and water birds in Yorkshire and the surrounding counties. Although they specialise in the rehabilitation and release of swans and water birds, they aim to help all forms of wildlife. Contact to assist as a volunteer.

Contact details:
Mail address: Yorkshire Swan & Wildlife Rescue Hospital, Stearsby Farm, Brandsby, Near York, North Yorkshire YO61 4SH
www.ysrh.org.uk
info@ysrh.org.uk

Yorkshire Wildlife Trust has worked for more than 50 years to protect vulnerable wildlife of all types - animals, birds, plants - and the places where they live. Their work is helping to secure the future of many important habitats and species, which might otherwise be lost. Contact to assist as a volunteer.

Contact details:
1 St George's Place, York, YO24 1GN
Tel: 01904 659570
Fax: 01904 613467
www.ywt.org.uk
info@ywt.org.uk

NORTH AMERICA

United States of America

"I care not much for a man's religion whose dog and cat are not the better for it." - Abraham Lincoln

2nd Chance 4 Pets, California is a non-profit organisation staffed by volunteers. They work throughout the state and across the nation to provide pet owners with comprehensive information about lifetime care solutions to ensure that pets will always be cared for. They are committed to providing assistance to pet owners in making lifetime care decisions for their pets. Based on the overwhelming response and requests for assistance they have received from pet owners, animal rescue groups, shelters, hospices and veterinarians, our programs have made a significant impact on preventing unnecessary euthanasia.

Contact details:
Mail address: 2nd Chance 4 Pets, 1484 Pollard Road, No. 444, Los Gatos, CA. 95032
Tel: 408 871 1133
www.2ndchance4pets.org
info@2ndchance4pets.org

American Humane Association American Humane's Emergency Services Volunteers are animal lovers committed to making sure animal needs are met during times of crisis. These volunteers are trained by American Humane to respond to the needs of animals, bringing vital skills in animal handling as well as necessary supplies for setting up temporary shelters.

Contact details:
National Headquarters: American Humane Association, 63 Inverness Drive East, Englewood, CO 80112
Tel: (800) 227-4645 or (303) 792-9900
Fax: (303) 792-5333
www.americanhumane.org
info@americanhumane.org

Contact details:
Capitol Hill Office: American Humane Association, 1400 16th Street NW, Suite 360, Washington, DC 20036
Tel: (202) 302-8357
www.americanhumane.org
info@americanhumane.org

American Humane's Animal Emergency Services Volunteers help communities care for animals by offering support in: communications, safety, equipment, logistics, administration, finance, public relations, animal control, resource distribution, temporary animal shelters, care and exercising of animals. All volunteers are required to be ready to travel to a disaster site within six hours of being called. Contact for more information.

Contact details:
www.americanhumane.org

Alley Cat Allies, USA is the national non profit clearinghouse for information on feral and stray cats. For more than a decade Alley Cat Allies has advocated Trap-Neuter-Return (TNR) - the most humane and effective method to reduce feral cat populations.

Contact details:
7920 Norfolk Avenue, Suite 600, Bethesda, MD 20814-2525
Tel: 240-482-1980
Fax: 240-482-1990
www.alleycat.org

Alliance for Contraception in Cats and Dogs (ACCD) has a mission to expedite the successful introduction of methods to non-surgically sterilise dogs and cats and to support the distribution and promotion of these products to humanely control cat and dog populations worldwide. Contact to assist as a volunteer.

Contact details:
www.acc-d.org
info@acc-d.org

Animal Rescue League of Boston aims to be a leader among animal welfare organisations in providing rescue and law enforcement services and promoting a compassionate and responsible attitude towards all living beings. The organisation envisions a day when all pets are cherished, and animals are no longer threatened with abandonment, neglect, abuse, exploitation, or extinction. Their three Animal Care and Adoption Centers and administrative offices often need volunteers to help with everything from animal care to general office support; from staffing special events to working on creative projects. "Whether it's feeding our shelter animals or applying your communications, writing, graphic design or office skills, we have numerous and meaningful ways for you to get involved".

Contact details:
Mail address: 10 Chandler Street, Boston, Massachusetts 02116
Tel: (617) 426-9170
Fax: (617) 426-3028
www.arlboston.org
dvogel@arlboston.org

Animal Shelter Inc, Massachusetts is a non-profit organisation and no-kill shelter. The shelter provides humane sheltering and care for stray, unwanted, abused and neglected animals. The organisation is dedicated to finding good homes for adoptable pets and they promote responsible pet ownership to improve the quality of life for the animals and people in the community. They welcome volunteers, contact to assist.

Contact details:
Mail address: 17 Laurelwood Road, Sterling, MA 01564
Tel: 978-422-8585
www.sterlingshelter.org
melissa@sterlingshelter.org **or** staff@sterlingshelter.org

Appalachian Bear Rescue works to rehabilitate orphaned and injured bears for release to the wild; to educate the public about black bears and the regional threats facing them; and to research bear attributes which may help solve other environmental or health related issues. They welcome volunteers, contact to assist.

Contact details:
Mail address: Appalachian Bear Rescue, P.O. Box 364, Townsend, Tennessee 37882
Tel: 865 448 0143
Fax: 865 448 014
www.appalachianbearrescue.org
jcburgin@kramer-rayson.com

Big Cat Rescue, Florida has a vision of no more big cats in cages. This non profit educational sanctuary, is devoted to rescuing and providing a permanent home for wild cats who have been abused, abandoned, bred to be pets, retired from performing acts, or saved from being slaughtered for fur coats, They aim to educate the public about these animals and the issues facing them in captivity and in the wild. The sanctuary houses the most diverse population of exotic cats in the world, with 16 of the 35 species of wild cat represented among the approximately 150 residents. These include tigers, lions, leopards, cougars, bobcats, lynx, ocelots, caracals and others, many are threatened, endangered, or now extinct in the wild. Volunteers assist with a variety of animal jobs.

Contact details:
Big Cat Rescue, 12802 Easy Street, Tampa, FL 33625
Tel: 813 920 4130
Fax: 866 571 4523
www.bigcatrescue.org
info@bigcatrescue.org **or** volunteer@bigcatrescue.org

Bucks County SPCA, Pennsylvania aims to prevent of cruelty to animals, to offer shelter to stray or unwanted animals, to place all adoptable animals into permanent homes, and work with state legislature to improve upon Pennsylvania's Animal Laws.

Contact details:
Mail address: Bucks County SPCA, 1665 Street Road, P.O. Box 277, Lahaska, PA 18931
Tel: 215 794 7425
Fax: 215 794 2750
www.bcspca.org
info@bcspca.org

Canine Assistants, national volunteer programme After having completed training requirements, volunteers are eligible to participate in and assist with support activities such as presentations, special events and fund raisers. Those interested in working directly with the C.A.S.E. (Canine Assistants Special Educators) dog in their area will undergo additional training and successful completion of a training exam required to become a certified handler. Once certified, volunteers will be able to work directly with the C.A.S.E. dog which will include taking the dog on outings and providing educational presentations to schools, businesses and community groups as well as doing fundraising in their hometown. Contact to get involved.

Contact details:
Canine Assistants, 3160 Francis Road, Milton, Georgia 30004
Tel: 770 664 7178
Fax: 770 664 7820
www.canineassistants.org
frances@canineassistants.org **or** sueharrison@canineassistants.org

Canine Companions for Independence, national volunteer programme Volunteers are crucial to the success of their programs. The organisation relies on volunteers in countless ways, including fundraising, special events, campus tours, washing dogs and administrative assistance. Contact you nearest regional centre to learn more about volunteer activities in your area.

Contact details:
National Headquarters mail address: 1-866-CCI-DOGS (224-3647), P.O. Box 446, Santa Rosa, CA 95402-0446
www.cci.org

Capital Area Humane Society (CAHS) their mission is to promote the humane treatment of companion animals through protection, placement, education and example. Their wide variety of programs and services exist to serve the animals and the people of the mid-Michigan community. Contact to participate in their volunteer programme.

Contact details:
Mail address: Capital Area Humane Society, P.O. Box 21445, Columbus, OH 43221-0445
Shelter address: Capital Area Humane Society, 3015 Scioto-Darby Executive Court, Hilliard, OH 43026-8990
Tel: (614) 777 7387
Fax: (614) 777 8449
www.cahs-pets.org
questions@cahs-pets.org

Central Vermont Humane Society (CVHS) their mission is to ensure the humane treatment of all domestic animals and to promote the advancement of animal welfare. They welcome volunteers to assist their work.

Contact details:
Mail address: P.O. Box 687 Montpelier, VT 05601
Shelter address: 1589 VT Route 14S, East Montpelier, VT 05651
Tel: (802) 476-3811 **or** (802) 476-3811 x108 **(volunteers)**
Fax: (802) 470-7833
www.cvhumane.com
info@cvhumane.com **or** volunteer@cvhumane.com

Chimp Haven serves as The National Chimpanzee Sanctuary. They are an independent, non profit organisation whose mission is to provide lifetime care for chimpanzees who have been retired from medical research, the entertainment industry or no longer wanted as pets. The organisation was founded in 1995 by professionals from the primatological, pharmaceutical, animal protection, zoo and business communities. Chimp Haven opened its doors to the first chimpanzees in April, 2005 and may also serve as an umbrella organization for several national sanctuaries in the future. They require volunteers to assist with education programmes.

Contact details:
Chimp Haven, 13600 Chimpanzee Place, Keithville, LA 71047
Tel: (318) 925 9575
Fax: 318 925 9576
www.chimphaven.org
volunteers@chimphaven.org

Connecticut Humane Society their mission is, "to promote humanity and kindness, and to prevent cruelty to man and animals, by information, statistics, appropriate literature, and by all lawful means which they may deem wise and best, and by assisting in prosecution of crimes of a cruel and inhumane nature; and generally to encourage justice and humanity and to discourage injustice and inhumanity". They rely on volunteers to help them achieve their mission. They offer an array of exciting opportunities for people who love animals to become involved with Connecticut's oldest animal welfare organisation.

Contact details:
Waterford Shelter and Companion Animal Sanctuary, 169 Old Colchester Road, Waterford, CT 06375
Tel: 860-442-8583
www.cthumane.org

Contact details:
Newington Shelter and Administrative Offices, 701 Russell Road, Newington, CT 06111
Tel: 1-800-452-0114
www.cthumane.org

Contact details:
Westport Shelter and Companion Animal Sanctuary, 455 Post Road East, Westport, CT 06880
Tel: 203-227-4137
www.cthumane.org

Days End Farm Horse Rescue (DEFHR), Maryland Volunteers offer invaluable support to DEFHR. They serve a vital role in horse rehabilitation, help with education and outreach activities, and have fun! Contact to assist as a volunteer.

Contact details:
1372 Woodbine Road, Woodbine, MD 21797
Mail address: P.O. Box 309, Lisbon, Maryland 21765
Tel: 301/854-5037 or 410/442-1564
www.defhr.org
info@defhr.org

Delta Society, Washington aims to improve human health through service and therapy animals. Delta Society's Pet Partners Program trains volunteers and screens volunteers and their pets for visiting animal programs in hospitals, nursing homes, rehabilitation centers, schools and other facilities.

Contact details:
Delta Society, 875 124th Ave NE #101, Bellevue, WA 98005, U.S.A.
Tel: (425) 679-5500
Fax: (425) 679-5539
www.deltasociety.org
info@DeltaSociety.org

Dogs for Deaf and Disabled Americans, Massachusetts has opportunities for volunteers in many different areas. Volunteers are needed to walk and feed dogs, raise puppies and give presentations to organisations, and staff trade show booths.

Contact details:
NEADS National Campus: 305 Redemption Rock Trail South Princeton, MA 01541
Mail address: NEADS, Dogs for Deaf and Disabled Americans, P.O. Box 213, West Boylston, MA 01583
Tel: (978) 422-9064
Fax: (978) 422-3255
www.neads.org

Elephant Sanctuary, Tennessee Interns are chosen for their field of study, experience and future goals. Internships are awarded to students studying veterinary science, zoology, wildlife management, and related fields, as well as to individuals drawn to the Sanctuary for spiritual reasons.

Contact details:
Mail address: The Elephant Sanctuary, P.O. Box 393, Hohenwald, TN 38462
Tel: (931) 796-6500 **or** (931) 796-13
www.elephants.com
elephant@elephants.com

Emergency Animal Rescue Service (EARS), California volunteers are the backbone of our efforts to provide lifesaving care and sheltering for animal victims of natural and human-caused disasters. Volunteers come from across the country and all walks of life, but they have one thing in common: a commitment to helping animals in need.

Contact details:
United Animal Nations, 1722 J Street, Suite 11, Sacramento, CA 95811
Mail address: United Animal Nations, P.O. Box 188890, Sacramento, CA 95818
Tel: (916) 429-2457
Fax: (916) 429-2456
www.uan.org
info@uan.org

Farm Animal Reform Movement (FARM), Maryland advocates a plant-based diet and humane treatment of farmed animals through a variety of grassroots programs. They require volunteers to assist with office duties, special projects and more - contact to assist.

Contact details:
FARM (Farm Animal Rights Movement), 10101 Ashburton Ln., Bethesda MD. 20817
Tel: 301-530-1737
www.farmusa.org
info@farmusa.org

Grey2K USA at commercial racetracks across the country, thousands of dogs live in warehouse-style kennels, confined for long hours each day in cages barely large enough for them to stand up or turn around. Every year, thousands of dogs are seriously injured while racing, and thousands more are killed when they are no longer able to compete. Grey2K USA is a national, non-profit organisation dedicated to ending this cruelty. They work to pass stronger dog protection laws and close down existing greyhound racetracks. They also offer adoption referral information to help the thousands of dogs still racing. Volunteers are needed to display and distribute information about greyhounds nationwide. The organisation will send you all the materials for free - brochures, stickers, signs and more - and you can take it from there!

Contact details:
Mail address: GREY2K USA P.O. Box 442117 Somerville, MA 02144
Tel: (617) 666-3526
Fax: 617-666-3568
www.grey2kusa.org
Info@GREY2KUSA.org

Greyhound Friends Inc, Massachusetts is a small non-profit organisation dedicated to saving racetrack greyhounds and placing them in responsible loving homes. They need volunteers to help with kennels jobs, transport, fostering and more - see website for details.

Contact details:
Greyhound Friends Inc., 167 Saddle Hill Road, Hopkinton, MA 01748
Tel: 508-435-5969
www.greyhound.org
ghfriend@greyhound.org

Guide Dogs of America, California There are many types of volunteering roles, including puppy raising.

Contact details:
Guide Dogs of America, 13445 Glenoaks Boulevard, Sylmar, CA 91342
Tel: (818) 362-5834
Fax: (818) 362-6870
www.guidedogsofamerica.org
mail@guidedogsofamerica.org

HawkWatch International (HWI), New Mexico has a mission to conserve our environment through education, long-term monitoring, and scientific research on raptors as indicators of ecosystem health. They require volunteers to assist with publicity and administration.

Contact details:
Salt Lake City Main Office: HawkWatch International, 2240 South 900 East, Salt Lake City, UT 84106
Tel: (801) 484-6808
Fax: 801-484-6810
www.hawkwatch.org
hwi@hawkwatch.org

New Mexico mailing address: HawkWatch International – New Mexico, P.O. Box 35706, Albuquerque, NM 87176
Tel: (505) 255-7622
www.hawkwatch.org

Hawaiian Humane Society serves as a shelter for homeless animals, a rescue operation, a placement agency, an educational and advocacy organisation and a pet care resource center. They have over 1,000 volunteers and run a comprehensive volunteering programme and require assistance in a number of ways.

Contact details:
Tel: 808.356-2216 **(volunteers)**
www.hawaiianhumane.org
hhs@hawaiianhumane.org

Helen Woodward Animal Centre (HWAC) is a unique, private, non-profit organisation dedicated to saving the lives of animals and enriching the lives of people. For more than 30 years, their no-kill Center has provided humane care and adoption for orphaned animals, as well as animal-centered educational and therapeutic programs for people. The Center is a dynamic, evolving institution that is an agent of change for the animal welfare world. They have a variety of volunteering opportunities available - see their website for more information.

Contact details:
Mail address: Helen Woodward Animal Center, P.O. Box 64, Rancho Santa Fe, CA 92067
Location address: 6461 El Apajo Road, Rancho Santa Fe, CA 92067
Tel: (858) 756-4117
Fax: (858) 756-1466
www.animalcenter.org

House Rabbit, California is looking for volunteers for tasks ranging from hands-on care of rabbits to administration duties.

Contact details:
148 Broadway, Richmond, CA 94804
Tel: (510) 970-7575
Fax: (510) 970-9820
www.rabbit.org
rabbit-center@rabbit.org

Houston SPCA is Houston's first and largest animal protection organisation and shelter. Their mission is to promote commitment to and respect for all animals and free them from suffering, abuse and exploitation. They have over 500 volunteers assisting their work, volunteer application forms are available from their website.

Contact details:
900 Portway Drive, Houston, Texas 77024-8022
Tel: (713)-869-7722
www.houstonspca.org
info@hspca.org

Humane Society of Berks County their mission is to serve Berks County through: education and outreach in the community, medical services for needy animals, humane investigation, safe shelter for homeless animals and strong sterilization and adoption programs to ensure that every companion animal lives in a safe, loving and secure home. They rely on volunteers to assist their work.

Contact details:
Humane Society of Berks County, 1801 N. 11th Street, Reading, PA 19604
Tel: 610-921-2348
Fax: 610-921-5833
www.berkshumane.org
hsbc@berkshumane.org

Humane Society of Broward County provides shelter, aid and responsible adoptions to animals entrusted to their care, and educates the community about respect and kindness to all animals. One and a half hour-long orientations are provided twice a month to prospective volunteers. During these sessions, Humane Society of Broward County's philosophies will be explained and different volunteer positions will be reviewed. At the end of the orientation, you will be asked to schedule your personal interview with the Director of Volunteer Services to answer any questions and to discuss your volunteer position and necessary training. The organisation does require at least a 6 month commitment to their Volunteer Programme.

Contact details:
2070 Griffin Road, Fort Lauderdale, Florida 33312
Tel: 954-266-6814 (Volunteer Services)
www.humanebroward.com
info@hsbroward.com

Los Angelos SPCA is dedicated to the prevention of cruelty to animals through education, law enforcement and intervention. Contact to assist as a volunteer.

Contact details:
Administrative office: 5026 West Jefferson Boulevard, Los Angeles, CA 90016
Tel: (888) SPCA-LA1 (772-2521)
Fax: (323) 730-5333
www.spcala.com
info@spcala.com **or** volunteer@spcaLA.com

International Wolf Centre, Minnesota advances the survival of wolf populations by teaching about wolves, their relationship to wild lands and the human role in their future. The organisation welcomes volunteers and has a wide variety of roles available.

Contact details:
Ely, Minnesota: International Wolf Center, 1396 Highway 169, Ely, MN 55731-8129
Tel: (218) 365-4695
Fax: (218) 365-3318
www.wolf.org

Contact details:
Minneapolis, Minnesota: International Wolf Center, 3410 Winnetka Avenue North, Ste. 101, Minneapolis, MN 55427
Tel: (763) 560-7374
Fax: (763) 560-7368
www.wolf.org

Kansas Specialty Dog Service Becoming a Puppy Raiser is one way to volunteer. Other animal volunteer opportunities include assistance from painters, carpenters, plumbers, individuals capable of doing odd jobs, yard work, mailings, tour guides, playing with puppies at the Canine Housing Unit and many more.

Contact details:
Mail address: 124 W. 7th St., Washington, KS 66968
Tel: (785) 325-2256
Fax: (785) 325-2258
www.ksds.org
ksds@ksds.org

Last Chance for Animals (LCA), Los Angelos this organisation recognises that animals have the ability to experience pain, and as such they deserve certain basic rights protecting them from pain caused by humans. LCA believes that animals should not be subjected to suffering and exploitation as alternatives exist for nearly every traditional "usage" of animals. Last Chance for Animals is always looking for other dedicated animal volunteer to get involved, speak up and make a difference for animals.

Contact details:
Last Chance for Animals, 8033 Sunset Blvd. #835, Los Angeles, CA 90046
Tel: 310-271-6096
Fax: 310-271-1890
www.lcanimal.org
volunteer@lcanimal.org

Labs4rescue, Connecticut is a non-profit organisation dedicated to providing a new life for rescued or displaced Labrador Retrievers and Labrador Mixes. Their biggest need is for foster homes and we have a great system that makes it easy for you to help! There are many other rewarding opportunities available for those interested in volunteering including home visits, marketing, advertising etc. Contact to assist.

Contact details:
Mail address: Labs4rescue, Inc., P.O.Box 955, Killingworth, CT, 06419
http://labs4rescue.com

Marin Humane Society (MHS), California Founded in 1907, the Marin Humane Society is a progressive, award-winning animal shelter, offering refuge and rehabilitation to nearly 8,000 animals each year through a myriad of community services, including adoptions, foster care, behavior and training, humane education, lost-and-found pet services, low-cost clinics, and more. Contact to assist as a volunteer.

Contact details:
The Marin Humane Society, 171 Bel Marin Keys Blvd., Novato, CA 94949
Tel: 415 883 4621
Fax: 415 382 1349
www.marinhumanesociety.org

Marine Mammal Center, California is dedicated to the rescue, rehabilitation and release of injured, sick and orphaned marine mammals. Originally founded by three volunteers, the Center relies heavily on a dynamic volunteer work force comprised of over 800 individuals from Mendocino through San Luis Obispo counties. In their expanding and exciting environment, the energy and dedication of many kinds of people are needed to keep the Center running smoothly. While some volunteer assignments require you to be at least 18 years of age, there are special youth opportunities for those under 18.

Contact details:
The Marine Mammal Center, 2000 Bunker Road, Fort Cronkhite, Sausalito, CA 94965-2619
Tel: 415 289 7325 **or** 415.289.7374 **(volunteers)**
Fax: 415 289 7333
www.marinemammalcenter.org
volunteer@tmmc.org

Massachusetts Society for the Prevention of Cruelty to Animals - Angell Animal Medical Centre (MSPCA-Angell) is a national and international leader in animal protection and veterinary medicine. Founded in 1868, it is the second-oldest humane society in the United States. Their services include animal protection and adoption, advocacy, humane education, law enforcement and the highest-quality veterinary care. They provide direct hands-on care to more than 250,000 animals each year. The organisation is committed to providing each volunteer with a rewarding and productive experience. They offer a well-structured volunteer program and provide all necessary orientation and training.

Contact details:
MSPCA-Angell Headquarters, 350 South Huntington Avenue, Boston, MA 02130
Tel: (617) 522-7400
http://mspca.pub30.convio.net
questions@mspca.org

Marine Animal Rescue, Florida is dedicated to the conservation of marine mammals through rescue, rehabilitation, research and education. They are always looking for volunteers in Southeast Florida.

Contact details:
Mail address: Marine Animal Rescue Society, P.O. Box 833356, Miami, Florida 33283
Tel: (305) 546-1111
www.marineanimalrescue.org
mars@marineanimalrescue.org

Michigan Humane Society (MHS) has a mission to end companion animal homelessness, to provide the highest quality service and compassion to the animals entrusted to our care, and to be a leader in promoting humane values. Visit their website for a volunteer application form.

Contact details:
Admin Office: Michigan Humane Society, 30300 Telegraph Road, Suite 220, Bingham Farms, MI 48025-4507
Tel: 248-283-1000
Fax: 248-283-5700
www.michiganhumane.org

Midwest Avian Adoption and Rescue Service (MAARS) their first function is to educate the public and people who already live with birds about proper bird care. The organisation believes that education about bird care and behavior helps people to provide the best homes possible for the birds already in captivity. Their second function is to accept and rescue surrendered, abandoned, neglected, and abused parrots and other captive exotic birds for health care, behavioral therapy, and placement in a new home or sanctuary. Volunteers assist with transportation, avian veterinary care, grooming, education, consultation, fundraising, administration, and other crucial tasks.

Contact details:
Mail address: P.O. Box 821, Stillwater, MN 55082
Tel: (651) 275-0568
Fax: (651) 275-0457
www.maars.org
volunteers@maars.org **or** birds@maars.org

Montgomery County SPCA is a non profit organisation established in 1909, dedicated to caring for unwanted, lost and abused domestic animals. See their website for comprehensive information about their volunteer programme.

Contact details:
www.montgomerycountyspca.org
mcspca@voicenet.com

Naperville Area Humane Society (NAHS) is a non profit, limited admission animal shelter accepting cats and dogs.They have a variety of volunteer opportunities available, contact to assist.

Contact details:
Naperville Area Humane Society, 1620 W. Diehl Road, Naperville, IL 60563
Tel: (630) 420-8989
Fax: (630) 420-9380
www.napervillehumanesociety.org
info@NapervilleAreaHumaneSociety.org

Nashville Humane Association is committed to: promoting humane treatment of animals, finding good homes for stray or abandoned dogs and cats, educating the public about their responsibility to help control the pet population, and providing treatment and care to ensure the well being of animals in their community. They encourage volunteers to assist them in their work.

Contact details:
Nashville Humane Association, 213 Oceola Avenue, Nashville, TN 37209
Tel: (615) 352-1010
www.nashvillehumane.org

National Cat Protection, USA works to assist with the rescue and re-homing of cats.

Contact details:
Spring Valley Shelter: 9031 Birch Street, Spring Valley, CA 91977
Tel: 619-469-8771
Fax: 619-469-2454
www.natcat.org
springvalley@natcat.org

Contact details:
Newport Beach Shelter: 6904 W. Coast Highway, Newport Beach, CA 92663
Tel: 949-650-1232
Fax: 949-650-7367
www.natcat.org
newport@natcat.org

New Hampshire SPCA (NHSPCA) mission is: "to bring together compassionate individuals to support and assist in the daily operations of the NHSPCA; to enhance the lives of the animals in their care; to present a positive image of the Society; and to promote an environment of dignity and respect for all living creatures". The NHSPCA depends greatly on over 200 volunteers who donate their time and talent to help the animals. Without volunteers they could not accomplish or advance their mission.

Contact details:
Mail address: New Hampshire SPCA, P.O. Box 196, Stratham, NH 03885
Tel: 603-772-2921
Fax: 603-778-7804
www.nhspca.org
volunteer@nhspca.org **or** info@nhspca.org

New York Horse Rescue works to prevent the inhumane slaughter of injured, abused, and unwanted horses. Their goal is to rehabilitate and place these horses in qualified adoptive homes. Volunteers are required to assist with events and fundraising.

Contact details:
Mail address: New York Horse Rescue Corporation, P.O. Box 435, Manorville, New York 11949
Tel: 631-874-9420
Fax: 631-878-3306
www.nyhr.org
mona@nyhr.org

Noah's Ark Animal Rehabilitation Centre is a rehabilitation center for animals and a group home for children from birth to 18 years old. The non-profit facility is home to over 1,000 animals and is licensed by the State of Georgia to provide residential care for up to 24 children. The wildlife from the rehabilitation center and the children from the Children's Care Home play a vital role for each other. The children participate in "pet therapy," nurturing the baby wildlife as the animals are rehabilitated in hopes of eventually being returned to their natural habitat. This is important because many of the children have been abused or abandoned and may have a hard time relating to people. They're able to learn to care for the animals that, in turn, are receiving much needed affection and attention. They have a volunteer programme, see their website for further information.

Contact details:
Noah's Ark, 712 LG Griffin Road, Locust Grove, GA 30248
Tel: 770 957 0888
Fax: 770 957 1181
www.noahs-ark.org
the roar@noahs-ark.org

Noah's Wish, California the mission of Noah's Wish is to save animals during disasters with their rescue and recovery services and to mitigate the impact of disasters on animals through their educational outreach programmes. Their unique in-field training program offers individuals a new way in which they can help animals. This program is the only training offered in the United States or Canada that prepares volunteers to respond to disasters by setting up a simulated temporary shelter and giving volunteers the opportunity to experience most aspects of mobilisation. What this means for trainees is that they spend the evening on site, just as they would do in a real disaster response. Students also must bring enough food, water and gear to "rough it" for the 48 hours of training. The purpose for this simulation is to give potential disaster responders the opportunity to experience what to expect if they deploy with Noah's Wish.Once volunteers complete their training, they become a valuable resource to Noah's Wish and other disaster response organisations.

Contact details:
Mail address: P.O. Box 4288, El Dorado Hills, CA 95762
Tel: (916) 939-9474
Fax: (916) 939-9479
www.noahswish.info
info@noahswish.info **or** training@noahswish.info

Contact details:
Mail address Canada: 1524 Marine Drive Suite 207, West Vancouver BC V7T 1B9
www.noahswish.info

North County Humane Society and SPCA is a non profit organization that provides support and compassionate care for the well being of animals and people. The organisation has a vision of a world where all animals receive humane treatment and people are stewards giving respect and compassion to all living creatures. The organisation welcomes volunteers to assist with a variety of tasks.

Contact details:
Gaines St. Campus: 5500 Gaines St., San Diego, CA 92110
Tel: (619) 299-7012
www.sdhumane.org
volinfo@sdhumane.org

Contact details:
North Campus: 2905 San Luis Rey Road, Oceanside, CA 92058
Tel: (760) 757-4357
Fax: (760) 757-3547
www.sdhumane.org

Our Companions Domestic Animal Sanctuary, Connecticut their mission is to create a humane movement to protect and advocate for the lives of companion animals by building a sanctuary to rescue those who would otherwise be destroyed, by offering innovating life-saving programs, and by collaborating with the animal welfare community to affect public policy, ensuring that every animal's life is valued. Contact to assist as a volunteer.

Contact details:
Mail address: Our Companions Domestic Animal Sanctuary, P.O. Box 673, Bloomfield, CT 06002
Tel/Fax: (860) 242-9999
Tel: (860) 242-9999 x300 (Volunteer Opportunities)
www.ourcompanions.org

Orangutan Conservancy, California is dedicated to protecting orangutans and the rain forest. The organisation provides funding to a variety of orangutan protection programmes. They are a non profit organisation and are entirely reliant on volunteers.

Contact details:
Mail address: P.O. Box 513, 5001 Wilshire Blvd. #112, Los Angeles, CA 90036 USA
http://www.orangutan.com
doug@orangutan.com

People for the Ethical Treatment of Animals (PETA) their volunteers are highly valued and come from diverse backgrounds and include teachers, doctors, retired adults, young adults, computer programmers, and artists. No matter what your talents are, they have a place for you!

Contact details:
501 Front Street, Norfolk, VA 23510
Tel: 757-622-7382
Fax: 757-622-0457
www.peta.org

Primate Rescue, Kentucky their mission is to alleviate the suffering of primates wherever it occurs by: Providing sanctuary or referral to appropriate facilities, working to end the illegal trade in primates both in the United States and abroad, educating the public to the plight of primates caught in the breeder/dealer cycle, assisting researchers and zoo personnel in finding appropriate placement for their surplus primates, encouraging compliance with applicable local, state, and federal laws and animal welfare statute.

Contact details:
Primate Rescue Center, Inc. 2515 Bethel Road, Nicholasville, KY 40356
Tel: (859) 858-4866
Fax: (859) 858-0044
www.primaterescue.org
admin101@primaterescue.org

Puppies Behind Bars, New York this volunteer opportunity is an amazing one in that it allows people to help the handicapped or law enforcement while you spend time with a loving, playful and well-behaved Labrador retriever puppy. You can watch "your" dog grow and be a vital part in the process of working to create guide and explosive-detection dogs.

Contact details:
Puppies Behind Bars, 10 East 40th Street, 19th Floor, New York, NY 10016
Tel: 212-680-9562
Fax: 212-689-9330
www.puppiesbehindbars.com
programs@puppiesbehindbars.com

Peace River Refuge and Ranch, Florida is a sanctuary dedicated to the lifetime care of abused, neglected, confiscated or unwanted exotic animals to prevent them from being destroyed. The animals that they rescue range from big cats such as tigers, cougars and leopards to wolves, bears, primates, small wild cats, bats and more. The animals are given permanent homes and most have come from situations that were potentially harmful for the animals. They do not sell, transfer or give away any of the animals we rescue and they are not used for breeding; they are simply protected from harm. There are a variety of volunteer opportunities available.

Contact details:
Mail address: P.O. Box 1127, 2545 Stoner Lane, Zolfo Springs, Florida 33890
Tel: (863) 735-0804
Fax: (863) 735-0805
www.peaceriverrefuge.org
volunteer@peaceriverrefuge.org **or** info@peaceriverrefuge.org

Richmond SPCA is a non-profit, no-kill humane organisation dedicated to the principle that every life is precious. As a national leader in humane care and education, the Richmond SPCA is aggressively tackling the problem of pet overpopulation through education, adoption, rehabilitation and spay/neuter. The organization saves the lives of 3,000 homeless animals each year and cares for approximately 350 cats and dogs daily. Volunteers are essential to their work.

Contact details:
Robins-Starr Humane Center, 2519 Hermitage Road, Richmond, VA 23220
Tel: 804-643-6785 or 804-521-1329 (Volunteers)
Fax: 804-644-8327
www.richmondspca.org
lclement@richmondspca.org

Sacramento SPCA (SSPCA) was established 1894 and is dedicated to ensuring the humane treatment of all animals in the Sacramento area. They provide a safe and nurturing environment for unwanted, abandoned and mistreated pets until they can be placed into loving homes. Through proactive intervention, public education and community outreach, the Sacramento SPCA seeks to promote respect for all life by breaking the cycle of abuse, neglect and pet overpopulation. Volunteers welcomed.

Contact details:
Mail address: Sacramento SPCA, 6201 Florin-Perkins Road, Sacramento, California 95828
Tel: (916) 383-7387 or (916) 383-7387 Ext 9147 (Volunteers)
Fax: (916) 383-7062
http://sspca.convio.net

San Diego Humane Society and SPCA provides vital services to animals and people alike through sheltering and adopting animals, providing positive reinforcement behavior training for adoptable animals and for owned animals through public training classes, investigating animal cruelty and neglect, providing adult and youth education programs, sharing animals through Pet-Assisted Therapy and rescuing animals in emergency situations. The organisation has over 500 volunteers and operates a structured volunteering programme.

Contact details:
Gaines St. Campus: 5500 Gaines St., San Diego, CA 92110
Tel: (619) 299-7012
www.sdhumane.org
volinfo@sdhumane.org

Contact details:
North Campus: 2905 San Luis Rey Road, Oceanside, CA 92058
Tel: (760) 757-4357
Fax: (760) 757-3547
www.sdhumane.org

San Francisco SPCA (SFSPCA) is a national leader in saving lives and raising the status of companion animals. Its innovative programs and services include: Maddie's Pet Adoption Center; Community Veterinary Services, including the SF/SPCA Animal Hospital and Spay/Neuter Clinic; Humane Education; public Dog Training classes; Feral Cat Assistance Program; and Animal Assisted Therapy. They have a comprehensive volunteer programme and a wide variety of volunteering opportunities.

Contact details:
Mail address: SF/SPCA, 2500 16th Street, San Francisco CA 94103
Campus address - administration: 2500 16th Street, San Francisco CA 94103
Tel: 415-554-3000 or 415-522-3523 **(volunteers)**
www.sfspca.org
volunteers@sfspca.org

Search Dog Foundation, California the mission of the Search Dog Foundation is to produce the most highly trained canine disaster search teams in the nation. You don't need to live in Ojai to become an SDF Agency Angel Volunteer! Some of their Angels live down the street--some on the other side of the country.

Contact details:
Search Dog Foundation, 501 E. Ojai Ave., Ojai, CA 93023
Tel: (888) 459-4376 (Ext 103 Volunteers & General Information)
Fax: (805) 640-1848
www.searchdogfoundation.org
Rescue@ndsdf.org **or** Jennifer@ndsdf.org (Volunteers)

Service Dogs for America, North Dakota trains service dogs for people with disabilities. They require volunteers to assist with socialising and training dogs.

Contact details:
Mail address: Service Dogs for America, Great Plains Assistance Dogs Foundation Inc., 920 Short Street, P.O. Box 513, Jud, North Dakota 58454
Tel: 701-685-2242
Fax: 701-685-2290
www.greatplainsdogs.com
info@greatplainsdogs.com

Southeastern Guide Dogs, Florida in both the training kennel and puppy kennel, volunteers work regularly with staff members to exercise and play with our dogs, as well as to expose them to new people and situations.

Contact details:
Southeastern Guide Dogs, 4210 77th Street East, Palmetto, FL 34221
Tel: 941.729.5665
Fax: 941.729.6646
www.guidedogs.org

Spay Neuter Assistance Programme (SNAP), Texas Homeless cats and dogs wander every neighborhood -- destined for suffering or euthanasia. SNAP works to reduce the overpopulation of unwanted animals through sterilization and education. They require volunteers to assist with a variety of roles at their Houston and San Antoinia offices and at many of their events.

Contact details:
Admin Office: SNAP Inc., 401 Studewood, Suite 350, Houston, Texas 77007
Mail address: P.O. Box 70286, Houston, Texas 77270
Tel: 713-862-3863 **or** 800-762-7762
Fax: 713-880-3172
www.snapus.org

Tree House Animal Foundation, Chicago is a humane organisation that promotes the inherent value of every animal and strives to educate the public about proper and responsible animal care, with a focus on the care and placement of stray cats with special physical and emotional needs.

Contact details:
Main office: Tree House Humane Society, 1212 W. Carmen Ave., Chicago, IL 60640-2999
Tel: (773) 784-5488
Fax: (773) 784-2332
www.treehouseanimals.org
volunteer@treehouseanimals.org **or** info@treehouseanimals.org

Contact details:
Bucktown: Tree House Bucktown Branch, 1629 N. Ashland Ave., Chicago, IL 60622
Tel: (773) 227-5535
Fax: (773) 342-1239
www.treehouseanimals.org
bucktown@treehouseanimals.org

United Animal Nations (UAN), California was founded in 1987, United Animal Nations (UAN) is North America 's leading provider of emergency animal sheltering and disaster relief services and a key advocate for the critical needs of animals. UAN assists animals by helping to prevent, mitigate and resolve crises. They accomplish this by sharing expertise, resources and information to empower others to help more animals.

Contact details:
United Animal Nations, 1722 J Street, Suite 11, Sacramento, CA 95811
Mail address: United Animal Nations, P.O. Box 188890, Sacramento, CA 95818
Tel: (916) 429-2457
Fax: (916) 429-2456
www.uan.org
info@uan.org

United Hope for Animals (UHA), California is a non-profit organisation committed to ending the suffering and mistreatment of dogs and cats in Tijuana and Southern California. "Through us, these animals benefit from spay and neuter services in areas where families cannot afford them; rescue, adoption and foster care where- and whenever possible; and additional support and education for those who will care for them". There are a variety of volunteer opportunities available.

Contact details:
Mail address: United Hope for Animals, P.O. Box 2349, Pasadena, CA 91102-2349
Tel: 909-801-0012 or 714-469-8339
www.hope4animals.org
kerryo@hope4animals.org **or** anne@hope4animals.org

VeterinaryVentures is a non profit organisation bringing quality veterinary care and humane population control to the world's under-served animal populations. Contact to assist as a volunteer.

Contact details:
Mail address: Veterinary Ventures, C/O Amber Holland, 2613 NW Raleigh Street, #25, Portland OR 97210
www.veterinaryventures.com
vetventures@gmail.com

WildCare, California depends upon the commitment of over 300 volunteers to help staff their programs, including their core animal aid and education programs. Each year over 35,000 hours of time are given to educate 40,000 Bay Area children and adults and treat more than 3,000 wild animals. If you care deeply about our connection with wildlife and want to help ensure a healthy co-existence between humans and animals, please volunteer. All training is provided.

Contact details:
Mall address: Wildcare, 76 Albert Park Ln., San Rafael, CA 94901
Tel: 415-453-1000
Fax: 415-456-0594
www.wildcarebayarea.org
volunteer@wildcarebayarea.org **or** Info@wildcarebayarea.org

"What is a man without the beasts? If all the beasts were gone, men would die form great loneliness of spirit, for whatever happens to the beasts also happens to man." - Chief Seattle

Canada

"In a gentle way, you can shake the world." - Mahatma Gandhi

Action for Animals In Distress Society is a registered non-profit organisation located in Burnaby, British Columbia, Canada. Action is dedicated and committed to the needs of homeless, abandoned, neglected, sick and injured animals. Contact to assist as a volunteer.

Contact details:
Mail address: Unit 652, 141-6200 McKay Avenue, Burnaby, BC Canada V5H 4M9
Tel: (604)724-7652
Fax: (604)431-7652
www.actionforanimals.net
info@actionforanimals.net

Alberta Animal Rescue Crew Society (AARCS) works to rescue abandoned, surrendered, or abused animals in Central Alberta. They have a structured volunteer programme, contact to assist.

Contact details:
Mail address: Alberta Animal Rescue Crew Society, P.O. Box 99076, Calgary, AB, T1Y 6M6
Tel: (403) 804-4334
www.albertaanimalrescuecrew.com
volunteer@albertaanimalrescuecrew.com **or** info@albertaanimalrescuecrew.com

Big Heart Rescue this organisation relies on volunteers to assist with their fostering project - they do not have a shelter and therefore rely on foster homes.

Contact details:
Mail address: Big Heart Rescue Society, PO Box 6, Gabriola BC V0R 1X0
Tel: 604-583-DOGS (3647)
http://bigheartrescue.com
spiritsmission@shaw.ca

British Colombia SPCA (BC SPCA) is a non-profit organisation dedicated to protecting and enhancing the quality of life for domestic, farm and wild animals in BC. Through its 36 branches located around BC and its provincial office in Vancouver, the BC SPCA provides a wide range of services for more than 40,000 homeless, abused, injured and abandoned animals around the province. Volunteers assist this organisation in a number of ways. Visit their website to download a volunteer application form.

Contact details:
www.spca.bc.ca

Calgary Humane Society aims to prevent cruelty to animals. Volunteers are an integral part of all services offered by the Calgary Humane Society and they state that "every animal benefits from their commitment and dedication".

Contact details:
4455 110th Ave SE, Calgary, Alberta, T2C 2T7
Tel: 403-205-4455 **or** 403-723-6020 (Volunteers)
Fax: 403-723-6050
www.calgaryhumane.ca
volunteer@calgaryhumane.ca **or** general.inquiries@calgaryhumane.ca

Cochrane Ecological Institute (CEI) is a charitable, not -for -profit organisation devoted to breeding endangered species for reintroduction, wildlife rescue, rehabilitation, and release, educating the public, monitoring habitat and species, and developing non intrusive wildlife survey methods. The organisation relies on volunteers.

Contact details:
Mail address: Cochrane Ecological Institute, P.O. Box 484, Cochrane, Alberta, Canada T4C 1A7
Tel: +1 403 932-5632
Fax: +1 403 932-6303
www.ceinst.org
cei@nucleus.com

Cochrane and Area Humane Society is a charitable organisation dedicated to promoting and preserving the well-being of animals, sustained by volunteers and the community. They state "we have a wide range of volunteer opportunities that allow you to develop new skills while making a much-needed contribution to our organisation and your community. We strive to ensure that volunteer participation meets expectations and is a rewarding experience".

Contact details:
Cochrane & Area Humane Society, 62 Griffin Industrial Point, Cochrane, AB T4C 0A3
Tel: (403) 932-2072
Fax: (403) 709-0009
www.cochranehumane.ca
shelter@cochranehumane.ca

Critter Care Wildlife Society receives, rehabilitates and releases back to the wild injured and orphaned mammals native to British Columbia. These include deer, raccoons, coyotes, skunks, flying squirrels, Douglas squirrels, gray squirrels, opossums, beaver, rabbits, marmots and bears. The organisation is made up entirely of volunteers and is always looking for help in all areas of its work.

Contact details:
Critter Care Wildlife Society, 481-216th Street, Langley, BC, V2Z 1R6
Tel: 604-530-2064 **or** 604-530-2054 (Volunteers)
Fax: 604-532-2009
www.crittercarewildlife.org
info@crittercarewildlife.org **or** volunteer@crittercarewildlife.org

Donkey Sanctuary of Canada (DSC) is dedicated to the rescue, rehabilitation and protection of abandoned, neglected or abused donkeys, mules and hinnies. Animals admitted to the DSC are given a lifelong home. Volunteers form a vital part of this organisation's work.

Contact details:
Mail address: The Donkey Sanctuary of Canada, 6981 Puslinch Conc. 4, R.R. #6, Guelph, ON, N1H 6J3
Tel: 519-836-1697
Fax: 519-821-0698
www.thedonkeysanctuary.ca
info@thedonkeysanctuary.ca

Global Action Network (GAN) is a nationally incorporated non-profit organisation, dedicated to fostering environmental awareness and action. The organisation believes that animal abuse and the destruction of our environment has an ultimate consequence - the degradation of the human species. They achieve their mandate through education, grassroots organising, coalition building, and political networking.Global Action Network works in seven program areas: Sustainable Agriculture, Oceans, Wildlife, Animals in Entertainment, Animals in Biomedical Research and Companion Animals. Contact to assist in a variety of ways as a volunteer.

Contact details:
372, rue Ste-Catherine West, Suite #319, Montreal, Quebec H3B 1A2
Tel: (514) 939-5525
www.gan.ca
contact@gan.ca.

Humane Animal Rescue Team (HART) is a non-profit organisation committed to: rescue stray, abandoned and unwanted dogs and cats from rural areas including First Nations surrounding Edmonton, Alberta and placing them in permanent homes. They also provide programs that promote responsible pet ownership, and prevent cruelty to animals. They have a variety of ways that volunteers can get involved - see website for further information.

Contact details:
Mail address: P.O. Box 62102, Edmonton, Alberta T5M 4B5
Tel: 780 455-4278
Fax: 780 447-4034
www.humaneanimalrescueteam.ca
info@humaneanimalrescueteam.ca

London Humane Society works to improve the lives of animals in the community by providing temporary shelter and appropriate new families for unwanted or cruelly treated animals, and by providing education and advocacy, and by assisting animals in distress. Each year they offer shelter and care to hundreds of animals. Their Investigations department responds to more than 1,000 complaints of animal cruelty each year. They have a comprehensive volunteer programme; see their website for further information.

Contact details:
Mail address: London Humane Society, 624 Clarke Road, London, ON, N5V 3K5 Canada
Tel: (519) 451-0630 (Ext 222 volunteers)
Fax: (519) 451-8995
administration@londonhumane.ca **or** jtremblay@londonhumane.ca **(Volunteers)**

No Whales In Captivity is a non-profit, grassroots, law-abiding, fully volunteer-run organisation based in Vancouver, Canada. They need volunteers to hold rallies and set up display tables at environmentally-friendly events. They also need volunteers to write letters, and organise and participate in public and government meetings.

Contact details:
Mail address: No Whales in Captivity, Box 461 – 1755 Robson Street, Vancouver, B.C. V6G 3B7, Canada
Tel: (604) 736-9514 **or** (604) 377-6444 (volunteers)
www.vcn.bc.ca/cmeps/11.html
info@whaleprotection.org **or** ericka@catcahelpanimals.org **(Volunteers)**

Ontario SPCA Through its province-wide network of 25 Ontario SPCA Branches and 31 affiliated member Humane Societies, the Ontario SPCA is one of the largest, most responsive animal welfare organisations in the country, providing care and shelter for tens of thousands of animals every year. The organisation requires volunteers to assist hand-on with the animals and with fundraising and other office tasks, see website for more information.

Contact details:
16586 Woodbine Avenue, RR 3, Newmarket, ON, L3Y 4W1
Tel: 1-888-668-7722
www.ontariospca.ca
info@ospca.on.ca

Ottawa Humane Society is a not-for-profit organisation that has provided shelter and medical care for thousands of animals since 1888. They state that "a lot of what we do for both the animals and the community is made possible by the assistance of our volunteer team". Contact to assist.

Contact details:
The Ottawa Humane Society, 101 Champagne Ave., Ottawa, ON, K1S 4P3
Tel: 613-725-3166 (Ext 231 volunteers)
Fax: 613-725-5674
www.ottawahumane.ca
volunteer@ottawahumane.ca

Seeing Eye, Toronto is the oldest dog guide school in the world. Twelve times a year, as many as 24 students at a time, discover the exhilarating experience of traveling with a Seeing Eye dog. They need volunteers to assist with puppy rearing and fostering.

Contact details:
Mail address for Canada: The Seeing Eye Organisation, C/o TH1017, P.O. Box 4283, Station A, Toronto, Ontario M5W 5W6
www.seeingeye.org
info@seeingeye.org

Contact details:
Mail address for United States: The Seeing Eye Inc., 10 Washington Valley Road, P.O. Box 375, Morristown, NJ 07963
Tel: 973-539-4425
Fax: 973-539-0922
www.seeingeye.org
info@seeingeye.org

Veterinarians Without Borders (VWB) All of their programs are grounded in the philosophy that the health of animals, people, and the ecosystems we share cannot be treated as separate problems. Their projects are: Education: they share our expertise with local animal health workers and farmers' groups in developing communities. They create and deliver training materials, offer short courses, and facilitate curricula development. Food Security and Public Health: they develop programs for small-holder farmers that improve the health and sustainability of animal agriculture. They facilitate regional networks in developing countries for sharing expertise and resources among animal health workers. Canine/Feline Population and Disease Control: they build community-based strategies to improve public and animal health with an emphasis on controlling dog overpopulation and preventing diseases transmitted to people such as rabies. Wildlife Health: they work to improve the health of wildlife, the ecosystems they live in, and the communities whose livelihoods depend on them. There are a variety of voluntary opportunities available, see their website for further information.

Contact details:
Mail address: VWB/VSF – Canada, Head Office P.O. Box 8373, Victoria, BC, V8W 3R9
Tel: 250-590-3340
www.vwb-vsf.ca
info@vwb-vsf.ca

Voice for Animals Humane Society their mission is to speak out for animals who are in exploitative situations created by humans. This includes animals in food production, vivisection, fashion, sport, companion animal, and entertainment industries. Their aim is not to moderate the behaviour of animal exploiters, but rather, to remove the exploitation completely by advocating against the view that animals are human property to do with as we see fit. The organisation requires volunteers to assist with animal rescue, driving, fundraising, etc.

Contact details:
Mail address: Voice for Animals Humane Society, P.O. Box 68119, 162 Bonnie Doon Mall, Edmonton, AB, T6C 4N6, Canada
Tel: 780-490-0905
Fax: 780-922-5287
www.v4a.org
info@v4a.org

Whistler Animals Galore Society (WAGS) works to protect and enhance the lives of lost, unwanted, and homeless animals. They aim "to bring about a time in our communities when all animals are treated humanely and with respect, and when every cat or dog ever born is guaranteed a loving home for the duration of its life". They require volunteers to assist with dog walking, kennel work, cattery assistance duties, fostering and more.

Contact details:
Mail address: P.O. Box 274, Whistler, BC, V0N 1B0
Tel: 604-935-8364
Fax: 604-935-8328
www.thewagway.com
gmelenka@thewagway.com **or** djones@thewagway.com

"All beings tremble before violence. All fear death. All love life. See yourself in others. Then whom can you hurt? What harm can you do?" Buddha

SOUTH AMERICA

"The purity of a person's heart can be quickly measured by how they regard animals." - Anonymous

Volunteer Latin America their mission is to help protect Latin America's flora and fauna, its biodiversity, and to offer the most cost effective way to become an environmental volunteer in Mexico, Central or South America. The projects we offer have been specially selected and range from building homes to monitoring small wildcats. There are hundreds of reputable organisations looking for international wildlife and conservation volunteers and you can see some examples of the projects available on their web site.

Contact details:
Mail address: Volunteer Latin America, Office 1728, PO Box 6945, London W1A 6US, UK
Tel: +44 (0)20 7193 9163
www.volunteerlatinamerica.com
info@volunteerlatinamerica.com

Anguilla

Anguilla Animal Rescue Foundation (AAAF) works to promote, develop and generally to assist in the humane treatment and care of animals in Anguilla. Contact to assist with socialising, feeding, fundraising, animal care and more.

Contact details:
Mail address: AARF, P.O. Box RI-4228, Anguilla, BWI AI-2640
Tel: (264) 476 2731
www.aarf.ai
aarfinfo@aarf.ai

Antigua

Antigua and Barbuda Humane Society works to improve the welfare of animals through humane education and the prevention of cruelty, and to offer shelter and humane care to all animals in need of protection in the State of Antigua and Barbuda. Contact to assist their work as a volunteer.

Contact details:
Mail address: Antigua & Barbuda Humane Society Inc., P. O. Box 205, St. John's, Antigua
Tel: (268) 461-4957
Fax: (268) 460-8843
www.antiguaanimals.org
abhumane@candw.ag

Argentina

Asociación para la Defensa de los Derechos del Animal (ADDA) this organisation condemns any type of discrimination to animals and works to represents all of them: farm animals, companion animals, wild animals, mammals, birds, insects, fishes, amphibians, etc. Contact to assist as a volunteer.

Contact details:
Tel: 4856-7028 Extension # 7
www.adda.org.ar
adda@fibertel.com.ar

The Argentine Foundation for Animal Welfare (FABA) is a non-profit organisation dedicated to providing health care and promoting education in order to improve the quality of life of animals. The organisation teaches respect for all living beings. Contact to assist as a volunteer.

Contact details:
www.fabaonline.com

Aruba

Animal Rights Aruba (ARA) is a non-profit Animal Welfare Image Organisation that aims to protect all Fauna, Flora and Marine Life on and around the island of Aruba. This organisation is run entirely by volunteers, contact to assist with their neutering, education and re-homing work.

Contact details:
Animal Rights Aruba, Mabon 7A, San Nicolas, Aruba
Tel: (mob) (297) 594 5393
www.animalrightsaruba.org
ara@setarnet.aw

Barbados

Ark Animal Welfare Society this organisation requires volunteers to assist with their adoption and fostering projects, educational programs to promote awareness of animal needs and rights and their low-cost spay/neuter program to reduce the unwanted litters of domestic animals on the Island. Contact if you can help.

Contact details:
Mail address: P.O. Box 199W, Christ Church, Barbados, West Indies
Tel: (246) 435-4108
www.arkanimalwelfarebarbados.com
ark@caribsurf.com

The Hope Sanctuary this organisation rescues, re-homes and rehabilitates animals in need. The Hope Sanctuary recognises that volunteers form a crucial element of their work. They rely on volunteers to assist with walking, socialising, fundraising, grooming, maintenance, adoption, publicity, education, etc.

Contact details:
Mail address: The Hope Sanctuary, Charity No. 590, P.O. Box 1015, Bridgetown, Barbados, West Indies
Tel: (246) 266-0986
www.thehopesanctuary.com
info@thehopesanctuary.com

Belize

Saga Humane Society their mission is: "preventing cruelty and promoting kindness to all animals". This is achieved first and foremost through the humane education program that Saga is working to implement within the community of San Pedro. Contact to assist as a volunteer.

Contact details:
Saga Humane Society, San Pedro Town, Ambergris Caye, Belize
Tel: +501 226 3266
http://sagahumanesociety.org
saga@btl.net

Bermuda SPCA has a mission to provide effective, lawful means for the prevention of cruelty to animals. To promote the education of the general public about the care and well being of all animals and to encourage and promote kindness to animals. They require voluntary help with walking dogs, socialising cats, fundraising and more. They offer orientation sessions for volunteers - see website for further information.

Contact details:
Mail address: PO Box WK 94, Warwick, WK BX
Street Address: 32 Valley Road, Paget PG 05
Tel: (441) 236-7333
Fax: (441) 236 6185
www.spca.bm
info@spca.bm

Bolivia

Animals SOS is the biggest non profit animal protection organisation in Bolivia. They run a variety of animal welfare projects, contact to assist as a volunteer.

Contact details:
Mail address: P.O. Box #5100, La Paz - Bolivia
Tel: (591)2- 230 808
www.animalessos.org
bolivia@animalessos.org

Brazil

Projeto Mucky works to rescue and care for Marmoset monkeys and currently have over 100 in their care. Contact to assist as a volunteer in a variety of ways.

Contact details:
www.culturaambientalnasescolas.com.br/noticia/meio-ambiente/conheca-o-projeto-mucky-:-protegendo-primatas-brasileiros

Costa Rica

Mc Kee Project approaches the suffering of companion animals at the root, in the community. They state: "we do not use euthanasia, because it does not work, likewise, we do not spend limited community resources on shelters, which do not solve the issue of overpopulation and which are inhumane storage and killing facilities". Instead, they build sustainable community solutions by teaching local veterinarians, governmental veterinarians & university veterinarians in advanced spay neuter techniques. Contact to assist.

Contact details:
www.mckeeproject.org

Pretoma is a marine conservation and research organisation working to protect ocean resources and promote sustainable fisheries policies in Costa Rica and Central America. Their structured volunteer programme enables people to get involved and to help protect and preserve endangered sea turtles and their precious habitat. Volunteers get involved with community-based conservation through stays of one week to five months. To assist, see their website for more detailed information.

Contact details:
www.pretoma.org

Dominican Republic

Friends of the Animals of Sosua provide emergency care for animals in need as well as running neutering projects, veterinary care, vaccinations and parasite treatments for street animals. They require voluntary assistance to help in a variety of hands-on ways.

Contact details:
US Mail Address: Asociación De Amigos Por Los Animales De Sosúa, EPS D4145, P.O. Box 02-5648, Miami, FL, 33102
Tel: 809-571-1167
www.aaasosua.com
info@aaasosua.com

El Salvador

Zoological Foundation of El Salvador (FUNZEL) operates the only wildlife rescue and re-habilitation centre in El Salvador. Their work is extremely important as unfortunately, there is a high demand for wild animals in El Salvador. Once captured, animals are illegally trafficked across the Honduran/Salvadoran border and approximately 95% are sent for sale as pets in the Central Market of San Salvador. This organisation requires volunteers to assist with their work and they offer training - see their website for further information.

Contact details:
7a. Calle Pte. #5150 San Salvador, El Salvador
Tel: (503) 262 1817 / 263 1071
www.elsalvador-online.com/esol/funzel/ingles.phpwww.elsalvador-online.com
funzel@navegante.com.sv

Grenada

Grenada SPCA their programs include: low cost and free spay / neuter clinics, feral cat program, education program, vaccination clinics, volunteer vet scheme and community outreach programs for unwanted, abused, neglected or stray animals. In addition, they travel the island in a mobile surgery van when volunteer vets are available. The organisation recognises the importance of volunteers and have a visitors volunteering programme for those visiting the area - volunteers are able to assist with a variety of jobs.

Contact details:
www.grenadaspca.org
pegalex@spiceisle.com

Guatemala

Animal Welfare Association - Rescue/Education (AWARE) this organisation works to rescue and re-habilitate domestic animals and state that they could not continue without the vital help provided by volunteers. "With over 200 dogs and nearly 100 cats we always need help with anything from building dog-runs or putting up fences to bathing, brushing, or walking dogs, providing some human company for both the dogs and the cats, or helping out with our educational programs. From time to time we need help with our spay/neuter and rabies vaccination clinics, garage sales, and other fund-raising events". Contact to assist.

Contact details:
Mail address: AWARE A-371, P.O. Box 669004, Miami Springs, FL 33266, USA
Street address: Granja Montecito, Pachaj, Sumpango
Tel: +502 7833-1639
www.animalaware.org
xenii-2@usa.net

Jamaica

Jamaica SPCA has been working in Jamaica for over one hundred years, to protect animals from cruelty, neglect, injury and abandonment, and to defend and promote animal rights. They encourage volunteers to assist them and have a volunteer application form on their site.

Contact details:
The Jamaica Society for The Prevention of Cruelty to Animals, 10 Winchester Road, Kingston, Jamaica
Tel: (876) 929-0320
Fax: (876) 754-4594
www.jspca.info

Noah's Ark Spay and Neuter Group work to improve the lives of Jamaica's street animals by providing free neutering, health care, and humane education programs. Contact to assist as a volunteer.

Contact details:
15127 Perdido Drive, Orlando, FL 32828, USA
Tel: (407) 482 8326
www.noahsarkjamaica.org

Mexico

Animal Protection Association of Cuernavaca (APAC) offers food, medical attention, shelter, vaccinations and neutering. They also work with the local authorities to control rabies. They have 150 dogs and 75 cats in their shelter, contact to assist as a volunteer.

Contact details:
Tel: 777 380 02 65
http://asilodecuernavaca.blogspot.com

Baja Dogs La Paz their mission is "to teach the children to respect and care for animals, promote disease prevention through community education and reduce the dog population through an aggressive spay and neuter program". They rely on volunteers to spend time with the animals in their care and to assist with their projects.

Contact details:
Tel: 044 612 155 8948
www.bajadogshelplineoflapaz.org
BDLP@bajadogslapaz.org

Fundacion Tomy has a vision of being an organisation "that plays a key role in cultural change, promoting healthy co-existence of society with animals in their habitat, based on the philosophy of respect for life". Visit their website to download a volunteering form.

Contact details:
www.fundaciontomy.org
avivas@fundaciontomy.org

Panama

Spay Panama is a non governmental organisation that provides an intensive neutering programme to control the companion animal numbers. They also promote the adoption of homeless animals. Contact to assist.

Contact details:
Mail address - Panama: Spay/Panama, Box 0818-00423, Bethania, Panama, Rep. de Panama
Tel: (507) 261-5542/ (507) 6671-0246
www.spaypanama.org/
doctor@spaypanama.org

Contact details:
Mail address - States
Spay/Panama, PTY 4689, P.O.Box 025724, Miami, Fl 33102-5724

Puerto Rico

Amigos de los Animales (ADLA) rescues, rehabilitates and re-homes abused and abandoned companion and farm animals, and also facilitates the rescue of such animals alongside other rescue organizations in Puerto Rico. ADLA successfully wages cruelty investigations when necessary, and is involved in Humane Education efforts/campaigns island wide. ADLA continually has its eye on the "big picture" for Puerto Rico, and is not limited in its involvement in planning for a humane Puerto Rico. Contact to assist as a volunteer.

Contact details:
www.amigosdelosanimalespr.org

Save A Sato is a non-profit organisation dedicated to easing the suffering of Puerto Rico's homeless and abused animals. "Sato" is slang for street dog. The organisation rescues Satos from the streets and beaches, gives them medical care, food and shelter, and plenty of love. When they are healthy, they are sent to one of their shelter partners for adoption into loving homes. Contact to assist as a volunteer with bathing, feeding, cleaning and loving the shelter dogs. They also require assistance with fostering and transporting dogs.

Contact details:
Mail address: Save a Sato Foundation, Inc. P.O.Box 37694 San Juan, Puerto Rico 00937-0694
www.saveasato.org
tracey@saveasato.org

St Lucia

St Lucia Animal Protection Society is dedicated to improving the welfare of all the animals on the island of St Lucia, in the West Indies. Contact to assist as a volunteer.

Contact details:
Mail address: St Lucia Animal Protection Society, P.O. Box 148, Castries. St Lucia
Tel: +1 758 457-5277
www.stluciaanimals.org/index.php
slaps@candw.lc

"Non-violence leads to the highest ethics, which is the goal of all evolution. Until we stop harming all other living beings, we are still savages." - Thomas A. Edison

USEFUL LINKS

Volunteering England works to support and increase the quality, quantity, impact and accessibility of volunteering throughout England.

Contact details:
Volunteering England, Regent's Wharf, 8 All Saints Street, London N1 9RL UK
Tel: +44 (0)20 7520 8900
Fax: +44 (0)20 7520 8910
www.volunteering.org.uk
volunteering@volunteering.org.uk

Volunteering Wales information and opportunities about volunteering throughout Wales.

Contact details:
www.volunteering-wales.net

Volunteer Scotland information and opportunities about volunteering throughout Scotland.

Contact details:
www.volunteerscotland.org.uk

Volunteering Development Agency Northern Ireland works to promote and develop volunteering

Contact details:
Volunteer Development Agency 2009, 129 Ormeau Road, Belfast, BT7 1SH
Tel: 028 9023 6100
Fax: 028 9023 7570
www.volunteering-ni.org
info@voluntecring-ni.org

TimeBank finds ways for you to give your time that suit who you are

Contact details:
TimeBank, 2nd Floor, Downstream Building, 1 London Bridge, SE1 9BG
Tel: 0845 456 1668
Fax: 0845 456 1669
www.timebank.org.uk
info@timebank.org.uk

VolunteerMatch USA volunteer placements in the USA

Contact details:
Mail address: VolunteerMatch, 717 California St., Second Floor, San Francisco, CA 94108
Tel: (415) 241-6868
Fax: (415) 241-6869
www.volunteermatch.org
support@volunteermatch.org

Jobs with Animals

If you want to work with animals, you'll find that there are many different options and a huge array of job opportunities. You may want to work directly with animals: e.g. as a vet, dog warden, RSPCA Inspector, animal care assistant, ranger, animal behaviourist, etc. Or, you may want to work with animals in a less hands-on way, in an office based environment in management, administrative, fundraising or personnel positions. For many employers, volunteer experience, interest, aptitude and commitment can be more important than initial entry qualifications. It is advisable to be well equipped with as many related skills as possible when seeking employment. Through volunteering, you'll acquire many new skills that will help you when applying for jobs or course placements. It is advisable for anyone wanting to work with animals, from would-be veterinary surgeons to animal care assistants, to do some sort of voluntary work before embarking on their chosen career.

Volunteering can be an excellent way of landing your perfect job, as it is common for volunteers to be offered permanent positions. By enrolling as a volunteer you will gain a thorough and invaluable understanding of the work involved. Training and qualifications can be equally important when seeking your job working with animals. There is fierce competition for animal care related jobs at all levels. If you don't have previous experience, an animal care qualification will greatly improve your job prospects. It is worth considering enrolling on online animal care courses as these enable you to study in your own time, at your own pace, and at home. There are many courses out there and we provide several that will provide qualifications to enhance many different careers with animals. Click here for more information about online animal diploma courses offered by Animal Jobs Direct

Jobs with animals in this ebook is divided into the following sections:

1. Animal Charity Jobs
2. Jobs working with Horses
3. Wildlife Jobs
4. Veterinary Jobs
5. Jobs working with Cats and Dogs
6. Zoo Jobs
7. Marine Jobs

Each listing in this ebook contains a summary about the organisation and a link directly to the latest jobs. This information is kept up to date, but please be aware that not all the listings have job vacancies all of the time and it is worth re-checking the links regularly for new jobs. Some listings may appear in several sections. This has been done so as to ensure that you don't miss out on a job listing if you only regularly check the category that most interests you. If you want to extend your job search around the world, please remember to visit:

Animal Jobs Direct America

Animal Jobs Direct Africa

Animal Jobs Direct Asia

Animal Jobs Direct Australia

Animal Jobs Direct Europe

Animal Jobs Direct New Zealand

If you are actively seeking employment, please register your details on the Animal Jobs Direct Job Board where you can upload your CV and search for the latest jobs in your area.

Animal Charity Jobs

Introduction

Animal charities have incredibly busy working environments. There are many different animal charities and, consequently, a large variety of jobs. Animal charities vary in size and function: there are several large international organisations with offices in the UK, such as the World Society for the Protection of Animals (WSPA) and the International Fund for Animal Welfare (IFAW). Both of these organisations are examples of charities that deal with international animal welfare issues, their work largely involves campaigning to end animal suffering around the world.

There are several large national charities such as the Blue Cross, People's Dispensary for Sick Animals (PDSA), Battersea Dogs & Cats Home, Dogs Trust, National Animal Welfare Trust and Cats Protection - all of these operate a variety of national programmes and initiatives. Most of them operate a number of clinics, hospitals and rescue homes around the country and employ a variety of staff in different roles. There are also many smaller charities; often these are predominently community based, working locally to provide animal welfare services, to promote animal adoptions and to deal with animal welfare problems as they arise.

Some animal charities have the primary role of campaigning for animal rights, eg: Animal Aid, BUAV, National Anti-vivisection Society, League Against Cruel Sports. Their work is largely office based, with few having animal holding facilities of any sort. Although the jobs offered by these charities are not directly with animals, the organisations assist many animals through education, raising awareness of animal suffering, raising funds to assist hands-on organisations, and campaigning for better legislation for the protection of animals.

Becoming a member of an animal charity could improve your chances of getting a job offer. Memberships enable you to receive regular updates and newsletters about the work of the charity; this will give you a better understanding of the work they do and will ensure that you are better informed should you be offered an interview.

Animal Charity Jobs

<u>Alderney Wildlife Trust</u> was launched in May 2002, in response to concerns about the lack of land management in Alderney and to combat the ensuing loss of habitat and took over from the existing Alderney Conservation Volunteers organisation.

Contact details:
Alderney Wildlife Trust, 51 Victoria Street, Alderney, Channel Islands GY9 3TA
Tel: +44 (0) 1481 822935
www.alderneywildlife.org
info@alderneywildlife.org

<u>Animal Defenders International (ADI)</u> works to educate, create awareness, and promote the interest of humanity in the cause of justice, and the suppression of all forms of cruelty to animals; wherever possible to alleviate suffering, and to conserve and protect animals and the environment.

Contact details:
UK/Europe: Animal Defenders International, Millbank Tower, Millbank, London SW1P 4QP
Tel: +44 (0)20 7630 3340
Fax: +44 (0)20 7828 2179
www.ad-international.org
info@ad-international.org

Contact details:
USA: 6100 Wilshire Boulevard, Suite 1150, Los Angeles, CA 90048, USA
Tel: +1 323-935-2234
www.ad-international.org
usa@ad-international.org

Contact details:
South America: Apartado Postal 359888 BOGOTA, Colombia
www.ad-international.org
infolatam@ad-international.org

<u>Animal Aid</u> is the UK's largest animal rights group and one of the longest established in the world, having been founded in 1977. They campaign peacefully against all forms of animal abuse and promote a cruelty-free lifestyle. They investigate and expose animal cruelty, and our undercover investigations and other evidence are often used by the media, bringing these issues to public attention.

Contact details:
Mail address: The Old Chapel, Bradford Street, Tonbridge, Kent TN9 1AW
Tel: +44 (0)1732 364546
Fax: +44 (0)1732 366533
www.animalaid.org.uk
info@animalaid.org.uk

Animal Protection Agency (APA) is the UK organisation committed to ceasing the trade in wildlife for pets. Perhaps unbelievably, it is still legal in Britain to sell wild animals captured from other countries. The majority of wild-trapped animals die from the stress and disease that is associated with every stage of their harrowing journey. Next to habitat destruction, collection of animals for the pet trade is the main reason for the decline in many species.

Contact details:
Animal Protection Agency, Brighton Media Centre, 68 Middle Street, Brighton BN1 1AL
Tel: +44 (0)1273 674253
Fax: +44 (0)1273 674927
www.apa.org.uk
info@apa.org.uk

Bat Conservation Trust works on a number of levels to create a better world for bats. They run a range of different projects and initiatives. The breadth and depth of their work is driven by their passion for bats, and their vision of bats and people living in harmony.

Contact details:
Mail address: Bat Conservation Trust, 5th Floor, Quadrant House, 250 Kennington Lane, London SE11 5RD
Fax: 020 7820 7198
www.bats.org.uk
enquiries@bats.org.uk

Battersea Dogs & Cats Home has been rescuing lost and unwanted dogs since 1860 and cats since 1883. The organisation works to rescue, rehabilitate, re-unite and re-home dogs and cats. They have rescue centres in Battersea London, Windsor and Brands Hatch.

Contact details:
Battersea, London: 4 Battersea Park Road, London SW8 4AA
Tel: 020 7622 3626
www.battersea.org.uk
info@battersea.org.uk

Contact details:
Battersea, Old Windsor: Priest Hill, Old Windsor, Windsor SL4 2JN
Tel: 01784 432929
www.battersea.org.uk
info@battersea.org.uk

Contact details:
Battersea, Brands Hatch: Crowhurst Lane, Ash, Brands Hatch TN15 7HH
Tel: 01474 874994
www.battersea.org.uk
info@battersea.org.uk

Berkshire, Buckinghamshire and Oxfordshire Wildlife Trust was established in 1959 by local ecologists who could see the extent of harm being done to the wonderfully rich natural environment of the three counties. This is the only voluntary organisation in the region concerned with all aspects of nature conservation. Their vision is to create a region rich in wildlife and appreciated by all.

Contact details:
Head Office: The Lodge, 1 Armstrong Road, Littlemore, Oxford OX4 4XT
Tel: 01865 775476
Fax: 01865 711301
www.bbowt.org.uk
info@bbowt.org.uk **or** recruitment@bbowt.org.uk **or** jobs@bbowt.org.uk

Blue Cross aims to: "ensure the welfare of animals by providing practical care, highlight the benefits of companionship between animals and people and promote a sense of respect and responsibility towards animals in the community". The organisation provides support to the nation's pets and their owners by: treating pets whose owners cannot afford private veterinary treatment, finding permanent homes for unwanted or abandoned animals and educating the public in responsible animal ownership.

Contact details:
The Blue Cross, Shilton Road, Burford, Oxon OX18 4PF
Tel: 01993 822651
Fax: 01993 823083
www.bluecross.org.uk
info@bluecross.org.uk **or** jobs@bluecross.org.uk

Bedfordshire, Cambridgeshire, Northamptonshire, Peterborough Wildlife Trusts
is a wildlife conservation charity that works for a better future for all kinds of wildlife across Bedfordshire, Cambridgeshire, Northamptonshire and Peterborough. Their mission is to protect and improve habitats and wildlife in our local area as well as helping people to enjoy and understand their local wildlife.

Contact details:
Bedfordshire Office: Priory Country Park, Barkers Lane, Bedford MK41 9DJ
Tel: 01234 364213
Fax: 01234 328520
www.wildlifebcnp.org
bedfordshire@wildlifcbcnp.org

Contact details:
Cambridgeshire Office: The Manor House, Broad Street, Great Cambourne, Cambridge CB23 6DH
Tel: 01954 713500
Fax: 01954 710051
www.wildlifebcnp.org
cambridgeshire@wildlifebcnp.org

Contact details:
Northamptonshire Office & Lings Environmental Centre: Lings House, Billing Lings, Northampton NN3 8BE
Tel: 01604 405285
Fax: 01604 784835
www.wildlifebcnp.org
northamptonshire@wildlifebcnp.org

Contact details:
Peterborough Office & Peterborough Community Education Service: Eco Innovation Centre, Peterscourt, City Road, Peterborough PE1 1SA
Tel: 01733 294543
Fax: 01733 554459
www.ecoinnovationcentre.co.uk
peterborough@wildlifebcnp.org

Bath Cats and Dogs Home works to shelter and care for unwanted animals in the Bath; North East Somerset and West Wiltshire areas, until they are successfully re-homed. The organisation recognises the valuable and unique contributions volunteers can make to its work and aims to maximise the opportunities for volunteer involvement at all levels of the organisation and in shaping and delivering the organisational objectives.

Contact details:
Bath Cats and Dogs Home, The Avenue, Claverton Down, Bath BA2 7AZ
Tel: 01225 787321
www.bathcatsanddogshome.org.uk

Birmingham and Black County Wildlife Trust was founded in 1980 as the Urban Wildlife Group, in 1982 they became the first urban Wildlife Trust, one of 47 covering the whole UK, they have been working to make Birmingham and the Black Country a better place for wildlife and people. Click on the left navigation bar on the 'contact us' button and then on the 'jobs' button for latest vacancies.

Contact details:
28 Harborne Road, Edgbaston, Birmingham B15 3AA
Tel: +44 (0)121 454 1199
Fax: +44 (0)121 454 6556
www.bbcwildlife.org.uk
info@bbcwildlife.org.uk

British Divers Marine Life Rescue (BDMLA) trains over 400 volunteer Marine Mammal Medics a year and have 20 whale rescue pontoons located at strategic points throughout the UK, waiting to help stranded whales and dolphins. This is a voluntary organisation - their training courses may be of great benefit to those seeking marine employment._

Contact details:
British Divers Marine Life Rescue, Lime House, Regency Close, Uckfield, East Sussex TN22 1DS
Tel: 01825 765546
Fax: 01825 768012
www.bdmlr.org.uk
info@bdmlr.org.uk

Celia Hammond Trust provides care and refuge for feral cats and kittens and for those animals which on the basis of age, temperament or appearance would not normally be taken in elsewhere. The organisation strives to: promote the welfare of animals through example and education, provide low cost treatment in their clinics for sick/injured animals, provide low cost neuter/vaccination clinics, operate a rescue service for animals, both domestic and feral in emergency situations, provide long and short-term sanctuary accommodation and re-homing facilities for rescued animals and to investigate complaints of cruelty and neglect and to take appropriate action.

Contact details:
Head Office: Celia Hammond Animal Trust, High Street, Wadhurst, East Sussex, TN5 6AG
Tel: 01892 783367
Fax: 01892 784882
www.celiahammond.org
headoffice@celiahammond.org

Contact details:
London – Canning Town: Neuter Clinic and Rescue Centre, 151-153 Barking Road, Canning Town, London E16 4HQ
Tel: 020 7474 8811
www.celiahammond.org
canningtown@celiahammond.org

Contact details:
London – Lewisham Branch: Neuter Clinic and Rescue Centre, 233-235 Lewisham Way, Lewisham SE4 1UY
Tel: 020 8691 2100
www.celiahammond.org
lewisham@celiahammond.org

Contact details:
Kent – Tunbridgewells Branch: -
Tel: 01892 514655
www.celiahammond.org
tunwells@celiahammond.org

Contact details:
East Sussex – Greenacres Sanctuary: Animal Sanctuary & Rescue Centre, Greenacres, Stubb Lane, Brede, Near Hastings, East Sussex
Tel: 01424 882198
www.celiahammond.org
brede@celiahammond.org

Cumbria Wildlife Trust is the only voluntary organisation devoted solely to the conservation of the wildlife and wild places of Cumbria. The Trust stands up for wildlife, creates wildlife havens, and seeks to raise environmental awareness.

Contact details:
Head Office: Cumbria Wildlife Trust, Plumgarths, Crook Road, Kendal, Cumbria LA8 8LX
Tel: 01539 816300
Fax: 01539 816301
www.cumbriawildlifetrust.org.uk
mail@cumbriawildlifetrust.org.uk

Contact details:
Carlisle Office: Gosling Sike Farm, Houghton, Carlisle CA3 0LD
Tel: 01228 829570
Fax: 01228 631811
www.cumbriawildlifetrust.org.uk

Contact details:
South Walney Office: No 1 Coastguard Cottages, South Walney Nature Reserve, Barrow in Furness, Cumbria LA14 3YQ
Tel: 01229 471066
www.cumbriawildlifetrust.org.uk

Cat and Rabbit Rescue Centre (CRRC) is located in rural Sidlesham, an ideal location for their long term residents who enjoy total freedom of the whole site. This is an unusual shelter that prides itself on the quality of accommodation and freedom given to the animals.

Contact details:
The Cat and Rabbit Rescue Centre, Holborow Lodge, Chalder Lane, Sidlesham, Chichester, West Sussex PO20 7RJ
Tel: 01243 641409
www.crrc.co.uk
info@crrc.co.uk

Care for the Wild International (CWI) is an animal welfare and conservation charity that funds practical projects around the world. They make areas safe from poachers, rehabilitate sick or injured animals and provide sanctuary for those animals that cannot return to the wild. They also act as a global voice for wildlife through research, education and advocacy and expose animal cruelty and wildlife crime.

Contact details:
The Granary, Tickfold Farm, Kingsfold, West Sussex RH12 3SE
Tel: +44 (0)1306 627900
Fax: +44 (0)1306 627901
www.careforthewild.com
info@careforthewild.com

Devon Wildlife Trust was established as a registered charity in 1962, the Devon Wildlife Trust has a unique and influential position. Unique because it is the only organisation concerned with all aspects of wildlife conservation in Devon. Influential because it is a member of The Wildlife Trusts partnership, a nationwide network dedicated to the achievement of a UK richer in wildlife. They have over 50 full time staff.

Contact details:
Devon Wildlife Trust, Cricklepit Mill, Commercial Road, Exeter, Devon EX2 4AB
Tel: 01392 279244
Fax: 01392 433221
www.devonwildlifetrust.org
contactus@devonwildlifetrust.org

Dorset Wildlife Trust is the largest conservation charity in Dorset with over 25,000 members.

Contact details:
Dorset Wildlife Trust HQ, Brooklands Farm, Forston, Dorchester DT2 7AA
Tel: 01305 264620
Fax: 01305 251120
www.dorsetwildlifetrust.org.uk
mail@dorestwildlifetrust.org.uk

Diana Brimblecombe Animal Rescue Centre (DBARC) assists and provides shelter for a variety of animals in need in the Berkshire area. Click on the 'job vacancies' button on the left navigation bar.

Contact details:
Diana Brimblecombe Animal Rescue Centre, Nelsons Lane, Hurst, Nr. Wokingham, Berkshire RG10 0RR
Tel: 0118 9341122
Fax: 0118 9706762
www.dbarc.org.uk

Durham Wildlife Trust works to protect wildlife and promote nature conservation in County Durham, the City of Sunderland and the Boroughs of Gateshead, South Tyneside and Darlington. They are one of the most active environmental organisations in the region, managing 25 Nature Reserves, a variety of species and habitat recovery projects and four Visitor Centres. They also manage an extensive environmental education programme that aims to engage schools, community groups, whole communities and individuals in issues around nature conservation and the wider environment.

Contact details:
Headquarters: Rainton Meadows, Durham Wildlife Trust, Rainton Meadows, Chilton Moor, Houghton-le-Spring, Tyne & Wear DH4 6PU
Tel: 0191 5843112
www.durhamwt.co.uk
mail@durhamwt.co.uk

Derbyshire Wildlife Trust aims to raise awareness of potential threats to wildlife and encourage individuals and organisations to take responsibility for caring for their local environment.

Contact details:
Derbyshire Wildlife Trust, East Mill, Bridge Foot, Belper, Derbyshire DE56 1XH
Tel: 01773 881188
Fax: 01773 821826
www.derbyshirewildlifetrut.org.uk
enquiries@derbyshirewt.co.uk

Essex Wildlife Trust is the leading conservation body in Essex. It has 32,000 members and 450 corporate members who enable to Trust to conduct campaigns for wildlife conservation and to protect over 7,250 acres of land on 87 Nature Reserves, 1 Nature Park and to run their 7 Visitor Centres.

Contact details:
Essex Wildlife Trust Headquarters, Abbotts Hall Farm, Great Wigborough, Colchester CO5 7RZ
Tel: 01621 862960
Fax: 01621 862990
www.essexwt.org.uk
admin@essexwt.org.uk

Foal Farm Animal Rescue Centre aims to take in as many sick, distressed and unwanted animals as possible and restore them to health and happiness. The animals are kept on a 26 acre farm where they are neutered, micro-chipped, vaccinated and given any other medical assistance necessary.

Contact details:
Foal Farm Animal Rescue Centre, Jail Lane, Biggin Hill, Kent TN16 3AX
Tel: 01959 572 386
www.foalfarm.org.uk
info@foalfarm.org.uk **or** volunteering@foalfarm.org.uk

Gloucestershire Wildlife Trust was formed in 1961 to work for wildlife conservation in Gloucestershire. The Trust employs professional staff to carry out the increasingly technical work associated with conserving wildlife with the support of over 300 volunteers.

Contact details:
Gloucestershire Wildlife Trust, Conservation Centre, Robinswood Hill Country Park, Reservoir Road, Gloucester GL4 6SX
Tel: 01452 38 33 33
Fax: 01452 38 33 34
www.gloucestershirewildlifetrust.co.uk
info@gloucestershirewildlifetrust.co.uk

Gables Farm Dogs and Cats Home founded in 1907, the organisation now looks after some 2,000 cats and dogs every year. They enforce a strict non-euthanasia policy and are committed to providing the best environment possible.

Contact details:
Gables Farm Dogs' & Cats' Home, 204 Merafield Road, Plymouth PL7 1UQ
Tel: 01752 331602
Fax: 01752 331604
www.gablesfarm.org.uk
info@gablesfarm.org.uk

Hampshire and Isle of Wight Wildlife Trust is a charity dedicated to conserving, protecting and enhancing local wildlife - whatever it is and wherever in the two counties it may be.

Contact details:
Hampshire and Isle of Wight Wildlife Trust Headquarters, Beechcroft House, Vicarage Lane, Curdridge, Hampshire SO32 2DP
Tel: 01489 774400
Fax: 01489 774401
www.hwt.org.uk
feedback@hwt.org.uk

HorseWorld is a charity that specialises in rescuing, rehabilitating and re-homing.

Contact details:
Charity Headquarters: HorseWorld, Delmar Hall, Keynes Farm, Staunton Lane, Whitchurch, Bristol BS14 0QL
Tel: 01275 832425
Fax: 01275 836909
www.horseworld.org.uk

Hertfordshire and Middlesex Wildlife Trust is the only charity dedicated solely to protecting local wildlife and wild spaces, engaging our diverse communities through access to nature reserves, campaigning, volunteering and education. They manage over 43 nature reserves and campaign to save important wildlife habitats, volunteering programmes and wildlife education work. Click on 'jobs' button on the left navigation menu.

Contact details:
Herts and Middlesex Wildlife Trust, Grebe House, St Michael's Street, St Albans, Herts AL3 4SN
Tel: 01727 858901
Fax: 01727 854542
www.hertswildlifetrust.org.uk
info@hmwt.org

Home for Unwanted and Lost Animals (HULA) operates from a 17 acre site which provides sanctuary for dogs, cats, rabbits, and other domestic animals until new homes can be found. They also have a number of resident animals including goats, pigs, sheep, cows, ponies, and a donkey who are permanently retired.

Contact details:
Mail address: HULA Animal Rescue, Glebe Farm, Salford Road, Aspley Guise, Milton Keynes MK17 8HZ
Tel: 01908 584000
Fax: 01908 282020
www.hularescue.org
hularescue@tiscali.co.uk

Kent Wildlife Trust works to protect Kent's native wildlife for future generations to enjoy. The challenges of protecting wildlife in Kent increase each year with new pressures placed on our countryside, habitats and species.

Contact details:
Head Office Address: Kent Wildlife Trust, Tyland Barn, Maidstone, Kent ME14 3BD
Tel: 01622 662012
www.kentwildlifetrust.org.uk
info@kentwildlife.org.uk

Lancashire, Manchester and North Merseyside Wildlife Trust was formed in 1962 by a group of naturalists who wanted to help protect the wildlife of the old county Lancashire. It is now the leading local environmental charity in this region. Their mission is to work for a region richer in wildlife by the protection and enhancement of species and habitats, both common and rare.

Contact details:
The Barn: Head Office: Wildlife Trust for Lancashire, Manchester & North Merseyside, Berkeley Drive, Bamber Bridge, Preston, Lancashire PR5 6BY
Tel: 01772 324129
Fax: 01772 628849
www.lancswt.org.uk
info@lancswt.org.uk

League Against Cruel Sports was established in 1924, and works to end cruelty to animals in the name of sport.

Contact details:
Mail address: League Against Cruel Sports, New Sparling House, Holloway Hill, Godalming, Surrey GU7 1QZ
Tel: 01483 524 250
www.league.org.uk
info@league.org.uk

Lincolnshire Wildife Trust is a voluntary charitable organisation which cares for Lincolnshire's wildlife and countryside. The Lincolnshire Wildlife Trust is one of the oldest of these county trusts, having been founded in 1948. The Trust covers the whole of the historic county of Lincolnshire – from the Humber to the Wash.

Contact details:
Headquarters Mail Address: Banovallum House, Manor House Street, Horncastle, Lincolnshire LN9 5HF
Tel: 01507 526667
Fax: 01507 525732
www.lincstrust.org.uk
info@lincstrust.co.uk

London Wildlife Trust is the only charity dedicated solely to protecting the capital's wildlife and wild spaces. They manage over fifty London-wide reserves and campaign to save important wildlife habitats, engaging London's diverse communities through access to their nature reserves, volunteering programmes and education work.

Contact details:
London Wildlife Trust, Skyline House, 200 Union Street, London SE1 0LX
Tel: 020 7261 0447
www.wildlondon.org.uk
enquiries@wildlondon.org.uk

Mayhew Animal Home has a vision of a world where all companion animals are wanted. They aim to set the standards in animal welfare. The Mayhew offers a wide variety of community services providing advice, care and assistance to animals and their carers whatever their circumstances and strives to tackle the companion animal welfare crisis from every possible angle.

Contact details:
The Mayhew Animal Home, Trenmar Gardens, Kensal Green, London NW10 6BJ
Tel: 020 8969 0178
Fax: 020 8964 3221
www.mayhewanimalhome.org
info@mayhewanimalhome.org

National Animal Welfare Trust (NAWT) aims for the provision of care and shelter for stray, neglected and unwanted animals of all kinds; the protection of animals of all kinds from ill-usage, cruelty and suffering; and in particular, to rescue and provide care and shelter for stray, neglected and unwanted animals of all kinds and find suitable homes for any such animals.

Contact details:
Head Office: Tyler's Way, Watford-By-Pass, Watford, Hertfordshire WD25 8WT
Tel: 020 8950 0177
Fax: 020 8420 4454
www.nawt.org.uk

Northumberland Wildlife Trust is the leading charity dedicated to wildlife conservation and environmental education in North East England. Their mission is to conserve local wildlife, promote nature conservation and provide the means by which everyone can become involved.

Contact details:
Mail address: Northumberland Wildlife Trust, St Nicholas Park, Gosforth, Newcastle upon Tyne, Tyne and Wear NE3 3XT
Tel: 0191 284 6884
Fax: 0191 284 6794
www.nwt.org.uk
mail@northwt.org.uk

North Clwyd Animal Rescue (NCAR) works to rescue, care for and re-home animals in this area.

Contact details:
North Clwyd Animal Rescue, Maes Gwyn, Glan yr Afron Road, Trelogan, Nr Holywell, Flintshire CH8 9BD
Tel: 01745 560546
reception@ncar.org.uk (general enquiries) **or** nickyowen@ncar.org.uk (vacancy enquiries)

Norfolk Wildlife Trust cares for over 50 nature reserves and other protected sites around the county including ten kilometres of coastline, nine Norfolk broads, nine National Nature Reserves and five ancient woodlands. They have a positive influence over a great deal of the Norfolk countryside through their planning and advisory functions.

Contact details:
Norfolk Wildlife Trust, Bewick House, 22 Thorpe Road, Norwich NR1 1RY
Tel: 01603 625540
www.norfolkwildlifetrust.org.uk
info@norfolkwildlifetrust.org.uk

Organisation Cetacea (ORCA) promotes the conservation of the marine environment through research, partnership and education and provides a forum for the enjoyment of whales, dolphins, seabirds and other marine life.

Contact details:
ORCA, Brittany Centre, Wharf Road, Portsmouth PO2 8RU
www.orcaweb.org.uk
info@orcaweb.org.uk

Peoples Dispensary for Sick Animals (PDSA) works to care for the pets of needy people by providing free veterinary services to their sick and injured animals and promoting responsible pet ownership. They are the largest private employer of fully qualified veterinary surgeons and veterinary nurses in Europe. PDSA is non-campaigning, and non-political.

Contact details:
Mail address: Head Office, Whitechapel Way, Priorslee, Telford, Shropshire TF2 9PQ
Tel: 01952 290999
Fax: 01952 291035
www.pdsa.org.uk

Royal Society for the Protection of Animals (RSPCA) has a vision of a world in which all humans respect and live in harmony with all other members of the animal kingdom. Their mission is to prevent cruelty, promote kindness to and alleviate suffering of animals.

Contact details:
RSPCA Enquiries Service, Wilberforce Way, Southwater, Horsham, West Sussex RH13 9RS
Tel: 0300 1234 555
Fax: 0303 123 0100
www.rspca.org.uk

Royal Society for the Protection of Birds (RSPB) was founded in 1889 and since then has grown into Europe's largest wildlife conservation charity with more than a million members. From its initial stance against the trade in wild birds' plumage, the issues which the Society tackles have grown hugely in number and size.

Contact details:
UK Headquarters: The Lodge, Potton Road, Sandy, Bedfordshire SG19 2DL
Tel: 01767 680551
www.rspb.org.uk

Royal Society of Wildlife Trusts (RSWT) although a charity in its own right, RSWT also operates as an umbrella group for the 47 local Wildlife Trusts that have been formed across the UK, helping to co-ordinate their activities and campaigning at a UK level.

Contact details:
Mail address: The Kiln, Waterside, Mather Road, Newark, Nottinghamshire NG24 1WT
Tel: 01636 677711
Fax: 01636 670001
www.wildlifetrusts.org
enquiry@wildlifetrusts.org

Raystede Animal Welfare Centre aims to prevent and relieve cruelty to animals and to protect them from unnecessary suffering. Over 1,500 unwanted and abandoned animals arrive at the centre annually. Dogs, cats and other companion animals are found new caring homes while others remain in Raystede's care for the rest of their days.

Contact details:
Raystede Animal Welfare, Ringmer, East Sussex BN8 5AJ
Tel: 01825 840252
Fax: 01825 840995
www.raystede.org
info@raystede.org

Somerset Wildlife Trust has a vision for A Living Landscape involving enlarging, improving and joining-up areas of land on nature reserves, in towns and in partnership with other landowners. Their Living Landscape schemes in Somerset - on Mendip and the Brue Valley - are creating inspirational, accessible landscapes - full of wildlife and rich in opportunities for learning, better health and well-being, alongside sustainable economic development.

Contact details:
Head Office: Somerset Wildlife Trust, Tonedale Mill, Tonedale, Wellington TA21 0AW
Tel: 01823 652400
Fax: 01823 652411
www.somersetwildlife.org
enquiries@somersetwildlife.org **or** volunteering@somersetwildlife.org

Contact details:
Mendip Office: Somerset Wildlife Trust, Callow Rock Offices, Shipham Road, Cheddar BS27 3DQ
Tel: 01823 652400
www.somersetwildlife.org
enquiries@somersetwildlife.org **or** volunteering@somersetwildlife.org

Scottish Society for the Prevention of Cruelty to Animals (SSPCA) was established in 1839 to prevent cruelty to animals and promote kindness and humanity in their treatment, the Scottish Society for the Prevention of Cruelty to Animals is Scotland's leading animal welfare charity. Today, its work is as necessary as ever. The Scottish SPCA is a reporting agency for the enforcement of animal protection laws.

Contact details:
Scottish SPCA, Kingseat Road, Halbeath, Dunfermline KY11 8RY
Tel: 03000 999 999
www.scottishspca.org

Shropshire Wildlife Trust are the county's leading environmental charity, currently supported by 10,000 members. With strength of numbers and 45 years of experience behind them, they are an increasingly effective champion for local wildlife.

Contact details:
Shropshire Wildlife Trust, 193 Abbey Foregate, Shrewsbury, Shropshire SY2 6AH
Tel: 01743 284280
Fax: 01743 284281
www.shropshirewildlifetrust.org.uk

Sheffield Wildlife Trust is the city's largest environmental charity, working to promote conservation, protection and improvement of the physical and natural environment of Sheffield. Targeted work to protect vulnerable habitats and species is happening alongside initiatives to boost the general wildlife value of parks and green spaces across Sheffield.

Contact details:
Mall address: Sheffield Wildlife Trust, Victoria Hall, 37 Stafford Road, Sheffield S2 2SF
Tel: 0114 2634335
Fax: 0114 2634345
www.wildsheffield.com
mail@wildsheffield.com **or** recruitment@wildsheffield.com

Suffolk Wildlife Trust aims to create a Living Landscape where wildlife flourishes in countryside, towns and villages. They care for more than 50 nature reserves and their conservation advisors work with farmers and local communities to improve their land for wildlife and create networks of linked up habitat across Suffolk.

Contact details:
Suffolk Wildlife Trust, Brooke House, Ashbocking, Ipswich IP6 9JY
Tel: 01473 890089
Fax: 01473 890165
www.suffolkwildlifetrust.org
info@suffolkwildlifetrust.org

Surrey Wildlife Trust currently manage 80 nature reserves covering over 4,000 hectares of Surrey's countryside. As well as managing their own reserves, they also manage land under access agreements with private landowners.

Contact details:
Head Office: Surrey Wildlife Trust, School Lane, Pirbright, Woking, Surrey GU24 0JN
Tel: 01483 795440
Fax: 01483 486505
www.surreywildlifetrust.org
info@surreywt.org.uk

Tiggywinkles Wildlife Hospital is the world's busiest wildlife hospital and cares for sick & injured hedgehogs, badgers, wild birds, foxes, even reptiles & amphibians. They are a specialist hospital, using all available veterinary welfare skills, dedicated to rescuing and rehabilitating all species of British wildlife.

Contact details:
Tiggywinkles, Aston Road, Haddenham, Aylesbury, Buckinghamshire HP17 8AF
Tel: 01844 292292
Fax: 01844 292640
www.sttiggywinkles.org.uk
mail@sttiggywinkles.org.uk

<u>Vale Wildlife Rescue</u> offers help to thousands of wildlife casualties every year by treating them and where possible release them back in to the wild. They are on call 24 hours a day, every single day of the year.

Contact details:
Vale Wildlife Hospital & Rehabilitation Centre, Station Road, Beckford, Nr Tewksbury, Gloucestershire GL20 7AN
Tel: 01386 882288
Fax: 01386 882299
www.valewildlife.org.uk
info@valewildlife.org.uk

<u>Wildlife Trust</u> has 47 branches across the whole of the UK, the Isle of Man and Alderney. They are the largest UK voluntary organisation dedicated to conserving the full range of the UK's habitats and species, whether they be in the countryside, in cities or at sea. The organisation envisages an environment rich in wildlife for everyone. Their mission is to rebuild biodiversity and engage people with their environment.

Contact details:
Mail address: The Kiln, Waterside, Mather Road, Newark, Nottinghamshire NG24 1WT
Tel: 01636 677711
Fax: 01636 670001
www.wildlifetrusts.org
enquiry@wildlifetrusts.org

<u>Wildlife Trust of South and West Wales</u> works for a better future for all kinds of wildlife across South and West Wales. Their mission is to protect and improve habitats and wildlife in the local area as well as helping people to enjoy and understand their local wildlife.

Contact details:
Mail address: Nature Centre, Parc Slip, Fountain Road, Tondu, Bridgend, Mid Glamorgan CF32 0EH
Tel: 01656 724 100
Fax: 01656 726 980
www.welshwildlife.org
info@welshwildlife.org

<u>Whale and Dolphin Conservation Society (WDCS)</u> is the global voice for the protection of whales, dolphins and their environment. They have offices in Argentina, Australia, Germany, the UK and the USA, as well as a worldwide network of field projects and consultants.

Contact details:
Brookfield House, 38 St Paul Street, Chippenham, Wiltshire SN15 1LJ
Tel: (44) (0)1249 449500
Fax: (44) (0)1249 449501
www.wdcs.org.uk
<u>info@wdcs.org</u>

<u>Wiltshire Wildlife Trust</u> is unique in being the only organisation concerned with all aspects of the environment in Wiltshire. They are one of the UK's most successful nature conservation charities.

Contact details:
Mail address: Wiltshire Wildlife Trust, Elm Tree Court, Long Street, Devizes, Wiltshire SN10 1NJ
Tel: 01380 725670
Fax: 01380 729017
www.wiltshirewildlife.org

<u>Wood Green Animal Shelter</u> has been rescuing and re-homing animals since 1924. The charity has two sanctuaries – in London and Cambridge and takes in over 6,000 animals a year.

Contact details:
London Shelter: 601 Lordship Lane, Wood Green, London N22 5LG
Tel: 0844 248 8181
Fax: 0208 889 0245
www.woodgreen.org.uk
info@woodgreen.org.uk (please specify which Shelter you would like to contact) **or**
jobs@woodgreen.org.uk

Heydon Shelter: Highway Cottage, Heydon, Herts SG8 8PN
Tel: 0844 248 8181
Fax: 01763 838824
www.woodgreen.org.uk

Godmanchester Shelter (HQ): King's Bush Farm, London Road, Godmanchester, Cambs PE29 2NH
Tel: 0844 248 8181
Fax: 01480 832815
www.woodgreen.org.uk

<u>Warwickshire Wildlife Trust</u> is the leading local charity protecting wildlife throughout Warwickshire, Coventry and Solihull.

Contact details:
Warwickshire Wildlife Trust, Brandon Marsh Nature Centre, Brandon Lane, Coventry CV3 3GW
Tel: 024 7630 2912
Fax: 024 7663 9556
www.warwickshire-wildlife-trust.org.uk
enquiries@wkwt.org.uk

<u>Worcestershire Wildlife Trust</u> is the county's leading local charity working to conserve and restore wildlife and wild places.

Contact details:
Mail address: Lower Smite Farm, Hindlip, Worcester, Worcestershire WR3 8SZ
Tel: 01905 754919
Fax: 01905 755868
www.worcswildlifetrust.co.uk
enquiries@worcestershirewildlifetrust.org

Yorkshire Wildlife Trust has worked for more than 50 years to protect vulnerable wildlife of all types - animals, birds, plants - and the places where they live. Their work is helping to secure the future of many important habitats and species, which might otherwise be lost.

Contact details:
1 St George's Place, York YO24 1GN
Tel: 01904 659570
Fax: 01904 613467
www.ywt.org.uk
info@ywt.org.uk

Jobs with Horses

Most horses in the UK are owned by individuals. Their owners and riders spend over 900 million pounds per year on them. As a result there are a large number of employment possibilities across the equine industry. The largest sector is racing; horse racing is a multi-million pound industry and there are dozens of different roles, including racecourse personnel and betting industry careers - some offer excellent remuneration. There are also many animal charities that specifically care for abandoned, unwanted and abused horses and we have also included these organisations below.

Animal Health Trust (AHT) is a charity that has been helping horses, dogs and cats for more than half a century. They provide specialist veterinary clinical, diagnostic and surgical services and their successes in research have ranged from major breakthroughs in anaesthesia and surgical techniques to the development of vaccines against diseases such as equine influenza.

Contact details:
Animal Health Trust, Lanwades Park, Kentford, Newmarket, Suffolk CB8 7UU
Tel: 01638 751000 or 01638 555669
Fax: 01638 750410
www.aht.org.uk
recruitment@aht.org.uk

British Horse Society (BHS) works to promote and advance the education, training and safety of the public in all matters relating to the horse. They also promote and facilitate the prevention of cruelty, neglect or harm to horses and to promote the relief, safety, sanctuary, rescue and welfare of horses in need of care, attention and assistance.

Contact details:
The British Horse Society, Abbey Park, Stareton, Kenilworth, Warwickshire CV8 2XZ
Tel: 0844 848 1666
Fax: 02476 840501
www.bhs.org.uk
jobs@bhs.org.uk

British Horse Racing Board (BHB) is the Governing Authority for Racing, working to promote the interests of horse racing. They seek to maintain and promote horse racing as a competitive and attractive sport and betting medium. BHB wishes to see the best possible training and working conditions for those employed in the industry, and the highest possible standards of care for horses.

Contact details:
British Horseracing Authority, 75 High Holburn, London WC1V 6LS
Tel: 020 7152 0000 **or** 020 7152 0060 (Human Resources Department)
www.britishhorseracing.com **or see** careersinracing.com
info@britishhorseracing.com **or** recruitment@britishhorseracing.com

Blue Cross aims to: ensure the welfare of animals by providing practical care, highlight the benefits of companionship between animals and people and promote a sense of respect and responsibility towards animals in the community. They have equine centres in Burford and Northiam.

Contact details:
The Blue Cross, Shilton Road, Burford, Oxon OX18 4PF
Tel: 01993 822651 **or** 01993 822454 (Equine)
Fax: 01993 823083
www.bluecross.org.uk
info@bluecross.org.uk **or** jobs@bluecross.org.uk **or** burford@bluecross.org.uk

Contact details:
The Blue Cross – Northiam Equine sanctuary
Tel: 01797 253908
Fax: 01797 252948
www.bluecross.org.uk
northiamequine@bluecross.org.uk

Donkey Sanctuary aims of to prevent the suffering of donkeys worldwide through the provision of high quality, professional advice, training and support on donkey welfare. In the UK and Ireland permanent sanctuary is provided to any donkey in need of refuge.

Contact details:
The Donkey Sanctuary, Sidmouth, Devon EX10 0NU
Tel: +44 (0)1395 578222 **or** +44 (0)1395 573089 (UK vacancies) **or** +44 (0)1395 573094 (Overseas vacancies)
Fax: +44 (0)1395 579266
http://drupal.thedonkeysanctuary.org.uk

Elisabeth Svendsen Trust for Children and Donkeys (EST) aims to bring enjoyment and pleasure into the lives of children with special needs and disabilities and to give them the satisfaction that comes with the achievement of learning riding skills. Jobs advertised when they arise.

Contact details:
EST Head Office: The Elisabeth Svendsen Trust, Slade House Farm, Sidmouth, Devon EX10 0NU
Tel: +44 (0)1395 573133
Fax: +44 (0)1395 579266
www.elisabethsvendsentrust.org.uk

Contact details:
EST Belfast, Ballymartin Road, Templepatrick BT39 0BS
Tel: 028 93324647
www.elisabethsvendsentrust.org.uk

Contact details:
EST Birmingham, Pilkington Donkey Centre, Sutton Park, Sutton Coldfield, Birmingham B74 2YT
Tel: +44 (0)121 354 9444
Fax: +44 (0)121 354 9444
www.elisabethsvendsentrust.org.uk

Contact details:
EST Ivybridge, Filham Park, Godwell Lane, Ivybridge, Devon PL21 0LE
Tel: +44 (0)1752 690200
Fax: +44 (0)1752 690200
www.elisabethsvendsentrust.org.uk

Contact details:
EST Leeds, The Donkey Centre, Swan Lane, Eccup, Leeds LS16 8AZ
Tel: +44 (0)113 261 9249
Fax: +44 (0)113 261 9249
www.elisabethsvendsentrust.org.uk

Contact details:
EST Manchester, Green Fold, Abbey Hey, Manchester M18 8RJ
Tel: +44 (0)161 301 4051
Fax: +44 (0)161 301 4051
www.elisabethsvendsentrust.org.uk

Contact details:
EST Sidmouth, Slade Farm House, Devon EX10 0NU
Tel: +44 (0)1395 573009
Fax: +44 (0)1395 579266
www.elisabethsvendsentrust.org.uk

Equine Classified lists horse related jobs.

Contact details:
Mail address: P.O. Box 235, Uckfield, Sussex TN22 9AJ
Tel: 07958 245 023
www.adhorse.com
info@adhorse.co.uk

Equine Online horse related jobs advertised.

Contact details:
Linford Stables, Buckingham Road, Singleborough, Milton Keynes, Buckinghamshire MK17 0RB
Tel: +44 (0)126 712180
www.equine-online.net

Foal Farm Animal Rescue Centre takes in sick, distressed and unwanted animals – including horses; to restore them to health and happiness, and to place them in good, vetted homes. No healthy animal is ever destroyed, and if no home can be found, the animal remains for the rest of its life at Foal Farm.

Contact details:
Foal Farm Animal Rescue Centre Jail Lane Biggin Hill Kent TN16 3AX
Tel: 01 959 572 386
www.foalfarm.org.uk
volunteering@foalfarm.org.uk **or** volunteering@foalfarm.org.uk

Home for Unwanted and Lost Animals (HULA) operates from a 17 acre site which provides sanctuary for animals including horses and donkeys.

Contact details:
HULA Animal Rescue, Glebe Farm, Salford Road, Aspley Guise, Milton Keynes MK17 8HZ
Tel: 01908 584000
Fax: 01908 282020
www.hularescue.org
hularescue@tiscali.co.uk

Horse World, (Friends of Bristol Horses Society) was formed by volunteers in 1952 to care for unwanted horses and ponies from agricultural and industrial backgrounds, such as farming and the coal mines. Many of these animals still had several years of life left, and the organisation saved as many as possible from unnecessary slaughter. Today the charity has evolved into a respected equine organisation, concentrating on rescuing, rehabilitating and re-homing horses, ponies and donkeys in need.

Contact details:
Headquarters: HorseWorld, Delmar Hall, Keynes Farm, Staunton Lane, Whitchurch, Bristol BS14 0QL
Tel: 01275 832425
Fax: 01275 836909
Visitor Centre: HorseWorld, Staunton Manor Farm, Staunton Lane, Whitchurch, Bristol, BS14 0QJ
Tel 01275 540173
Fax: 01275 540119
www.horseworld.org.uk

Horse and Hound Magazine classified section containing current jobs with horses.

Contact details:
www.horseandhound.co.uk

Island Farm Donkey Sanctuary is located in Oxfordshire. The organisation is a registered charity that cares for and protects abused and ill-treated donkeys and other animals. Vacancies are shown on the home page as and when they arise.

Contact details:
Island Farm Donkey Sanctuary, Old Didcot Road, Brightwell-Cum-Sotwell, Wallingford, Oxfordshire OX10 0SW
Tel: 01491 833938
Fax: 01491 833938
www.donkeyrescue.org.uk
mail@donkeyrescue.org.uk

Raystede Centre for Animal Welfare was founded in 1952 to prevent and relieve cruelty to animals and to protect them from unnecessary suffering. Around 1,500 unwanted and abandoned animals arrive at the centre annually. Horses and donkeys are cared for along with a variety of other animals.

Contact details:
Raystede Animal Welfare, Ringmer, East Sussex, BN8 5AJ
Tel: (01825) 840252
Fax: (01825) 840995
www.raystede.org
info@raystede.org

Redwings Horse Sanctuary was established in 1984 and today has grown to be the largest horse charity in the UK, working to save horses, ponies, donkeys and mules whose future would otherwise be bleak. The organisation exists to provide and promote the welfare care and protection of horses, ponies, donkeys and mules. Every year they provide a safe, secure home for rescued animals who, through no fault of their own, have fallen upon difficult times and are in need of help and care.

Contact details:
Redwings Horse Sanctuary, Hapton, Norwich NR15 1SP
Tel: 01508 481000
www.redwings.org.uk
workforus@redwings.co.uk

World Horse Welfare operates internationally as one of the world's leading equine welfare charities working to improve the lives of many horses. Their political campaigners, international training teams, UK Field Officers and Rehabilitation Centres are all working towards a world where the horse is used but never abused.

Contact details:
World Horse Welfare, Anne Colvin House, Ada Cole Avenue, Snetterton, Norfolk NR16 2LR
Tel: 01953 498682
Fax: 01953 498373
www.worldhorsewelfare.org
info@worldhorsewelfare.org

World of Horses jobs with horses listed.

Contact details:
Tel: 01772 36 80 82
www.worldofhorses.co.uk
worldofhorses@live.co.uk

Wildlife Jobs

Jobs working with wildlife require good communication skills and may involve tough physical outdoor work. You will need to be physically fit, healthy, hard working, have plenty of stamina and enjoy exercise. Some wildlife jobs wildlife may require you to live on site, to have a driving license and be confident driving off-road vehicles.

Different jobs may include; conducting wildlife and ecological surveys, monitoring wildlife habitats and populations, protection and rescue of animals from natural and man-made disasters and rehabilitation of sick or injured animals.

Animal Protection Agency (APA), UK exposes the wasteful practices and consequences of the trade in exotic pets and the suffering endured by captured wild animals. By working alongside government agencies and local authorities, and by building public support and awareness, APA seeks to end the cruel confinement of wild animals as pets.

Contact details:
Animal Protection Agency, Brighton Media Centre, 68 Middle Street, Brighton BN1 1AL
Tel: +44 (0)1273 674253
Fax: +44 (0)1273 674927
www.apa.org.uk
info@apa.org.uk

Animal Defenders International (ADI), UK exists too educate, create awareness, promote the end of all forms of cruelty to animals, alleviate suffering, and to conserve and protect animals and the environment.

Contact details:
Animal Defenders International, Millbank Tower, Millbank, London SW1P 4QP, UK
Tel: +44 (0) 20 7630 3340
Fax: +44 (0) 20 7828 2179
www.ad-international.org
info@ad-international.org

Contact details:
USA: 6100 Wilshire Boulevard, Suite 1150, Los Angeles, CA 90048, USA
Tel: +1 323-935-2234
www.ad-international.org
usa@ad-international.org

Contact details:
South America: Apartado Postal 359888 BOGOTA, Colombia
www.ad-international.org
infolatam@ad-international.org

Alderney Wildlife Trust was launched in May 2002, in response to concerns about the lack of land management in Alderney and to combat the ensuing loss of habitat and took over from the existing Alderney Conservation Volunteers organisation.

Contact details:
Alderney Wildlife Trust, 51 Victoria Street, Alderney, Channel Islands GY9 3TA
Tel: +44 (0) 1481 822935
www.alderneywildlife.org
info@alderneywildlife.org

Berkshire, Buckinghamshire and Oxfordshire Wildlife Trust was established in 1959 by local ecologists who could see the extent of harm being done to the wonderfully rich natural environment of the three counties. This is the only voluntary organisation in the region concerned with all aspects of nature conservation. Their vision is to create a region rich in wildlife and appreciated by all.

Contact details:
Head Office: The Lodge, 1 Armstrong Road, Littlemore, Oxford OX4 4XT
Tel: 01865 775476
Fax: 01865 711301
www.bbowt.org.uk
info@bbowt.org.uk **or** recruitment@bbowt.org.uk **or** jobs@bbowt.org.uk

Bedfordshire, Cambridgeshire, Northamptonshire, Peterborough Wildlife Trusts
is a wildlife conservation charity that works for a better future for all kinds of wildlife across Bedfordshire, Cambridgeshire, Northamptonshire and Peterborough. Their mission is to protect and improve habitats and wildlife in our local area as well as helping people to enjoy and understand their local wildlife.

Contact details:
Bedfordshire Office: Priory Country Park, Barkers Lane, Bedford MK41 9DJ
Tel: 01234 364213
Fax: 01234 328520
www.wildlifebcnp.org
bedfordshire@wildlifebcnp.org

Contact details:
Cambridgeshire Office: The Manor House, Broad Street, Great Cambourne, Cambridge CB23 6DH
Tel: 01954 713500
Fax: 01954 710051
www.wildlifebcnp.org
cambridgeshire@wildlifebcnp.org

Contact details:
Northamptonshire Office & Lings Environmental Centre: Lings House, Billing Lings, Northampton NN3 8BE
Tel: 01604 405285
Fax: 01604 784835
www.wildlifebcnp.org
northamptonshire@wildlifebcnp.org

Contact details:
Peterborough Office & Peterborough Community Education Service: Eco Innovation Centre, Peterscourt, City Road, Peterborough PE1 1SA
Tel: 01733 294543
Fax: 01733 554459
www.ecoinnovationcentre.co.uk
peterborough@wildlifebcnp.org

Birmingham and Black County Wildlife Trust was founded in 1980 as the Urban Wildlife Group, in 1982 they became the first urban Wildlife Trust, one of 47 covering the whole UK, they have been working to make Birmingham and the Black Country a better place for wildlife and people. Click on the 'contact us' button and then on the 'jobs' button for current vacancies.

Contact details:
28 Harborne Road, Edgbaston, Birmingham B15 3AA
Tel: +44 (0)121 454 1199
Fax: +44 (0)121 454 6556
www.bbcwildlife.org.uk
info@bbcwildlife.org.uk

Care for the Wild International (CWI) is an animal welfare and conservation charity that funds practical projects around the world. They make areas safe from poachers, rehabilitate sick or injured animals and provide sanctuary for those who can not return to the wild. They also act as a global voice for wildlife through research, education and advocacy and expose animal cruelty and wildlife crime.

Contact details:
The Granary, Tickfold Farm, Kingsfold, West Sussex RH12 3SE, UK
Tel: +44 (0) 1306 627900
Fax: +44 (0) 1306 627901
www.careforthewild.com
info@careforthewild.com

Cumbria Wildlife Trust is the only voluntary organisation devoted solely to the conservation of the wildlife and wild places of Cumbria. The Trust stands up for wildlife, creates wildlife havens, and seeks to raise environmental awareness.

Contact details:
Head Office: Cumbria Wildlife Trust, Plumgarths, Crook Road, Kendal, Cumbria LA8 8LX
Tel: 01539 816300
Fax: 01539 816301
www.cumbriawildlifetrust.org.uk
mail@cumbriawildlifetrust.org.uk

Contact details:
Carlisle Office: Gosling Sike Farm, Houghton, Carlisle CA3 0LD
Tel: 01228 829570
Fax: 01228 631811
www.cumbriawildlifetrust.org.uk

Contact details:
South Walney Office: No 1 Coastguard Cottages, South Walney Nature Reserve, Barrow in Furness, Cumbria LA14 3YQ
Tel: 01229 471066
www.cumbriawildlifetrust.org.uk

Cornwall Wildlife Trust founded in 1962, this charity fulfils a role occupied by no other countryside organisation. They are concerned solely with Cornwall and deal with all aspects of conserving the county's wildlife and habitats. They have established many nature reserves, in which examples of each of Cornwall's habitats may give refuge to nationally rare and endangered species.

Contact details:
Cornwall Wildlife Trust, Five Acres, Allet, Truro, Cornwall TR4 9DJ
Tel: 01872 273939
Fax: 01872 225476
www.cornwallwildlifetrust.org.uk

Devon Wildlife Trust was established as a registered charity in 1962, the Devon Wildlife Trust has a unique and influential position. Unique because it is the only organisation concerned with all aspects of wildlife conservation in Devon. Influential because it is a member of The Wildlife Trusts partnership, a nationwide network dedicated to the achievement of a UK richer in wildlife. They have over 50 full time staff.

Contact details:
Devon Wildlife Trust, Cricklepit Mill, Commercial Road, Exeter, Devon EX2 4AB
Tel: 01392 279244
Fax: 01392 433221
www.devonwildlifetrust.org
jobapps@devonwildlifetrust.org **or** contactus@devonwildlifetrust.org

Dorset Wildlife Trust is the largest conservation charity in Dorset with over 25,000 members.

Contact details:
Dorset Wildlife Trust HQ, Brooklands Farm, Forston, Dorchester DT2 7AA
Tel: 01305 264620
Fax: 01305 251120
www.dorsetwildlifetrust.org.uk
mail@dorestwildlifetrust.org.uk

<u>Durrell Wildlife Organisation</u> works to save species from extinction. The organisation believes that with scientific expertise and dedication, extinction can be prevented.

Contact details:
Durrell Wildlife Conservation Trust, Les Augres Manor, La Profonde Rue, Trinity, Jersey, Channel Islands JE3 5BP
Tel: +44 (0)1534 860000
Fax: +44 (0)1534 860001
www.durrell.org
recruitment@durrell.org

<u>Derbyshire Wildlife Trust</u> aims to raise awareness of potential threats to wildlife and encourage individuals and organisations to take responsibility for caring for their local environment.

Contact details:
Mail address: Derbyshire Wildlife Trust, East Mill, Bridge Foot, Belper, Derbyshire DE56 1XH
Tel: 01773 881188
Fax: 01773 821826
www.derbyshirewildlifetrut.org.uk
enquiries@derbyshirewt.co.uk

<u>Durham Wildlife Trust</u> works to protect wildlife and promote nature conservation in County Durham, the City of Sunderland and the Boroughs of Gateshead, South Tyneside and Darlington. They are one of the most active environmental organisations in the region, managing 25 Nature Reserves, a variety of species and habitat recovery projects and four Visitor Centres. They also manage an extensive environmental education programme that aims to engage schools, community groups, whole communities and individuals in issues around nature conservation and the wider environment.

Contact details:
Headquarters: Rainton Meadows, Durham Wildlife Trust, Rainton Meadows, Chilton Moor, Houghton-le-Spring, Tyne & Wear DH4 6PU
Tel: 0191 5843112
www.durhamwt.co.uk
mail@durhamwt.co.uk

<u>Environment Job</u> a job site that contains employment and volunteering opportunities in the environmental sector.

Contact details:
Working Planet Limited, The Innovation Centre, University of Exeter Campus, Exeter EX4 4RN
Tel: 01392 491578
www.environmentjob.co.uk
admin@environmentjob.co.uk

Essex Wildlife Trust is the leading conservation body in Essex. It has 32,000 members and 450 corporate members who enable to Trust to conduct campaigns for wildlife conservation and to protect over 7,250 acres of land on 87 Nature Reserves, 1 Nature Park and to run their 7 Visitor Centres.

Contact details:
Essex Wildlife Trust Headquarters, Abbotts Hall Farm, Great Wigborough, Colchester CO5 7RZ
Tel: 01621 862960
Fax: 01621 862990
www.essexwt.org.uk
admin@essexwt.org.uk

Frontier Want to have the best time of your life while gaining academic qualifications at the same time? Join a Frontier expedition and save endangered wildlife and threatened ecosystems while gaining an A-level. Learn to run expeditions and gain an AS-level. Teach English and get TEFL trained. Whichever you choose, you'll be off the beaten track having adventures beyond anything you've ever imagined! They have projects in Africa, Asia, Fiji & the Pacific Isles, Indonesia, South and Central America, and Nepal.

Contact details:
THE SOCIETY FOR ENVIRONMENTAL EXPLORATION (operating as 'Frontier'),
50-52 Rivington Street, London, EC2A 3QP, UK
Tel: +44 (0) 20 7613 2422
Fax: +44 (0) 20 7613 2992
info@frontier.ac.uk
www.frontier.ac.uk

Forestry Commission delivers practical programmes to make sure that, as communities and individuals, we can get the most from forests and woods. The organisation works with a whole range of partners from private sector landowners to sports clubs, local communities to national businesses, on a whole host of recreation, regeneration and educational schemes. Their responsibilities span research, commercial timber production, sustainability programmes and policy, as well as learning and leisure. Their goal is always to ensure that, "at a practical level, Britain can use its forests to contribute positively to as many of the nation's needs as we can while sustaining this great resource for the future".

Contact details:
Forestry Commission, Silvan House, 231 Corstorphine Road, Edinburgh EH12 7AT
Tel: 0131 334 0303
www.forestry.gov.uk
Contact details:
Forest Research Station, Alice Holt Lodge, Wrecclesham, Farnham, Surrey GU10 4LH
Tel: 01420 22255
www.forestry.gov.uk

Gloucestershire Wildlife Trust was formed in 1961 to work for wildlife conservation in Gloucestershire. The Trust employs professional staff to carry out the increasingly technical work associated with conserving wildlife with the support of over 300 volunteers.

Contact details:
Gloucestershire Wildlife Trust, Conservation Centre, Robinswood Hill Country Park, Reservoir Road, Gloucester GL4 6SX
Tel: 01452 38 33 33
Fax: 01452 38 33 34
www.gloucestershirewildlifetrust.co.uk
info@gloucestershirewildlifetrust.co.uk

Graduate Link promotes graduate jobs and careers in the Yorkshire and Humber region for graduates throughout the UK. Graduate Link is owned and operated by the University careers services. Environmental and wildlife job vacancies are advertised.

Contact details:
Graduates Yorkshire, University of Sheffield, 4 Hounsfield Road, Sheffield S3 7RF
Tel: 0114 222 0954
Fax: 0114 222 0950
www.graduatesyorkshire.co.uk
info@graduatesyorkshire.co.uk

Hertfordshire and Middlesex Wildlife Trust is the only charity dedicated solely to protecting local wildlife and wild spaces, engaging our diverse communities through access to nature reserves, campaigning, volunteering and education. They manage over 43 nature reserves and campaign to save important wildlife habitats, volunteering programmes and wildlife education work.

Contact details:
Herts and Middlesex Wildlife Trust, Grebe House, St Michael's Street, St Albans, Herts AL3 4SN
Tel: 01727 858901
Fax: 01727 854542
www.hertswildlifetrust.org.uk
info@hmwt.org

Hampshire and Isle of Wight Wildlife Trust is a charity dedicated to conserving, protecting and enhancing local wildlife - whatever it is and wherever in the two counties it may be.

Contact details:
Hampshire and Isle of Wight Wildlife Trust Headquarters, Beechcroft House, Vicarage Lane, Curdridge, Hampshire SO32 2DP
Tel: 01489 774400
Fax: 01489 774401
www.hwt.org.uk
feedback@hwt.org.uk

IFAW International Fund for Animal Welfare From the outset, the founders of the International Fund for Animal Welfare (IFAW), rejected the notion that the interests of humans and animals were separate. Instead they embraced the understanding that the fate and future of harp seals - and all other animals on Earth - are inextricably linked to our own.

Contact details:
International Headquarters, 290 Summer Street, Yarmouth Port, MA 02675 United States
Tel: (508) 744 2000 or (800) 932 4329
Fax: (508) 744 2099
www.ifaw.org
info@ifaw.org

Contact details:
United Kingdom, 87-90 Albert Embankment, London SE1 7UD
Tel: +44 207 587 6700
Fax: +44 207 587 6720
www.ifaw.org
info-uk@ifaw.org

Institute of Zoology (IoZ) is the research division of the Zoological Society of London (ZSL). It is a government-funded research institute specialising in scientific issues relevant to the conservation of animal species and their habitats. The Institute is based at ZSL's Regents Park site, London.

Contact details:
Institute of Zoology, Zoological Society of London, Regent's Park, London NW1 4RY
Tel: 020 7449 6610
Fax: 020 7586 2870
www.zsl.org
enquiries@ioz.ac.uk

Kent Wildlife Trust works to protect Kent's native wildlife for future generations to enjoy. The challenges of protecting wildlife in Kent increase each year with new pressures placed on our countryside, habitats and species.

Contact details:
Head Office Address: Kent Wildlife Trust, Tyland Barn, Maidstone, Kent ME14 3BD
Tel: 01622 662012
www.kentwildlifetrust.org.uk
info@kentwildlife.org.uk

Lancashire, Manchester and North Merseyside Wildlife Trust was formed in 1962 by a group of naturalists who wanted to help protect the wildlife of the old county Lancashire. It is now the leading local environmental charity in this region. Their mission is to work for a region richer in wildlife by the protection and enhancement of species and habitats, both common and rare.

Contact details:
The Barn: Head Office: Wildlife Trust for Lancashire, Manchester & North Merseyside, Berkeley Drive, Bamber Bridge, Preston, Lancashire PR5 6BY
Tel: 01772 324129
Fax: 01772 628849
www.lancswt.org.uk
info@lancswt.org.uk

London Wildlife Trust is the only charity dedicated solely to protecting the capital's wildlife and wild spaces. They manage over fifty London-wide reserves and campaign to save important wildlife habitats, engaging London's diverse communities through access to their nature reserves, volunteering programmes and education work.

Contact details:
London Wildlife Trust, Skyline House, 200 Union Street, London SE1 0LX
Tel: 020 7261 0447
www.wildlondon.org.uk
recruitment@wildlondon.org.uk **or** enquiries@wildlondon.org.uk

Lincolnshire Wildife Trust is a voluntary charitable organisation which cares for Lincolnshire's wildlife and countryside. The Lincolnshire Wildlife Trust is one of the oldest of these county trusts, having been founded in 1948. The Trust covers the whole of the historic county of Lincolnshire – from the Humber to the Wash.

Contact details:
Headquarters Mail Address: Banovallum House, Manor House Street, Horncastle, Lincolnshire LN9 5HF
Tel: 01507 526667
Fax: 01507 525732
www.lincstrust.org.uk
info@lincstrust.co.uk

Monkey Sanctuary has been home to a colony of woolly monkeys since 1964. The original aim was to provide a stable setting in which woolly monkeys, rescued from lives of isolation in zoos or as pets, could live as naturally as possible. The Trust has evolved and is now campaigning to stop the primate pet trade in the UK. They are able to offer sanctuary to a few of the monkeys in Britain who desperately need a safe and socially stimulating environment. Jobs are advertised from time to time.

Contact details:
Wild Futures' Monkey Sanctuary, Murrayton House, St Martins, Looe, Cornwall PL13 1NZ
Tel/Fax: +44 (0)844 272 1271 (If based in Guernsey please use Tel: 01503 262532)
www.monkeysanctuary.org
info@wildfutures.org

Marine Animal Rescue Society is dedicated to the conservation of marine animals through, rescue, rehabilitation, research, and education.

Contact details:
Mail address: Marine Animal Rescue Society, P.O. Box 833356, Miami, Florida 33283
Tel: (305) 546-1111
www.marineanimalrescue.org
mars@marineanimalrescue.org
http://www.mcsuk.org/info/aboutmcs/vacancies
Marine Conservation Society (MCS) is the UK charity dedicated to caring for our seas, shores and wildlife. MCS campaigns for clean seas and beaches, sustainable fisheries, and protection for all marine life.

Contact details:
Mail address: Marine Conservation Society, Unit 3, Wolf Business Park, Alton Road, Ross-on Wye, Herefordshire HR9 5NB
Tel: 01989 566017
Fax: 01989 567815
www.mcsuk.org

North Wales Wildlife Trust works to protect the wildlife that remains and improve habitats for the wildlife of North Wales.

Contact details:
Head Office: 376 High Street, Bangor, Gwynedd LL57 1YE
Tel: 01248 351541
www.northwaleswildlifetrust.org.uk
nwwt@wildlifetrustswales.org

Northumberland Wildlife Trust is the leading charity dedicated to wildlife conservation and environmental education in North East England. Their mission is to conserve local wildlife, promote nature conservation and provide the means by which everyone can become involved.

Contact details:
Mail address: Northumberland Wildlife Trust, St Nicholas Park, Gosforth, Newcastle upon Tyne, Tyne and Wear NE3 3XT
Tel: 0191 284 6884
Fax: 0191 284 6794
www.nwt.org.uk
mail@northwt.org.uk

Natural England works with regional partners to develop robust frameworks for decision making and actions to achieve sustainable development. They seek to secure and enhance wildlife and geology through regional working.

Contact details:
Head Office: Natural England, 1 East Parade, Sheffield S1 2ET
Tel: 0300 060 6000
Fax: 0300 060 1622
www.naturalengland.org.uk
enquiries@naturalengland.org.uk

Norfolk Wildlife Trust care for over 50 nature reserves and other protected sites around the county including ten kilometres of coastline, nine Norfolk broads, nine National Nature Reserves and five ancient woodlands. They have a positive influence over a great deal of the Norfolk countryside through their planning and advisory functions.

Contact details:
Norfolk Wildlife Trust, Bewick House, 22 Thorpe Road, Norwich NR1 1RY
Tel: 01603 625540
www.norfolkwildlifetrust.org.uk
info@norfolkwildlifetrust.org.uk

Organisation Cetacea (ORCA) promotes the conservation of the marine environment through research, partnership and education and provides a forum for the enjoyment of whales, dolphins, seabirds and other marine life. They seek to provide a forum for raising interest and participation in conservation research.

Contact details:
ORCA, Brittany Centre, Wharf Road, Portsmouth PO2 8RU
www.orcaweb.org.uk
info@orcaweb.org.uk

Radnorshire Wildlife Trust (RWT) is one of the youngest wildlife trusts in the UK. Established in 1987 as a volunteer only group they have grown to an organisation with 19 reserves across the county covering a range of habitats from woodland to moorland, wetland to meadow. Where possible, RWT has an open access policy to allow enjoyment of the reserves for all. Even those with some restrictions are accessible in part or at certain times of the year.

Contact details:
Radnorshire Wildlife Trust, High Street, Llandrindod Wells, Powys LD1 6AG
Tel: 01597 823298
Fax: 01597 823274
www.rwtwales.org
info@rwtwales.org

Royal Society for the Protection of Birds (RSPB) Since its founding in 1889, the RSPB has grown into a wildlife conservation charity with more than a million members. It has offices across the UK and, since its successful first campaign to end the plumage trade, it has widened its sphere of influence to include a huge range of issues that affect wildlife and habitats.

Contact details:
UK Headquarters – The Lodge, Potton Road, Sandy, Bedfordshire SG19 2DL
Tel: 01767 680551
www.rspb.org.uk
volunteers@rspb.org.uk

Royal Society of Wildlife Trusts (RSWT) although a charity in its own right, RSWT also operates as an umbrella group for the 47 local Wildlife Trusts that have been formed across the UK, helping to co-ordinate their activities and campaigning at a UK level.

Contact details:
Mail address: The Kiln, Waterside, Mather Road, Newark, Nottinghamshire NG24 1WT
Tel: 01636 677711
Fax: 01636 670001
www.wildlifetrusts.org
enquiry@wildlifetrusts.org

Sheffield Wildlife Trust is the city's largest environmental charity, working to promote conservation, protection and improvement of the physical and natural environment of Sheffield. Targeted work to protect vulnerable habitats and species is happening alongside initiatives to boost the general wildlife value of parks and green spaces across Sheffield.

Contact details:
Mail address: Sheffield Wildlife Trust, Victoria Hall, 37 Stafford Road, Sheffield S2 2SF
Tel: 0114 2634335
Fax: 0114 2634345
www.wildsheffield.com
mail@wildsheffield.com **or** recruitment@wildsheffield.com

Somerset Wildlife Trust has a vision for A Living Landscape involving enlarging, improving and joining-up areas of land on nature reserves, in towns and in partnership with other landowners. Their Living Landscape schemes in Somerset - on Mendip and the Brue Valley - are creating inspirational, accessible landscapes - full of wildlife and rich in opportunities for learning, better health and well-being, alongside sustainable economic development.

Contact details:
Head Office: Somerset Wildlife Trust, Tonedale Mill, Tonedale, Wellington TA21 0AW
Tel: 01823 652400
Fax: 01823 652411
www.somersetwildlife.org
enquiries@somersetwildlife.org **or** volunteering@somersetwildlife.org

Contact details:
Mendip Office: Somerset Wildlife Trust, Callow Rock Offices, Shipham Road, Cheddar BS27 3DQ
Tel: 01823 652400
www.somersetwildlife.org
enquiries@somersetwildlife.org **or** volunteering@somersetwildlife.org

Surrey Wildlife Trust currently manage 80 nature reserves covering over 4,000 hectares of Surrey's countryside. As well as managing their own reserves, they also manage land under access agreements with private landowners.

Contact details:
Head Office: Surrey Wildlife Trust, School Lane, Pirbright, Woking, Surrey GU24 0JN
Tel: 01483 795440
Fax: 01483 486505
www.surreywildlifetrust.org
info@surreywt.org.uk

Shropshire Wildlife Trust is the county's leading environmental charity, currently supported by 10,000 members. With strength of numbers and 45 years of experience behind them, they are an increasingly effective champion for local wildlife.

Contact details:
Shropshire Wildlife Trust, 193 Abbey Foregate, Shrewsbury, Shropshire SY2 6AH
Tel: 01743 284280
Fax: 01743 284281
www.shropshirewildlifetrust.org.uk

Scottish Natural Heritage (SNH) aims to help people enjoy Scotland's natural heritage responsibly, understand it more fully and use it wisely so that it can be sustained for future generations.

Contact details:
Headquarters: Great Glen House, Leachkin Road, Inverness IV3 8NW
Tel: 01463 725000
Fax: 01463 725067
www.snhjobs.co.uk **or** www.snh.gov.uk

Suffolk Wildlife Trust aims to create a Living Landscape where wildlife flourishes in countryside, towns and villages. They care for more than 50 nature reserves and their conservation advisors work with farmers and local communities to improve their land for wildlife and create networks of linked up habitat across Suffolk.

Contact details:
Suffolk Wildlife Trust, Brooke House, Ashbocking, Ipswich IP6 9JY
Tel: 01473 890089
Fax: 01473 890165
www.suffolkwildlifetrust.org
info@suffolkwildlifetrust.org

Sussex Wildlife Trust looks after over 3,000 acres of downland, woodland, wetland and heath. Their work also includes environmental education, working with land owners, companies and local communities to conserve Sussex.

Contact details:
Sussex Wildlife Trust, Woods Mill, Henfield, West Sussex BN5 9SD
Tel: 01273 492630
Fax: 01273 494500
www.sussexwt.org.uk

Scottish Wildlife Trust (SWT) offers practical conservation solutions through habitat management. SWT has continuously contributed to the enhancement and preservation of habitats and wildlife throughout the country. They believe that through encouraging access to wildlife, we can involve people in understanding, conserving and shaping our landscape for the better.

Contact details:
Mail address: Scottish Wildlife Trust, Cramond House, 3 Kirk Cramond, Edinburgh EH4 6HZ
Tel: 0131 312 7765
www.swt.org.uk

Sea Mammal Research Unit (SMRU) is one of the foremost research institutions carrying out research about marine mammals in the world. The mission of the SMRU is to carry out fundamental research into the biology of upper trophic level predators in the oceans and, through this, to provide support to the Natural Environment Research Council so that it can carry out its statutory duty to advise the UK government.

Contact details:
SMRU Administration, Sea Mammal Research Unit, Gatty Marine Laboratory, University of St Andrews, St Andrews, Fife KY16 8LB
Tel: (0)1334 462630
Fax: (0)1334 463443
www.smru.st-andrews.ac.uk
smru@st-andrews.ac.uk

Tiggywinkles Wildlife Hospital is the world's busiest wildlife hospital and cares for sick & injured hedgehogs, badgers, wild birds, foxes, even reptiles & amphibians. They are a specialist hospital, using all available veterinary welfare skills, dedicated to rescuing and rehabilitating all species of British wildlife.

Contact details:
Tiggywinkles, Aston Road, Haddenham, Aylesbury, Buckinghamshire HP17 8AF
Tel: 01844 292292
Fax: 01844 292640
www.sttiggywinkles.org.uk
mail@sttiggywinkles.org.uk

Vale Wildlife Rescue this organisation helps thousands of wildlife casualties every year by treating them and where possible release them back in to the wild. They have rescue staff on call 24 hours a day, every day of the year.

Contact details:
Vale Wildlife Hospital & Rehabilitation Centre, Station Road, Beckford, Nr Tewksbury, Gloucestershire GL20 7AN
Tel: 01386 882288
Fax: 01386 882299
www.valewildlife.org.uk
info@valewildlife.org.uk

Veterinary Laboratory Agency (VLA) is an Executive Agency of the Department for Environment, Food and Rural Affairs (Defra). VLA is a regional network of 16 veterinary laboratories, including one in Scotland, two in Wales, and a central facility near Weybridge in Surrey. VLA provides all sectors of the animal health & environment industry with animal disease surveillance, diagnostic services and veterinary scientific research.

Contact details:
Tel: +44 (0)1932341111
Fax: +44 (0)1932347046
www.vla.defra.gov.uk

Warwickshire Wildlife Trust is the leading local charity protecting wildlife throughout Warwickshire, Coventry and Solihull.

Contact details:
Warwickshire Wildlife Trust, Brandon Marsh Nature Centre, Brandon Lane, Coventry CV3 3GW
Tel: 024 7630 2912
Fax: 024 7663 9556
www.warwickshire-wildlife-trust.org.uk
enquiries@wkwt.org.uk

Wildlife Conservation Research Unit (WildCRU) is determined to span the gulf between academic theory and practical problem solving to tackle the emerging biodiversity crisis. The WildCRU was formally launched with the establishment of Britain's first University-based research fellowship in wildlife conservation. The organisation has grown to become renowned worldwide.

Contact details:
Wildlife Conservation Research Unit, Department of Zoology, University of Oxford, Recanati-Kaplan Centre, Tubney House, Abingdon Road, Tubney, Oxfordshire OX13 5QL
Tel: +44 1865 611 100
Fax: +44 1865 611 101
www.wildcru.org
wildsec@zoo.ox.ac.uk

Worcestershire Wildilfe Trust is the county's leading local charity working to conserve and restore wildlife and wild places.

Contact details:
Mail address: Lower Smite Farm, Hindlip, Worcester, Worcestershire WR3 8SZ
Tel: 01905 754919
Fax: 01905 755868
www.worcswildlifetrust.co.uk
enquiries@worcestershirewildlifetrust.org

Wildlife Trust has 47 branches across the whole of the UK, the Isle of Man and Alderney. They are the largest UK voluntary organisation dedicated to conserving the full range of the UK's habitats and species, whether they be in the countryside, in cities or at sea. The organisation envisages an environment rich in wildlife for everyone. Their mission is to rebuild biodiversity and engage people with their environment.

Contact details:
Mail address: The Kiln, Waterside, Mather Road, Newark, Nottinghamshire NG24 1WT
Tel: 01636 677711
Fax: 01636 670001
www.wildlifetrusts.org
enquiry@wildlifetrusts.org

Wiltshire Wildlife Trust is unique in being the only organisation concerned with all aspects of the environment in Wiltshire. They are one of the UK's most successful nature conservation charities.

Contact details:
Mail address: Wiltshire Wildlife Trust, Elm Tree Court, Long Street, Devizes, Wiltshire SN10 1NJ
Tel: 01380 725670
Fax: 01380 729017
www.wiltshirewildlife.org

Wildlife Trust of South and West Wales works for a better future for all kinds of wildlife across South and West Wales. Their mission is to protect and improve habitats and wildlife in the local area as well as helping people to enjoy and understand their local wildlife.

Contact details:
Mail address: Nature Centre, Parc Slip, Fountain Road, Tondu, Bridgend, Mid Glamorgan CF32 0EH
Tel: 01656 724 100
Fax: 01656 726 980
www.welshwildlife.org
info@welshwildlife.org

Wildlife and Countryside Link was set up in recognition that better co-ordination was needed between voluntary organisations with similar core objectives. Wildlife Link merged with Countryside Link in 1990, creating the organisation whose interests span the breadth of wildlife and countryside issues.

Contact details:
Wildlife and Countryside Link, 89 Albert Embankment, London SE1 7TP
Tel: 020 7820 8600
Fax: 020 7820 8620
www.wcl.org.uk
enquiry@wcl.org.uk **or** jobs@wcl.org.uk

Wilderness Foundation UK was established in 1974 by Sir Laurens van der Post, writer, explorer and philosopher, and Dr. Ian Player DMS, international conservationist renowned for saving the white rhino and founder of the World Wilderness Congress movement. They work closely with their sister organisations The Wilderness Foundation in South Africa, The WILD Foundation in the USA and other groups in Europe and Asia. Together they share a common belief in the irreplaceable value of wilderness, which contains the wonders of pristine nature, and enables us to return to our origins and draw a deep sense of belonging and inspiration.

Contact details:
Mail address: Wilderness Foundation UK, No 8 (Unit D) Whitbread Business Centre, Whitbread Farm Lane, Chatham Green, Chelmsford, Essex CM3 3FE
Tel: 01245 443073
Fax: 01245 360942
www.wildernessfoundation.org.uk

Yorkshire Wildlife Trust has worked for more than 60 years to maximise the region's modern landscape by protecting wildlife and wild places, and educating, influencing and empowering people. They manage 80 of the best sites and help others to manage theirs. Their work is helping to secure the future of many important habitats and species, which might otherwise be lost.

Contact details:
1 St George's Place, York, YO24 1GN
Tel: 01904 659570
Fax: 01904 613467
www.ywt.org.uk
info@ywt.org.uk

Zoological Society of London (ZSL) is a charity devoted to the worldwide conservation of animals and their habitats. Their scientists in the laboratory and the field, animal management teams and veterinarians contribute wide-ranging skills and experience to both practical conservation and to the scientific research that underpins this work. The charity is made up of five operating divisions: London Zoo, Whipsnade Wild Animal Park, Institute of Zoology, Conservation Programmes and Fellowship Services.

Contact details:
Institute of Zoology, Zoological Society of London, Regent's Park, London NW1 4RY
Tel: 020 7449 6610
Fax: 020 7586 2870
www.zsl.org
enquiries@ioz.ac.uk

Contact details:
ZSL London Zoo, Outer Circle, Regent's Park, London NW1 4RY
www.zsl.org
hr@zsl.org

Contact details:
ZSL Whipsnade Zoo, Dunstable, Bedfordshire LU6 2LF
www.zsl.org
hr@zsl.org

Contact details:
Conservation Department
www.zsl.org
cp@zsl.org

Contact details:
ZSL Fellowship: Fellowship Executive, Zoological Society of London, Regent's Park, London NW1 4RY
Tel: 020 7449 6228
www.zsl.org
fellowship@zsl.org

Veterinary Jobs

Veterinary staff may be required to make difficult decisions regarding the animals in their care, and sometimes they have to deal with distressing situations. To enjoy this type of work, its important to be willing to communicate effectively with people, and be able to keep a level head in emergency situations. Livestock and wildlife veterinary work may require some tough physical outdoor work and it is advantageous to be physically fit and have plenty of stamina.

Animal Health Trust (AHT) is a charity that has been helping dogs, cats and horses for more than half a century. They provide specialist veterinary clinical, diagnostic and surgical services and their successes in research have ranged from major breakthroughs in anaesthesia and surgical techniques to the development of vaccines against diseases such as canine distemper and equine influenza. Knowledge is passed on to benefit the maximum number of animals.

Contact details:
Animal Health Trust, Lanwades Park, Kentford, Newmarket, Suffolk CB8 7UU
Tel: 01638 751000 or 01638 555669
Fax: 01638 750410
www.aht.org.uk
recruitment@aht.org.uk

British Veterinary Association (BVA) is the national representative body for the veterinary profession with over 11,000 members. In promoting and supporting the interests of our members, and the animals under their care, the BVA is committed to developing and maintaining channels of communication not least with government, parliamentarians and the media.

Contact details:
British Veterinary Association, 7 Mansfield Street, London W1G 9NQ
Tel: 020 7636 6541
Fax: 020 7908 6349
www.bva.co.uk
bvahq@bva.co.uk

Battersea Dogs & Cats Home has been rescuing lost and unwanted dogs since 1860 and cats since 1883. The organisation works to rescue, rehabilitate, re-unite and re-home dogs and cats. The organisation has a veterinary department that deals with veterinary emergencies, neutering and general veterinary welfare.

Contact details:
Battersea, London, 4 Battersea Park Road, London SW8 4AA
Tel: 020 7622 3626
www.battersea.org.uk
info@battersea.org.uk

Contact details:
Battersea, Old Windsor, Priest Hill, Old Windsor, Windsor, Berkshire SL4 2JN
Tel: 01784 432929
www.battersea.org.uk
info@battersea.org.uk

Contact details:
Battersea, Brands Hatch, Crowhurst Lane, Ash, Brands Hatch, Kent TN15 7HH
Tel: 01474 874994
www.battersea.org.uk
info@battersea.org.uk

Blue Cross aims to: ensure the welfare of animals by providing practical care, highlight the benefits of companionship between animals and people and promote a sense of respect and responsibility towards animals in the community. The organisation provides support to the nation's pets and their owners by: treating pets whose owners cannot afford private veterinary treatment, finding permanent homes for unwanted or abandoned animals and educating the public in responsible animal ownership.

Contact details:
The Blue Cross, Shilton Road, Burford, Oxon OX18 4PF
Tel: 01993 822651
Fax: 01993 823083
www.bluecross.org.uk
info@bluecross.org.uk **or** jobs@bluecross.org.uk

Celia Hammond Trust provides care and refuge for feral cats and kittens and for those animals that on the basis of age, temperament or appearance would not normally be taken in elsewhere. The organisation strives to: promote the welfare of animals through example and education, provide low cost treatment in their clinics for sick/injured animals, provide low cost neuter/vaccination clinics, operate a rescue service for animals, both domestic and feral in emergency situations, provide long and short-term sanctuary accommodation and re-homing facilities for rescued animals and to investigate complaints of cruelty and neglect and to take appropriate action.

Contact details:
Head Office and Charity Shop: Celia Hammond Animal Trust,High Street, Wadhurst, East Sussex, TN5 6AG
Tel: 01892 783367
Fax: 01892 784882
www.celiahammond.org
headoffice@celiahammond.org **or** info@celiahammond.org

Contact details:
East Sussex – Greenacres Sanctuary: Animal Sanctuary & Rescue Centre, Greenacres, Stubb Lane, Brede, Near Hastings, East Sussex
Tel: 01424 882198
www.celiahammond.org
brede@celiahammond.org

Contact details:
London - Lewisham Branch: Neuter Clinic and Rescue Centre, 233-235 Lewisham Way, Lewisham SE4 1UY
Tel: 020 8691 2100
www.celiahammond.org
lewisham@celiahammond.org

Contact details:
London - Canning Town: Neuter Clinic and Rescue Centre, 151 – 153 Barking Road, Canning Town, London E16 4HQ
Tel: 020 7474 8811
www.celiahammond.org
canningtown@celiahammond.org

Department of Veterinary Medicine, Cambridge is at the forefront of veterinary science and education and is a centre of excellence for teaching and research. Their mission is to improve the prevention and treatment of diseases of animals by defining and applying best clinical practice, by understanding and developing the science underpinning best practice, and by embedding an education programme in the veterinary sciences that delivers the best veterinary practitioners, academics and research scientists.

Contact details:
Mail address: University of Cambridge, Department of Veterinary Medicine, Madingley Road, Cambridge CB3 0ES
www.vet.cam.ac.uk
enquiries@vet.cam.ac.uk

Eduserve Veterinary Vacancies advertise vet jobs as they arise.

Contact details:
www.vacancies.ac.uk

Eastcott Veterinary Clinic and Hospital, Wiltshire is a Veterinary Hospital treating only dogs, cats and other small domestic pets base. They are equipped with state of the art medical and surgical facilities.

Contact details:
Eastcott Veterinary Clinic and Hospital, 59 Bath Road, Swindon, Wiltshire SN1 4AU
Tel: 01793 528 341
Fax: 01793 491066
www.eastcottvets.co.uk
enquiries@eastcottvets.co.uk

Contact details:
Eastcott Vets Cricklade Road, 6 Clive Parade, Swindon, Wiltshire SN2 1AJ
Tel: 01793 528 341
www.eastcottvets.co.uk
enquiries@eastcottvets.co.uk

International Zoo Veterinary Group (IZVG) was founded in 1976, by the association of two veterinary practices that were involved in full-time freelance zoo animal medicine. The group works with zoos, parks and marinelands around the world, treating wild, rare and endangered species.

Contact details:
Tel: +44 (0)1535 692000
Fax: +44 (0)1535 690433
www.izvg.co.uk
office@izvg.co.uk

Liphook Equine Hospital is a specialist veterinary practice dedicated to the horse world providing both a highly experienced ambulatory equine practice and an expert, fully equipped equine referral hospital. The practice has developed over the last 25 years into one of the largest equine hospitals in the country.

Contact details:
Mail address: The Liphook Equine Hospital, Forest Mere, Liphook, Hampshire GU30 7JG
Tel: 01428 727200 /01428 723594/01428 727727
Fax: 01428 722263
www.liphookequinehosp.co.uk
enquiries@theLEH.co.uk

Parkvets Veterinary Group operate from a large veterinary hospital and six veterinary clinics situated on the borders of South East London and North West Kent.

Contact details:
Headquarters of Parkvets Group: Parkvets Veterinary Hospital, 53-55 Maidstone Road, Footscray, Kent DA14 5HB
Tel: 020 8300 8111
Fax: 020 8300 0199
www.parkvets.com

Peoples Dispensary for Sick Animals (PDSA) works to care for the pets of needy people by providing free veterinary services to their sick and injured animals and promoting responsible pet ownership. They are the largest private employer of fully qualified veterinary surgeons and veterinary nurses in Europe. PDSA is non-campaigning, and non-political. Complete online application form for job information.

Contact details:
Head Office: Whitechapel Way, Priorslee, Telford, Shropshire TF2 9PQ
Tel: 01952 290 999 (Recruitment Team)
Fax: 01952 291035
www.pdsa.org.uk

Royal Veterinary College (RVC) is the UK's first and largest veterinary school and a constituent College of the University of London, it is one of the leading veterinary research centres in Europe. The RVC provides support for the veterinary profession through its three referral hospitals, diagnostic services and continuing professional development courses.

Contact details:
Camden Campus: The Royal Veterinary College, Royal College Street, London NW10 0TU
Tel: +44 (0)20 7468 5000
www.rvc.ac.uk

Contact details:
Hawkshead Campus: The Royal Veterinary College, Hawshead Lane, North Mymms, Hatfield, Hertforshire AL9 7TA
Tel: +44 (0)1707 666333
www.rvc.ac.uk

Royal College of Veterinary Surgeons (RCVS) is the regulatory body for veterinary surgeons in the UK. Its role is: to safeguard the health and welfare of animals committed to veterinary care through the regulation of the educational, ethical and clinical standards of the veterinary profession, thereby protecting the interests of those dependent on animals and assuring public health. To act as an impartial source of informed opinion on animal health and welfare issues and their interaction with human health.

Contact details:
Royal College of Veterinary Surgeons, Belgravia House, 62-64 Horseferry Road, London SW1P 2AF
Tel: 020 7222 2001
Fax: 020 7222 2004
www.rcvs.org.uk
info@rcvs.org.uk

RSPCA has a vision of a world in which all humans respect and live in harmony with all other members of the animal kingdom. Their mission statement is to prevent cruelty, promote kindness to and alleviate suffering of animals.

Contact details:
RSPCA Enquiries Service, Wilberforce Way, Southwater, Horsham, West Sussex RH13 9RS
Tel: 0300 1234 555
Fax: 0303 123 0100
www.rspca.org.uk

Tiggywinkles Wildlife Hospital is the world's busiest wildlife hospital and cares for sick & injured hedgehogs, badgers, wild birds, foxes, even reptiles & amphibians. They are a specialist hospital, using all available veterinary welfare skills, dedicated to rescuing and rehabilitating all species of British wildlife.

Contact details:
Tiggywinkles, Aston Road, Haddenham, Aylesbury, Buckinghamshire HP17 8AF
Tel: 01844 292292
Fax: 01844 292640
www.sttiggywinkles.org.uk
mail@sttiggywinkles.org.uk

University of Bristol, faculty of Veterinary Science veterinary vacancies advertised as they arise.

Contact details:
University of Bristol, Senate House, Tyndall Avenue, Bristol BS8 1TH
Tel: 0117 954 6947
Fax: 0117 925 9473
www.bristol.ac.uk
recruitment@bristol.ac.uk

University of Glasgow, faculty of Veterinary Science veterinary vacancies advertised as they arise.

Contact details:
University of Glasgow, Glasgow, Scotland G12 8QQ
Tel: +44 (0)141 330 3898 **or** +44 (0)141 330 3594 (HR Dept)
Fax: +44 (0)141 330 4921
www.gla.ac.uk
c.bevan@admin.gla.ac.uk **or** humanresources@glasgow.ac.uk

University of Edinburgh, faculty of Veterinary Science veterinary vacancies advertised as they arise.

Contact details:
Mail address: Human Resources, The University of Edinburgh, Charles Stewart House, 9-16 Chambers Street, Edinburgh EH1 1HT
www.ed.ac.uk
jobs@ed.ac.uk

University of Liverpool, faculty of Veterinary Science veterinary vacancies advertised as they arise.

Contact details:
Human Resources Department, Hart Building, Mount Pleasant, Liverpool L3 5TQ
Tel: 0151 794 6771
Fax: 0151 795 4674
www.liv.ac.uk
jobs@liv.ac.uk

Veterinary Laboratory Agency (VLA) is an Executive Agency of the Department for Environment, Food and Rural Affairs (Defra). VLA is a regional network of 16 veterinary laboratories, including one in Scotland, two in Wales, and a central facility near Weybridge in Surrey. VLA provides all sectors of the animal health & environment industry with animal disease surveillance, diagnostic services and veterinary scientific research.

Contact details:
Tel: +44 (0)1932341111
Fax: +44 (0)1932347046
www.vla.defra.gov.uk

Veterinary Practice Management Association (VPMA) is the Association for those involved in veterinary practice management. They have a useful employment register which contains current veterinary related jobs.

Contact details:
VPMA Ltd., 76 St John's Road, Kettering, Northants NN15 5AZ
Tel: 07000 782324
Fax: 0870 836 2250
www.vpma.co.uk
secretariat@vpma.co.uk

Veterinary Record is the British Veterinary Association's official journal and has been published weekly since 1888. It contains news, comment, letters and clinical research papers on a wide range of veterinary topics. Its classified advertisement section includes an extensive list of veterinary and veterinary-related jobs.

Contact details:
Veterinary Record, Classified Advertising, Mezzanine Floor, BMA House, Tavistock Square, London WC1H 9JR
www.vetrecordjobs.com

VetBuzz is a veterinary portal with current veterinary jobs.

Contact details:
www.vetbuzz.co.uk
info@vetbuzz.com
admin@vetbuzz.com

Vetclick provides internet services for busy veterinary professionals and has veterinary jobs advertised.

Contact details:
www.vetclick.com
info@vetclick.com

Jobs with Cats and Dogs

Jobs working hands-on with cats and dogs can be grubby and may involve tough physical outdoor work. It's crucial that you don't mind working outdoors in all types of weather as many catteries are based outside and dogs need to be excercised in all weathers. You will need to be physically fit, hard working, enjoy exercise, have plenty of stamina and not be squeamish as some parts of the work can be messy and unpleasant.

Dogs and cats being cared for in a boarding environment need care twenty-four hours a day, seven days a week and therefore, the working hours can be unpredictable and varied; you may be required to work at weekends and bank holidays. That's the downside of this type of work and we hope this hasn't put you off! Working directly with companion animals can be extremely rewarding and satisfying.

Animal Rescue Centres UK scroll down to the animal charity section with information and links to animal rescue centres in the UK – some offering jobs with cats and dogs. For those organisations who don't have a specific vacancies section on their website, it may be worth contacting them regarding any vacancies or sending in your CV.

Contact details:
www.animalresources.co.uk

Battersea Dogs & Cats Home has been rescuing lost and unwanted dogs since 1860 and cats since 1883. The organisation works to rescue, rehabilitate, re-unite and re-home dogs and cats.

Contact details:
Battersea, London, 4 Battersea Park Road, London SW8 4AA
Tel: 020 7622 3626
www.battersea.org.uk
info@battersea.org.uk

Contact details:
Battersea, Old Windsor, Priest Hill, Old Windsor, Windsor, Berkshire SL4 2JN
Tel: 01784 432929
www.battersea.org.uk
info@battersea.org.uk

Contact details:
Battersea, Brands Hatch, Crowhurst Lane, Ash, Brands Hatch, Kent TN15 7HH
Tel: 01474 874994
www.battersea.org.uk
info@battersea.org.uk

Blue Cross aims to: ensure the welfare of animals by providing practical care, highlight the benefits of companionship between animals and people and promote a sense of respect and responsibility towards animals in the community. The organisation provides support to the nation's pets and their owners by: treating pets whose owners cannot afford private veterinary treatment, finding permanent homes for unwanted or abandoned animals and educating the public in responsible animal ownership.

Contact details:
Shilton Road, Burford, OXON, OX18 4PF
Tel: 01993 822651
Fax: 01993 823083
www.bluecross.org.uk
info@bluecross.org.uk **or** jobs@bluecross.org.uk

Bath Cats and Dogs Home works to shelter and care for unwanted animals in the Bath; North East Somerset and West Wiltshire areas, until they are successfully re-homed. The Home encourages good health, welfare and improved quality of life for all animals through promoting responsible pet ownership.

Contact details:
Bath Cats and Dogs Home, The Avenue, Claverton Down, Bath, BA2 7AZ
Tel: 01225 787321
www.bathcatsanddogshome.org.uk

Celia Hammond Trust provides care and refuge for feral cats and kittens and for those animals that on the basis of age, temperament or appearance would not normally be taken in elsewhere. The organisation strives to: promote the welfare of animals through example and education, provide low cost treatment in their clinics for sick/injured animals, provide low cost neuter/vaccination clinics, operate a rescue service for animals, both domestic and feral in emergency situations, provide long and short-term sanctuary accommodation and re-homing facilities for rescued animals and to investigate complaints of cruelty and neglect and to take appropriate action.

Contact details:
Head Office and Charity Shop: Celia Hammond Animal Trust,High Street, Wadhurst, East Sussex, TN5 6AG
Tel: 01892 783367
Fax: 01892 784882
www.celiahammond.org
headoffice@celiahammond.org **or** info@celiahammond.org

Contact details:
East Sussex – Greenacres Sanctuary: Animal Sanctuary & Rescue Centre, Greenacres, Stubb Lane, Brede, Near Hastings, East Sussex
Tel: 01424 882198
www.celiahammond.org
brede@celiahammond.org

Contact details:
London - Lewisham Branch: Neuter Clinic and Rescue Centre, 233-235 Lewisham Way, Lewisham SE4 1UY
Tel: 020 8691 2100
www.celiahammond.org
lewisham@celiahammond.org

Contact details:
London - Canning Town: Neuter Clinic and Rescue Centre, 151 – 153 Barking Road, Canning Town, London E16 4HQ
Tel: 020 7474 8811
www.celiahammond.org

Dogs for the Disabled founded in 1986 to work with disabled people allowing them to have assistance from a dog partnership. The organisation has to date trained over 300 partnerships.

Contact details:
Dogs for the Disabled, The Frances Hay Centre, Blacklocks Hill, Banbury OX17 2BS
Tel: 01295 252600
www.dogsforthedisabled.org
info@dogsforthedisabled.org

Regional Centres:
Contact details:
The Gillow Suite, Nostell Estate Yard, Nostell, Wakefield WF4 1AB
Tel: 01924 860699
www.dogsforthedisabled.org
info@dogsforthedisabled.org

Contact details:
C/o RNIB, Still House Lane, Bedminster, Bristol BS3 4EB
Tel: 01179 341729
www.dogsforthedisabled.org
info@dogsforthedisabled.org

Foal Farm Animal Rescue Centre is a registered charity located in Biggin Hill, Kent England. Its aim is to take in as many sick, distressed and unwanted animals as possible and restore them to health and happiness.

Contact details:
Foal Farm Animal Rescue Centre Jail Lane Biggin Hill Kent TN16 3AX
Tel: 01 959 572 386
www.foalfarm.org.uk
info@foalfarm.org.uk **or** volunteering@foalfarm.org.uk

Guide Dogs for the Blind Association envisages a world in which all people who are blind and partially-sighted enjoy the same rights, opportunities and responsibilities as everyone else. Their mission is to provide guide dogs, mobility and other rehabilitation services that meet the needs of blind and partially-sighted people.

Contact details:
The Guide Dogs for the Blind Association, Burghfield Common, Reading RG7 3YG
Tel: 0118 983 5555
Fax: 0118 983 5433
www.guidedogs.org.uk
guidedogs@guidedogs.org.uk

Gables Farm Dogs' and Cats' Home founded in 1907, the organisation now looks after some 2,000 cats and dogs every year. They enforce a strict non-euthanasia policy and are committed to providing the best environment possible.

Contact details:
Gables Farm Dogs' & Cats' Home, 204 Merafield Road, Plymouth PL7 1UQ
Tel: 01752 331602
Fax: 01752 331604
www.gablesfarm.org.uk
info@gablesfarm.org.uk

Hearing Dogs for Deaf People was launched in 1982. Since then they have continued to train dogs to alert deaf people to specific sounds, whether in the home, workplace or public buildings. To date they have placed nearly 1,300 hearing dogs throughout England, Scotland, Wales, Northern Ireland and the Channel Islands.

Contact details:
Head Office: The Grange, Wycombe Road, Saunderton, Princes Risborough, Buckinghamshire HP27 9NS
Tel: 01844 348 100
Fax: 01844 348 101
www.hearingdogs.org.uk
info@hearingdogs.org.uk

Contact details:
The Beatrice Wright Training Centre, Hayton Road, Bielby, York, East Yorkshire YO42 4JP
Tel: 01759 322299
Fax: 01759 322298
www.hearingdogs.org.uk
info@hearingdogs.org.uk

Kennel and Cattery Magazine advertise situations vacant, including boarding catteries and kennels for sale - this may be of use to those considering setting up their own pet boarding business.

Contact details:
Albatross Publications, P.O. Box 523, Horsham, West Sussex RH12 4WL
Tel: 01293 871201
www.kennelandcattery.com

Last Chance Animal Rescue, Kent rescues dogs, some saved from destruction in Welsh pounds others handed in to them for whatever reason. They provide medical care, food, shelter and love for them all and ultimately find them loving homes. Volunteer assistance required and paid animal jobs are advertised as they arise - click on the navigation bar (how can you help us and then on the job opportunities button).

Contact details:
Last Chance Animal Rescue, Hartfield Road, Edenbridge, Kent TN8 5NH
Tel: 01732 865530
Fax: 01732 865838
www.lastchanceanimalrescue.co.uk

Manchester and Cheshire Dogs' Homes rescues, cares for and re-homes dogs in need in Greater Manchester, parts of Derbyshire and Lancashire. They have over 150 dogs in their care.

Contact details:
Head Office: Manchester & Cheshire Dogs' Home, Crofter's House, Moss Brook Road, Harpurhey, Manchester M9 5PG
Tel: 0844 504 1212
www.dogshome.net

Contact details:
Cheshire Dogs' Home, 225 Knutsford Road, Grappenhall, Warrington WA4 3JZ
Tel: 0844 504 1212
www.dogshome.net

National Animal Welfare Trust has re-homing centres in Berkshire, Somerset, Cornwall, Thurrock and Watford. The organisation seeks to assist in the provision of care and shelter for stray, neglected and unwanted animals of all kinds. They work for the protection of animals of all kinds from ill-usage, cruelty and suffering, and in particular, to rescue and provide care and shelter for stray, neglected and unwanted animals of all kinds and find suitable homes for any such animals.

Contact details:
NAWT Head Office & London & Home Counties Animal Rescue Centre: Tyler's Way, Watford-By-Pass, Watford, Hertfordshire WD25 8WT
Tel: 020 8950 0177 (0900 to 1700 Mon-Fri)
Fax: 020 8420 4454
www.nawt.org.uk
watford@nawt.org.uk

Contact details:
NAWT Berkshire: Trindledown Farm Animal Rescue Centre, Trindledown Farm, Wantage Road, Great Shefford, Berkshire RG17 7DQ
Tel: 01488 638584
Fax: 01488 638141
www.nawt.org.uk
trindledown@nawt.org.uk

Contact details:
NAWT Cornwall: Cornish Animal Rescue Centre, Wheal Alfred Kennels, Wheal Alfred Road, Hayle, Cornwall TR27 5JT
Tel: 01736 756005
Fax: 01736 756536
www.nawt.org.uk
CornwallReception@nawt.org.uk

Contact details:
NAWT Somerset: Somerset Animal Rescue Centre, Heavens Gate Farm, West Henley, Langport, Somerset TA10 9BE
Tel: 01458 252656
Fax: 01458 253806
www.nawt.org.uk
hg.reception@nawt.org.uk

Contact details:
NAWT Essex: Tel: 01375 376682
www.nawt.org.uk

Newcastle Dog and Cat Shelter has been in operation since 1896 caring for the stray, neglected, injured and abandoned animals throughout the North East. They receive between 4,000 and 6,000 animals per year and between their two shelters can hold up to 250 dogs and 200 cats.

Contact details:
Newcastle Dog and Cat Shelter, Benton North Farm, Benton Lane, Newcastle upon Tyne NE12 8EH
Tel: 0191 215 0435
www.dogandcatshelter.com

Contact details:
Nwcastle Dog and Cat Shelter, Claremont Road, Newcastle upon Tyne NE2 4NL
Tel: 0191 232 2878
www.dogandcatshelter.com

Our Cats magazine have vacancies listed in the classifieds section of their site (on the left hand side).

Contact details:
Our Cats Publishing, 1 Lund Street, Manchester M16 9EJ
www.ourcats.co.uk

Petsmiles current vacancies from the Petsmiles website including kennel jobs, kennel manager vacancies, pet sitters.

Contact details:
Tel: 0845 895 1025
info@petsmiles.com
www.petsmiles.com

Peoples Dispensary for Sick Animals (PDSA) works to care for the pets of needy people by providing free veterinary services to their sick and injured animals and promoting responsible pet ownership. They are the largest private employer of fully qualified veterinary surgeons and veterinary nurses in Europe. PDSA is non-campaigning, and non-political. Complete online application form for job information.

Contact details:
Head Office: Whitechapel Way, Priorslee, Telford, Shropshire TF2 9PQ
Tel: 01952 290 999 (Recruitment Team)
Fax: 01952 291035
www.pdsa.org.uk

Raystede Centre for Animal Welfare was founded in 1952 to prevent and relieve cruelty to animals and to protect them from unnecessary suffering. Around 1,500 unwanted and abandoned animals arrive at the centre annually. Dogs, cats and other small companion animals are found new caring homes while others remain in Raystede's care for the rest of their days. There are at present over 1,000 animals enjoying a happy and peaceful life at the centre.

Contact details:
Raystede Animal Welfare, Ringmer, East Sussex, BN8 5AJ
Tel: (01825) 840252
Fax: (01825) 840995
www.raystede.org
info@raystede.org

RSPCA has a vision of a world in which all humans respect and live in harmony with all other members of the animal kingdom. Their mission statement is to prevent cruelty, promote kindness to and alleviate suffering of animals.

Contact details:
RSPCA Enquiries Service, Wilberforce Way, Southwater, Horsham, West Sussex RH13 9RS
Tel: 0300 1234 555
Fax: 0303 123 0100
www.rspca.org.uk

Scottish SPCA was established in 1839 to prevent cruelty to animals and promote kindness and humanity in their treatment, the Scottish Society for the Prevention of Cruelty to Animals is Scotland's leading animal welfare charity. Today, its work is as necessary as ever. The Scottish SPCA is a reporting agency for the enforcement of animal protection laws.

Contact details:
Scottish SPCA, Kingseat Road, Halbeath, Dunfermline KY11 8RY
Tel: 03000 999 999
www.scottishspca.org

Wood Green Animal Shelters has been rescuing and re-homing animals since 1924. The charity has two sanctuaries – in London and Cambridge and takes in over 6,000 animals a year.

Contact details:
Godmanchester Shelter (HQ):
King's Bush Farm, London Road, Godmanchester, Cambs PE29 2NH
Tel: 0844 248 8181
Fax: 01480 832815
www.woodgreen.org.uk
info@woodgreen.org.uk

Contact details:
London Shelter:
601 Lordship Lane, Wood Green, London N22 5LG
Tel: 0844 248 8181
Fax: 0208 889 0245
www.woodgreen.org.uk
info@woodgreen.org.uk

Contact details:
Heydon Shelter:
Highway Cottage, Heydon, Herts SG8 8PN
Tel: 0844 248 8181
Fax: 01763 838824
www.woodgreen.org.uk
info@woodgreen.org.uk

Zoo Jobs

The UK has taken the lead and campaigned for the adoption of the EU directive to establish minimum standards for zoos and this has led to a far greater focus on conservation and animal welfare issues. This means that zoos have changed purpose from existing purely for public entertainment, to now ensuring that some endangered wild species have a chance of survival.

As this emphasis on conservation increases, more zoos are employing specialist zoologists, conservation experts and ecologists. Sadly, not all zoos are forward thinking and unfortunately, many wild animals are still exhibited in appalling conditions with little attention paid to their physical or psychological wellbeing. Many countries still allow the building of zoos where wild animals are kept in cramped cages where they are not cared for properly – however, there is increasing pressure for these places to improve conditions.

With over a hundred million people visiting zoos every year, those working in zoos have an excellent opportunity to educate large numbers of people about the need for the conservation of wildlife and the importance of respecting animals. This responsibility assures a varied, interesting and rewarding career working with animals.

Anglesey Sea Zoo is the largest marine aquarium in Wales, nestling on the shores of the Menai Strait. With over 50 species, the Sea Zoo has re-created the habitats of the fauna and flora found around Anglesey and the North Wales coastline.

Contact details:
Anglesey Sea Zoo, Brynsiencyn, Isle of Anglesey LL61 6TQ
Tel: 01248 430411
Fax: 01248 430213
www.angleseyseazoo.co.uk
post@angleseyseazoo.co.uk

Association of British Wild Animal Keepers (ABWAK) The objectives of the Association are: to improve cooperation among animal keepers, both nationally and internationally; to provide, encourage and organise facilities for the meeting of keepers of wild animals; to improve, through education, the professional competence of all involved with wild animal husbandry; to support the conservation of wildlife through out the world. Jobs advertised as they arise.

Contact details:
Federation of Zoological Gardens of Britain and Ireland: Regents Park, London, NW1 4RY.
Tel: 020 7586 0230.
www.abwak.org
abwak-enquiries@live.co.uk

British and Irish Association of Zoos and Aquariums (BIAZA) are the professional body representing the best zoos and aquariums in Britain and Ireland. Their Member Collections pride themselves on their excellent animal welfare, education and conservation work. BIAZA supports them in their work and helps promote the work of good zoos and aquariums. They list jobs available from their member organisations.

Contact details:
BIAZA, Regents Park, London NW1 4RY
Tel: 020 7449 6351
Fax: 020 7449 6359
www.biaza.org.uk

Bristol Zoo Gardens maintains and defends biodiversity through conserving threatened species and habitats and promoting a wider understanding of the natural world.

Contact details:
Bristol Zoo Gardens, Clifton, Bristol BS8 3HA
Tel: 0117 974 7399
Fax: 0117 973 6814
www.bristolzoo.org.uk
information@bristolzoo.org.uk

Blackpool Zoo aims to provide new standards of animal care and to provide a stimulating, informative and enjoyable experience that demonstrates its role in the conservation of endangered species.

Contact details:
Blackpool Zoo, East Park Drive, Blackpool, Lancashire FY3 8PP
Tel: 01253 830 830
Fax: 01253 830 800
www.blackpoolzoo.org.uk
info@blackpoolzoo.org.uk

Banham Zoo aims to create a haven where not only the animals can enjoy a protected environment in which to thrive, but also where visitors of all ages can gain an appreciation of the diversity of the animal kingdom.

Contact details:
Banham Zoo, Kenninghall Road, Banham, Norfolk NR16 2HE
Tel: 01953 887771
Fax: 01953 887445
www.banhamzoo.co.uk

Colchester Zoo is constantly evolving to ensure their world class level of commitment to the animals in their care.

Contact details:
Colchester Zoo, Maldon Road, Stanway, Colchester, Essex CO3 0SL
Tel: 01206 331292
Fax: 01206 331392
www.colchester-zoo.com

Chester Zoo was founded in 1934 and receives no government funding It has grown to become one of the largest zoos in the UK. The zoo is a substantial employer for Chester with over 250 permanent staff, increasing to 400 in the summer season.

Contact details:
Chester Zoo, Upton-by-Chester, Chester CH2 1LH
Tel: 01244 380280 **or** 01244 389477 (recruitment line)
Fax: 01244 371273
www.chesterzoo.org
guest.services@chesterzoo.org **or** recruitment@chesterzoo.org

Edinburgh Zoo aims to inspire and excite visitors with the wonder of living animals, and so to promote the conservation of threatened species and habitats. They are committed to providing a world class visitor experience with the highest standards of animal welfare, education and research, supported by excellent visitor service.

Contact details:
The Royal Zoological Society of Scotland, Edinburgh Zoo, 134 Corstorphine Road, Edinburgh EH12 6TS
Tel: 0131 334 9171
Fax: 0131 314 0384
www.edinburghzoo.org.uk
info@rzss.org.uk

Environmental Investigation Agency (EIA) works to investigate, expose and campaign against the illegal trade in wildlife and the destruction of our natural environment. Working undercover to expose international environmental crime -such as the illegal trade in wildlife, illegal logging and trade in timber species, and the world-wide trade in ozone depleting substances - EIA has directly brought about changes in international laws and the policies of governments, saving the lives of millions of rare and endangered animals and putting a stop to the devastating effects of environmental criminals.

Contact details:
EIA UK: 62/63 Upper Street, London N1 0NY
Tel: +44 (0)20 7354 7960
Fax: +44 (0)20 7354 7961
www.eia-international.org
ukinfo@eia-international.org

Contact details:
EIA USA: P.O. Box 53343, Washington DC 20009, USA
Tel: +1 202 483 6621
Fax: +1 202 986 8626
www.eia-international.org
usinfo@eia-international.org

Institute of Zoology is the research division of the Zoological Society of London (ZSL). It is a government-funded research institute specialising in scientific issues relevant to the conservation of animal species and their habitats. The Institute is based at ZSL's Regents Park site, London. Vacancies advertised as they arise.

Contact details:
Institute of Zoology, Zoological Society of London, Regent's Park, London NW1 4RY
Tel: 020 7449 6610
Fax: 020 7586 2870
www.zsl.org
enquiries@ioz.ac.uk

Marwell Zoological Park is a registered charity, their mission is: "to contribute to the conservation of biological diversity, the conservation and management of wild species in their natural habitat, and by inspiring improved understanding, awareness and care of wildlife and the environment".

Contact details:
Human Resources Department, Marwell Wildlife, Colden Common, Winchester, Hampshire SO21 1JH
Tel: 01962 777407
Fax: 01962 777511
www.marwell.org.uk
marwell@marwell.org.uk **or** jobs@marwell.org.uk

Newquay Zoo has become one of the country's top zoos, with ground breaking and innovative conservation programmes. Winning 11 major awards since 1996, as well as passing the South West Tourism Visitor Attraction Quality Assurance assessment, it has proved itself to be one of the best attractions in the South West.

Contact details:
Newquay Zoo, Trenance Gardens, Newquay, Cornwall TR7 2LZ
Tel: (+44) 0844 474 2244
Fax: 01637 851318
www.newquayzoo.org.uk
info@newquayzoo.org.uk

Shepreth Wildlife Park has adopted many injured victims of road accidents, shootings etc. They have hand reared countless orphaned animals such as foxes, stoats, hedgehogs, squirrels, hares, rabbits, deer, polecats, bats, owls, kestrels, sparrowhawks, swans, geese, doves, ducks and many species of small birds. Many of the farm animals in the Park today were saved from the slaughterhouse - including the ponies which were destined for dog food. Many of the different exotic animals in the Park come from zoos that have closed down, or were unwanted pets.

Contact details:
Recruitment Manager, Shepreth Wildlife Park, Station Road, Shepreth, Nr Royston, Herts SG8 6PZ
Tel: 01763 26 22 26
www.sheprethwildlifepark.co.uk
office@sheprethwildlifepark.co.uk

Twycross Zoo is a charitable trust concentrating on conservation and education, and now assists endangered animals. Like most British zoos, Twycross receives no government funds and relies entirely on money spent by visitors to continue its work.

Contact details:
East Midland Zoological Society, Burton Road, Atherstone, Warwickshire CV9 3PX
Tel: 0844 474 1777
Fax: 0844 474 1888
www.twycrosszoo.org
info@twycrosszoo.org

Universities Federation for Animal Welfare (UFAW) is a unique scientific and technical animal welfare organisation. They use scientific knowledge and established expertise to improve the welfare of animals kept as pets, in zoos, and on farms and of wild animals with which we interact. They also award grants and scholarships.

Contact details:
Universities Federation for Animal Welfare, The Old School, Brewhouse Hill, Wheathampstead, Hertfordshire AL4 8AN
Tel: +44 (0)1582 831818
Fax: +44 (0)1582 831414
www.ufaw.org.uk
ufaw@ufaw.org.uk

World Association of Zoos and Aquariums (WAZA) their mission is to guide, encourage and support the zoos, aquariums, and like-minded organisations of the world in animal care and welfare, environmental education and global conservation.

Contact details:
WAZA Executive Office, IUCN Conservation Centre, Rue Mauverney 28, CH-1196 Gland, Switzerland
Tel: +41 (0)22 999 07 90
Fax: +41 (0)22 999 07 91
secretariat@waza.org
www.waza.org

Marine Jobs

Marine jobs may include; Conducting surveys, monitoring habitats and populations, rehabilitation of sick or injured marine life and the protection and rescue of animals from natural and man-made disasters. Marine jobs may have working hours that are unpredictable and you will probably be required to work at weekends and bank holidays. You will need to be physically fit, a competent swimmer, healthy, and have plenty of stamina. Some marine and careers require you to live on site.

Anglesey Sea Zoo is the largest marine aquarium in Wales, nestling on the shores of the Menai Strait. With over 50 species, the Sea Zoo has re-created the habitats of the fauna and flora found around Anglesey and the North Wales coastline.

Contact details:
Anglesey Sea Zoo, Brynsiencyn, Isle of Anglesey LL61 6TQ
Tel: 01248 430411
Fax: 01248 430213
www.angleseyseazoo.co.uk
post@angleseyseazoo.co.uk

British and Irish Association of Zoos and Aquariums (BIAZA) are the professional body representing the best zoos and aquariums in Britain and Ireland. Their Member Collections pride themselves on their excellent animal welfare, education and conservation work. BIAZA supports them in their work and helps promote the work of good zoos and aquariums. They list jobs available from their member organisations.

Contact details:
BIAZA, Regents Park, London NW1 4RY
Tel: 020 7449 6351
Fax: 020 7449 6359
www.biaza.org.uk

British Antarctic Survey (BAS) has, for almost 60 years, undertaken the majority of Britain's scientific research on and around the Antarctic continent. It now shares that continent with scientists from over thirty countries. BAS employs over 400 staff, and supports three stations in the Antarctic, at Rothera, Halley and Signy, and two stations on South Georgia, at King Edward Point and Bird Island. The Antarctic operations and science programmes are executed and managed from Cambridge, and rely on a wide-ranging team of professional staff.

Contact details:
British Antarctic Survey, High Cross, Madingley Road, Cambridge CB3 0ET
Tel: +44 (0)1223 221400
Fax: +44 (0)1223 362616
www.antarctica.ac.uk

British Divers Marine Life Rescue (BDMLA) trains over 400 volunteer Marine Mammal Medics a year and have 20 whale rescue pontoons located at strategic points throughout the UK, waiting to help stranded whales and dolphins. This is a voluntary organisation - their training courses may be of great benefit to those seeking marine employment.

Contact details:
British Divers Marine Life Rescue, Lime House, Regency Close, Uckfield, East Sussex TN22 1DS
Tel: 01825 765546
Fax: 01825 768012
www.bdmlr.org.uk
info@bdmlr.org.uk

Centre for Ecology and Hydrology (CEH) is the UK's Centre of Excellence for integrated research in terrestrial and freshwater ecosystems and their interaction with the atmosphere.

Contact details:
Wallingford - CEH Headquarters: Centre for Ecology & Hydrology, Maclean Building, Benson Lane, Crowmarsh Gifford, Wallingford, Oxfordshire OX10 8BB
Tel: +44 (0)1491 838800
Fax: +44 (0)1491 692424
www.ceh.ac.uk

Contact details:
Bangor: Centre for Ecology & Hydrology, Environmental Centre Wales, Deiniol Road, Bangor, Gwynedd LL57 2UW
Tel: +44 (0)1248 374500
Fax: +44 (0)1248 362133
www.ceh.ac.uk

Contact details:
Edinburgh: Centre for Ecology & Hydrology, Bush Estate, Pencuik, Midlothian EH26 0QB
Tel: +44 (0)131 4454343
Fax: +44 (0)131 4453943
www.ceh.ac.uk

Contact details:
Lancaster: Centre for Ecology & Hydrology, Lancaster Environment Centre, Library Avenue, Bailrigg, Lancaster LA1 4AP
Tel: +44 (0)1524 595800
Fax: +44 (0)1524 61536
www.ceh.ac.uk

Department for Environment, Food and Rural Affairs (Defra) works by integrating environmental, social and economic objectives - putting sustainable development into practice every day, and by championing sustainable development as the way forward for Government. See their marine section for relevant information and jobs as they arise.

Contact details:
Defra, Nobel House, 17 Smith Square, London SW1P 3JR
Tel: (Defra Helpline) 08459 33 55 77
www.defra.gov.uk
defra.helpline@defra.gsi.gov.uk

International Marine Trainers Association (IMATA) was founded to foster communication, professionalism, and co-operation among those who serve marine mammal science through training, public display, research, husbandry, conservation, and education. Become a member to see all the vacancies.

Contact details:
International Marine Animal Trainers' Association, 1200 South Lake Shore Drive, Chicago, IL 60605-2490, United States of America
Tel: 312-692-3193
Fax: 312-939-2216
www.imata.org
info@imata.org

Marine Mammal Conservancy aims to provide professional and effective response and care for stranded marine mammals and to add to the overall understanding of marine mammals on both the scientific and public fronts. Via data collection, they help ensure the success of an inspiring and threatened group of animals. They have internship information and this is beneficial to those seeking a marine career.

Contact details:
www.marinemammalconservancy.org
info@marinemammalconservancy.org

Mystic Aquarium & Institute for Exploration has been rescuing stranded marine mammals for over 25 years, and is a founding member of the Northeast Regional Stranding Network. The network consists of independent organisations dedicated to caring for sick and injured animals, and to learning more about the reasons that they come ashore.

Contact details:
Mystic Aquarium, 55 Coogan Blvd., Mystic, CT 06355-1997
Tel: 860 572 5955
Fax: 860 572 5969
www.mysticaquarium.org
info@mysticaquarium.org **or** humanresources@mysticaquarium.org

Marine Animal Rescue Society is dedicated to the conservation of marine animals through, rescue, rehabilitation, research, and education.

Contact details:
Mail address: Marine Animal Rescue Society, P.O. Box 833356, Miami, Florida 33283
Tel: (305) 546-1111
www.marineanimalrescue.org
mars@marineanimalrescue.org

Marine Conservation Society (MCS) is the UK charity dedicated to caring for our seas, shores and wildlife. MCS campaigns for clean seas and beaches, sustainable fisheries, and protection for all marine life.

Contact details:
Mail address: Marine Conservation Society, Unit 3, Wolf Business Park, Alton Road, Ross-on Wye, Herefordshire HR9 5NB
Tel: 01989 566017
Fax: 01989 567815
www.mcsuk.org

Natural Environment Research Council (NERC) funds world-class science in universities and our own research centres that improves knowledge and understanding of the natural world. They are tackling the 21st century's major environmental issues such as climate change, biodiversity and natural hazards. They lead in providing independent research and training in the environmental sciences.

Contact details:
Natural Environment Research Council, Polaris House, North Star Avenue, Swindon SN2 1EU
Tel: 01793 411500
Fax: 01793 411501
www.nerc.ac.uk

National Seal Sanctuary the organisation has over fifty years experience in seal rescue, rehabilitation and release.

Contact details:
Work Placement Coordinator, National Seal Sanctuary, Gweek, Nr Helston, Cornwall TR12 6UG
Tel: 01326 221361 **or** 0871 423 2110
www.sealsanctuary.co.uk
seals@sealsanctuary.co.uk

National Oceanography Centre, Southampton (NOCS) is the national focus for oceanography in the UK with a remit to achieve scientific excellence in its own right as one of the world's top five oceanographic research institutions. NOCS activities encompass major ocean technology development, long-term observations, managing international science programmes, promoting enterprise and knowledge transfer, providing advice to Government, business and charities, and the engagement between science and society. Moreover, the Centre is also specifically charged with working with the wider science community to provide strategic leadership, coordination and facilitation for the whole of the UK marine and related earth sciences.

Contact details:
National Oceanography Centre, Southampton, University of Southampton Waterfront Campus, European Way, Southampton SO14 3ZH
Tel: 00 44 23 8059 6666
www.noc.soton.ac.uk

Organisation Cetacea (ORCA) promotes the conservation of the marine environment through research, partnership and education and provides a forum for the enjoyment of whales, dolphins, seabirds and other marine life.

Contact details:
ORCA, Brittany Centre, Wharf Road, Portsmouth PO2 8RU
www.orcaweb.org.uk
info@orcaweb.org.uk

Proudman Oceanographic Laboratory (POL) is a fully-owned research laboratory of the Natural Environment Research Council. Their world-class research includes: physics of estuarine, coastal and shelf sea circulation; wind wave dynamics & sediment transport processes; global sea level science and geodetic oceanography and marine technology & operational oceanography.

Contact details:
National Oceanography Centre, Joseph Proudman Building, 6 Brownlow Street, Liverpool L3 5DA
Tel: +44 (0)151 795 4800 **or** +44 (0)151 795 4836/4841
Fax: +44 (0)151 795 4801
www.pol.ac.uk

SeaWeb International is a communications-based non-profit organisation that uses social marketing techniques to advance ocean conservation. By raising public awareness, advancing science-based solutions and mobilising decision-makers around ocean conservation, they are leading voices for a healthy ocean. They have offices in Paris, London and the USA.

Contact details:
Atlantic Ocean Offices: Washington, D.C., USA, 8401 Colesville Road, Suite 500, Silver Spring, MD 20910
Tel: 1.301.495.9570
Fax: 1.301.495.4846
www.seaweb.org
contactus@seaweb.org

Contact details:
Atlantic Ocean Offices: Paris, France, 51, rue le Peletier, 75009, Paris, France
Tel: 33.1.73.02.50.63
www.seaweb.org
contactus@seaweb.org

Contact details:
Atlantic Ocean Offices: London, England, 32-36 Loman Street, London SE1 0EH
Tel: 44.207.922.7780
Fax: 44.207.922.7706
www.seaweb.org
contactus@seaweb.org

Contact details:
Pacific Ocean Offices: San Francisco, CA, USA, 75 Broadway, Suite 203, San Francisco, CA 94111
Tel: 1.415.913.7224
Fax: 1.415.520.9888
www.seaweb.org
contactus@seaweb.org

Contact details:
Pacific Ocean Offices: Port Moresby, Papua New Guinea, P.O. Box 44144, Boroko, NCD 111, Papua New Guinea
Tel: 675.72130611
www.seaweb.org
contactus@seaweb.org

Contact details:
Pacific Ocean Offices: Suva, Fiji, 15 Ma'afu Street, Private Mail Bax, Suva, Fiji
Tel: 679.3319084 Ext 21
www.seaweb.org
contactus@seaweb.org

Sea Mammal Research Unit (SMRU) is one of the foremost research institutions carrying out research about marine mammals in the world. The mission of the SMRU is to carry out fundamental research into the biology of upper trophic level predators in the oceans and, through this, to provide support to the Natural Environment Research Council so that it can carry out its statutory duty to advise the UK government.

Contact details:
SMRU Administration, Sea Mammal Research Unit, Gatty Marine Laboratory, University of St Andrews, St Andrews, Fife KY16 8LB
Tel: (0)1334 462630
Fax: (0)1334 463443
www.smru.st-andrews.ac.uk
smru@st-andrews.ac.uk

Universities Federation for Animal Welfare (UFAW) is a unique scientific and technical animal welfare organisation. They use scientific knowledge and established expertise to improve the welfare of animals kept as pets, in zoos, and on farms and of wild animals with which we interact. They also award grants and scholarships.

Contact details:
Universities Federation for Animal Welfare, The Old School, Brewhouse Hill, Wheathampstead, Hertfordshire AL4 8AN
Tel: +44 (0)1582 831818
Fax: +44 (0)1582 831414
www.ufaw.org.uk
ufaw@ufaw.org.uk

Whale and Dolphin Conservation Society (WDCS) is the global voice for the protection of whales, dolphins and their environment. They have offices in Argentina, Australia, Germany, the UK and the USA, as well as a worldwide network of field projects and consultants.

Contact details:
WDCS UK: Brookfield House, 38 St Paul Street, Chippenham, Wiltshire SN15 1LJ
Tel: (44) (0)1249 449500
Fax: (44) (0)1249 449501
www.wdcs.org.uk
info@wdcs.org

Contact details:
WDCS Australasia: P.O. Box 720, Port Adelaide Business Centre, South Australia, Australia 5015
Tel: 1300 360 442
Fax: (0)8 8242 1595
www.wdcs.org.au
info@wdcs.org.au

Contact details:
WDCS North America: Whale and Dolphin Conservation Society (North America), 7 Nelson Street, Plymouth, MA 02360-4044, USA
Tel: (508) 746-2522
www.wdcs.org
contact@whales.org

WorldFish Center is an autonomous, non-profit organisation, and was established as an international centre in 1977. The Center is an operational entity with programs funded by grants from private foundations and governments. They strive to be the science partner of choice for delivering aquaculture and fisheries solutions in developing countries. Worldwide vacancies are advertised on their website.

Contact details:
Headquarters: The WorldFish Center – Malaysia Office, Jalan Batu Maung, Batu Maung, 11960 Bayan Lepas, Penang, Malaysia
Mail address: P.O. Box 500, GPO 10670, Penang, Malaysia
Tel: (+60-4) 626 1606
Fax: (+60-4) 626 5530
www.worldfishcenter.org
worldfishcenter@cgiar.org

A Prayer For Animals

"Hear our humble prayer, Oh God, for our friends the animals, especially for ones who are suffering; for any that are hunted or lost or deserted or frightened or hungry; for all that must be put to death. We entreat for them all Thy mercy and pity, and for those who deal with them, we ask a heart of compassion and gentle hands and kindly words. Make us, ourselves, to be true friends to animals and to share the blessings of the merciful" - Albert Schweitzer